BLACK ECONOMIC DEVELOPMENT
Analysis and Implications

An Anthology

Edited by

William L. Cash, Jr., and Lucy R. Oliver

Division of Research ● Graduate School of Business Administration
The University of Michigan ● Ann Arbor

Editors' Acknowledgments

Acknowledgment is made to the copyright owners who gave permission to reprint these articles from the following publications:

Getting It together: Black Businessmen in America: John Seder and Berkeley G. Burrell, "Getting It together," © 1971 by John Seder and Berkeley G. Burrell. Reprinted with permission of Harcourt Brace Jovanovich, Inc.

Black Business Digest: Jesse Jackson, "The Rev. Jesse Jackson Tells It like It Is" (May 1971);
Theodore L. Cross, "A White Paper on Black Capitalism" (November 1971), © 1971 by Theodore Cross.

Journal of Finance: Henry S. Terrell, "Wealth Accumulation of Black and White Families: The Empirical Evidence" (May 1971);
W. J. Garvin, "The Small Business Capital Gap: The Special Case of Minority Enterprise" (May 1971);
Fred E. Case, "Housing the Underhoused in the Inner City" (May 1971).

Review of Black Political Economy: Thomas Sowell, "Economics and Black People" (Spring 1971);
Robert S. Browne, "The Constellation of Politics and Economics: A Dynamic Duo in the Black Economy" (Fall 1971), and "Barriers to Black Participation in the American Economy" (Winter/Spring 1971);
Courtney N. Blackman, "An Eclectic Approach to the Problem of Black Economic Development" (Fall 1971);
Frank G. Davis, "Problems of Economic Growth in the Black Community: Some Alternative Hypotheses" (Summer 1971);
Rawle Farley, "Black Banking: A Comment on the Andrew Brimmer Bias" (Spring 1972);
Thomas Vietorisz and Bennett Harrison, "Ghetto Development, Community Corporation, and Public Policy" (Fall 1971);
Peter Labrie, "Black Central Cities: Dispersal or Rebuilding" (Winter/Spring 1971);
James Hefner and Marguerite R. Barnett, "Implications of Revenue Sharing for Black Political and Economic Goals" (Summer 1971);
Richard F. America, "Savings, Voluntary Taxes, and the National Fund" (revised from Winter 1971);
June G. Hopps, "A Planning Model for Black Community Development" (Spring 1973).

Harvard Business Review: Michael Brower and Doyle Little, "White Help for Black Business" (May-June 1970), © 1970 by the President and Fellows of Harvard College.

Journal of Economics and Business: Garrett A. Vaughn, "The Role of Residential Racial Segregation in Perpetuating Inferior Housing for Lower-Income Nonwhites" (Fall 1972).

American Journal of Economics and Sociology: William L. Henderson and Larry C. Ledebur, "Programs for the Economic Development of the American Negro Community: The Militant Approach" (October 1970), and "Programs for the Economic Development of the American Negro Community: The Moderate Approach" (January 1971).

Journal of Bank Research: John T. Boorman, "The Prospects for Minority-Owned Commercial Banks: A Comparative Performance Analysis" (Winter 1974).

Law and Contemporary Problems: John E. Oxendine and Alvin N. Puryear, "Profit Motivation and Management Assistance in Community Economic Development";
Milton Kotler, "The Politics of Community Economic Development";
Samuel I. Doctors and Sharon Lockwood, "New Directions for Minority Enterprise," reprinted with permission from a symposium, Community Economic Development—Part I, appearing in Vol. 36, no. 1 (Winter 1971). Published by the Duke University School of Law, Durham, N.C., © 1971 by Duke University.

Journal of Marketing: Fred C. Allvine, "Black Business Development" (April 1970). Published by the American Marketing Association.

Land Economics: Charles H. Levine, "Black Entrepreneurship in the Ghetto: A Recruitment Strategy" (August 1972), © 1972 by *Land Economics,* University of Wisconsin Press.

Black Enterprise Magazine: Pat Patterson, "Community Development Corporations" (July 1972).

The Bankers Magazine: Thomas F. Murray, "Problems and Techniques in Financing Ghetto Housing" (Spring 1969).

Yale Review of Law and Social Action: Charles Hampden-Turner, "A Proposal for Political Marketing" (Winter 1970). Reprinted from Vol. 1, nos. 2–3. Published quarterly by the students at the Yale Law School.

About the Editors

William L. Cash, Jr., is active in the affairs of the Michigan Office of Minority Enterprise. He is Assistant to the President of The University of Michigan, Professor of Education, Lecturer in Psychology, and a Certified Consulting Psychologist. Cash earned his Ph.D. at The University of Michigan after receiving Collegiate and Professional Graduate degrees from Fisk University and Oberlin College. He has been a member of the faculty at Prairie View A & M University, Texas, the Universities of North Dakota, Southern California, Minnesota, Hawaii, Nevada, and Sarasota. His consulting assignments have been with the U.S. Office of Education, the Educational Testing Service, MINCOMP, American Institute for Research, and consulting editor for the *Journal of Counseling Psychology*. Cash is a member of the American Psychological Association, American Personnel and Guidance Association, and the Sigma Xi, Phi Kappa Phi, Phi Delta Kappa, and Psi Chi honor societies.

Lucy Reuben Oliver has studied at the University of Ghana, West Africa, and earned an A.B. in Economics at Oberlin College and an M.B.A. in Finance from the University of Michigan. She served on the executive board of the Oberlin College Association for Black Culture and on the University of Michigan student-faculty committee on Afro-American Studies and she was a Junior Counselor to the Afro-American House. During 1970 Ms. Oliver participated in the Cooperative Urban Studies Center, Cleveland, Ohio, and was assigned to the Hough Area Development Corporation. She is currently a Financial Analyst with the Ford Motor Company, Dearborn, Michigan, on leave to pursue doctoral studies at the Graduate School of Business Administration, The University of Michigan.

Table of Contents

Foreword xiii
          Alfred L. Edwards

Introduction xv

I. Analysis

HISTORICAL

Getting It together 3
          John Seder, Berkeley G. Burrell

CONTEMPORARY

The Rev. Jesse Jackson Tells It like It Is 16
          Jesse Jackson

A White Paper on Black Capitalism 24
          Theodore L. Cross

Wealth Accumulation of Black and White Families:
The Empirical Evidence 36
          Henry S. Terrell

Economics and Black People 52
          Thomas Sowell

Topics for Discussion and Further Study 66

Suggested Readings 67

II. Problems

ASSESSMENT

The Constellation of Politics and Economics: A Dynamic
Duo in the Black Economy 71
          Robert S. Browne

Barriers to Black Participation in the American Economy 80
  Robert S. Browne

White Help for Black Business 89
  Michael Brower, Doyle Little

The Role of Residential Racial Segregation in Causing and
Perpetuating Inferior Housing for Lower-Income Nonwhites . . 100
  Garrett A. Vaughn

ALTERNATIVE STRATEGIES

An Eclectic Approach to the Problem of Black Economic
Development 114
  Courtney N. Blackman

Problems of Economic Growth in the Black Community:
Some Alternative Hypotheses 134
  Frank G. Davis

Topics for Discussion and Further Study 163

Suggested Readings 164

III. Programs

OVERVIEW

Programs for the Economic Development of the American
Negro Community: The Moderate Approach 169
  William L. Henderson,
  Larry C. Ledebur

Programs for the Economic Development of the American
Negro Community: The Militant Approach 186
  William L. Henderson,
  Larry C. Ledebur

SPECIFIC PROGRAMS

CAPITAL

The Prospects for Minority-Owned Commercial Banks:
A Comparative Performance Analysis 200
John T. Boorman

Black Banking: A Comment on the Andrew Brimmer Bias . . . 224
Rawle Farley

The Small Business Capital Gap: The Special Case of
Minority Enterprise 233
W. J. Garvin

MANAGEMENT AND TECHNICAL ASSISTANCE

Profit Motivation and Management Assistance in Community
Economic Development 247
John E. Oxendine, Alvin N. Puryear

Black Business Development 256
Fred C. Allvine

Black Entrepreneurship in the Ghetto: A Recruitment
Strategy 269
Charles H. Levine

COMMUNITY DEVELOPMENT CONCEPTS

Community Development Corporations 276
Pat Patterson

The Politics of Community Economic Development 282
Milton Kotler

Ghetto Development, Community Corporations, and Public
Policy 292
Thomas Vietorisz, Bennett Harrison

HOUSING AND THE MORTGAGE MARKET

Problems and Techniques in Financing Ghetto Housing 304
Thomas F. Murray

Housing the Underhoused in the Inner City 314
Fred E. Case

Black Central Cities: Dispersal or Rebuilding 334
Peter Labrie

Topics for Discussion and Further Study 351

Suggested Readings 353

IV. Proposals and Implications

New Directions for Minority Enterprise 357
Samuel I. Doctors and
Sharon Lockwood

Implications of Revenue Sharing for Black Political and
Economic Goals 375
James Hefner and
Marguerite R. Barnett

Savings, Voluntary Taxes, and the National Fund 393
Richard F. America

A Proposal for Political Marketing 400
Charles Hampden-Turner

A Planning Model for Black Community Development 411
June G. Hopps

Topics for Discussion and Further Study 425

Suggested Readings 425

Foreword

Economic development of the emerging nations of the world has been of concern to and studied by social scientists since World War II. Only in recent years have attempts been made to apply the same rigorous analytical framework to black economic development.

It is well documented that the problems common to the developing nations of the world are common to American black society. In describing both of these societies, one finds parallels: a relatively low per-capita income, a high birth rate, and a small middle class. The population is composed mostly of unskilled workers with a high incidence of unemployment. Relatively little saving takes place and capital is scarce. External funds, i.e., welfare payments and other government transfers, are needed to meet the requirements of the area. Other similarities are too numerous to mention here.

When the plight of the black community became highly visible during the upheaval of the sixties, public policy was directed mainly toward developing black enterprise. This was done under a variety of headings, "black capitalism," "black entrepreneurship," "compensating capitalism," and so on. The attempt was to provide blacks with a "piece of the action" in developing on-going business concerns. Scholarly attention and academic interest dwelled on analyzing the process by which business could succeed in this new environment.

Whether or not the programs were successful or met their goals can be debated. What is clear, however, is the recognition that these initiatives attacked only part of the problem of the black community. What was needed then, and is still required, is a comprehensive program that will create an economically viable community and erase the differences with the mainstream of American life.

The papers in this volume pursue the comprehensive analytical framework necessary for a systematic study of black economic development. They present both analysis and assessment of problems linked in a fashion which will further understanding of the larger goal of development. The reader is given an anlysis of black economic development in a historical and contemporary perspective. Within the various major groupings, the views of the academician, the practitioner, and the polemicist are shared. These divergent views and policy recommendations provide a useful setting for a basic understanding of the processes needed and the paths to follow toward the economic development of the black community. Hopefully a wider dissemination of these views will broaden scholarly interest and insight into the issues, and contribute to even more rigorous analysis of the problems of the underdeveloped segment of American society.

This book is part of a series of publications dealing with issues of the black economy published by the Division of Research. We are grateful for the efforts of the Editors of the volume and the support of all who made it possible.

ALFRED L. EDWARDS

Director, Division of Research
Graduate School of Business Administration
The University of Michigan

Introduction

Parallel to the ever accelerating accumulation of knowledge is a need for integration of information from various sources. This is particularly true for those who are interested in the course and process of black economic development, and thus such integration is the purpose of this anthology.

The readings here are grouped according to particular areas of economic development to facilitate selection by the reader of pertinent chapters which will yield a maximum of relevant information.

This volume is designed to serve as an authoritative source on black economic development in the United States. The articles were written by authors who are well known and respected for their contributions to some phase of black economic development. The author's prominence was not, however, the sole criterion for inclusion of an article. Each was selected because it concisely and clearly presents a point of view or discusses an unusual aspect of development which merits attention.

As the reader progresses through these readings and develops his own structures, frame of reference, or interpretive background, he may find it beneficial to return, re-read, and reassess some of the selections in order to gain deeper insight into the nature of the problems and issues in black economic development.

By definition, black economic development is the process by which the total quantity and quality of resources available in and to the black or minority community is increased in relation to the total resources of the white or majority community. In order to achieve this objective, the existing as well as the new businesses in the black community must be black owned and controlled. When this is accomplished, increased employment and the increased welfare of black people should come about as a result of increased demand for black employees by the expanded new black businesses, community-based organizations, etc. As black people seek their equitable share of the nation's wealth and benefits, economic activity and opportunities within the black community can be favorably increased.

Businesses expand to meet the increased *demands* of the market place. Usually, new businesses come into being to *supply* new or improved products or services, or to increase the supply of products or services already in existence. The essential policy question the black community must decide on is whether it would rather have a few large, diversified, corporate-type businesses or many small businesses. If the community chooses large, corporate-type businesses, it must then decide which industries would most profit from a concentration of developmental efforts. The choice of industry, of course, should reflect the economic as well as social needs of the black community. This should be thoroughly analyzed to determine what resources are already available to the community and what additional resources are needed in order to achieve community objectives. If the necessary resources for success do not presently exist within the community, plans should be made either to import them or to create them within the community. This could mean an increased investment in people to create human capital.

After the desired industries are agreed on by the black community, specific businesses within the designated industry should be selected. These choices should be made with the community's objectives and resources fully in mind. In selecting specific business ventures, careful consideration should be given to each business's overall potential, its source of capital, management, and any other assistance that may be required. Once selected, business must be implemented by applying good sound business principles to their day-to-day operation. The business always must be operated to earn, at the least, a reasonable profit. It is, therefore, necessary that the organization's management team devote the majority of its time and energy to the managerial functions of organizing, planning, directing, actuating, and controlling instead of to other, nonmanagerial activities.

It should be remembered that the definition of a problem is the difference or "gap" between existing conditions and desired conditions. It is also important to remember that the problem-solving process consists essentially of four steps: (1) problem definition, identification, and formation, (2) the search for alternative solutions to the problem, (3) evaluation and assessment of alternatives, and (4) selection of the best alternative. It should be obvious that if a selected alternative does not solve the problem, it was probably not the "best" alternative for that problem, probably because the problem was not adequately or accurately defined or diagnosed. One should always seek a precise problem definition which first should be analyzed in light of facts and then resolved so as to be consistent with certain explicit as well as implicit principles.

It is our hope that these readings can provide the sketchy outlines of a black economic development portrait.

Acknowledgments

Special recognition is due Esau Jackson, M.B.A., Western Michigan University and a University of Michigan law student, with whom the idea for this book originated. He worked on the earliest stages of the collection, although unfortunately he was unable to contribute significantly before revisions, additions, and reorganization gave the book its present form.

We also wish to thank the following faculty and staff members of The University of Michigan for their encouragement and assistance: Paul Root, former Director, Division of Research, and Alfred W. Swinyard, Associate Dean, School of Business Administration; Donald N. Smith, Director, and Lawrence Crockett, former Assistant Director, Industrial Development Division, Institute for Science and Technology.

Although we cannot begin to list the names of all who helped, we are especially grateful to Henrietta Slote and Alice Preketes, editorial staff, Division of Research, School of Business Administration, for invaluable aid in the final editing and printing of the book.

Finally, we are indebted to the authors whose works appear here as well as to Alfred L. Edwards, Director, Division of Research, School of Business Administration, who has been a most helpful critic.

I
Analysis:
Historical and
Contemporary

Getting It together

John Seder and
Berkeley G. Burrell

Before Emancipation

The conciliatory spirit of the Revolutionary War was short-lived and deceptive, for the attitude of American society towards blacks in the early years of the Republic was charged with the character of slavery. The moral indignation of the new abolitionist movement was confined to isolated groups and areas, one of which was New England. But while writers and orators delivered their tirades in that abolitionist stronghold, New England merchants continued to sell African black men into Southern slavery.

In both North and South, the black man struggled to secure a measure of economic independence in an atmosphere of subordination, subservience and contempt for his personality. Although Northern blacks were under generally less severe restrictions and suffered less outright cruelty, they fared no better economically than those in the South. In a way, their situation was worse—a slaveowner usually at least fed his slaves. Even the abolitionists were silent on the issue of employing blacks in the higher pursuits of labor. Competition with Northern whites in even the most menial jobs made it very difficult for free blacks to earn a livelihood. Thus entrepreneurship was often a last-resort endeavor.

Among the free blacks who sought economic independence in the post-Revolutionary period, Paul Cuffe was one of the earliest and most outstanding. He was born in New Bedford, Massachusetts, in 1759 of an African freedman father and an Indian mother. Possessing very little formal education, he was nevertheless determined to make his way in that settlement of seafarers and soon excelled in mathematics and navigation.

In a brave and significant act during the Revolutionary War, Cuffe and one of his brothers refused to pay tax in Massachusetts on the grounds that they and all other blacks were denied the right to vote. Their protest went all the way to the state legislature, which honored their suit by passing a law granting free blacks full citizenship with all accompanying rights and privileges.

3

Cuffe had gone to sea at sixteen. Five years later, in 1780, he began to build and operate his own ships, starting with a small open boat of less than ten tons, which made regular runs to New York and points farther south. By 1806, he had moved into the fleet class with one large ship, two brigs and several small vessels; he also had sizable holdings of real estate. His operations later extended to the West Indies and England.

Along the way he joined the Quakers, becoming deeply interested in improving the lot of his fellow blacks. He went to Sierra Leone on one of his ships in 1811 to investigate the possibilities of establishing free black colonies in Africa. Three years later he took thirty-eight people to Sierra Leone in an unsuccessful attempt at colonization that cost him almost $4,000. Paul Cuffe died in 1817, leaving an estate of over $20,000 from his shipping empire.

In New York City, Samuel Fraunces opened a restaurant where George Washington often dined and where the New York State Chamber of Commerce was organized. Fraunces Tavern is still in business—under white ownership.

During the early 1800s, the seat of black affluence was Philadelphia. As early as 1789, free blacks ran small shops throughout the city, and by 1820 the black population of 12,000 persons owned about $250,000 worth of property. Richard Allen, founder of the African Methodist Episcopal Church, was one of these influential black leaders. He owned a boot-and-shoe store and, with his friend Absalom Jones, also a minister and businessman, he formed the Free African Society of Philadelphia, Pennsylvania. This nonsectarian religious organization operated a mutual-aid society, which marked the beginning of the black insurance business.

Perhaps the most successful Philadelphia entrepreneur was James Forten, a Revolutionary War veteran who made a fortune as a sail manufacturer. Starting as an errand boy around the docks, he learned the trade through apprenticeship to a white man who recognized young Forten's exceptional abilities. Upon the death of his mentor, Forten took over the business and expanded it until there were more than forty employees, including whites. The company continued to prosper until steam navigation came into general use.

James Forten was an active abolitionist and a close associate of William Lloyd Garrison. As a financial angel for the antislavery movement, he is credited with saving Garrison's famous paper, the *Liberator*. Forten also championed a movement to hold periodic national conventions of free blacks in order to attack the mounting problems confronting them.

By the time of Forten's death in 1842, black business in Philadelphia had succumbed to a series of setbacks. The influx of competitive European immigrants resulted in racial clashes that often erupted into riots. Black citizens in the City of Brotherly Love had been deprived of the right to vote in 1836, and subsequently the number of black businessmen and women there dropped sharply.

In Cincinnati, a black cabinetmaker named Henry Boyd built a factory for the manufacture of bedsteads when local prejudice prevented him from practicing his trade. Boyd invented a machine to produce rails for beds and obtained a patent for it in a white man's name. His furniture-making operation occupied four buildings and at one time employed fifty men.

The settlement that later became Chicago, Illinois, was founded shortly after the Revolution by a black trapper and fur trader named Jean Baptiste Point du Sable. Neighboring Indians reportedly had a saying: "The first white man to settle in Chicago was a Negro."

Black merchants also ventured into the newly opened Western territories. William Alexander Leidesdorff, who became a rancher, merchant and land speculator in California, was born in the Virgin Islands, the son of a Danish planter and an African mother. At an early age he was sent to New Orleans to work in the office of his brothers, who were in the cotton business. When the brothers died, leaving him a fortune, Leidesdorff adventurously sold his property, bought a 106-ton schooner and set sail for San Francisco Bay, which he reached months later after a hazardous voyage around Cape Horn. This same ship made several voyages to Hawaii in Leidesdorff's export-import business.

Pre-gold-rush California, thinly populated and still under Mexican domination, was coveted by both the United States and England. Leidesdorff was able to capitalize on this international intrigue. He had himself appointed American consul in California, and then became naturalized as a Mexican citizen. He entertained officials from both countries in his impressive home and was able to wheel and deal his way to fortune. He built stores and a warehouse in San Francisco, the latter on a street bearing his name. In 1844, he obtained a grant of 35,000 acres of land on a bank of the American River.

The political intrigue ended when the U.S. Marines landed and captured Monterey in 1846, but Leidesdorff continued to expand his holdings. In 1847, he launched the first steamship to pass through the Golden Gate; when he died a year later, at the age of thirty-eight, his estate totaled about $1,000,000.

In the South, the majority of blacks were slaves and could neither trade freely nor purchase goods. But a few were free and their presence was a constant embarrassment to the slaveholders, for it seemed to undermine the very foundation upon which slavery was built, the alleged inferiority of blacks. Southern whites considered it in their best interest to keep them "in their place."

A rash of restrictive laws affected the legal and property rights—even freedom of movement—of free blacks. Some states passed specific economic proscriptions. In 1805, Maryland prohibited free blacks from selling corn, wheat or tobacco without a license. A North Carolina law of 1831 required licenses, which were difficult if not impossible to obtain, for all free black traders and peddlers. Other legislation barred them from certain trades and occupations.

Nevertheless, a few black men had a natural business acumen that enabled them to achieve success in the Southern states. Lunsford Lane, a servant for a wealthy citizen in Raleigh, also ran errands for merchants and he learned much by observing their business operations. Since the state legislature met in Raleigh and its members were heavy smokers, he started a business to supply them with pipes and tobacco. Later he expanded to cover a large part of the state.

With his profits Lane bought freedom. Since that was still illegal in North Carolina, he went to New York with his master's agent to complete the transaction. Returning to Raleigh, he continued his tobacco business and opened a general merchandise store and lumberyard. Although he grew quite wealthy and counted the well-to-do people of Raleigh among his patrons, he was unpopular among poor whites, who demanded that he be expelled from the state under a law forbidding free blacks from other states to reside in North Carolina. Finally, all of his property was taken from him by force and he was tarred and feathered and driven out of town.

An earlier North Carolina businessman, John C. Stanley, had been freed by a legislative act in 1798. He was a prosperous barber who invested in plantations and bought and freed many blacks. It is reported that his net worth of more than $40,000 made him one of the wealthiest men in Craven County, North Carolina.

Black entrepreneurship emerged even in Washington, D.C., which was perhaps the most notorious slave market in the country until 1850. William Wormley was a wealthy man who owned and operated the largest livery stable in Washington. Unfortunately, Wormley's health and business declined after repeated acts of vandalism and persecution following the riots of 1835.

A number of free black merchants prospered in Louisiana, where they owned sugar and cotton plantations—with slaves—and a variety of thriving businesses. By 1860, their property was said to be worth more than $15,000,000. Thomy Lafon, a New Orleans cotton broker, had accumulated half a million dollars at the time of his death and had contributed so much to the city that the state legislature ordered a bust of him to be carved and placed in the state museum.

Thus there was black entrepreneurship in the United States even before the Civil War. The outstanding achievements of these black men in a hostile society were testimonials to their exceptional shrewdness and determination. But they were not only unusual; they were few in number. The fact that the vast majority of the black population lived in bondage made it impossible for free black men to develop a broad business class.

After Emancipation

Abraham Lincoln's Emancipation Proclamation, which freed only the Southern slaves and which he acknowledged to be primarily a military expedient aimed at undermining the South's position, took effect on January 1, 1863. Northern slaves were not freed until early 1865, on the eve of victory. After the war, the newly emancipated blacks fought an uphill battle to participate in a shattered national economy. The grant of freedom did not and could not alter the conditioning of a slave society or the dearth of capital, experience and training. A strong entrepreneurial tradition and inclination was lacking among the freedmen, and the number of blacks in business in the years just after the Civil War was not substantially greater than before.

Emancipation understandably made less change in the status of blacks in business in the North than in the South. With the exception of the grant of civil rights, which had generally been withheld, Northern blacks had nothing new in their lives. The vigorous postwar industrial development of the North and West left behind the small local pursuits of the black businessman. Barbers, caterers and restaurant keepers continued to eke out meager incomes, just as they had before the war.

There were, however, some exceptional entrepreneurial efforts in the North and Border States. One, the Chesapeake and Marine Railway and Dry Dock Company, was organized in 1865 by a group of blacks in Baltimore, Maryland. Created to protect black mechanics from the competition and prejudice of their white counterparts, it was capitalized at $40,000. By 1870 the company was prosperous enough to buy a shipyard, but profits began to decline in 1877 and it went out of business in 1883.

In the South, the release of 4,000,000 people from bondage had enormous implications for the economy. White Southerners grudgingly accepted emancipation, but they had no interest in helping the freedmen achieve economic independence; indeed, they fought any attempt to raise the black race out of poverty. Legal and monetary difficulties were created for any black man who sought to engage in business in competition with whites. They were even driven out of those industries and crafts that they had mastered as slaves. In fact, the activities of black businessmen were limited and experimental until almost 1900.

Still, there were, as always, important exceptions. As early as 1866, James Tate was running a fine grocery in Atlanta, Georgia. Elijah Cook was the highly prosperous proprietor of an undertaking establishment in Montgomery, Alabama. A store owned by Samuel Harris in Williamsburg, Virginia, brought in over $50,000 a year. Other individually owned enterprises flourished in cities such as Charleston, New Orleans, and Memphis. Southern blacks also engaged in co-operative farming ventures—a number of large plantations were owned and successfully managed by blacks who had combined their resources to purchase the property and pooled their labor to provide a work force.

The most serious blow to black economic development after the Civil War was the collapse of the Freedmen's Savings Bank and Trust Company, an enterprise that was neither initiated nor managed by blacks. The bank was authorized by an act of Congress in March 1865, and it began operating in May of that year. Its main office was first located in New York, then moved to Washington, with branches established in many cities throughout the South.

Although the bank was not an agency of the federal government, it was clearly the intent of Congress to create an institution of unimpeachable integrity. The bank was managed by a board of trustees consisting of fifty wealthy and prominent citizens who were presumably also dedicated and public-spirited. These men were expected to protect the hard-earned savings of black people, most of whom were newly freed slaves. The trustees were required to serve without salary. However, no security or bond was required of the officers, and strangely enough there was no penalty for misconduct. (Only later, when the bank was virtually bankrupt, did Congress amend the Act of Incorporation to provide for punishment of misconduct as a misdemeanor, with a maximum five-year sentence upon conviction.)

Black people all over the country believed Freedmen's to be a United States government institution. Promotional literature distributed by the bank further enforced this belief, as did many speeches made by bank officers. Blacks rushed in such numbers to place their deposits that by 1872 there were 70,000 depositors in thirty-four branches of the bank. The Freedmen's Bank was controlled by white men, and at the beginning almost all of its employees were white. Later, increasing numbers of blacks were employed as tellers and clerks and in lower supervisory posts. However, almost to the end of the bank's existence, there was no room for blacks at the top of their own major financial institution.

Dr. Abram L. Harris gives this vivid description of the national climate that led to the failure of the Freedmen's Bank:

> The period from 1866 to the panic of 1873 was one of reckless speculation, over-capitalization, stock manipulation, intrigue and bribery, and downright plundering. In this welter of corruption, high finance, and fraud, the Bank played a passive role. The persons responsible for its failure were irresponsible plunderers, typical of a large group of financial speculators who rose to ascendancy in the country's economic life during this period. Such persons welcomed any opportunity which gave them control over other people's funds that could be used in speculative, if not fraudulent, ventures. Falling into the hands of such characters, small wonder that the Bank failed.[1]

Recognizing the progressive weakening of the bank's condition, many of the white trustees withdrew their accounts. Others resigned, including many who had participated in authorizing the speculation that led to the difficulties. As the news spread, other depositors also began to withdraw.

In a last-ditch attempt to save the Freedmen's Bank, the trustees decided to bring in the great black orator and statesman, Frederick Douglass, to serve as president. (This was, and is, a common white tactic—to select a popular black figure to restore the confidence of the black community in a faltering venture.) It was widely believed at the time that the trustees deliberately concealed the true condition of the bank from Douglass. Blacks were also added to the board of trustees and the advisory councils of the branches. But these moves were too little and too late. Confidence in the bank had been so completely shattered within the black community that it closed its doors forever in June of 1874.

The failure was disastrous, both in its financial repercussions and in its moral consequences. It was not merely that many blacks lost faith in savings banks at a time when they desperately required them; nor was it merely that the dollars lost were needed so badly. The worst aspect was that black people were convinced that they had been deliberately swindled by the United States government.

Because they understood that the Freedmen's Bank had never been under their direction, many blacks saw the need for banks of their own. The first two were established in 1888—the Savings Bank of the Grand Fountain United Order of True Reformers in Richmond, Virginia, and the Capital Savings Bank in Washington, D.C. A year later, the Mutual Trust Company was organized in Chattanooga, Tennessee, and in 1890 the Alabama Penny Savings and Loan Company was started in Birmingham. No fewer than twenty-eight banks had been started by blacks by 1905.

Most of these early financial institutions were short-lived. Starting with limited capital, they soon faltered as a result of ill-advised long-term loans, speculation and misappropriation of funds by bank officials. Although both ineptness and larceny were common in banking and business at this time regardless of the race of the owning and controlling interests, these early failures produced an unfortunate image that plagues black banks even today.

In the gold-mining boom town of Denver, Colorado, a former fugitive slave named Barney Ford established the Inter-Ocean Hotel in 1873 and made it a showplace for millionaires and Presidents. Strangely, he was beleaguered all his life by townspeople convinced that his source of wealth was actually gold from a nearby hill rather than his prosperous hotel and restaurant business.

Ford was deeply concerned about the removal of voting rights for blacks from the territorial constitution and led a fight to block statehood for Colorado until they were restored. Perhaps as a result of Ford's campaign, President Andrew Johnson vetoed the Colorado-statehood bill. If he had signed it Colorado's two Senators-designate, known to be anti-Johnson, would have provided the crucial votes to defeat Johnson in the impeachment trial and remove him from office.

Later, in 1880, a special commission was appointed to decide the winner of the bitterly contested presidential election between Samuel Tilden and Rutherford B. Hayes. Barney Ford was extremely close to the Colorado representatives on the commission, and it was widely believed that his influence produced the commission's decision in favor of Hayes by a single vote. Thus it is possible that this fugitive slave changed the course of presidential history not once but twice.

About this time, benevolent and fraternal insurance and burial societies, under the influence and control of churches, were organized in many black communities. Ministers used the spiritual bonds of their congregations to establish mutual-aid societies, which assured dignified burial for members of the congregation and provided access to insurance coverage—something very difficult for blacks to obtain. A number of these societies evolved into national organizations. Eighteen ninety-eight saw the founding of what is now the largest black-controlled business institution in the world, the North Carolina Mutual Life Insurance Company. Another pioneer insurance venture was Atlanta Life Insurance Company, a stock company.

A study of black business progress was undertaken in 1899 and 1900 by Dr. W. E. B. DuBois under the auspices of Atlanta University. The study covered 1,906 enterprises with $500 or more of capital. It showed that many had evolved from the occupations dictated by slavery. House servants became barbers, restaurant keepers and caterers; field hands became gardeners, grocers, florists and millowners. Those who had been plantation craftsmen used their talents to become builders and contractors, brickmasons, painters and blacksmiths.

In 1896 the Coleman Cotton Mills were established in Concord, North Carolina, by seven black men, including R. B. Fitzgerald, E. A. Johnson, and W. C. Coleman. The founders had made a feasibility study by communicating with black people all over the country to determine whether they thought that such a mill was desirable and practical. The responses were very favorable and led in some cases to substantial individual investments in the enterprise. The plant consisted of a huge three-story brick building with power facilities, adjacent structures and grounds.

Coleman Cotton Mills manufactured cotton yarns and goods using the latest equipment and machinery; its work force of about 250 people included many skilled craftsmen. Only a few black businesses of that size exist today. The company shipped goods all over the United States and to parts of Africa and several cities in England. From this mill and the efforts of one of its employees, a black master mechanic, there also grew a wool mill, established in 1901.

Among other ventures founded during the last years of the nineteenth century were Mount Alto Mining and Land Company of Virginia, a real estate brokerage and contracting firm incorporated in 1880; several large denominational publishing boards, including the National Baptist Publishing Board of Nashville, Tennessee; Wormley's Hotel in Washington, established by James Wormley, who died leaving an estate of over $100,000; a firm of truck gardeners in Charleston, South Carolina, established before 1870, which had 500 acres under extensive cultivation and shipped several carloads of produce to Northern markets each week; and the Baltimore *Afro-American* newspaper, which is now published by the second-, third- and fourth-generation descendants of the founder, John Henry Murphy, Sr.

Other businesses were built by H. C. Haynes, inventor of the Haynes Razor Strap in Chicago; James N. Vanderall and Z. T. Evans, mattress manufacturers in Orange, New Jersey, and New Orleans; John S. Hicks, owner of a bakery and ice-cream and candy plants in Erie, Pennsylvania; and Junius Graves, known as the "Negro Potato King" in Kansas in the 1880s and 1890s.

One of the most successful businesswomen, black or white, that America has produced was Mme. C. J. Walker. Born in Louisiana in 1869, she was orphaned at the age of six. She married at fourteen and at twenty was a widow with a small child to support. After moving to Saint Louis, Missouri, she worked as a washerwoman and laundress and then married Charles J. Walker. Mme. Walker's claim to fame and riches was her invention of a hair-styling formula and process that included a hair softener and a special straightening comb. Later she moved to Indianapolis, Indiana, and founded the world's first black cosmetics company. It grew rapidly into a thriving manufacturing business with more than 2,000 sales agents, and sales-training schools in many cities. The more enterprising of the salespeople became franchised dealers for the "Walker System" of hair preparation. The company is still in business.

Another outstanding business venture still in operation is the Chicago *Defender*, founded in 1905 by Robert S. Abbott. The *Defender* has now expanded from a weekly to a daily newspaper. Operated by the three Sengstacke brothers, nephews of the founder, the *Defender* also owns the Pittsburgh *Courier*, which was started by Robert L. Vann in 1910, and two other weeklies.

The Overton Hygienic Products Company was organized in Chicago in 1911 by Anthony Overton. This company manufactures and distributes baking powder, flavor extracts and various toilet articles. Overton was involved in several other ventures including the Douglas National Bank.

Against this background of black business development, Booker T. Washington called in 1900 for the formation of the National Negro Business League. That same year more than 400 delegates, about eighty percent of them from the South, attended the organizing convention in Boston, Massachusetts. Washington saw to it that a large part of the convention's program was devoted to individual accounts of business achievement by black people from every section of the country, from cities and rural areas, in many fields of endeavor. These success stories, told in simple, dignified terms and recounted extensively in the newspapers, provided a powerful motivation for black men interested in careers in business.

Washington noted that wherever a black man succeeded in business, in either the North or South, he was treated with respect by the white community. He hoped that, as these examples multiplied in city after city, they would rapidly provide a solution to the race problem. Although that hope proved to be wildly optimistic, the basic idea was sound—when an individual produces what the world wants and needs, the world does not inquire as to his skin color before buying.

Washington made clear to the delegates that the league was to be open to all black businessmen in the communities—no matter how small or insignificant. His objective was to reach all of them and encourage habits of thrift, self-reliance and self-respect; he hoped that they in turn would instill such habits in the black masses so that they might become the consumer class that black business desperately needed.

As the league achieved widespread acceptance and influence in black communities throughout the nation, many local chapters were organized. The next conventions were held in Chicago in 1901, Richmond in 1902, Nashville in 1903, Indianapolis in 1904 and New York City in 1905.

During the years between 1900 and 1920, committees were formed within the structure of the league that developed into the major business and trade organizations still serving black communities across the nation. These include the National Negro Funeral Directors' Association, National Negro Press Association, National Negro Bar Association, National Negro Bankers Association, National Negro Farmers Association and National Negro Insurance Association.

Through World War and Depression

While there had been a gradual northward movement of blacks after 1890, the first mass migrations from the South occurred during and immediately after World War I. Prior to 1914, the country was absorbing almost 1,000,000 immigrant laborers a year from Europe, but the war made it impossible for them to get to America. Northern industry was busy manufacturing munitions and supplies, first for the European combatants and later for the U.S. war effort, and it needed large numbers of workers. Black people moved North to take these jobs.

However, the black migrants soon became painfully aware that the black belts of the cities held no dream-fulfilling prospects. In most instances the migrants were forced to live in old houses that were the hand-me-downs of whites fleeing the black "invasion" and proved to be run-down, rat-infested, dirty and poorly provided with sanitation facilities. When the war ended, the government's need for supplies and services was cut back sharply; contracts with suppliers were canceled and many plants either closed or drastically reduced operations. This brought a worsening labor market and a return to the familiar pattern—blacks, who had been the last to be hired, were the first to be fired.

Black disenchantment found expression in the back-to-Africa movement championed by Marcus Garvey's Universal Negro Improvement Association. Garvey stressed economic self-sufficiency for blacks and urged that they establish their own retail, distribution and production outlets. He also appealed to pride of race and taught the virtues of the rich African heritage of black Americans. A brilliant organizer, political tactician and leader, Garvey had grandiose designs for a black economy. He started the Black Star Line, a steamship company, the Universal Improvement Corporation, and other ventures. All of them failed, however, perhaps because he did not seek the assistance of technical and financial experts.

Meanwhile, mass migration from the South had created a black market in Northern cities, where black workers were paid higher wages than they had been receiving in rural Southern areas. Black businesses were established to serve these people. For the year 1920 the United States Department of Commerce estimated black purchasing power at $2 billion.

Thousands of black businesses were founded in the 1920s, most but not all of them small retail and service shops. A number of insurance companies, banks, and savings and loan associations came into being, many of which survived the Depression and are operating today. People's Finance Corporation, a small loan company, sprang up in Saint Louis. The Greenfield (Ohio) Bus Company manufactured bus bodies. The Cannolene Company of Atlanta manufactured cosmetics and sold them door to door and by mail. A man named H. Omohundro owned the Norfolk (Virginia) Mirror Company, which manufactured plate glass and stained glass as well as mirrors. There were also a number of building contractors in Norfolk.

One of the best-known businesses of 1920s was a music-publishing house started by Harry H. Pace and the composer W. C. Handy. The white recording companies had only recently been persuaded to sign black artists and performers. However, this breakthrough was considerably tainted, for they did not allow the artists their full range of expression and talent but insisted on "molding" them in "acceptable" styles. Many of these companies refused to permit any black compositions except certain kinds of blues and minstrel numbers.

Pace felt strongly that blacks should be represented as manufacturers in the phonograph-record industry in order to provide black concert, religious and jazz artists with the proper material, media and setting for their talents. He also believed that such a company could be a sound financial venture providing a good return to the investors. He dreamed of records sung, played, recorded and manufactured by black people.

The white record companies, recognizing the threat of this showcase for black talent, threw up obstacles in Pace's path. When Pace attempted to purchase a record-pressing plant, a large white company bought it just to keep him out. Eventually, he was forced to resign as president of Pace and Handy in order to free the company from threatened reprisals. Nevertheless, the company managed to record a number of classical, popular, jazz and blues artists under the Black Swan Label. All of these recordings are valuable classics today.

During the 1920s the National Negro Business League continued to grow in membership and influence. In the early twenties its president, Robert R. Moton, proposed the formation of a corporation that would finance business enterprises among blacks. This National Negro Finance Corporation came into being in 1924 with pledges of $150,000 of capital. Subsequently, Dr. Moton became ill; without his driving spirit the enterprise never really got off the ground.

The Colored Merchants Association (CMA) was begun in August 1928 in Montgomery, Alabama, by twelve local black grocers headed by A. C. Brown. It was a "voluntary" chain: that is, a joining together of a number of independent store owners to act collectively. The purchase orders of the group were combined into one large unit, and wholesale grocers in Montgomery were invited to bid on the combined order. Uniform accounting systems were used as well as cooperative advertising.

Albon Holsey of Tuskegee was the national organizer for the CMA chain. He instituted an educational program among the store owners and operators stressing provision of sufficient variety of fresh stock of good quality, and at prices comparable to those of white groceries and service. Race pride was to be only an incidental factor in attracting customers under this program.

A warehouse was opened in New York City, stocking canned goods, coffee, tea and other staples with CMA labels. Under Holsey's organizational efforts, the chain found outlets in Manhattan, Brooklyn, Philadelphia, Richmond, Winston-Salem, Nashville, Detroit, Chicago, Dallas and other cities. It was just beginning to get on its feet at the time of the stock-market collapse in 1929, and was not strong enough to survive ten years of depression.

Black businesses, especially the larger ones, were devastated by the Depression. As the economic distress of the nation deepened, more and more insurance companies and commercial establishments failed and were liquidated. Those that survived cut their work forces drastically.

Across the nation thirteen black banks failed during the period, some them after twenty years in operation. Dozens of white banks also failed in the early 1930s, and in most cases the depositors lost every penny of their savings.

While most businesses at that time were foundering, a few managed to get started: Crayton's Southern Sausage Company, the Industrial Bank of Washington, organized in 1934, and Virginia Mutual Benefit Life Insurance Company, founded in 1933.

In black communities during the Depression, emphasis shifted back to the economic boycott, the organizing of purchasing power so that blacks might obtain employment in the stores in black neighborhoods. Many communities converted these into "Buy Black—Support Your Own" plans. Chicago had exceptionally effective selective-buying programs.

The election in 1932 of Franklin D. Roosevelt offered hope to a despairing nation, especially to its black people. For the first time since Ulysses S. Grant, there was a man in the White House who seemed to have a slight perception, a tiny glimmer of understanding about what black people were enduring in this country. For the first time since the dreams of freedom were shattered in the Reconstruction era, some thought they saw light at the end of the long, long tunnel. One of the achievements of his New Deal was the opening of aid programs to black people. By 1939 the Works Progress Administration, a large federal job-creation effort, was employing a million black men on its projects throughout the country, even though it was operated in a discriminatory manner in the South.

Another significant event of the 1930s was the establishment of the Congress of Industrial Organizations, which splintered away from the highly exclusive, craft-based American Federation of Labor and created a new type of industrial union that welcomed all the workers in an industry. For the first time blacks were able to join, and by 1940 an estimated 210,000 had become members of various CIO unions.

One of the most important events of the twentieth century for black people—one which foreshadowed a new era and set an example for the 1960s—never happened at all. In 1941, A. Philip Randolph and other black leaders and national organizations called for a march on Washington to dramatize and publicize dissatisfaction with employment opportunities in defense industries. Despite booming production in these plants, blacks in most instances were hired only in the most menial, unskilled categories.

In a desperate last-minute move to head off the march, which would have involved 100,000 blacks in a powerful demonstration of unity and determination, President Roosevelt finally yielded to the demands of the sponsors and issued Executive Order 8802, which stated the federal government's policy against discrimination in employment.

The Fair Employment Practices Committee was established with a field staff to investigate violations, process complaints and hold public hearings. As a result, employment opportunities were opened for blacks and other minorities, especially in the aircraft industry and the shipyards, which were important centers of the war effort. Also, black women were hired in much larger numbers and at higher levels in government departments, agencies and bureaus.

Once again, in 1941 as in 1861, the nation turned its total energies to a terrible war—and once again black people thought that when it was over they might be free at last. Sadly, many of these dreams have been frustrated once more, but not entirely—as the stories that follow will illustrate.

NOTES

1. Dr. Abram L. Harris, *The Negro as Capitalist* (Philadelphia, Pa.: American Academy of Political and Social Science, 1936), p. 33.

The Rev. Jesse Jackson
Tells it like it is

The Rev. Jesse Jackson

The greatness of the Interracial Council for Business Opportunity (ICBO) is expressed in its ability to hear, and be willing to accept, the demands of change. Not so much that history is bringing, history is a rather abstract notion much like time is. And in the course of history and in time, the people organize their minds and demand what is theirs; things will change for the better for them in time. And a bad history can become a good future. I stand here—with my basic roots in the black community fully recognizing that our getting out of the hole that we're in is not going to be any picnic, nor is it going to be easy. Nor once we begin to demand the sharing of our power will we be able to take some of the friends on in that are now with us at this stage of the game. Leaders are dying. But the ideas they left behind are being born in this age, being born with children that the press cannot keep up with; nor can the present establishment leadership identify. Not even anymore by hair style and dress style. Truly an idea has come in its own time and it's in the universe. And it's almost going to be a you cut us in or you cut it out. It's all of our thing . . . or it's nobody's thing.

Some fundamental changes are going to have to come, with the young whites in my generation, if there's going to be peace, because—as I told a young white man, twenty-eight-years-old, who is the head of a major newspaper in Chicago, the other day—the both of us are going to have some serious dialogue about our relationship, since, with other things being equal, both of us are going to be living in Chicago for awhile. Because I know I was not going to be to him as my daddy was to his daddy, and he needs to prepare to be different to me than his daddy was to my daddy. Now, I didn't know where his daddy was, or what he was, but something fundamental had changed, because I changed. Something had reminded me on the inside that the rights that we are now volleying for are my God-given rights. They already belong to me. And something on the outside tells me, when I see black men like me who develop once they get an iota of a chance; something on the outside reminds me that these rights can be obtained.

The black man is in a dilemma. After more than 300-odd years of a kind of injustice we like to pass over very fast, we still are trapped trying to prove ourselves in a situation that is essentially still the black man's burden and the white man's shame. And yet, seeking self-pity is no solution for our problem, or our own inner health and our own outer functioning; we are called on to be as productive and resourceful and as understanding as anybody. As resourceful as those who have never known oppression and exploitation. This is our dilemma. We're called upon to be at the finish line with the same people who left before we left. And even though they left before we left, and we were behind—our ankles went in chains and then our minds,—yet we still are expected to do the impossible. It is enough to make a racer give up in despair. And yet for some reason, this ain't the stuff we're made out of. And I want to share with you perhaps what may not make you comfortable, but if you will hear, a little more aware. Racism has always been the excuse and the scapegoat for the whites, but we've spent a disproportionate amount of time arguing about black-white, moral-immoral, good-evil. Why are we using social argument about an economic situation? The situation has always been profit-loss, assets-liability.

Blacks were not the first slaves on this soil; whites were. And when it ceased to be economically profitable for whatever the international circumstance was, they shifted to the red man. His character development was so strong, his sense of somebodiness was so in harmony with the universe, he was not capable of being enslaved and exploited. Not racially . . . not sexually . . . but economically. And it was through the rape of Africa and the corruption on that continent, and the relationship with the exploiters from other continents, and the Middle passage and the right back-breaking process, and the personality-splitting processes that the black man became capable of being enslaved, but for economic purposes. Racism became an ideological scapegoat for the ignorant white who was kept ignorant for economic reasons in order that the laws of supply and demand would keep an abundant and cheap labor supply. You'll always have too many poor blacks, too many poor whites, too many poor browns, and too many poor reds competing for jobs that did not exist, for they became preoccupied with each other's skin color. They could never deal with the economic situation and so even now we speak of polarization in the nation, we're arguing about the emotional or the sexual relationships, when black men and white women or white men and black women get together. We don't speak of quality education . . . we talk about integration, suggesting a sexual relationship. Never getting to the heart of the matter, that is, the crisis between black men and white men.

The black men have been made boys, therefore whites have ended up appearing to be supermen. I went along with the superman theory for awhile. I even became so careless in my rationale for being poor that I assumed white folk didn't work and black folk did. That isn't true. White folk work hard everyday. Always did work hard . . . except, they worked for themselves. And black folk worked hard . . . except, we worked for white folk. So it's two people working for the white folk, and nobody working for us. Sometimes we continue to beg the question of black preparation. I hear it in bits and pieces, black progress has never been in proportion to black preparation, but always in proportion to the self-interest economically of the mental wealth of the American white male. We were ready to play baseball before '47. Prepared. We were prepared to sit on the front of a bus before '55. We were prepared to vote before '65. Black progress is in proportion to black opportunity, which usually comes with the organization of blacks and concerned whites to take power, because they're seldom ever given a share.

Argue with the record. Even through black genius or drastic national conditions, or international circumstances, we've made progress. You show me the progress made during the era of Abraham Lincoln, I'll show you a black genius named Frederick Douglass right behind him . . . I'll show you a circumstance of the Civil War. You show me the major progress made during the era of Franklin D. Roosevelt, I'll show you an A. Philip Randolph prodding him and the circumstance of a national depression. You show me the progress made during the era of a John F. Kennedy, I'll show you a Martin Luther King, prodding him and the circumstance of international embarrassment as nations rose to independence in Africa.

I would tell my brothers to be aware and sensitive to the nature of this crisis. We're involved in a struggle right now with A & P in this city, and it's war time! They aren't going to give us anything. With a break here and there. I don't feel good, to have you dole out on your timetable what is already mine.

Yeah, we made good progress with A & P in Chicago, because of the 72 stores, 40 were in the black community. And we didn't change the heart of the president, we changed the economic alternatives under which he made decisions. We cut off his marginal profit. It did not increase his love for us, but we were not seeking a personal relationship where love was necessary. We were seeking an institutional relationship where justice and respect is the issue. And our banks grooved, 'cause we fed the 40 stores in the black community and put our money in our banks, that all future stores in our community be built by us; that we have priority of our products on the shelves of our community. The Freedom National Bank in the last three months has received only $3 million from the Hall Clothiers, not because of a manifestation of goodness, but power. Now, we can take this for what it's worth. Being up North and being intimidated, being a "country preacher" like I am, I don't get enough of these kinds of audience to get used to them no-how. So, if I wasn't to get back, I couldn't get too upset, 'cause I wouldn't be missing nothing.

But I suspect you all knew who I was before I got here, so I'll go on and represent that, that I represent. It's a strange notion that black folk only represent at the level of leadership, black folk. There has never been a sound idea offered by black leaders for black folk that did not help white folk. What is good for the black community is good for America, but what is good to the white community is not necessarily good for anybody in the world. So, I'm going to use lack of black symbolic leadership as a reason why blacks are not making progress now. Didn't need any one national black leader to tax us. Didn't need any one national black leader to draft us. Didn't need any black national leadership to enslave us.

The fact of the matter is the polarization is not half as great at the base of the economy between the poor who are trapped in the arguing of social issues. The real polarization is not horizontal between poor black and poor white, it is vertical between the haves and have-nots; between the greedy and the needy—that is a serious polarization and that pole is extended. The fact is the rich are getting richer and taxed less, and the poor are getting poorer, and the foundation money which amounts to the chump-change of the industry is not enough to pick up the base of the American economy. Let's look at who's at the base. I looked at it—*Time* and *Newsweek* two or three weeks ago, and it attempted to depict or project a welfare project, still giving the implication by pictures, if not by words, that welfare was a black crisis. Oh, I read the fine print—said that more whites on welfare than more blacks. But you know, one picture is worth a thousand words. The fact of the matter is that welfare came into existence for white folk. It was during the white Depression of the 30s that welfare came into existence. If welfare was as a result of an objective economic status, that is what we would have received when forty acres and a mule was reneged on—but welfare was a response to white poverty. So in America, there are more poor whites on welfare than blacks and there have always been. War on poverty was not a response to rats in Harlem, but poverty in West Virginia. That's why blacks must at least be rational enough to know that we may not be brothers in love with poor whites, but we are economic brothers and survivors, and we are at the bottom class. Either ride together like brothers or stay at the bottom and suffocate like fools. That's based on the desire to live. Who's at the base of the economy? 40 million poor people in a nation of 200 million. Of the 40 million listed as malnourished, 28 million are white. Of the 14 million rural poor, 11 million are white. On the question of laziness and energy of the 40 million, 30 million live in a household where somebody works every day. They just made such little money, until their working is in vain. What is the problem? The top 1 percent of the nation owns absolutely 26 percent of the wealth and controls 84 percent. And the bottom 20 percent of the nation, owns less than 5.4 percent of the wealth. At no other time has an economic order had that great a gap between the greedy and the needy. What you in fact have, no matter what words you use, is an aristocracy under the veneer of a democracy and it needs the largest military on earth to suppress revolution. That's what we've got on our hands.

It ain't no accident that the federal budget of $157 billion, $85 billion is for killing programs; $13 billion for veterans of past wars; $10 billion for the national debt, $108 of $157 billion, 69.9 percent for killing and only 12.2 percent for health, welfare, and education, collectively, and that was the first part of the budget. Cut that. That does not mean that the nation is mean—it means that it is sick—and it is losing meaning. The genius of Whitney Young was that Whitney knew that organizing the poor black folk on a corner in Harlem would not address itself to this problem. Picking up some pitiful Negro, giving him a newspaper stand and a box of candy was not going to deal with this crisis. Even though it made him unpopular as a scientist, he went directly to the seat of power, and challenged those who have the ability to solve the problem, if they have the will. All black leaders from the most conservative to the most militant all have the will, but collectively we don't have the ability to free our people. White leadership has the ability, but not the will. That's why I suggested last week that we're going to test the sickness of racism, to deal with the crisis of lack of black business. We need to run a black man for President. And the only reason it does not make sense, even to the blacks who have been affected and cramped by racism, is that our expectation of black is national, rather than universal. This nation cannot afford any more to run an Eisenhower for president and assume that Ralph Bunche does not even exist in the universe, simply because he's black. Can't afford that no more. Right now, Congressmen Diggs, Conyers, Clay, Carl Stokes, Art Fletcher, men here now capable of leading this nation, 'cause they've always had experience of taking little and doing much. White leadership by and large has forfeited the right to lead. It cannot lead its family, it cannot lead its children, it cannot lead the nation. It is disrespected throughout the world.

I was in Africa two weeks ago, and America's respect is based on obedience to military power, not loyalty to moral truth. That is what made Toynbee so profound when he said "America is in the path of the 26 great previous civilizations that died from the inside out." I'm proud of the struggling black businessmen. Number one, in Africa, where there are underdeveloped nations just like Harlem, south-side Chicago, Fillmore District, and Watts, they do not call an underdeveloped nation a ghetto. Ghetto is the terminology of sociologist, which implies people gravitating for social reasons to a given geographical area. The Africans recognize themselves to be trapped in colonialism, a geographical area set up for at least four reasons. We must understand that the black colony is an American business. The black community itself is a conglomerate. It is a business. It is America's cheap labor base, still, that fits somewhere in business. The marginal profit of every major item produced and sold in America comes from the black community. Our consumer rate is at least 40 billion dollars a year, larger than all the nations in the world except six. That's why our boycotts are effective, because the margin of profit, even of General Motors, is in the black community, and anytime a man has the margin of profit of a major corporation in his mouth and chooses to beg that corporation rather than bite, he's a sick man, an insensitive man. I ain't going to beg nobody in my community to respect me.

Cheap labor base; margin of profit; soldiers during the time of war come out of the black community, disproportionate to our race. That's an economic investment. I want y'all to hear me. I want you to hear this: Whites who cannot get executive jobs in the white community usurp the executive jobs in the black community. That's why whites feel the pinch of the Depression last.

We thought we got whipped with bricks when we wanted to live next door to white folks in open housing, but when we demanded the right to let white folk alone, saying no, we won't live with, y'all don't like us no more, we just want to build the school next door; we just want to build the chain store on the block; when we demanded the right to build where we live, that is when white resistance became violent to the point National Guard was called out and presidential sanction was given to it. White hats . . . we argued about it as a social phenomenon; as an economic phenomenon of asking to build in our own community.

If we can't build in our own community, we have no choice but to tear it down, we have no self-interest in its growth, because there is no relationship between its growth and our growth. Black underdevelopment is a social predicament. A special social-economic predicament. Black development, therefore, will have to be a special social-economic development. In other words, for the 300 years of discrimination, since technology moves so fast until it can go off distance and time with speed, and since the black man of today is not the black man of 350 years ago, for discrimination there will have to be a program of compensation, not reverse discrimination. See, reverse discrimination puts the hook on the wrong side. It assumes that somebody's doing black folk a favor. It is not reverse discrimination; it is compensation to blacks for white discrimination. So you owe to us the development of our community, simply because you tore it up, just that simple.

Black folks ain't smuggling no dope in this country. Black folks are not absentee landlords. Nigeria, under the leadership of General Gowan, passed out an order a few weeks ago, saying, "There will be no more outside corporations in Nigeria. By six o'clock on the given day, all corporations will become Nigerian corporations, or we will seize their assets." They did not choose. They did not choose to say all white folk get out. They didn't say that. They said, that for white folks staying on in our land, with our laborers, we have the right to tax you and to use our tax money for our development. Now, let's transfer it over to Harlem. Suppose the tax money from Harlem went in the black bank of Harlem. Would the president of the black bank have to be grateful for some damned contribution? We can't put our tax money in our banks, and the rationale is that our banks are too small to hold our money, and they show us a law that says that. You know, if my pocket is too small to hold my money, which may be logical, if I got a lot of money, the answer to it is not "You hold my money." If my pockets are too small to hold my money, the answer is "Let me get bigger pockets." So the answer to the tax money of Harlem not going in Freedom National Bank ain't that Freedom National Bank is too small, therefore, downtown banks hold our money to invest in South Africa—that ain't the answer.

In closing, white man, black man, those who are concerned about the serious nature of the crisis, black folk have two choices: we can either go to the white power structure and do some enlightened begging and ask you, to give us what is ours, on the basis of benevolence, or we can try to prove to you that it is to your enlightened self-interest to give us what is ours—which is an effective technique. It is an effective technique. But then, the other answer is for us to organize ourselves so as to control our margin of profit and be able to demand what's ours. It may be, given a new insight, as I gather from watching African Economic Development—they say, no, we're not going to run the oil wells out, because we're not prepared to run the oil wells. But we are prepared to learn how to run them, and we are prepared to tax them because the oil is coming out of our soil. So, maybe the answer will be as opposed to getting a black businessman with the desire to go in business with no ability. The answer may be to get a struggling white who has the techniques, but not the consumer, and a struggling black who has the consumer but not the techniques, and maybe SBA ought to form both of them in the integration of economics, not of sexes. The integration of economics, as opposed to the white man's being able to run back to his community out of a job, and the black man's being left there with a store he can't run—perhaps both of them ought to survive, but with the black man having the controlling interest since it's in his community.

That is, a development process of economic growth. Now, just making this speech to the black businessmen won't work, because they do not have the power to make that decision, but they do have the obligation to make that demand, that in Harlem, Tanzania and Zambia—somehow we think we're a little more civilized, we think we're ahead of them— everything in Tanzania and Zambia—60 percent has to be owned by the people who live there. They're not running white folks out. They running black folks in, and developing a new relationship. We must develop process, we must develop power—find out if my spiritual tradition as a minister of the gospel, moving toward the ultimate community of respect—I still believe in love, but I know that genuine, authentic, anthological love has to have justice as its content, just as an enameled tooth has to have substance as its content. A love without justice is a powerless and weak and feeble love. And yet, justice without love is crude and vicious, so we must have a love-filled drive with justice as our motivating factor. I would hope that our education would no longer be measured by our ability to memorize poems, to determine a level of literacy. If a child graduates from a school in Harlem, and cannot help develop Harlem, he is illiterate. If a Ph.D. walks the streets of Harlem and is not conscious enough to transform unconscious energy into production, he is still illiterate, he is functionally illiterate. Man must be able to use his hands and produce.

All them great speeches made on 125th Street and 7th Avenue—all them great fiery speeches going back to the nineteenth century—we are still on that corner, and it wouldn't be so bad if it was o-w-n the corner, but it's just o-n that corner. Just still on it. I'm glad to see the rich and the established and the educated and the powerful here, because if you have a genuine desire to put forth a collective formula—not just an individual business here and there, but what Whitney used to call a domestic market plan, a formula for the development of a whole community, and with that, a value system, and in that value system we need more teachers— teachers who will teach for life, 'cause they can't help it, not just teach for a living. Surely we need more doctors, doctors who will study medicine 'cause of their concern for public health, not just a commitment to personal wealth; lawyers, more lawyers, new lawyers, who have studied the art of law in order that they might be able to distribute justice, not just acquire a judgeship. We would then see the fruits of that tradition established by the likes of Medgar, and Malcolm, and Martin, and Whitney . . . then our living and our gathering will not have been in vain.

A White Paper on Black Capitalism

Theodore L. Cross

Three years have passed since the nation suddenly noticed that its black citizens were capital poor. But there has been something better than symbolic change. Twenty-eight minority enterprise venture capital funds have been licensed to do business. There are a handful of new Negro-run automobile dealerships, one black manufacturing company with its shares trading on the American Stock Exchange, and scores of new start-ups of mini-capitalism in the inner cities. But the fundamental condition of 22 million American Negroes as nonowners and noncontrollers of the engines of modern enterprise remains the same. And the question of public policy, too, is still with us. Should federal power be used to assist black citizens to forge and acquire entrepreneurial institutions? If so, how do people who have no capital get it?

Let's start at the beginning.

We in America acquire resources in an incentive-activated economy Under this system the volume of economic demand for commercial acts—whether directed at white, black, or brown people—persuades labor to train itself, encourages capital and savings to form, and induces goods to be manufactured. This proposition also has its negative: the withholding of economic demand—especially when it is done systematically and collectively—causes a pool of labor to atrophy, money to get spent rather than saved, capital to shrink, manufacturers to suspend or lose interest in production, and people to tire of arming themselves with skills.

During the 100 years or more that laws in the United States have allowed Negroes to respond to economic forces rather than to a master's command to work, demand in all markets of the country has been very satisfactory for black people wielding a broom, lifting a suitcase, making a Pullman bed, and tending a steel furnace. But the great marketplaces of the nation never acquired a desire for blacks holding certain other well-specified commercial positions. Sometimes this categorical preference became, instead, a solid aversion. Indeed, for many generations there have been powerful forces at work to discourage and prevent the need for

24

whites to trade with or employ blacks, and therefore to discourage also the assumption or pursuit by black Americans of the commercial roles that such trading or employment would entail.

The results of this were quite predictable under rules set out for us by Adam Smith 200 years ago. Black people, who in 1865 started without even the mule they had been promised, became very good at getting, doing, and keeping the special jobs for which they were in demand. This has been so ever since the first emancipated slave discovered—perhaps to his surprise, since the nation had fought a long and bloody war to make him free—that the white artisan still preferred to hire a white apprentice. Thus, most Negro waiters, busboys, and dishwashers—who were both efficient and hardworking in these jobs where society viewed them with complacency—had no reason to school themselves to be restaurant or hotel managers. They would, indeed, have been quite foolish to do so. Nor did a majority of the *sons* of hardworking black porters and chauffeurs have any pragmatic need to equip themselves to be both hard-working and well-educated porters and chauffeurs.

Today in Philadelphia, Pennsylvania (notwithstanding the fair employment plan named after it) and in most other places, the market is not very good for plumbers and electricians who are black—save only for the stage props who, for the edification of federal inspectors, are shuttled by motorcycle from one job site to another. In consequence, there are precious few black people in Philadelphia (or anywhere else in America) who are very good at fitting pipes or wiring skyscrapers. Moving one step up, the completely evident and catastrophic shortage of black bankers, accountants, engineers, lawyers, managers, and hucksters, is a simple fulfillment of the prediction of the classical economist—the direct, foreseeable, and *certain* result of the sustained withdrawal (or, if you prefer, nondevelopment) of serious economic demand for black people in these bigger economic roles.

The almost total suspension of market demand directed at a race has also operated in a predictable way on its attainments as entrepreneurs and capitalists. Black traders, dealers, and producers came to be in short supply because the economy never furnished adequate wants or demands for goods that might be made, sold, or serviced by black people. If conventional wisdom about black people missing a tradition of entrepreneurship, ownership, and a "need for achievement" holds even a grain of truth, it is a statement not of an original condition but of an assured economic result of the sustained and collective preference of white people not to trade or exchange commercial promises with black people.

This negative preference was not limited to goods and services originating with blacks. White capital had a selective preference to employ white entrepreneurs. And so the great possessors of capital in our society never chose to furnish any economic wants or shortages for black entrepreneurs acting as bidders for, or rewarders of, money. Conversely, Negro banks are toy banks, and other black-controlled money institutions are specks of gold dust in the $1 trillion private capital and credit markets of America. And this did not happen because black people are "present-oriented'' and therefore do not save money. It occurred because a white society, which controlled all worthwhile opportunities for money to grow, consistently avoided offering any interesting investment demand or opportunity reward for any capital which blacks might go about getting together. Today, such black capital as exists is assuredly far more unemployed and underemployed than black people themselves.

Two centuries of total exile from commerce, followed by a third century of what was at best mercantile disinterest and at worst an intensely virulent form of economic discrimination, explain almost all of the economic inequalities that black people struggle with today. While generally unorganized, often benevolent, and in certain parts of the country almost conspiratorial, this powerful economic boycott (the word is harsh but only slightly less than accurate) had a very long, and sometimes profitable, run in America.

If my proposition is correct, and if we choose to look, the path suddenly clears. As a nation, we now face the very interesting possibility that we may be able to get out of this mess by the way we came in. My proposition necessarily means, too, that the very minor things we are presently doing to connect black people with capital will not help very much even if we do many more of them.

But it once seemed so simple. Surely education and training were the answer. If no one could find qualified black bankers, accountants, and businessmen, why not graduate more of them? If the great business school at Harvard during the years 1908 through 1969 graduated only forty-one black MBAs, obviously the solution was to admit seventy to this year's freshman class. If black people failed in commerce because they were denied grubstake capital and seed loans, it seemed sensible enough to issue a government fiat for a national chain of venture-capital funds, meanwhile jawboning the banks to put up more money for blacks who had a commercial swagger. If the white man's diagnosis of the black entrepreneur was ''slow commercial death for lack of business expertise,'' surely the plan should be to spoon-feed technical assistance to the patient.

But who are to be the customers of all those new black automobile dealerships that are to be so carefully erected by the minority enterprise ''one-stop packaging stations''? Will they be black people who, like the rest of us, are more interested in continuing repair and service from a solvent dealer than in feeding the entrepreneurial aspirations of a black capitalist? For black customers know, too, that the brother, who has been ''granted'' a dealership and handed a loan and a cigar by the local Small Business Administration director, can't insure the cars while he is trying to sell them, much less pay for them when he *does* with those perfectly sound but entirely nonbankable installment notes that his customers are going to give him. Or will the customers of the black dealer be those ''concerned'' whites who give regularly to liberal causes, whose notes can be discounted at any bank, but who have bought new cars for the last ten years from 30,000 white dealers known for both their services and solvency?

Plainly there are no customers, black or white, for those plucky little inner-city enterprises that we fund and publicize so assiduously.

Yet when the heat is on the temptations are great to build a few monuments to black affluence. And the unanimous message of the recent report of the President's Council on Minority Enterprise calls for nearly $1 billion of new federal grants to be committed almost entirely on direct acts to increase the visible *supply* of black and brown people standing next to machinery and doing their commercial thing.

But these plans are not unsound; they are commendable and worthy. You are always in deep commercial trouble if there is no supply around when demand for what you can do (or might do) suddenly hits the market. Yet I find it strange that this should be the total strategy in a *market* economy where the best way to increase the supply of something you want has always been to make sure there is a very solid demand for it.

If black capitalism has failed in America for lack of economic wants or shortages in a black economy that was poor (and indeed sometimes distrustful of its own entrepreneurs) and in a white marketplace that was always indifferent and sometimes hostile, it suddenly makes sense to stop trying to push an economic string. The way to foster entrepreneurs among black people is not to fuss around with increasing the supply of them. We need, instead, to shape new forces of market needs and scarcities that will put the black entrepreneur in *short* supply and in excessively *great* demand. Stated another way, the nation which Lord Keynes taught so well and wisely how to rig markets must do important things to diminish the profit or raise the cost of not trading with black people. There is no other way—whether you are talking about unemployed people, underutilized capital, or underdeveloped entrepreneurs.

So training and education is not the magic key. The most graceful white entrepreneurs I know never went to college. The black entrepreneur, too, is alive and well. Like other entrepreneurs, he enjoys risk and counts accurately, but at the moment he has more interesting things on his mind. Only the sudden appearance of compelling shortages and needs for his doing something else will make careers of dealing in capital a highly possible and attractive pursuit for him and his children. When all the froth and jive disappear and real opportunities emerge, the black American, for the first time in our history, will acquire an economic stake—a great deal to lose if he doesn't behave like a mover and user of money.[1]

And so all those hearts-and-minds programs to provide black people with an equal business opportunity to compete with the sharks will not help much. The businessmen who swim in markets out there are not wicked, but they are white, and, above all, they have a handle on economic power—markets, management, and sources of money that they command and almost never entreat. Enterprise capitalists, big or small, are designed to share these turfs with no one—even if he is black, sports a new loan from the Freedom National Bank, and holds a fresh degree from a leading business college.

Sooner or later, if we as a nation are serious about minority business enterprise, we will begin to work with the only side of the bargaining equation that can be controlled. We will then set aside—either through tax incentives, direct rewards, legal sanctions, or through a redirection of government purchasing—a segment of national economic scarcities that can be satisfied *only* by the mercantile acts and employment of disadvantaged people and of their neighborhood corporations.

Now, in a free state the most important economic force that the sovereign can get a grip on is its own purchasing power. For our special purposes here in America, this power is a very remarkable thing to behold. First, the purchasing power of the United States is a vast reservoir of highly controllable economic wants. Last year, outside government payrolls, the executive branch spent $99.7 billion on direct purchases of goods and services for housekeeping and defense. Yet, of this money, $25 million (or about $1 per year for each black and brown citizen in the country) was allocated to minority enterprise or to community-based self-help efforts of the white and black poor.

Therefore, not everything that makes sense in the economic development of disadvantaged communities requires an act of Congress or even a specific appropriation of money. The biggest economic power level of all is already held by the President who, in this important matter, *is* the United States of America. The most interesting fact of all is that Congress, in addition to established and specific direct ''set-aside'' authority, has given the executive branch of the government a very broad power and mandate to use federal spending for the purposes we are concerned with here.[2]

Under a broad Presidential executive order, great new vistas open up. Should, for example, the government purchase a $300 million computer, as it recently did, without requiring a *reviewable good faith effort* on the part of all bidders (competing on equal terms) to subcontract a small but fixed percentage of the prime contract in favor of self-help enterprises in hard-core areas of poverty or distress?[3] (Ten percent of the value of this single contract would exceed all of last year's federal procurement ''set-asides'' for minority enterprise.) And if the prime contractor cannot find a qualified community-based supplier, is there any serious objection to requiring the contractor to demonstrate instead that its purchasing department is subcontracting the equivalent value elsewhere in ghettos, barrios, reservations, or in white Appalachia? Failing that, why not require, for the duration of the contract, the prime contractor to keep a small percentage of the procurement award as fully protected working capital deposits in inner-city banking institutions serving only areas of concentrated blight?

For a year or more I have urged such a broad new program of federal Non-Racial Subcontracting Quotas (NSQ) in favor of community corporations of the poor and other development units in areas of economic disadvantage. Such a plan would be applied to all government contract awards exceeding $1 million. By way of preliminary exploration an experimental NSQ effort—a Southern California Procurement Demonstration Plan—would be shaped in the Los Angeles area serving large groups of segregated blacks, Chicanos, and traveling ghettos of migrant whites.

The agenda should be very broad. Should the Department of the Interior let contracts for harvesting or planting national forests, or for maintenance work in its parks, without seeing that a portion of the award has been subcontracted in favor of rural corporations organized by and employing the poorest of the poor—the seasonal and migrant agricultural workers? Would there be any fundamental objection if the Navy called on its installations near big cities to purchase a fixed amount of soft drinks at established prices from inner-city bottlers who train and employ the unemployable? As long as prices and quality are in order, isn't the Army procurement officer in Santa Fe, New Mexico, who, like most of us, is more interested in his own tenure than in the long-term objectives of federal procurement policy, better off if he is required (not asked) to allocate a fixed percentage of beef or lamb purchases to cooperative feed lots serving the Spanish-speaking, low-income cattle herders of the northern part of the state? In the interests of cleaner air, government vehicles currently use only low-lead fuels at a premium cost of $5.4 million a year. The petroleum industry has not been among the laggards in concern for minorities and the poor. Yet, should the government buy gasoline and oil *at all* from major oil companies that drag their heels on assigning filling station franchises to neighborhood-development units which are also providing housing, day-care, and health services to the dispossessed?

Franchising, the nation's fastest-growing industry, now accounts for one-tenth of our gross national product. Last year it claims to have delivered $100 billion of goods and services to the American economy. The construction industry—an industry almost completely closed to the disadvantaged—is headed for $150 billion in annual volume in just a few years. Should government subsidies or aid be extended to any part of these great industries without making sure, not only that employment discrimination does not occur, but also that the contractors and suppliers set up by community-development corporations of the white and black poor get an established part of the business action?

But the government is bashful about disclosing how much it spends. Government procurement has a second face that the Office of Budget and Management does not measure or predict. The slightly less than $100 billion for goods and services is only part of the wealth and benefits the agencies and departments confer each year on its citizens. Hasn't the time come to shape a new policy at the Federal Communications Commission (FCC) which would award, under expanded doctrines of fairness, one of every ten new TV, cable TV, or FM licenses to community corporations of the poor? Will hundreds of millions of dollars in value of new microwave, data-transmission station licenses be handed out in the next few months by the FCC in the usual way to established telecommunications companies? Shouldn't our government cease to confer valuable rights to develop publicly owned resources except in favor of those who, in a very specific way, also agree to look after or affiliate with those who attend to, other national goals and needs? Total isolation from the means of mass communication is one of the most serious aspects of the impotence of the poor. Cleveland's (Ohio) Hough Development Corporation, Brooklyn's

(New York) Bedford-Stuyvesant Redevelopment Corporation, and dozens of similar reconstruction units, act for hundreds of thousands of constituents who are currently powerless to speak effectively to the many except through riots, boycotts, and sit-ins.

And if 200,000 black servicemen are paying the government $40 a year each in premiums for nonmilitary risk life insurance, wouldn't it be better for all citizens if the $80 million in annual premiums were not simply turned over to a pool of insurance companies in which most black-owned companies are too small to participate? Surely it would be better, at the very least, to allocate these premiums as a competitive award to those companies, both black and white, who in the past year invested the largest proportion of their resources in investments in commercial improvements in distressed areas that do not qualify for federal subsidies and guarantees.

In 1969, mutual life insurance companies (another industry which has responded concretely to the needs of minorities)—after investing $400 million or more in fully guaranteed inner city mortgages—distributed $3 billion in dividends to policyholders. If a gentle nudge from the government were to persuade the companies to defer only 1 percent of these dividends to future years, a $30 million venture-capital fund could be created for the enterprises of the poor—a fund which under present law an agency of the federal government would be obligated to match up to *fifteen* times over.

So the executive branch is not bound by an intransigent Congress. No one has even begun to explore the vast opportunities for the creative use of federal economic power. Why not award a community-development corporation in a poor white section of Boston a preferential right on the disposal of surplus federal property? Would it be possible to give neighborhood-development corporations everywhere a first crack at the licensing of the 20,000 patents owned by the federal government and at the concessions at federally assisted highways and airports? Why should black people be the first buyers who come to mind when an obsolete division of a company is to be sold? What about all those established and successful businesses that must be spun-off each year under the antitrust laws? Consider, too, the many ways in which the corporations of the poor could import money and resources into their communities by participating in the exploitation of government-owned timber, shale oil, and offshore oil deposits.

I have left the biggest federal lever to the end. Many governments abroad, such as those of West Germany, the Netherlands, and Japan—countries not known for their fondness for collectivist approaches to economics—regularly use their central banks as a force for internal development and change. Shouldn't we in America—where 30 million are racial minorities and 17 million are white and poor—work toward the allocation of more banking resources to inner-city communities where the credit markets are ruled by criminal loan sharks who, each year, siphon off hundreds of millions of dollars of federal welfare payments? Only one five-thousandth of the $500 billion of America's banking money is currently working for minority enterprise and for community corporations set up by the poor. If bank holding company privileges, federal deposit insurance benefits, and federal loan guarantees influenced an allocation of only 1 percent of the nation's bank deposits to urban and rural self-help enterprises, a new development fund of $5 billion would be created. There has been consistent resistance in the Treasury to linking government deposit balances to economic-development loans. Yet all big banks perform government fiscal functions with equal skill. No longer can we afford to ignore other criteria for receiving the benefit of deposits of public funds.

For many years I have been stumping for automatic and categorical money incentives—preferably through the federal tax system—to raise the bargaining power of black people by making their assurances of work, goods, and services more valuable in the greater economy. But I am not an idealogue. All of that requires an act of Congress. I now turn to modest redirections of federal purchasing power as the single most impressive way of demonstrating, without need for immediate legislation, the opportunity to deal with poverty by drawing the poor into the national bargaining contest. The goal is to create new cradles of economic power in poor neighborhoods by leveraging scarcities in the national demand market so that it suddenly acquires a hunger for the commercial endeavors of the disadvantaged and for those who would employ them.

I continue to have faith, too, in the essential good sense of our first tentative step to shape an independent national funding corporation to insure, warrant, and rediscount the contracts and undertakings of the institutions and enterprises of the poor. I also view the bonding powers and incentive-payment privileges of the national funding corporation as the single most effective way of stimulating private business and financial corporations, as well as cities and towns, to allocate some of their purchasing and lending powers to untried efforts of community self-help rather than to established enterprises of demonstrated competence and strength. I see the national funding corporation as a first step to removing that great barrier to trade between blacks and whites and between the poor and the nonpoor—the still unproven and often irrational fear of nonfulfillment of a mercantile covenant or undertaking.

For those of you who have come with me this far I owe an explanation. Why should a multiracial society in 1971, with anywhere from 20 to 50 percent of its ghetto blacks out of jobs and living in squalid housing, be interested in how its races share or control the ownership of private capital?

Jobs and housing continue to be the most urgent problems of black people in America. But democratic capitalism, as it is practiced in a stage of advanced development, has become an economic scrimmage that allocates resources, not according to need or necessarily even to productivity, but according to success in the struggle for economic power. It happens that holding the job one must have in order to continue to eat and live has absolutely nothing to do with economic power. Yet the man or institution who stands at the gate (because of position, title, wealth, or constituency) and is able to say to the others, "You shall not book labor, rent apartments, or invest capital except through me," is, in fact, in *possession* of jobs, housing, and capital. And so I say black people must have some power, not because power is intrinsically good, but because other people have it and the possession of it has consistently worked against those who lack it. All the wailing and prayers for jobs, housing, and education will never equalize the maldistribution of resources unless black people get a grip on the structure that controls jobs, housing, and education.

In consequence, I hold that assigning black people today an *exclusive* goal of the direct pursuit of fuller employment is a concession of black inferiority, if not a form of new servitude. When most of us settle back to a four-day week, living partly off the productivity of the machines we own, what is to happen to the 30 million newcomers of all races who will finally win their jobs but who are still poor in capital? And so I say "watch out" for those in our society (mostly white) who now say to black people: "Fellows, capitalism is not for you. Stay out of the big game. You will only go to the cleaners." Some of these gatekeepers are great-grandchildren of gatekeepers who, fifty years ago, urged Negroes in the south to tend to their jobs in the fields rather than worry about trying to own or control some of the machines that ultimately put them out of work.

I believe, too, that education and job training, so effective in beginning to reduce poverty among whites but so impotent among groups who have been denied opportunity, will take hold for black people only when the nation starts doing things that dramatically improve the income of black people who are already *above* the poverty level. During a recent visit to the Soviet Union, I discussed economic development with the chairman of the Soviet State Bank and others on his staff. I have watched the gradual emergence of new economic incentives for the regulation of resources in that country; I have viewed the signs of creeping *embour-geoisement* of the economy of East Germany. I have followed, too, all those remarkably candid reports from Cuba in which the government virtually concedes that economic disaster has proceeded from its inability to frame an adequate system of work incentives. So I continue to harbor a middle-class conviction in the powerful effect on personal initiative of startling examples of achievement by others—a belief that people, black and white, will go through long periods of uncompensated education and training only if they see a spread of rewards between the bottom and the top.

I believe, too, that the most stunning mercantile successes at the top will continue to be men and women working as entrepreneurs, bootstrapping money, and probing the mysteries of economic synergism. Popular myth and thesis writers to the contrary, the obituaries for small business are premature. For whites it has never been easier to make it big. As Peter Drucker has observed, eight to ten thousand new businesses got going in America in each year between 1959 and 1969, all important and successful enough to have notified the Securities and Exchange Commission of their existence.[4] Underwriting firms no one had heard of ten years ago are now picking up the pieces after the recent reversals on Wall Street. And it is our big steel that is in trouble in foreign markets and our big aircraft makers that are sinking at home—not the innovation and technology that emerges from an over-mortgaged garage. I yield the point that the highly visible black vice-president of the large company is also a model of great value, but he will draw others to his side only when corporations finally learn how to fire him for incompetency and promote him for achievement.

I believe, too, that the way black people are winning civil and political rights points to solutions of their final problem, which quite plainly is economic. Fifteen years ago great civil rights victories for blacks began to happen when they decided to act for a collective purpose. But there had been no progress until there emerged a tough cadre of organized leaders and lawyers who fought the boycotts of Montgomery, Alabama, organized the voter-registration drives in Selma, Alabama, and laboriously pushed the civil-rights cases through the kangaroo courts of Mississippi. Black people in America are now winning political power and rights everywhere, not on account of the agitation of a concerned, liberal, white establishment, but through developing a new class of black political professionals. Could we draw the final conclusion that economic inequality will be overcome only when black people, too, organize a powerful entrepreneurial class of bankers, builders, and executives creating and managing business corporations in the traditional way and marshalling the meager resources of the black poor in community-based efforts of self-help?

I believe, finally, in giving the greatest weight to what black people think will help them most. This includes hearing the message of a recent Harris poll that 93 percent of a test sampling of black people mentioned "starting more businesses" as a route to making real progress—a goal, the poll reported, exceeded only in importance, in the view of those interviewed, by "getting more blacks better educated."

These are all things I believe and cannot prove, but there are undeniable facts of inequality that I can see. For example, I know that black people in America own only a handful of very shaky automobile dealerships. They control in big cities thirty segregated institutions of banking with resources, all told, less than only one of the white-controlled banks in Grand Rapids, Michigan. I know that the prize example of American black capitalism is a stagnant life insurance industry with total capital that is a good deal less than the amount of money a few of the giant life insurance companies will flick off their books in the Penn Central bankruptcy. I know, too, that Negro families have on average $300 in the bank compared to $2,860 for whites, own securities of about $38 per family compared to $2,603 for white families, and hold about $382 per family in all financial assets (money in banks, government bonds, and stocks) as against $5,924 for the average white family.[5]

Jobs alone will not correct such grave inequality and injustice. The inequality will persist until there are a few thousand black people earning $80,000 a year serving on powerful executive committees of large corporations. It will continue until there are ten-thousand black millionaires, instead of fifty. In America full economic equality means that black men, holding stock options and heading syndicates financed on Wall Street, execute dramatic takeovers of major corporations. It means that the one or two black executives now working in the ranks of the 3,182 senior officers who run the five-hundred largest corporations must increase to three hundred. Pursuit of equality will lead black people into developing new high technology companies as a major source of national innovation and penetration of foreign markets, rather than rural chicken coops and ghetto-bound fast-food operations. Equality means black people's negotiating sales and leasebacks, major mergers, spin-offs, and split-ups. Indeed, equality requires that a few black people have misunderstandings with their government and breaking antitrust laws as well as traffic laws. Equality calls for black people's clipping bond coupons, paying mortgages on second homes, and losing their shirts in the commercial paper of the Penn Central Railroad as well as in those brave, little inner-city transit companies financed by a benevolent suburban corporation that left the inner-city and a thousand jobs behind.

To many in America, all of this has become a drab pursuit. But do not confuse the question of whether capitalism is still good with the wholly different issue of whether, in a nation of capitalists, the advancement of black capitalism is bad. Whatever the future of democratic enterprise, the instruments of capital and economic power will long be with us. And in a just society black people must have them, or have a handle on them, until such time as whites, or black and whites together, decide it is better to give them up.

NOTES

1. My thesis is not without support in history. The fortunes made by blacks in undertaking, hair preparations, and life insurance were achieved in areas of commerce where there was solid economic demand which the greater society refused to fill. Blacks did not have to fight their way into these businesses. Consider, too, the black professional athlete. There has always been a strong supply of professional black prizefighters because the demand for them was there. Up until 1945, there was no demand in major markets for black baseball players. And, until quite recently, there was no demand for black basketball and black football players. Today blacks dominate the basketball scene, and they are very prominent in the football area, far out of proportion to their numbers in the population. This did not come about because black people are stronger or more agile than whites. Certainly it did not occur because we suddenly instituted training programs for black athletes. That was not necessary. When the demand opened up, the supply grew.

2. A provision of the Economic Opportunity Act of 1964 (largely, but not intentionally, overlooked) provides that the Director of the Office of Economic Opportunity (the head of the antipoverty program that functions under law in the executive office of the President) "shall take such steps as may be necessary and appropriate in coordination and cooperation with the heads of other Federal departments and agencies, so that contracts, subcontracts and deposits made by the Federal Government, or in connection with programs aided with Federal funds are placed in such a way as to further the purposes of this part."

As I write, the OEO enabling law, due to expire in June 1971, has been recommended for extension by the President and leading members of both parties in the Congress. Even if the Act were to lapse, the constitutional powers of the President (and of those serving at his pleasure) to direct procurement spending continue to be very broad.

3. Congressional injunctions in appropriation acts against paying price differentials must be obeyed. But many federal appropriations do not prohibit differentials. Moreover, "bid-matching" and "set-aside techniques" are common practices of the procurement officer. Linked bank deposit plans and purchases at established posted prices do not involve differentials. The question is whether the government lawyer—sensing a positive or negative mandate—is looking for obstacles or for opportunities. The provisions of the OEO Act I have mentioned provide solid ground from which to defend a very broad Presidential order calling for quantitative procurement goals to reinforce antipoverty grants.

If a mandatory executive order were issued calling for percentage purchasing in favor of communities of the poor, the obvious channel would be the urban and rural community capitalism efforts funded by specific authority and requirement of the "special impact" provisions of the federal antipoverty law. Unlike the Philadelphia Plan (calling for "quota" hiring of blacks in construction trades), there is no question under the Civil Rights Act of 1964 of the propriety of requiring prime government contractors to subcontract a percentage of their business to community development corporations. These units, although largely serving segregated minorities in ghettos, barrios, and reservations, also serve poor whites. The community development corporations are based in rural and urban poverty areas designated, not according to race or even cultural disadvantage, but according to established nonracial indices of poverty and unemployment.

4. "The New Markets and the New Capitalism," *The Public Interest,* Fall 1970, p. 49.

5. Bureau of Census, *Survey of Economic Opportunity,* 1967.

Wealth Accumulation of Black and White Families: The Empirical Evidence

Henry S. Terrell

Considerable amounts of research activity have been focused recently on understanding the relative economic status of the black minority population, in the United States. In general these studies have considered income and earnings as the relevant variables, primarily because data on these flow magnitudes have been readily available.[1] Flow magnitudes, such as income and earnings, do not, however, provide a complete picture of the relative economic position of the black population, because they fail to account for the relative wealth position of black family units. Wealth accumulation is very important in assessing economic status as many economic decisions, such as retirement and the acquisition of human capital, depend on wealth accumulation.

To date virtually no information has been available on the relative wealth position of the black population. The 1967 Survey of Economic Opportunity (SEO) has helped to fill this critical data void. The SEO asked comprehensive questions on assets and liabilities and the oversampling in poor and predominantly black areas has resulted in relatively small sampling errors for the black population.

This study will utilize the data in the 1967 SEO to present evidence on the size, composition, and concentration of net wealth accumulation among black families compared to white families. The final section presents and tests a simple econometric model of the estimated relationship between income and wealth for black and white families. In preparing this paper it was well understood that survey data are notoriously unreliable on assets and liabilities. Larger samples do not remove the errors if there is a tendency for a distinct subgroup to misreport its assets or liabilities. A rather extensive literature has evolved concerning the errors in survey data on assets and liabilities and is noted.[2] At various stages of the analysis the findings from the SEO are compared to results from the comprehensive *Survey of Financial Characteristics of Consumers*.

Relative Size of Black Wealth Accumulation

The simplest way to assess the relative wealth accumulation of black families is to compare total wealth accumulation of black and white families at similar levels of income.[3] Table 1 presents data on wealth accumulation standardized by income level.[4] The data in Table 1 are very convincing in one simple respect; on average, black families have less than one-fifth the total wealth accumulation of white families, and differences in observed income levels alone are not nearly sufficient to explain relative differences in wealth accumulation since black families at each tabulated income level had less than one-half the wealth accumulation of white families in the same income bracket. The average white family had a wealth accumulation roughly two and one-half times as great as its observed income, while black families on average had a wealth-to-income ratio of less than one.

The figures in Table 1 are of further interest because they show what appears to be a slight tendency for the ratio of black to white wealth to rise with higher levels of income, although this rise in relative accumulation is still of insufficient magnitude to prevent the absolute wealth gap from widening with income. In the $2,500–4,999 income class the black-to-white ratio was only 16.1 percent, but it rises steadily to 47.3 percent in the $15,000–19,999 income range. The sharp decline in the ratio to 29.9 percent in the over $20,000 income cell in large part reflects the fact that this cell is open-ended and refers to a substantially more affluent white population.[5]

TABLE 1
Total Net Wealth of White and Black Families, by Income Class
(mean amounts in dollars)

Income Class	Net Wealth		Ratio of Black to White Wealth	Wealth-Income Ratio*	
	White	Black	Wealth	White	Black
$ 0– 2,499	$ 10,681	$ 2,148	20.1	7.51	1.61
2,500– 4,999	13,932	2,239	16.1	3.75	0.62
5,000– 7,499	13,954	4,240	30.4	2.25	0.69
7,500– 9,999	16,441	6,021	36.6	1.91	0.70
10,000–14,999	24,304	8,694	35.8	2.04	0.74
15,000–19,999	43,413	20,533	47.3	2.58	1.22
20,000 & over	101,009	30,195	29.9	3.37	1.26
All units	20,153	3,779	18.8	2.58	0.81

*Evaluated at mean income within each income class.

The general conclusion from these simple tabulations is that black families at any observed income level have substantially less wealth than white families. This lower level of wealth for black families in any given income class can probably be explained by reference to the permanent income model developed by Milton Friedman. Friedman, in considering the determinants of consumption, noted "the inadequacy of measured income as an indicator of long-run income status."[6] In effect, observed income data are inadequate for comparing the relative long-run income status of black families because they fail to show the history of lower past incomes and the expected lower future incomes of black families.[7] Friedman utilized this model to explain the generally observed lower levels of black consumption out of given income.

> The higher average income (for whites) means that a given measured income corresponds to a higher permanent income for whites than for Negroes; and, therefore, according to our hypothesis, to a higher level of consumption.[8]

Richard Sterner recognized this same problem:

> In any given income group white families are much more likely than Negro families to 'have seen better days!' In a given income group, also, white families probably include a larger proportion which have reason to anticipate higher earnings in the future.[9]

The data on wealth accumulation from the SEO appear to confirm the views of Friedman and Sterner. The lack of wealth accumulation of black families of given income levels combined with considerable evidence[10] of lower black consumption out of given income suggests clearly that the permanent or long-run income status of black families is substantially poorer than for white families of similar levels of observed income.

The Composition of Wealth

Having discussed the relative size of black wealth it is important to analyze its composition. Table 2 presents data on the average wealth portfolios of black and white families and the estimated share of the total wealth held by black families. The figures in Table 2 show very large structural differences in the wealth portfolios of black and white families.[11] The most noticeable difference between black and white families is the virtual total lack of financial asset holdings among black families. The SEO data estimated that the average black family held only $384 or 10.2 percent of its total wealth in financial assets. These meager financial asset holdings represented only 6.2 percent of the average financial accumulation of white families, and black families held an estimated 0.7 percent of all financial assets. Black families showed a particular lack of wealth accumulation in stocks, holding an average of only $39 per family which accounted for an estimated 0.13 percent of all stock accumulation.

The case of nonfinancial assets is considerably different. The SEO data estimated that black families held $3,395 in nonfinancial assets equivalent to 89.8 percent of their total wealth. This figure represented 24.1 percent of the average white accumulation and the black share of the total nonfinancial wealth was 2.6 percent, almost four times as great as the share of financial accumulation. Important differences occur between black and white families in the structure of nonfinancial wealth accumulation. Black families have a definite tendency toward accumulation in assets yielding consumption services (cars, trucks, and housing) while white families hold a greater share of their nonfinancial wealth in income-providing assets (farms, other real estate, and business equity). The SEO data suggest that 71.7 of black nonfinancial wealth holding is in assets yielding consumption services compared to only 53.5 percent for white families. This relatively high concentration by black families in assets yielding consumption services is not very surprising. Black family units, with their substantially lower levels of absolute wealth accumulation, are forced by necessity to hold a larger share of their lower wealth in assets yielding the essential consumption services of transportation and housing before financial and other nonfinancial assets may be acquired.

The data in Table 2 on the asset structure of white and black families offer some evidence on the economic impact of segregation and discrimination. Black families have conspicious underaccumulation in those forms of wealth whose acquisition requires access to national markets, and a relative overaccumulation (in percentage terms) of assets whose acquisition is directly affected by segregation. A specific way segregation has affected the asset portfolio of black families can be observed by the relative importance of business equity to stock ownership in the total wealth of black and white families. The average white family reported 1.38 times as much accumulation in stock ownership as in business equity, while for black families the ratio of stock ownership to business equity was only 0.18. The reasons for this rather striking difference in portfolio choice reflect the effects of segregation and economies of scale. Black businessmen have enjoyed a protective barrier of segregation within a rather limited market environment. The relatively small and predominantly local markets were not large enough to support a securities market but instead were more conducive to the acquisition of business equity.

The general conclusion from this section is that segregation and the smaller overall amount of wealth has affected the general composition of black wealth. The lower level of wealth of black families has meant that a greater proportion of wealth must be devoted to assets yielding consumption services, while segregation has led to a relative overconcentration of business ownership compared to stock ownership.

Concentration of Wealth among Black and White Families

Having discussed the relative size and composition of black wealth accumulation, it is important to examine the relative degree of concentration of wealth among black and white families. Concentration here refers to the equality of distribution of wealth holding among the different units. The most common measure of concentration utilized by economists is the Gini index.[12] The Gini index is "a mathematical expression of the relation between the Lorenz curve of actual distribution and the line of equal

TABLE 2
Net Wealth Accumulation, Distribution, and Aggregates for White and Black Families

Type of Asset	Mean Accumulation per Family (absolute amount)			Distribution of Total Holdings (percent)		Estimated Aggregate Holdings (billions of dollars)		Black Share of Total[1] (percent)
	White	Black	Ratio	White	Black	White	Black	
Nonfinancial Assets								
Equity in Home	$ 6,511	$2,125	32.6	32.3	56.2	$ 359.2	$12.7	3.4
Equity in Cars and trucks	1,033	309	29.9	5.1	8.2	57.0	1.9	3.2
Equity in Other								
Real Estate	1,868	436	23.3	9.3	11.5	103.1	2.6	2.5
Farm Equity	2,769	309	11.2	13.7	8.2	152.8	1.9	1.2
Business Equity	1,904	216	11.3	9.4	5.7	105.1	1.3	1.2
Subtotal	$14,085	$3,395	24.1	69.9	89.8	$ 777.2	$20.4	2.6
Financial Assets								
Value of Stocks	2,631	39	1.5	13.1	1.0	145.2	0.2	0.13
Money in Banks	2,955	296	10.0	14.7	7.8	163.0	1.8	1.1
Government Bonds	482	49	10.2	2.4	1.3	26.6	0.3	1.1
Subtotal	$ 6,068	$ 384	6.3	30.1	10.2	$ 334.8	$ 2.3	0.7
Total. All Assets	$20,153	$3,779	18.8	100%	100%	$1,112.0	$22.7	2.0

[1]This is the black share of the total for the entire black and white population and does not include holdings of the less than 1 percent of the nonblack minority population.

distribution."[13] Gini coefficients vary from 0 to 1.0 with a higher coefficient representing a less equal distribution. A Gini coefficient of zero would imply total equality of distribution with each unit having the same amount, while a coefficient of 1.0 implies total inequality of distribution.

Table 3 presents Gini coefficients for black and white wealth accumulation and its components, as well as for black and white income from both the SEO and Census data. One important finding from the SEO data which has been well known to empirical researchers is that wealth is substantially less evenly distributed than income.[14] This finding holds true for blacks, whites, and all family units taken together. A second important finding from the SEO data is the reconfirmation of the fact that income is less evenly distributed among black families than among white families.[15]

Table 3 presents Gini coefficients on total wealth accumulation of black and white families. The Gini coefficient of wealth concentration was 0.823 for black families, compared to 0.694 for white families. The Gini coefficients on wealth distribution, therefore, certainly reinforce the data on income distribution in showing that economic power is distributed much less evenly among blacks than among whites.

The Gini coefficients tabulated for the individual asset components comprising net wealth were much less satisfactory because the relatively few cases reporting accumulation in certain assets meant that the Gini coefficients were scarcely different from 1.0.[16] In three asset cases—equity in cars and trucks, equity in homes, and money in banks—ownership was sufficiently diffused that the Gini coefficients were

TABLE 3

Gini Coefficients of Wealth Distribution and Its Components among White and Black Families

Asset Type	All Families			Families Reporting Accumulation		
	White	Black	Total	White	Black	Total
Government Bonds	.942	.983	.946	.774	.785	.776
Money in Banks	.792	.914	.815	.739	.730	.744
Value of Stocks	.963	.994	.966	.783	.566	.784
Equity in Farm	.991	.992	.993	.621	.632	.629
Equity in Business	1.074	1.049	1.075	.773	.869	.777
Equity in Home	.682	.850	.700	.436	.483	.441
Equity in Other Real Estate	1.060	.978	1.061	.744	.641	.743
Equity in Cars and Trucks	.658	.903	.681	.553	.650	.561
Net Wealth	.694	.823	.715	.671	.712	.680
Family Income (SEO)	.383	.416	.392	.380	.412 [1]	.389
Family Income (Census, 1966)	.343	.385 [1]	.352	—	—	—

[1] Refers to all nonwhites.

considerably different from 1.0. In each of these three cases Gini coefficients showed quite clearly that wealth accumulation was much less evenly distributed among black families than among whites.

To account for the fact that the lack of diffusion of asset ownership in some areas made the overall Gini coefficients difficult to interpret, the coefficients were recomputed for those units reporting positive accumulation in specific asset types. These coefficients are also reported in Table 3 and have a considerably different interpretation. The recomputed Gini coefficients refer to the concentration of wealth accumulation among those units who hold wealth and omit units with zero accumulation.

The recomputed Gini coefficients in Table 3 yield some very interesting results. The new coefficients for income distribution have remained virtually the same since practically all units reported some income. The new coefficients on wealth accumulation, however, have been altered rather profoundly. The coefficients for white, black, and total have dropped considerably, as would be expected. In relative terms, however, the coefficient for the concentration of relative black wealth has dropped considerably more than the one for white accumulation. The recomputed Gini coefficients on wealth accumulation still show that wealth is much less evenly distributed among black families than among white families for those reporting wealth, but they also show that a substantial amount of the difference in relative wealth concentration between blacks and whites is explained by the fact that a large portion of the black population simply did not report any wealth accumulation at all.

The results for concentration of holdings of specific assets by those reporting accumulation were also quite interesting. Many of the coefficients appeared quite similar for both races. White accumulation, however, was significantly less equally distributed in stock ownership and equity in other real estate, and black accumulation less equally distributed in homes, cars and trucks, and businesses. The relatively higher levels of concentration among whites of those reporting stock ownership is probably due to the fact that there are virtually no large black investors who have chosen to hold their wealth in the form of common stocks, while for wealthy whites common stock is the largest single component of the wealth portfolio. The SEO estimated that only 14.7 percent of black stock ownership was by families reporting total stock ownership of $10,000 or more. For whites the corresponding figure was 86.1 percent and 70.8 percent of total white stock ownership was by families with total stock ownership of $25,000 or more. Clearly the large holdings of the small minority of affluent whites result in the relatively higher concentration of stock ownership among white families reporting ownership.

The case of the relatively larger concentration of wealth in home equity, car and truck equity, and business equity among blacks appears to follow the general pattern of the greater concentration of wealth among black families. Home equity is the most important asset in black accumulation, and since overall black accumulation is less equally distributed it would be expected that home equity would be less equally distributed also. The relatively higher index of white concentration in equity in other real estate is quite difficult to explain, and more research is needed to find out whether the category equity in other real estate means the same thing for blacks as for whites.

The general conclusion from this section is that the lower level of black wealth is much less evenly distributed than white wealth, just as the lower level of black family income is less equally distributed than white family income. It has also been shown that a substantial amount of the difference in concentration is due to the fact that many black family units reported no wealth.

Empirical Factors Associated with Wealth Accumulation

Previous sections have presented considerable tabular material on the wealth accumulation of black and white families. This section will develop multiple regression equations to estimate the empirical relationships between wealth accumulation and other factors for black and white families. Regression analysis is particularly useful because it permits a comparison of the importance of various factors of wealth accumulation for the two races by inspection of the size and statistical reliability of the estimated coefficients. Before presentation of the regression analysis it is important to discuss the expected relationships.

Wealth accumulation in general depends on: (1) the size of the stream of past income, (2) the rate of savings out of this past income stream, (3) the length of time of accumulation, (4) the rate at which accumulated wealth compounds itself, and (5) any influences of inherited wealth. All these factors merit attention, but the regression analysis is limited to those areas in which data exist, notably the factors expected to influence the average stream of past income, which will be discussed in detail later, and the length of time of accumulation which can be approximated by the age of the head of the family. As documented earlier, the empirical literature is rather convincing that black families tend to save more out of given observed income than white families. This observation *alone* would suggest that black families at similar levels of income ought to have more wealth than whites.

The question of comparing the rate at which wealth compounds itself for black and white families is much more difficult to handle. The traditional literature on the economics of discrimination developed by Becker[17] suggests that segregation will result in higher returns to black capitalists because capital is the relatively scarce factor of production within the segregated black economy. The tabulations presented on the composition of black wealth in Table 2 suggest that this analysis may simply be irrelevant to an estimation of the relative overall rates at which black and white wealth accumulate.

Table 2 shows that business-type assets comprise a very small share of the wealth portfolio of either race. The important fact is, however, that the lower level of black wealth means that a substantially larger share is invested in assets yielding housing and transportation services which probably do not offer the same prospects for appreciation. A second point which the Becker model neglects is that segregation has restricted the set of choices available to black families which in turn reduces their ability to increase the yield and/or lower the risk on their wealth portfolios. Thus, there is no strong *a priori* reason to expect the rate of compounding of wealth to be higher for black families than for whites, and it may in fact be lower.

The question of inheritor status cannot be handled directly in this analysis because the SEO simply did not gather any information on this subject. In general it would be expected that black families at given levels of income would have less inherited wealth because of the lower income experience of their predecessors, but this hypothesis is impossible to test with existing data. *The Survey of Financial Characteristics of Consumers*[18] considered the general question of inheritor status and found that only 5 percent of all units considered that inherited assets comprise a substantial portion of their total assets; and these were primarily families with income and estimated assets of over $50,000 in 1962. Given these general findings and the very low level of overall wealth held by black families, it appears safe to speculate that inherited wealth probably is of negligible importance to black families and only appears important to white families reporting relatively large amounts of wealth accumulation.[19]

Despite the lack of data for analyzing the rate of compounding of wealth and inheritor status, the single most important factor determining wealth accumulation remains the stream of past income, since the average size of past income determines the absolute amount of savings. The closest empirical proxy for average past income is observed current income. Families with high levels of current income will tend to be those who have had high average levels of past income. A second factor associated with wealth accumulation is the education level of the head of the family.

The general hypothesis is that, given observed income and age, a higher level of education will be associated with a greater amount of wealth accumulation. For example, of two families with an observed income of $10,000 per year and a head of a given age, the one headed by someone with a college degree is expected to have had a higher average past income than the one headed by someone with only an eighth grade education. By the same reasoning a family headed by someone with a college education at a fairly low observed income is probably only at that income because of transitory factors, such as illness or temporary unemployment, and has a much higher past income history than suggested by current income alone. Thus the hypothesis is that wealth accumulation will vary positively with the level of education of the head of the family.

Observed income, age, and education are important variables; however, the *Survey of Financial Characteristics of Consumers* also found that employment status was an important determinant of total wealth.[20] In general it was found that those reporting self-employment had substantially more wealth on average but had a less positive relationship between income and wealth than those reporting being employed by others. The self-employed on average do represent an entrepreneurial class whose income is more dependent on business than on human capital and thus would be expected to have more measurable wealth.

The final hypothesis to be tested concerns the influence of residential location on wealth accumulation. The SEO data permit the utilization of a dummy variable for urban and rural location. It is fairly well documented in the empirical literature on consumption that farm families tend to save more out of a given income.[21] Although all rural families are not farmers, their influence in the rural segment of the sample is important, and the hypothesis is that rural families, other factors constant, will on an average have greater wealth accumulation.

Given the hypotheses above, separate multiple regression equations were computed on wealth accumulation of the black and white populations. Following the precedent of the *Survey of Financial Characteristics of Consumers,* the expected relationship between wealth and observed income was logarithmic of the form:

(1) $W = a\ Y^b$ which can be estimated in the form,
(2) $\log W = \log a + b \log Y.$[22]

All the expected explanatory variables were entered as dichotomous dummy variables affecting the constant term; and, in addition, the observed coefficient between wealth and income was not assumed constant for the different employment groups, so an interaction term between income and employment status was utilized to estimate the effects of employment status on the relationship between wealth and income as well as its effect on total wealth.

Table 4 presents the estimated regression equations for wealth accumulation for the black and white population. In virtually all cases the T statistic indicated the coefficient was many times its standard error suggesting a high degree of statistical reliability.[23]

Examination of the regression equations in Table 4 shows that the most important difference between the two races with respect to wealth accumulation can be seen in the constant term and the elasticity of wealth with respect to observed income.[24] The estimated constant term for blacks in the regression equation is more than one full point lower than for whites. This lower constant term indicates the general degree to which black families have substantially less wealth than white families before allowing for those factors other than race alone which are associated with wealth accumulation.

The elasticity coefficient, however, is somewhat higher for blacks than for whites. This higher elasticity suggests that a given *percentage* increase in black income will be associated with a greater *percentage* in wealth accumulation. When all other factors are considered, the equations in Table 4 reinforce the previous finding that black wealth is less equally distributed than white wealth since a given percentage increase in black income, which is itself less equally distributed than white income, is associated with an even greater percentage increase in wealth accumulation.[25] It should be clearly noted that the higher elasticity coefficient for blacks applied to the much smaller constant term in the equations in Table 4 suggests that the absolute differences of black and white wealth will widen at higher income levels, although the ratio of black to white will narrow slightly.

TABLE 4
Multiple Linear Regression of Total Wealth (in Logarithms) on Income, Age, Employment Status, and Residential Status for White and Black Families

Variable	White Families		Black Families	
	Coefficient	T Value	Coefficient	T Value
Constant Term	−3.3956	24.31	−5.1666	26.12
Variables Affecting Constant Term				
Age of Head				
Under 35	−0.4351	19.35	−0.3538	8.40
55–64	0.3839	14.71	0.5346	10.78
Over 65	0.6592	21.44	0.7621	13.42
Education of Head				
0–7 Years	−0.3103	11.51	−0.0731	1.78
12 Years	0.2219	9.82	0.3579	7.32
13–15 Years	0.3306	10.52	0.6267	7.99
16+ Years	0.3944	12.96	1.0826	10.59
Rural	0.2894	13.36	0.7165	15.86
Self-Employed	4.8059	18.73	3.8009	6.47
Not Employed	3.8067	22.60	4.7504	19.34
Logarithm of Income	1.7505	48.86	1.9467	36.15
Variables Interacting with Income				
Self-Employed Times Income	−1.0743	15.99	−0.7278	4.24
Not Employed Times Income	−1.0356	22.41	−1.5286	21.17
$\bar{R}^2$	.33		.27	
F	506.56		219.90	
Sample Size	13,813		7,527	

The remainder of the regression coefficients from Table 4 tend to be larger for blacks than for whites. These larger coefficients for black families suggest that the factors associated with wealth accumulation tend to lead to wider proportionate variations in wealth accumulation for blacks than for whites, although the absolute differences will be much smaller for blacks since these proportions are computed over much smaller bases. Rural residence would be a good case in point, with the logarithm of wealth 0.2894 higher for whites and 0.7165 higher for blacks, suggesting that *ceteris paribus* a rural white family will have slightly less than twice as much wealth as its urban counterpart, while a rural black family will have about five times as much in wealth as its urban counterpart. The greater proportionate increase in black wealth associated with rural residence will close the relative gap but not the absolute gap, since it is applied to a smaller base.

From Table 4 it can be noted that the coefficients in education were generally larger for black families. These larger coefficients result in a narrowing proportionate and widening absolute gap between black and white wealth accumulation. This result can be more easily understood by reference to Table 5 which makes some sample calculations of estimated wealth for urban families with a head employed by someone else, by age, education, and three alternative income levels.[26] The simple calculations in Table 5 show how the proportionate gaps in black and white wealth accumulation narrow with income and education (when the lowest education group is eliminated) while the absolute gaps increase greatly with all factors associated with wealth accumulation.

The calculated data in Table 5 based on the regressions in Table 4 show one particularly significant difference between black and white families concerning the impact of education on wealth accumulation. The regression coefficient in Table 4 for the influence of a college diploma on wealth accumulation is $4559 higher for black families with a college degree than those with some college education, suggesting black families with a college degree have roughly 19 times as much wealth as black families headed by someone with some college education.[27] For white families a college degree raised the logarithm of net wealth by 0.1087, suggesting only 1.3 times as much wealth. The figures in Table 5 show that in many cases a black family headed by someone with a college degree has over half as much wealth as its white counterpart. These figures are especially noteworthy because the regression equations have already standardized for income levels and age. The especially high level of wealth accumulation of black families headed by someone with a college degree of given age and observed income suggests that these families have had a history of higher past incomes and perhaps a higher propensity to save out of this income than black families headed by someone with less education.

The figures in Table 5 are of interest, not only because they show the estimated effects of the primary determinants of wealth accumulation of black and white families, but also because they show that, after the important variables of age, education, income, residential location, and employment status have been considered, black families (with the exception of those headed by someone with a college degree) still only have between 10 and 35 percent of the wealth accumulation of white families with similar characteristics.

Summary and Conclusions

The most important conclusion from this study is that, regardless of any possible shortcomings in the data, the evidence appears overwhelming that the net wealth position of black families is substantially poorer

TABLE 5

Estimated Wealth Accumulation of Urban Black and White Families with an Employed Head, by Family Income, Age, and Education of Head

Hypothetical Level of Family Income and of Head's Education	Age of the Head of the Family											
	Under 35			35–54			55–64			Over 65		
	White	Black	Ratio	White	Black	Ratio	White	Black	Ratio	White	Black	Ratio
A. $5,000 Family Income												
0–7 yrs. education	216	48	.22	588	108	.18	1,420	371	.26	2,680	625	.23
8–11 yrs.	441	48	.11	1,200	108	.09	2,910	371	.13	5,480	625	.11
12 yrs.	735	160	.22	2,000	247	.12	4,840	845	.17	9,130	1,430	.16
13–15 yrs.	944	203	.22	2,570	458	.18	6,220	1,970	.32	11,600	2,200	.19
16 or more yrs.	1,090	579	.53	2,980	1,310	.44	7,210	4,480	.62	13,600	7,580	.56
B. $10,000 Family Income												
0–7 yrs. education	727	186	.25	979	417	.21	4,778	1,434	.30	9,018	2,416	.27
8–11 yrs.	1,484	186	.13	4,038	417	.10	9,792	1,434	.15	18,440	2,416	.13
12 yrs.	2,473	618	.25	6,730	955	.14	16,287	3,266	.20	30,722	5,527	.18
13–15 yrs.	3,177	785	.25	8,648	1,777	.21	20,930	7,614	.36	39,034	8,503	.22
16 or more yrs.	3,667	2,238	.63	10,028	5,063	.50	24,262	17,315	.71	45,764	29,297	.64
C. $25,000 Family Income												
0–7 yrs. education	3,606	1,107	.31	9,816	2,481	.25	23,699	8,532	.36	44,729	14,375	.32
8–11 yrs.	7,361	1,107	.15	20,078	2,481	.12	48,568	8,532	.18	91,462	14,375	.16
12 yrs.	12,266	3,677	.30	33,381	5,682	.17	80,784	19,433	.24	152,381	32,886	.22
13–15 yrs.	15,758	4,671	.30	42,894	10,573	.25	103,813	45,303	.44	193,609	50,593	.26
16 or more yrs.	18,188	13,316	.73	49,739	30,125	.61	120,340	103,024	.86	226,989	174,317	.77

than that of white families of similar characteristics. The reason does not appear to be related to a lack of thrift among black families, since the bulk of consumption studies show blacks save more at any given level of income, but rather to the fact that black families at any observed income level appear to have had a past history of lower average income than white families of that same income level.

The general findings on wealth accumulation demonstrate the pervasive effect of the past on the current economic status of the black minority population. Current income data alone, which generally show black families having roughly three-fifths[28] as much income as white families, are very misleading because they fail to account for the substantially poorer net wealth position of black families. These rather stark findings on wealth accumulation suggest that economic equality for black families will not be achieved when the current annual income gap between black and white families is eliminated because a considerable wealth gap will remain as a legacy of past economic deprivation.

NOTES

1. The most comprehensive work in this field which includes an excellent bibliography is Lester C. Thurow, *Poverty and Discrimination* (Washington, D.C.: The Brookings Institution, 1969).

2. The most complete work is Robert Ferber, *The Reliability of Consumer Reports of Financial Assets and Debts* (Urbana, Ill.: University of Illinois Press, 1966). A more recent contribution is Ferber *et al.*, "Validation of Consumer Financial Characteristics: Common Stock," *Journal of The American Statistical Association* 64 (June 1969): 415–32.

3. Following the precedent of the Federal Reserve's *Survey of Financial Characteristics of Consumers*, net wealth is defined as all assets minus all debts secured by these assets. From the SEO total wealth is the sum of bank accounts, stocks, Government bonds, housing equity, car and truck equity, farm equity, business equity, and equity in other real estate. The SEO data were collected in 1967 so that income figures refer to calendar 1966 and wealth data to the moment of survey within calendar 1967. It should also be noted that this study considers only nonhuman wealth accumulation.

4. The estimate of $20,153 mean accumulation for white families from the SEO compares with a mean total wealth of $20,982 from the *Survey of Financial Characteristics of Consumers*.

5. For example, the tabulated mean income for black families with income above $20,000 was $23,894; for white families it was $30,015, or 25.6 percent higher.

6. Milton Friedman, *A Theory of the Consumption Function*, (Princeton, N.J.: Princeton University Press, 1957), p. 37.

7. In another essay I have attempted to show how observed income data are inadequate for making short-run comparisons between black and white families since black family income (1) supports more people, (2) is not augmented to the same degree by returns to owner-occupied housing, (3) is earned by the efforts of more people, and (4) is spent on goods and services costing higher prices. It was estimated that the observed ratio of black-to-white mean family income for urban families in 1968 of 63.9 should have been reduced roughly 10 percentage points to account for those biases. See Henry S. Terrell, "The Data on Relative White-Nonwhite Income and Earnings Re-examined: A Comment on the Papers by Guthrie and Ashenfelter," *Journal of Human Resources* 6, No. 3 (1971): 384–91.

8. Friedman, *Theory of Consumption Function*, p. 80.

9. Richard Sterner, *The Negroes' Share: A Study of Income, Consumption, Housing, and Public Assistance* (New York: Harper & Brothers, 1943), p. 93.

10. For numerous citations see Friedman, *Theory of Consumption Function*, pp. 79–85.

11. The broader question of the influence of the size of wealth on its composition is considered in the study in progress noted earlier.

12. For a more complete discussion of the Gini Index see, U.S. Department of Commerce, Bureau of the Census, *Income Distribution in the United States*, by Herman P. Miller, (Washington, D.C.: U.S. Government Printing Office, 1966), pp. 220–21.

13. Board of Governors of the Federal Reserve System, Dorothy S. Projector and Gertrude Weiss, *Survey of Financial Characteristics of Consumers* (Washington, D.C.: Federal Reserve Board, 1966), p. 30.

14. The *Survey of Financial Characteristics of Consumers*, utilizing data collected in 1962 estimated a Gini coefficient for total wealth at 0.76 and 0.43 for family income which are remarkably close to the estimates in Table 3 based on the SEO data.

15. Differences in the absolute size of the Gini coefficients of income from the two different sources were surprisingly small and were due to differences in tabulating methods, different population samples, and the fact that the SEO data contained unrelated individuals, while the census data referred to family units of two or more related by blood, marriage, or adoption. In each case the SEO Gini coefficient was about .040 higher.

16. In some cases the Gini coefficient actually exceeded 1.0 by a small amount. This seeming paradox occurs when the individual reports a minus equity (debts greater than assets) in a specific asset whose distribution is already quite uneven. A simple numerical example can clarify this point. Assume that a society has $100,000 of net business equity divided among two individuals. One individual has a net business equity of $110,000, while the second one has an equity postition of $10,000. Clearly net business equity in this case is less evenly distributed than if one individual had the whole $100,000 of net business equity in that society, thus the Gini coefficient would be greater than 1.0.

17. Gary S. Becker, *The Economics of Discrimination* (Chicago, Ill.: University of Chicago Press, 1957).

18. *Survey of Financial Characteristics of Consumers*, Table A-32, p. 148.

19. For example, Table A-32 of *The Survey of Financial Characteristics of Consumers* reported inherited assets were considered a substantial portion of total assets by 8 percent of units reporting wealth of $25,000–$49,000, 14 percent of units reporting wealth of $50,000–$99,999, and 57 percent of units reporting wealth over $100,000. The SEO contained no information on inheritor status. Clearly inherited wealth will increase with age as the probability of one's parent's decease increases. Inherited wealth probably is positively related to education, as individuals from wealthier families will receive more encouragement to acquire education and will also receive financial assistance. In general the regression coefficients will overstate the effects of age and education on wealth by neglecting the effects of inherited wealth, but they are still important in assessing the relative accumulation of black and white families at given levels of age, income and education.

20. *Survey of Financial Characteristics of Consumers*, p. 7.

21. For extensive documentation see Friedman, *Theory of Consumption Function*, pp. 58–69.

22. Cases with zero and negative income and wealth were eliminated.

23. Higher $\overline{R^2}$ are attainable if the black and white samples are aggregated and are distinguished only by a dichotomous dummy variable, but this method fails to estimate any difference in the effects of the explanatory variables on wealth accumulation of the two races.

24. The coefficients in a double logarithmic relationship have an elasticity interpretation, i.e., in this case, the percentage change in observed wealth corresponding to any percentage change in observed income. It should also be noted that the estimated elasticity for whites of 1.75 compares with an estimated elasticity of 1.74 from the *Survey of Financial Characteristics of Consumers.*

25. In other words a doubling of income raises wealth proportionately more for blacks than for whites.

26. Similar calculations can be made for any group by finding the estimated logarithm of wealth from Table 4 and taking the antilogarithm.

27. Small sample size does not appear to be a problem as the SEO contained 263 black families headed by someone with a college degree.

28. For example, the SEO estimated that the mean 1966 income for black families was $4,460, or 59.5 percent of the estimated mean income of $7,801 for white families.

Economics and Black People

Thomas Sowell

Economics and black people are both poorly understood by the public at large. Economics is often confused with (1) business management, (2) general money making, or (3) moralistic evaluations of economic problems. Economics is essentially a *cause-and-effect* analysis of the production and distribution of goods and resources. Few, if any, economic principles apply exclusively to black people, and so in that sense there is no "black economics," any more than there is "black mathematics." Yet many of the problems of black people—and more importantly, the solutions to those problems—involve an understanding of economic concepts and analysis. In this sense, economics is not only "relevant" to black people but vitally important. This can be illustrated by the usefulness of the economic concept of "human capital" and by the economic analysis of various approaches to black economic development.

Human Capital

One of the more useful concepts of modern economics is the concept of "human capital." Capital is normally thought of as inanimate resources such as machinery, dams, etc., which are accumulated and organized for their future contribution to output and income, rather than for their direct use in the present. However, intangible things such as education can also be accumulated for the sake of future benefits, and the same underlying principles apply to investment in such "human capital" and to its rate of return. Simple as this idea is, many knotty problems are readily understood when human capital is taken into account. Historians have often wondered how nations recover so quickly from the widespread devastations of war—the "German miracle" of recovery after World War II being only the most recent example of something that has happened repeatedly over the centuries. The key fact is that only the devastated country's *physical* capital has been destroyed, for the vital accumulation of knowledge, skills and organizational experience—their human capital—remains intact and can reproduce the physical things, as they would have had to do anyway in the normal course of wear and tear.

Similarly, there has been much wondering and confusion as to how it is that refugees can arrive in the United States with only the clothes on their backs and within a few years be prosperous, while the domestic poor seem trapped in a vicious cycle of poverty. Some people will argue that this just proves that the native poor (sometimes, explicitly or by implication, black people) are just not trying, and others have argued that it proves that the deliberate barriers against the domestic poor are just too high. Actually, most refugees to the United States in the past several decades have come carrying an enormous investment in human capital even if they have left all of their physical belongings behind. They have had educational investments worth tens of thousands of dollars, as well as business, professional, and industrial skills accumulated in high-level positions abroad. Such things are the bulk of the real wealth of most middle-class people, foreign or domestic. The physical things that they own are worth only a fraction of the value of these intangible assets and are symptoms rather than causes of their earning power. The fact that human capital cannot be seen with the naked eye in no way reduces its economic importance.

The poverty of the domestic poor generally, or of black people specifically, is not only a poverty in terms of the physical things they own or don't own; their share of the human capital of the country is even more desperately small. To try to understand these differences in terms of years of formal schooling between black and white is barely to scratch the surface of the problem. Human capital does not consist solely or even primarily in the kinds of knowledge acquired in classrooms and certified by embossed pieces of paper. But if we consider formal education first, for the sake of convenience, it is clear that the amount invested in the children of the poor and black is far less than is invested in the children of middle-class or well-off parents. This is true even in the extreme case of states where "free" education is available from kindergarten to the Ph.D. These differences are due to a number of factors.

1. Expenditures per student are almost always lower in poorer neighborhoods. A large part of educational expenditures consists of teachers' salaries, but, although there are standard pay scales for teachers of a given level which apply everywhere in a given educational system, the schools in poor neighborhoods typically have a large proportion of temporary, substitute, and inexperienced teachers *and* larger classes. The combination drastically lowers the investment per child, sometimes to half of what it is in middle-class schools in the same city or state. Sometimes this is accompanied by dilapidated school buildings and inadequate equipment in the low-income sections, but although the physical dilapidation makes for dramatic photographs and attracts a disproportionate amount of attention, the differences in teaching are far more fundamental and can persist even after shiny new buildings are put into the ghettoes.

2. Even a perfectly equal investment per child per year would turn out to be a highly unequal total investment where different children attend school for different numbers of years—as children from high and low-

income families do. Another way of looking at the same thing is that government subsidies are much more widely available in the forms traditional to middle-class cultures—formal courses of study in school rooms—than in forms more in keeping with lower-income cultures—such as more direct job training, perhaps in the work place itself. "Vocational" public schools sometimes provide the latter, but very often they are simply dumping grounds for problem students, and the obsolescence and general uselessness of what is called vocational education is a well-known national scandal.[1]

3. The system of free college and university education in state institutions is another highly unequal set of investments, though often hotly defended as a system which equalizes opportunity for the poor. Actually, "free" tuition, without provision for living expenses, amounts to a *matching grant*—a subsidy available only to those who can raise substantial amounts of money of their own to make up the difference between the subsidy and the total cost. For example, where tuition costs would be about $2,000 in a similar private college and living expenses about the same, the state school in effect offers $8,000 for a four-year education to anyone who can come up with another $8,000 for living expenses over the same period. Not surprisingly, few poor people can take them up on such an offer. Moreover, poor people do not have the option of taking the $8,000 in the form of fully paid education for two years rather than half-paid education for four years. It is not surprising that study after study shows state colleges and universities populated primarily by students from families of above-average income. In states such as California where the poor contribute a higher share of state taxes than of students in the state-university system, the poor are in effect subsidizing the education of the rich.

4. In considering colleges and universities, differences in the quantity and quality of education become even more important than on the public-school level. The investment per year in a junior-college student is likely to be only a fraction of the investment per year in a doctoral candidate at the state university. The junior-college student is likely to be taught in large classes by a faculty member with modest credentials and modest salary while the doctoral candidate is more likely to be taught in small seminars, his dissertation directed personally by a leading authority in his field, who earns double or triple the salary of a junior-college instructor. Because of poor academic preparation, lower-income students constitute an ever smaller proportion of the total student body as you progress from the poorer quality junior colleges up through the better state colleges and universities, or as you proceed from the freshman year to the Ph.D. level. In addition, since low income and black students have less public school preparation, they are also more concentrated in easier and less remunerative fields, such as sociology, education, etc., rather than in more demanding fields, such as mathematics, engineering, medicine and law, which require far better educational background, and which constitute more expensive education in terms of both equipment needs and high-salaried faculty. Each of these inequalities in cost and quality compounds

the previous inequalities in human capital investment between rich and poor, black and white.

The pattern of cumulative inequalities in human capital investment in formal schooling is repeated in the other forms of human capital. The whole way of thinking and behaving as is appropriate to the more lucrative and responsible occupations comes freely, and even unconsciously, to people reared in families where such occupations have been common for generations; whereas such human capital comes to the low-income person only slowly, imperfectly and with great deliberate effort to break his natural patterns. Such basic traits as punctuality, efficiency, and long-run planning are of little use to people who have been limited to menial jobs for generations as with most black Americans. Everyone can understand the economic value of such traits as an abstract intellectual proposition, but to understand such qualities abstractly and to have such *habits* in reality are very different things. Those black people who have such traits have typically acquired them through persistent, and sometimes painful, adjustments which would be difficult to explain to people who grew up with these patterns as a free cultural inheritance.

In addition to the human capital represented by general intellectual skills and complementary economic behavior patterns, a good deal of human capital consists of economically valuable knowledge of particular situations and individuals. Such knowledge is not easily incorporated into theoretical analysis and so is likely to be neglected (or even disdained) by intellectuals analyzing the sources of wealth, but its value is enormous in either economic or social terms. There are people whose whole income and occupation depends upon such knowledge, ranging from community leaders in the ghetto to speculators on Wall Street. Knowledge of specifically where, how, and by whom to get things done is very unequally distributed and constitutes a tremendous handicap to the poor in a highly complex society. A ghetto youth with a knack for mathematics and a potential for engineering or chemistry probably does not know a single engineer or chemist who could give him some idea of what his avenues and alternatives are. One consequence is the simple direct loss of young black people's potential, because they have no realistic basis for organizing and directing their education and few concrete reasons to feel hopeful or enthusiastic about their prospects, even where, objectively, opportunity exists.

A more concealed but perhaps equally important loss is in the *misdirection* of such black talent, as each generation tends to crowd into a relatively few occupations which educated black people have traditionally entered, such as teaching, medicine and sociology. There are great unmet needs in all these areas—qualitatively perhaps more than quantitatively—but the range of talents of black people is not confined or specialized to the few areas which happened to have had openings in the past when other fields were closed. This is a handicap which some other ethnic minorities imposed on themselves in the past, but we can learn from their mistakes instead of repeating them. One of the reasons for the relatively slow rise of the Irish in America, for example, was their tendency to concentrate on being policemen, priests, and politicians, instead of spreading out into as many occupations as they could break into, as the Jews did. When a group diversifies its occupations to match the differences in its people, instead of trying to force square pegs into round holes, it not only realizes more of its potential in the current generation, it sets up lines of communications into a wide range of fields for the next generation.

In considering the economics of human capital, we consider not only the quantity, quality, and variety of human capital, but also the efficiency with which it is used. Any nation or group of people who are intent on increasing their rate of economic development should of course increase the rate of capital investment and reinvestment. A substantial part of the capital they create should be reinvested in producing more capital for the future rather than directed toward current consumption. With physical capital, this means using a good part of the newly created machines for producing *other* machines instead of producing cars or canned goods. With human capital it means using highly trained professionals and technicians to produce other highly trained professionals and technicians instead of exhausting their efforts in activities designed for an immediate payoff without providing for the replacement and growth of skills for the future.

Unfortunately, the development of highly trained black people has been the opposite of this. The number of black people receiving the Ph.D. has actually *declined* in recent years. No doubt this is because promising black graduate students are in great demand for current use in business, government and the universities, as directors of programs, consultants on projects or simply as symbolic representatives or window dressing. But, whatever the reason, it means that the rate of investment in this kind of human capital is *declining* for black people—from an already low level. This is the equivalent of consuming your capital in the present instead of building it up for the future—wearing out machines faster than replacements are being built or eating up the grain needed for next year's planting.

The use of black human capital of this sort tends also to be the opposite of the pattern necessary for accumulation. Black professors at leading universities are typically busy with miscellaneous campus activities which amount to public relations, social work, or crisis negotiation—all activities which may be worthwhile in themselves but which do not require a highly trained academic to perform them and which fragment his working days into pieces of time too small for serious professional work. Sometimes such tasks are taken up not because they seem intrinsically important to the black professional but because he feels a need to prove his concern for black people in general and black students in particular, in contrast to past instances of black middle-class indifference to the fate of the rest of their people. While the new feeling of concern marks an advance in thinking and responsibility, the cost of spending great amounts of time ''proving'' things to himself or others can be very high, not only to the black professional himself, but to black people generally, if it means that skill development is repeatedly sacrificed to image building. Sometimes the motivation is more opportunistic: for some individuals there may be more money to be made by giving popular lectures than by advancing intellectually, more job security in building a large campus following than in doing competent professional work, or more personal satisfaction in competing with white professors in political power terms than in competing in intellectual terms, for which whites have been given better preparation since childhood. But whether the motivation is sincere or selfish, the net result is the same. In the case of this scarce and valuable human capital the weighing of present advantages against future advantages, which is the essence of the investment process, is completely biased towards current advantages.

Another source of loss of black human capital is the fact that much of the best-trained black professional and technical talent does not teach at the black colleges but at other institutions which are already well supplied with such talent. Sometimes this is simply a matter of pursuing individual self-interest in terms of career opportunities. But in a very large proportion of cases it is because the atmosphere at black colleges is inhospitable or even hostile to the intellectual levels, values and priorities which such people represent. The faculties and administrations of black colleges are all in favor of raising standards, but without disrupting existing patterns, without threatening existing personnel, without undermining existing power and prestige relationships—in short, they are seeking fundamental improvement without fundamental change. The reasons for this situation and these attitudes are rooted in the complex social history of black people—and of white trustees and philanthropists—but the situation itself is painfully obvious, even though the late E. Franklin Frazier was vehemently attacked for pointing it out, as Jencks and Riesman have been attacked for doing so more recently.[2] A key piece of evidence is the incredible rate of faculty turnover at many black colleges, which indicates that the problem is not—as often claimed—the inability to *attract* people but the inability to *keep* people, once they discover the futility of bucking the system.[3]

While existing black professionals and technicians are important in terms of human capital formation and accumulation, the key factor is the black college students—greater in numbers than ever, from more diverse social backgrounds than in the past, and with a new commitment to the advancement of their people rather than to the pursuit of personal success. The great potential here is obvious, and yet offsetting tendencies, which may not be so obvious, may be no less powerful. Most black college students, whether at black institutions or white ones, have not received anything approaching an equal education in the public schools. On the whole, they must either continue to receive second-class education in college or give second-class performances in first-class education. These are the grim alternatives facing us, whatever we might prefer to believe. The second alternative offers better prospects because many students can develop quickly and overcome past deficiencies, in varying degrees, where they encounter high-quality education. Moreover, the process is cumulative, since the first generation to break out of the vicious cycle of undereducation tends to raise the next generation to still higher standards. The advantages of top-quality education, even for those not fully prepared for it, may be obvious in terms of the economics of human-capital formation, but politically it creates many problems and strains for faculty and administrators, and for the black students themselves, so that innumerable ways are found to avoid it, water it down, or grandly dismiss it as "irrelevant."

Despite the myth promoted by American teachers' colleges that good education is always interesting and inspiring, the cold fact is that many of the most valuable intellectual skills are dry, tedious, frustrating, and sometimes agonizing to learn. A very intelligent woman with a Ph.D. in economics from Harvard once confessed that the study of economic theory had given her a splitting headache. People vary, but anyone who plans to pursue seriously economics or any other technical field would do well to keep some aspirin handy. The question is, how many guilty white faculty members and timid white administrators are prepared to give black students splitting headaches? How many black students are prepared to accept headaches after twelve years of coasting through inferior public schools? The question answers itself. Much of the rhetoric, actions, and mystique of our time is an elaboration of that answer. The implications of that answer are also apparent in the small proportion of black students found in the solid and difficult courses which presuppose technical and mathematical skills, disciplined logic, and a mastery of language, in contrast to the high proportion found in loose courses which involve simply the transmission of general information, the airing of opinions, or excursions into the community. There are many ways of getting an inferior education, even at the best colleges and universities. Some football teams and fraternities have made a science of it, but they can usually afford it better than black students, few of whom are in a position to get a "gentleman's C" in sociology and go on to inherit their father's business.

Unfortunately, the question of hard education for future use versus more immediately satisfying classroom discussion has become mixed up with the emotionally charged opposition of integrationist and separatist visions of the future of black people in America. Too often, the argument for taking the more solid and demanding intellectual work has been that this is how you get a better-paying job with I.B.M. or General Motors[4]—an argument which presupposes an integrationist position which many black students question or reject. The underlying economic reality, of which the high salaries are merely symptoms, is that engineering, medicine, chemistry, etc., are more productive—in an all-white society, a multi-racial society, or an all-black society. The irony of the situation is that the kind of education advocated by the integrationists is absolutely essential for a separatist society—where black people would have to supply all their own technical skills and run their own industrial complexes—while the kind of education advocated by the separatists is primarily related to a society with black and white racial conflicts.

Black Economic Development

The question of "black capitalism," "community-owned businesses," "ghetto industries," or however else it is phrased, has been raised by a wide variety of groups and individuals. Sometimes the primary aim has been to replace white merchants with black merchants, in hopes of lower prices or more honest dealing, or simply because the presence of white merchants in a black community is offensive to racial pride. Sometimes there is a belief that business ownership offers a promising way out of poverty for black people—for the black businessmen themselves, and indirectly for the younger generation of black children who will be able to see black adult "models" doing responsible work independently of any white man's direction. Sometimes it is felt that the ghetto must be kept intact and made into an economically viable community rather than having its best talents co-opted into the larger society, leaving the others to languish in poverty. Where so many hopes are built up around one central idea, it is difficult to deal with its validity in all the different respects involved, except by considering them one by one.

Both scientific studies and casual observations confirm that prices are higher in the ghetto for the same items and sometimes for items inferior to those found elsewhere. There are, in addition, a variety of schemes designed to take advantage of various kinds of vulnerable people who live in the ghetto.[5] Such things are enough to arouse even the mildest person to anger, but finding villains is not the same as analyzing causes and effects. Wherever there are people in a position to be cheated there has always been someone rotten enough to cheat them, whatever their color or his. Cheating and abuse on a mass scale have been stopped only when the people being cheated and abused became individually sophisticated and collectively politically aware enough to make it no longer feasible. Some black merchants would undoubtedly be restrained by conscience from exploiting other members of their community. But to expect this to make a great difference, overall, would be naïve. Moreover, high prices are by no means a sign of profitable businesses. An efficiently run supermarket can make a penny profit on a dollar and be tremendously profitable because its stock turns over a couple of dozen times a year, making one percent each time. A small grocery store can make a nickel profit on the same dollar and, because of much slower turnover, be barely able to make ends meet. This is why the competition of supermarkets is destroying small grocery stores all over the country. Supermarket chains and other high efficiency enterprises tend to avoid the ghetto. As long as they do, and as long as no sizeable business class arises in the ghetto with sufficient experience to run large-scale enterprises efficiently, ghetto prices will continue to be high, even in the unlikely event that all the merchants become honest.

It is very hard for many people to believe that it takes much special experience or knowledge to run a business. *Most* small businesses fail within a few years of being established, and yet thousands of people set up new businesses with their life savings each year, because they believe that there is nothing complicated about it. In a sense they are right; a small business may have no single aspect that is intellectually complicated, and yet there may be dozens of small pieces of knowledge that *must* be acquired by experience—often disastrous experience—and the firm's assets may be gone before the owner learns why he should deal with one kind of supplier rather than another, prefer one location to another, have one kind of employee rather than another, deal with the public one way rather than another, etc., etc., etc. If it were simply an intellectual process, it could be taught in schools, so that a new business-man would know what to do from the outset, but much of the knowledge is the kind which can be acquired only by actual experience, including knowledge of particular people in a given trade or locality. The process of producing a whole class of experienced businessmen is necessarily a gradual one, whether one believes in gradualism as a principle or not. Driving white merchants out is relatively easy; replacing them with black businessmen is much harder, and people have to eat in the meantime. The high odds against the survival of a given small business makes business ownership a very doubtful way out of poverty for great numbers of black people. It has always been an easy way *into* poverty for many people who have put their life's savings into it.

Many of the reasons for wanting black businesses are completely valid in themselves and, in fact, the move to start producing a black business class, instead of blindly sending all of our best talent into a few stereotyped professions, is long overdue. But it will succeed only to the extent that the difficulties are seen in advance and expectations are geared to a trial-and-error process, rather than to an inspired formula for salvation.

One idea underlying many of the schemes for community-based enterprises is that prosperity will be increased if money is kept in the ghetto community instead of being siphoned off by white business interests. Here again economics can make a contribution, for this basic idea was at its peak of popularity two-hundred years ago in England under the name of ''mercantilism''—until it was destroyed by the rise of modern economic analysis. Firstly, wealth does *not* consist of money but of goods and services, so that maximizing the wealth of a nation or of a community does not mean keeping money from leaving but maximizing the flow of goods and services through the community during a given time. This is not simply a matter of different words but of policies with completely opposite implications. To keep money from leaving the community implies efforts at economic self-sufficiency, while maximizing the actual goods and services implies spending the money wherever it will buy the most. Actually, it is nearly impossible in practice to keep money from leaving or entering any community; this is what undermined mercantilism in practice even before its intellectual defects were brought out. The flow of money into and out of a community is a symptom of an underlying economic reality and treating symptoms is not going to change the basic fact of the earnings of their labor versus their cost of living, which is what determines whether they are prosperous or poor. To the extent that self-sufficiency means producing goods at higher cost than they can be bought from others, it makes the cost of living higher and the standard of living lower. To the extent that the locally produced goods are cheaper, no special policies are necessary to get people to buy them. This is easily seen in the case of international trade and the same principle applies to trade between communities.

It is difficult to shake loose from the idea that money is wealth. For an individual money *is* wealth, but in considering an economic *system*, it is just green pieces of paper. What matters are the goods and services available. Money flows *through* the black community, as it flows through all communities, and the very process which would reduce the flow *out*—increasing self-sufficiency—would also reduce the flow *in*, as fewer black people would earn incomes in the outside world. The real difference in economic well-being would be measured by the differences in goods and services available under internal production versus buying and selling wherever the best price is available. Trying to dam up the flow of money is futile and self-defeating.

Another important meaning of "keeping money in the community" is that community savings should be invested in community businesses instead of being used to finance ventures elsewhere. But just as ghetto residents are not going to be made more prosperous by working in the ghetto at wages lower than those available to them outside the ghetto, so the employment of black capital at a lower rate of return inside the ghetto than outside is not going to promote prosperity. The physical locations of jobs, investment, or money sources means nothing in itself; what matters is the flow of real wealth which results to the people who are located in the black community, regardless of where the flow originates. Capital is the most fluid of all resources. It goes wherever the rate of profit is highest, allowing for risk. If the ghetto were a high-profit location, nothing is more certain than that capital would be flowing in instead of avoiding it. Empirical evidence, thus far, suggests that new black businesses established in recent years have on the whole done poorly and so have the community banks which have financed them. This is a high price to pay for heady rhetoric and naïve economics. In particular cases there are striking successes for which "leaders" take credit, but failures are passed over in silence, creating a very misleading impression for those who judge results by the sounds that are heard. It is a fact of political life, not only in the black community but throughout society and around the world, that methods which produce "issues," "victories," and "achievements" for "leaders" are going to be preferred, whether they are economically best or not. Repeated disasters over a period of generations were required to discredit the mercantilist way of thinking in Europe and America, but black people have been through too many disasters already without repeating the mistakes that white people made in previous centuries.

Underlying many of the approaches to black economic development is the idea that the poverty of black people is a simple consequence of white people's taking away wealth from them in the higher prices they charge or in the lower wages they pay. To many people this seems so directly obvious that any complicated economic analysis seems pedantic at best and dishonest at worse. But despite the popular appeal of "exploitation" theories and the prevalence of cheating wherever people can be cheated, the fundamental cause-and-effect sequence in black poverty is very different. A black man who is born with the native ability to be a chemist and earn $20,000 a year can easily find himself so boxed in by discrimination that he ends up as a ditch-digger making $3,000 a year. He is worse off than if he were in fact exploited, but any policy based on the belief that his ditch-digging is underpaid is going to compound the problem. For example, if his wages are forced up on the assumption that his employer is making huge profits from his underpaid labor, the net result is likely to be that more machines will be used for ditch digging and his already meager income will be further reduced. The difference between denial of opportunity and exploitation is not merely a matter of verbal fastidiousness. Completely different economic policies are needed for dealing with the two things, and we cannot afford to pursue self-defeating policies because we have become attached to a label.

The "exploitation" label further complicates matters when the prosperity of white people is seen not as a consequence of better opportunities which have given them advantages in scientific and technical skills and managerial experience, but as simply a consequence of robbing black people, at home and abroad. A certain class of white merchants, slum landlords, etc., do, in fact, prosper by cheating black people, but the prosperity of the white 90 percent of the country can hardly be explained by what they take away from the black 10 percent.[6] Moreover, since only 5 percent of the total goods and services which make up the American standard of living comes from international trade, even if that trade represented complete robbery, it would account for little of that standard of living. The real problem is that deliberate discrimination, unconscious racism, and general neglect have left black people too poor to be robbed of anything that would make a difference on a national scale. Whenever one group oppresses another, it almost invariably does so by denying them opportunities for self-realization, *not* by allowing them to develop their potential and then taking away what they have produced. This means that a group rising out of oppression must recognize that the hard task of developing its potential lies ahead, that the mere removal of oppression will do little to improve this situation, that it cannot simply dismiss the skills it lacks as "irrelevant" or as morally tainted because the oppressors have such skills.

The difficulties of promoting black economic development through the kinds of programs that various groups have blueprinted does not mean that black economic development is not possible or likely by other routes, in less spectacular forms, and in less organized ways which provide little political mileage for black "leaders" or white "friends." In fact, *most* black economic progress has taken place in ways *not* mapped out by inspired messiahs or vocal partisans. So has the progress of most other people. The idea of drawing up a master plan for a whole society has great appeal, especially to those without actual experience in the management of massive organizations. The notion of controlling society or history is the kind of attractive idea which people give up only after the most obvious and repeated damaging experience. The mercantilism of the seventeenth and eighteenth century was abandoned only after gross fiascos and widespread inefficiencies plagued generation after generation. Socialist economies, from the Soviet Union to Yugoslavia, have been steadily retreating from central planning under the pressure of similar experience. The American belief that the United States could control the direction of world history has led to a similar string of political debacles (from the "loss of China" to the Bay of Pigs to the Vietnam war), which have caused even the supporters of aggressive foreign policies to turn toward disengagement.

The clash of separatist and integrationist, militant and moderate visions of the future is as unnecessary as it is divisive. No one can tell 20 million people what is best for them, and the attempt to "unite" people of widely differing philosophies behind one master plan is itself a major cause of disunity. What matters far more than whose ideology shall be dominant is the standard of living and the number and quality of options open to black people. The real problem is to raise the productivity and earnings of black people in order to lift them out of poverty. What they choose to do then is their own business individually, and no college degrees or inspired message or feeling of being blacker-than-thou gives anyone the right to decide what others should do. Black people have been dictated to for too long by white people to start dictating to each other now. Undoubtedly, some will want to spread out into the larger society while others will prefer to prosper among their own people and culture, while still others will alternate according to changing attitudes—their own and the white society's.

Far more fundamental than the distinction between "militant" and "moderate" approaches is the distinction between seeking concessions (whether moderate concessions or radical concessions) and seeking self-realization—the latter attitude being exemplified in the remark of football great Jim Brown: "Don't give me anything; just get off my back!" Concessionism—moderate or radical—gains some tangible benefits from whites but exacts an exhorbitant price from the black man who allows his aspirations to be oriented towards this basically subordinate and parasitic role. Some people see a great difference between going to the white man hat in hand and going to him with a list of demands (and perhaps the weapons to back them up), but basically it is still going to the white man, and becoming a *recipient* rather than a creator. Concessionism "works," but it works in the same way that Uncle Tomism worked—at a cost out of all proportion to what was gained, by abandoning creativity and independence.

It is not worth debating whether black people "deserve" concessions as a result of injustices. What is far more important is whether concessions help or hinder. Even a casual observation of the areas of the economy in which black people have been most successful—sports and entertainment, both ruthlessly competitive—and those in which they have done poorly—for example, the academic world, where "sympathetic" whites full of concessions and special allowances abound—should at least raise doubts about the value of concessions and the atmosphere they create. Nor is this simply a difference between intellectual and nonintellectual fields. Black *non*academic intellectuals, who have to compete on equal terms, with no allowance for "cultural deprivation" and the like, have been far more successful than black academicians. It is difficult to name black academic intellectuals of the calibre of such black *non*academic intellectuals as Richard Wright, Lorraine Hansberry, James Baldwin, Thurgood Marshall, etc., not to mention such musical composers as W. C. Handy, Duke Ellington, and others too numerous to list.

Whether discussing human capital or economic development, black students are a key, and perhaps *the* key, to the future. Their opportunities for advancing their people are matched only by the many lures and pressures on them to go off on some tangent and dissipate their time. To many universities, including some of the most prestigious in the country, they are so much window dressing, and policies are shaped not primarily to educate them but to keep them happy, or at least quiet. To many socio-political doctrinaires, they are so much cannon fodder to be thrown into battle for their special causes. They themselves are probably not quite sure what they are, which is what makes them so vulnerable to assorted opportunists. Neither kindness nor myths, nor remedial tutoring can give them the sense of personal worth necessary to sustain them in the impossible situation in which many find themselves. Their search for a sense of worth is all the more ironic since there are probably few people in the country who mean so much to the future. A white middle-class student who has been groomed for college since he was out of diapers may make a more impressive academic record, but another white doctor in a white middle-class community means simply shorter lines in the waiting room, while another black doctor in a ghetto or in the rural south may mean the difference between someone's getting medical attention and not getting it at all or getting it too late. A white graduate who can analyze financial records is just another useful employee for some corporation, but a black graduate who can do the same may be the difference between a flourishing business in the ghetto and one which collapses with many people's hard-earned savings in it. No one needs to *give* black students a sense of their importance; they need only to *realize* their importance and the responsibility this implies. A black student who wants to live up to this responsibility cannot, for example, play the popular game of grade-point averages, for an A in the sociology of the ghetto adds little to what he already knows, while a C in calculus can give him the foundation he needs for work in fields where he can render a lifetime of service. The existing generation of black academics and professionals can render a service to black students by helping them sort out their own priorities—a process which may also help the older generation to sort out theirs.

NOTES

1. See Edward P. Chase, "Learning to be Unemployable," *Harper's Magazine,* Apr. 1963: 33–40.

2. E. Franklin Frazier, *Black Bourgeoisie* (Detroit, Mich.: The Free Press, 1957); Christopher Jencks and David Riesman, "The American Negro College," *Harvard Educational Review* 37 (Winter 1967): 3–60.

3. During one year in the economics department of a black university, one constantly stressing its difficulties in finding good men, I noted the departure of men who went on to (1) teach at three Ivy League universities work as economists in (2) the world's largest corporation, (3) a leading bank in New York, and (4) a nationally known food products corporation. From my own knowledge of the men involved, there is little doubt that they would have been willing to spend their lives building that department and that university if they thought there was any real hope of doing so.

4. I have found myself misquoted to that effect.

5. See Warren G. Magnuson, *The Dark Side of the Marketplace* (Englewood Cliffs, N.J.: Prentice-Hall, Inc., 1968), chap. 2.

6. Even slavery, the number-one *moral* horror of American history, held nowhere near that position as a contribution to the *economic* development of the United States. The South, where slavery flourished, has always been one of the poorest regions of the country, and those parts of the South in which slavery was most widespread and most vicious—Mississippi, for example—has always been the poorest part of the South. Fortunes were made by some of the 5 percent of the white Southern population which owned slaves, but the distortions of the whole Southern economy and society caused by slavery make it doubtful that the region as a whole gained much by it (except a sense of racial superiority to comfort them in their poverty) and entirely possible that it lost, on net balance, as many economists have argued. Without even attempting to summarize the voluminous analyses of the economics of slavery, which stretch back over the past two centuries and which are still being debated, it may be worthwhile to note (1) the penetrating analysis of the social-economic effects of slavery on the South in the 1835 classic by Alexis de Tocqueville, *Democracy in America* (New York: Alfred A. Knopf, 1966), Vol. I, pp. 356–81, and (2) a survey of the various economic arguments about slavery, with valuable references to the original sources, in Harold D. Woodman, "The Profitability of Slavery: A Historical Perennial," *Journal of Southern History,* Aug. 1963: 303–25.

Topics for Discussion

1. Describe the economic and business climate in which blacks operated prior to the Civil War. What were the notable successes? Which of these remain?
2. Describe the banking activities, emphasizing effects of Freedmen's banks.
3. How did economic and political problems interact? How was political disenfranchisement used to impede and inhibit the economic advances of blacks? What were the responses of successful black businessmen?
4. The economic and business activities of black people have generally been circumscribed or dictated by the climate of the day. An understanding of these activities demands an understanding of the economic and political pressures to which blacks were subjected; for example, in addition to customary discrimination, specific laws and rules were formulated to inhibit economic advancement by black people. The extent to which this affected both the direction of and the basis for black economic development must be fully comprehended.
5. Black people have continuously sought economic power as a response to fight disenfranchisement and other forms of oppression and discrimination. Discuss this strategy in terms of (1) the pre-Civil War efforts of individuals and mutual-aid societies; (2) the philosophy of Booker T. Washington and the National Business League, and (3) Marcus Garvey's Universal Negro Improvement Association. Consider these efforts in terms of precedents for efforts in black economic development today.
6. Discuss the effects of the Depression in shifting the emphasis from building black businesses to opening employment opportunities.
7. Discuss the political philosophies and racial aspirations implied in an emphasis on black business ownership. Would such philosophy and aspirations be expected to change as the black economic thrust changes from businesses catering to a segregated market to businesses catering to more open markets? Would any differences in philosophies and aspirations appear in an emphasis on employment opportunities?

Suggested Readings

Anderson, R. C. "Black Employment in the Securities Industry." *Industrial Relations*, February 1973.

Corazzini, Arthur J. "Equality of Employment Opportunity in the Federal Civil Services," *Journal of Human Resources*, Fall 1972.

Emeka, Mauris Lee Porter. *Black Banks, Past and Present.* Kansas City, Mo.: Mauris L.P. Emeka, (5000 Walrind 64130).

Myrdal, Gunnar. *An American Dilemma: The Negro Problem and Modern Democracy.* New York: Harper and Row, 1962. ("The Negro in Business," pp. 307–18, and "Boosting Negro Business and Criticism of Negro Business Chauvinism," pp. 800–5.)

Harris, Abram L. *The Negro as Capitalist: A Study of Banking and Business among American Negroes.* Philadelphia, Pa.: American Academy of Political and Social Sciences, 1936.

Michelson, S. "Incomes of Racial Minorities." Unpublished doctoral dissertation, Stanford University, 1965.

Ritchie, R. "The Economic Situation of Blacks." *Federal Reserve Bank of Philadelphia Business Review,* June 1972.

Thieblot, Armand J., and Fletcher, Linda. *Negro Employment in Finance: A Study of Racial Policies in Banking and Insurance.* Philadelphia: University of Pennsylvania Press, 1970.

Tucker, David M. "Black Pride and Negro Business in the 1920's; George Washington Lee of Memphis." *Business History Review* 42 (Winter 1969): 435–51.

U.S. Department of Labor. *Black Americans: A Chartbook* (Bureau of Labor Statistics Bulletin, 1699). Washington, D.C.: Government Printing Office, 1971.

II
Problems

The Constellation of Politics and Economics: A Dynamic Duo in the Black Economy

Robert S. Browne

With 23 million people, one-third of them concentrated in fifteen cities, the black population of America constitutes a potential force of formidable dimensions in American political affairs. Its potential is further enhanced by its low median age and high growth rate compared to the white population. To be sure, these quantitative factors are heavily vitiated by a variety of qualitative characteristics of the black community which are likely to weaken its potential for political effectiveness. These characteristics include the low level of black voter registration and electoral participation, the legal and illegal disenfranchisement of significant portions of the black population, its subjection to gerrymandering at the hands of white majorities who can render the black ballot largely ineffective, and the traditional dependence of the more politically active portion of the black electorate and of its elected officials on one or the other of the two major political parties.

Black Electoral Politics

The above characteristics notwithstanding, it is increasingly clear that today we find ourselves entering a totally new era of black electoral political activity, an era which has had no counterpart in recent American history. Not since the little-known and ill-understood period of Reconstruction has the black voter or the black politician found himself speaking to the white political establishment with the degree of self-confidence which he feels today.

It would, of course, be a grave misreading of reality to describe the current political rumblings within the black community as an unambiguous index of growing black political power in America. On the contrary, recent secret meetings of top black elected officials, murmers of an incipient national black political party, and rumors of a black presidential candidate for 1972 could well turn out to be little more than high-level minstrel shows, extended ego trips for a few black political leaders who are reacting—perhaps subconsciously—against an unbearable realization of their own powerlessness in the giant, racist machine which constitutes American society. This would be a very defensible reading of the current activities in the black political community, for an unsentimental assessment of the power of black political leadership and its factionalized, quarreling, poverty-stricken constituency of 23 million, swallowed in a total population of 220 million, can hardly be other than pessimistic.

A contrary interpretation of the new black political thrust is, however, possible. This interpretation would accept that in 1971, almost eleven decades after Emancipation and five years away from America's 200th anniversary, the sons and daughters of former slaves have genuinely determined that the time has come for them to play a major role in fashioning the future of American society. That such a momentous decision might come at this particular moment in American history is hardly surprising. The entire thrust of the civil rights activities of the 1960s was laying the foundation for a political consciousness among blacks, and, given the unyielding racism of the nation's institutions, it could have been predicted that this political awareness would at some point in its development be obliged to consolidate as a black movement, at least for the formulation of its goals. A factor of perhaps equal, if not greater, strength in forging a black political movement at this historical moment is the recent discovery by blacks of the effectiveness of the negative political power which they can exercise in contemporary America. Indeed, the demographic figures on the black community, and its geographical distribution, are probably of less significance for their electoral potential than for what they suggest in terms of the black disruptive potential to the harmonious functioning of the society.

The pessimists are correct when they assess the electoral potential of the black community as being relatively low. James Madison himself during the formative years of the Republic wrote at length about his fears regarding the protection of minorities against the deliberate tyranny of the majority, and these fears haunt the black community today in terms of its very potential for survival in the face of intense racial polarization. A dozen black congressmen, or even the two score of them which would more closely reflect the black population percentage, must obviously remain forever vulnerable to the whims of their majority colleagues; so electoral politics by itself is admittedly of limited usefulness to blacks. Similarly, the power of disruption, or the threat of it—call it negative political power—is also a tool of limited utility in the black man's kit, whether used directly to bludgeon concessions from, or indirectly to dramatize injustices and heighten the moral sensitivity of, the white community.

Despite the limitations of both of these styles of political maneuvering, however, it is probably some combination of them to which one must credit such social and economic gains as the black community has achieved in recent years. It was only two years ago that the keynote speech at the Detroit (Michigan) Black Economic Development Conference stressed the total absence of black people from the boards of directors and from the upper executive echelons of the major corporations of America. Now, two years later, the appointment of blacks to major corporate boards has become almost a fad, with Chase Manhattan Bank, First National City Bank, Equitable Life Assurance Co., Metropolitan Life Insurance Co., General Motors, I.B.M., and others, each boasting of having appointed a black director to its board. Clearly, these blacks did not suddenly in 1970 and 1971 become qualified to be on the boards of major corporations. There were probably blacks just as qualified in 1965 and 1966, or even in 1955 and 1956. Obviously, factors completely external to these individuals were responsible for their being suddenly discovered by big business. And whatever these external factors were—and it may be difficult to obtain agreement on just what they were—they were certainly political in their nature.

Black Powerlessness

One complaint—perhaps the major complaint of the black man in America—is his relative powerlessness. Now that the larger society is recognizing this fact and perceiving the threat which black powerlessness poses to the nation, the white establishment is confronted with a grave dilemma—how to share its power without in fact sharing it. Resolving this riddle promises to be quite an act, and the black community is watching with intense curiosity.

In American society, political and economic power tend to be so closely entwined that they become largely inseparable at the summit. With some exceptions, however, the route to political power in America has generally lain through economic power rather than the reverse. This is not a route which is open to black Americans, for blacks lack the economic base—the accumulation of assets—which is necessary for launching a bid for a share of national power. Rather, the black political electorate constitutes virtually the only leverage either for placing a black hand on the nation's throttle or for appropriating for the black community a reasonably fair share of the national income and of the national wealth. It is this realization, no doubt, which lies behind the current audacious black political thrusts and most especially behind the movement toward a unified black political effort. It may appear desperate to the dispassionate, but it is probably the only path available which offers any hope for success.

The election of black mayors in several major cities and in a number of minor ones has thus far constituted the most dramatic demonstration of black political emergence. These victories have certainly not been unmixed blessings, for while they have unquestionably enhanced the black man's self-image, which is no small accomplishment, in most cases the cities involved are in serious social and economic straits and suffering from secular decline on a scale which renders them almost unsalvageable except by herculean outside assistance. This is particularly true of Newark, New Jersey, and largely true of Cleveland, Ohio. It is probably also true of Detroit, where blacks may well elect the next mayor. Indeed, every time this author passes a certain little storefront office in Harlem where a giant sign states "It's time for New York City to elect a black mayor" he is tempted to go inside and ask: "WHY?"

On the other hand, one should not overlook the very real opportunities which the mayor's seat offers for providing blacks with positions and experience which they have never before enjoyed, for providing black entrepreneurs with city contracts and with other benefits which have been the monopoly of white firms and contractors, and for using municipal monies in creative ways to assist the neglected black community instead of the favored white one. On balance, there seems to be little doubt that blacks stand to gain more than they lose through electing black mayors; so they should continue to pursue this type of effort when it appears to be achievable, although recognizing the real limitations which are inherent in such victories.

Another form in which black political power has been manifest has been the takeover of political units larger than municipalities—most notably in the election of a full slate of officials in Green County, Alabama. This type of effort has been confined to the South, specifically to those counties with strong black majorities. Heavy rural-to-urban migration has gravely reduced the number and strength of such majorities, which is unfortunate, for these black-run counties may offer the black man his best potential for building viable communities in which he can enjoy a measure of self-determination and economic independence. The counties where blacks are in the majority are almost invariably the poorest counties in their states (Green County, for example, has the unenviable status of being the fifth poorest county in all of America); so the task of developing these counties does not promise to be easier than the task of rendering the cities viable. But they do represent a significant opportunity for black people from all walks of life to pool their talents within a reasonably congenial atmosphere and attempt to build thriving, comprehensive communities where young black people can be trained and inspired to render useful service to themselves and to their people. Efforts are underway to assist these black-run counties to establish a sound economic base through attracting industry and halting the erosion of black land ownership. Because southern black people are even poorer than those in the North, northern blacks should be prepared to lend not only their financial support to these efforts but also to lend their skills, to the extent that this is possible.

Success at either of these levels of development will require a massive infusion of funds which is not likely to be forthcoming unless powerful pressure is put on the executive and legislative branches of the national government. Not only must national priorities be reordered, but the nation must be obliged to admit that the present distribution of income and wealth within the country is grossly intolerable and that a voluntary and drastic redistribution of it is absolutely essential if any semblance of an orderly society is to be preserved. Such a prescription, of course, speaks not only to the black condition in America, but to the total social condition of the country. A situation where 5 percent of the population disposes of 20 percent of the income and the top 1 percent of wealth holders dispose of 26 percent of the nation's total personal wealth can hardly be considered stable at this stage in America's history, although such inequality has admittedly been commonplace at earlier periods and exists today in some other countries.

Caucus of Black Congressmen

The foregoing suggests that, ultimately, it is at the national level that black politics must become the instrument for economic liberation. Hopefully, it is the beginnings of this thrust which blacks witnessed last spring. The recent creation of a Caucus of Black Congressmen, speaking with a unified voice, eschewing any tie to political machines and espousing instead a politics of principle over a politics of party, represents a breath of fresh air on the political horizon.

All blacks should contribute as generously as possible to the Caucus's fund-raising campaign, which will provide an urgently needed secretariat and research staff for its work. In addition to providing financial support, however, blacks must also monitor the Caucus's work carefully, while remaining alert to detect and deflect whatever "divide-and-conquer" tactics which may be devised to discredit it or render it ineffectual.

The sixty-one recommendations which the Black Caucus presented to the President, although deficient in their attention to concerns of the rural southern black, were generally well chosen and well formulated. They constituted a reasonable, achievable basic program for blacks during the remaining portion of President Nixon's term. In most cases the recommendations erred on the side of moderation, and they were clearly a substantial compromise from what some of the more militant of the black Congressmen would have wished. Despite this, however, the President's response was extremely disappointing. Consider a few examples of the President's unresponsiveness on the economic issues which were raised.

Of the sixty-one recommendations, the largest single group was the one devoted to Economic Security and Economic Development, which contained twenty-four recommendations. The three other categories were: Community and Human Development (twenty-one recommendations), Justice and Civil Rights (ten recommendations), and Foreign Policy (six recommendations). Among the economic recommendations submitted and flatly rejected by the President were:

1. A request for a public service job creation program which would provide a minimum of 1.1 million jobs within the first year. He dismissed this request as unnecessary in view of the public service jobs (unspecified in number) which were explicitly or inexplicitly included in the Administration's welfare reform and revenue-sharing bills.

2. A request for a new, independent quasi-public development bank, funded initially at $1 billion annually, for the purpose of addressing the problem of assisting minority enterprise. He rejected this as unnecessary in view of existing and planned programs, although no powerful voice for minority enterprise either exists or is envisioned in the Administration's plans, and minority development funds requested by the Administration for existing agencies total considerably less than the $1 billion requested by the Caucus.

3. A request for $50 million for funding community-development corporations (CDCs), a new form of all-purpose, community-run development agency which is having some success in a number of black communities. He rejected this request on the grounds that CDCs are experimental, so no new ones should be started until the present ones have proved their effectiveness. Passed over in silence was the fact that the *existing* CDCs need $50 million for their own expansion if they are to achieve all that is being expected of them.

4. A request for a federally financed guarantee organization similar to the Government National Mortgage Association to insure securities and obligations of CDCs. He rejected this on the grounds that "this would stigmatize CDCs as unable to compete with other firms in existing capital markets..." The reality, of course, is that by their very nature and newness the CDCs cannot hope to compete with other firms for capital, and that admission actually constituted the basis for the request for a guaranteeing agency.

The President's insensitivity to these reasonable and disconcertingly modest requests suggests that Washington is very far indeed from being disposed to deal with the more drastic kinds of economic demand which will have to be made on it in the coming months and years. A few hundred million or even a few billion dollars, administered through traditional or largely traditional types of institutions, are not capable of bringing about the changes which the society needs—nor is the $6500 per year guaranteed income which the black Congressmen also requested and which the President firmly rejected. The reasons which the President gave for this rejection, however, go to the heart of the matter; he argued that so generous a welfare plan would be fiscally irresponsible, would cost some $75 billion per year, and would lead to substantial reallocation of funds from other programs benefiting the poor. One wonders how he arrived at his $75 billion figure and why he suggested that one program to benefit the poor could only be funded by cutting back on other socially oriented programs.

The Black Economist's Role

This seems to suggest that black economists must join with black political leaders to formulate totally new challenges to the manner in which the nation's resources are being allocated. Not only must the government (not just the present incumbents but also the establishment which runs this country irrespective of who sits in the White House) abandon its preposterous external squandering of the national resources—in aggressive military adventures and posturing, in expensive space galas, and in international political intrigue—it must also take steps to see that resources are better distributed within the body politic. Our tax structure is long overdue for genuine reform, both because of its failure to redistribute wealth and because its inequities constitute an endless eroding of the national moral fiber. Public awareness that loopholes in the tax laws reduce effective rates of federal taxation actually paid by the rich to less than half the nominal rates, permitting hundreds of high-income recipients, including at least a score of millionaires, to escape federal taxes, totally, constitutes a revolutionary potential of considerable proportions. The capital gains provisions alone provide several billions of dollars of tax relief to the rich, lost revenues which must be compensated for by imposing higher rates on the poor, who cannot take advantage of capital gains. When this situation is superimposed on the burden created by the little-understood but scandalously unfair Social Security tax mechanism and then supplemented by the heavily regressive tax structures of the states and municipalities, blacks are confronted with a situation where the poor are, for all practical purposes, subsidizing the rich via the tax structures. In New York City, for example, residents are paying a combined city and state sales tax of 7 percent. The absence from our tax structure of a capital levy of strong estate and inheritance taxes further aggravates the bias in favor of those who possess accumulations of wealth, while bleeding those whose sole income is from wages and salaries.

Such inequities, which fall far harder on the black community than on the white, cannot be tolerated indefinitely. Whether one chooses to call the rectification of economic injustice by the name of tax reform, reparations, or some other term is immaterial. What is important is that the society realize that the gross inequities in the distribution of wealth between the white majority and the black minority must be corrected as a *sine qua non* for a stable American society. The reparations concept obviously speaks more directly to the black economic predicament, which is essentially a shortage of capital assets within the black community, occasioned by the historical circumstances of slavery, persecution and discrimination. The ill-fated Freedman's Bureau concept of special or preferential treatment to help rectify the devastating results of this historical injustice has slowly gained some degree of re-acceptance in American social thinking as reflected in programs such as the Department of Commerce's Section 8 (a) set-asides, Minority Enterprise Small Business Investment Companies (MESBICs), the liberalized Small Business Administration (SBA) regulations for minority enterprise, the Philadelphia Plan, and other minority-aid schemes—most of which, incidentally, look much better on paper than in practice. But discussion of an actual major capital transfer from the general society to the black community, a modern day Homestead Act of some sort, continues to remain a taboo subject.

A misplaced sense of pride on the part of many black people too often leads them to make public declarations that they do not want handouts, that they do not want welfare, that they do not want anything but a fair chance to compete. Unfortunately, these well-meaning blacks are perhaps unaware that a very sizable portion of our national budget, to which they are contributing heavily, is being used for handouts to cover the deficits of some of the largest industries in America and to subsidize the most prosperous farmers in our country. It is being used to pay subventions to some of the wealthiest governments in the world—such as Germany, which presumably wants U.S. troops but not badly enough to pay for them. Recently Congress voted to use poor people's tax payments to save a specific private company, the Lockheed Aircraft Corporation, from the bankruptcy which it faced because of executive incompetence. Corporations contracting with the Defense Department have made it standard operating procedure to submit deliberately understated bids for government contracts, confident that when their costs far exceed their estimates, the government will cover their deficit. With the national government thus favorably disposed toward giving welfare to the rich, further compounding the tax structure's already strong bias in favor of these very same groups, black people would appear to have little reason for hesitancy in demanding both a level of welfare adequate for human decency and a sizable payment in reparations to provide them an economic basis for a meaningful takeoff in the area of development. The obvious, a soundly based black politics is the prerequisite for rendering such a demand effective.

Clearly, the black economist, in conjunction with the black politician, will have to become much more active in analyzing and defining proper government economic policy from the perspective of the black community. For example, the black economist can no longer close his eyes to the fact that the present international monetary arrangements, with the dollar accorded key or reserve currency status, leads ultimately to a hardship's being visited upon the black community with no compensating gains to it. Far better that the United States be obliged to terminate its payment deficit and end its imperialist adventures than that interest rates be kept at levels which render new housing construction virtually impossible and all credit exorbitantly dear. Key currency status for the dollar is essentially a national prestige item and an American political asset; it is totally irrelevant to the destitute black community, which could not care less as to whether the United States is the number one or the number ten power in the world. Indeed, the ghetto's living conditions understandably cause it to identify more with the so-called underdeveloped nations than with any image of world leadership.

Conclusion

The black community has erred for too long on the side of subordinating its own best interests to those which were identified as "the national interest." Now that blacks are reaching political maturity they are beginning to discern that there is no such thing as "the national interest." There are merely a number of competing, conflicting, special interests—each greedily seeking to gain control over the largest possible share of the nation's wealth, income, and political apparatus. The task which lies before black people is to devise effective strategies through which they may insure that their lagging, beloved black community at long last obtains an equitable portion of these American prizes.

If the international enthronement of the dollar is condemning black people to poor housing, then the dollar must be dethroned. If Germany's security requires the presence of American troops, then Germany, not the poor black taxpayer, must pay for those troops. If American business is unwilling to build plants in the black-dominated counties of the American South, then blacks should invite Japanese capital to come in and help them. If Washington will not supply adequate funds for developing the ghettos, then blacks must seek them from the World Bank, from the United Nations, or from the Soviet Union, as dozens of other underdeveloped nations do. In short, blacks must liberate themselves from any artificial national restrictions which obstruct their progress.

For 300 years the impact of the black community on America has been passive, reactive, and involuntary. Henceforth, black political leaders must commit themselves to making the impact of blacks active, deliberate, and self-centered—ignoring the appeals to a mythological national interest and focusing on the swiftest possible development of the black economy. Hopefully, the more far-sighted elements of the white community will join blacks in this effort. For unless this business is attended to with unaccustomed speed it is highly possible that the United States as a nation will be unable to transcend the grave internal stresses which are already subjecting it to a considerable degree of domestic turmoil.

Barriers to Black Participation in the American Economy

Robert S. Browne

Attempting to chart a rational but effective path of economic development for black people in America is a peculiarly difficult task because of the *double* inequalities of American society. On the one hand, income and wealth (and inevitably, power) are so inequitably distributed in America, irrespective of race, that a powerful case can—indeed, must—be made, for a total restructuring of the economy as a necessary precondition for genuine black economic development. On the other hand, the society is so ridden with racial inequality and racial prejudice that astute black people are rightly skeptical about blindly supporting any of the numerous movements for revolutionary economic change in America. Such movements are inevitably led and financed by whites, so, even should they prove successful in bringing about revolutionary economic change, they offer no guarantee that white socialism would be any more free of racism than is white capitalism.

In a sense, this dilemma represents the economic aspect of the integrationist-separatist debate which is surging through black America at this moment. To the degree that the economic aspects of the black condition are separable from political and cultural ones, the question is this: to what extent can blacks entrust their future to alliances with liberal or radical whites, alliances in which blacks will inevitably be the weaker partner; and to what extent should they rely primarily on their own resources and those which they can extract from whites by the judicious use of black pressure? It is my personal belief that the millenium for the mass of black folks is only achievable within a separate black society of some form. Rather than to take a firm position on this question at this time, however, I would like to describe in some detail the nature of the American economy, to indicate the types of obstacle which confront us in our struggle, and possibly to point up directions in which we might move.

At the outset, it is important to have clearly in our minds exactly what struggle we are talking about, for there is a great deal of confusion within black circles arising from our failure to be explicit on this point. When we speak of black economic development, are we talking about raising the median family income of blacks, or are we talking about closing the gap between median family income of blacks and whites, or again, are we talking about securing for blacks an equitable share of the nation's income—and of its wealth and its power? These are not identical objectives, and while it is possible to view them as a continuum which one traverses step-by-step, it is likely that excessive focusing on one may in fact diminish one's ability or enthusiasm for dealing with the others.

I suspect we can assume that the mere raising of median family income of blacks is not in itself a satisfactory objective of black economic development. If it were, we should be feeling reasonably satisfied with ourselves today because family income for blacks has been rising steadily for the past twenty-five years.

Personally, I do not even feel that we should be content with the objective of "closing the gap" between white and black median family income. Indeed, this gap actually has been closed somewhat in recent years, a trend which has so deeply impressed presidential counsellor Daniel Moynihan that he has been led to call for a period of "benign neglect" toward blacks, overlooking the fact that the black-white income differential is still substantial ($8,936 for whites vs. $5,359 for blacks) and the equally significant fact that it requires the employment of one and one-half members of a black family as compared with only one member of a white family in order to achieve even this degree of income inequality.

But I have a more fundamental reason for rejecting equalized median family income between whites and blacks as a satisfactory goal of black economic development. I reject it because median family income does not tell us very much about the real plight of black people in this country. Median income has sometimes been criticized as a misleading measure of the economic condition of whites, but it is an even more inappropriate measure as regards blacks. Median income merely indicates the middle income in a ranked distribution of all incomes. Half of the population makes more than this income and half makes less. In 1968, for example, half of the white families earned more than $8,936 and half less; for blacks the figures divided at $5,359. But black economic development, it seems to me, must be crucially concerned with the *dispersion* around that median figure. Although we have no figures on the dispersion of black incomes, we do have data on general income distribution in the United States, data which suggest that the wealthiest 5 percent of the population receives about 20 percent of the national income, whereas the poorest 20 percent must make do with only 5 percent of the national income. Other figures inform us that a disproportionately large number of black families fall into this lowest 20 percent income category (more than 45 percent of black families). It is not unreasonable to conclude that the 50 percent of black incomes which are above the $5,359 median are not very far above it (80 percent of black families earned less than $10,000 in 1968), and the 50 percent which are below are probably concentrated well below (23 percent of black families earned less than $3,000). We conclude, then, that equalizing the median income of blacks and whites will still leave us far from enjoying an equitable participation in the economy, for it is the large incomes, the incomes well above the median, which are intimately tied to real power in American society.

Since the turn of the century the national income has fairly consistently allocated itself in the ratio of roughly one-fourth to the owners of property (in the form of rent, interest, and profits) and three-fourths to labor in the form of wages and salaries. The very large incomes, the incomes which are attached to significant power in the American society, are not, for the most part, the wage incomes which comprise the three-fourths of the national income pie, but are the incomes from property, which comprise the other quarter. We have some figures which suggest that 25 percent of the nation's wealth is owned by one-half of one percent of the total adult population. Researchers apparently did not feel it necessary to seek a racial breakdown of this affluent ruling class, although *Fortune* magazine in May 1968 listed America's wealthiest families, and I hardly need tell you that no blacks were included. Increasingly, it seems to me, it becomes necessary for black folk to deal with this question of the ruling class—of property income, or wealth—while of course not neglecting the more immediate, more visible struggle for a fairer share of the earned incomes: for better jobs, equalized pay scales, meaningful training programs, and similar accomplishments. Stated differently, equality of *earned* incomes as between whites and blacks, although extremely significant as a partial indicator of progress, nevertheless falls far short of representing achievement of an equitable share of the nation's income for blacks and is therefore an inadequate objective for black economic development.

It may be useful to emphasize here the distinction between the concepts of income and of wealth. *Income* is a "flow" and refers usually to the purchasing power which accrues to an individual over a period of time, either as a payment for services rendered (wages) or as a payment for the use of his assets (rent, interest, profits). *Wealth,* on the other hand, is a "stock" concept and refers to the assets themselves, the real estate, cash, property, or portfolio investments which an individual owns and *which produce an income for him.* (There is also a type of wealth which generally yields no monetary income to the owner but which is desired for consumption or display purpose. Personal possessions, such as jewelry, art treasures, and durable type consumer goods, including pleasure automobiles, comprise this category.) The fact that the bulk of the income-producing wealth in this country is owned by a relatively small group of people accounts for the great disparity in the distribution of income in America. The fact that the black population's ownership of income-producing assets is insignificant accounts in large measure for black powerlessness and argues for a major thrust by blacks to acquire a reasonable share of the nation's wealth.

It behooves me to state here that the task of acquiring a base of wealth for the black community is likely to be a far more arduous task than that of building up our earned incomes. We are starting from a base of virtual zero at a time when the frontier of the country has long been closed and when the level of technology in the society is so great that it is nearly impossible to acquire wealth unless one already has wealth. It is likewise an era in which consumption rather than saving is not only the fashion but is indeed the national policy. Thus, almost every route which has traditionally been followed to acquire wealth in America is effectively closed to black people, not solely because of their color but also because of objective conditions within the economy. Even the route of organized crime has become the virtual monopoly of one group and "no blacks need apply." The amassing of black wealth will not be easy.

At this point we encounter somewhat of a paradox, for the suggestion that blacks must set their sights on the acquisition of a significant portion of the nation's wealth would seem to violate the unmistakable spirit of the current movement for black development, which is a spirit of *collective* as opposed to *individual* advancement. Indeed, few terms have so quickly acquired a negative connotation within the black community as has the term "black capitalism." Let us admit that the paradox is a genuine one. On the one hand we are saying that equity for blacks cannot be achieved so long as there are white Rockefellers and Gettys and Mellons and Hunts but no blacks of comparable wealth, influence, and power. On the other hand, we are saying that we are not eager to create black Rockefellers and Gettys, whether because we feel it is undemocratic, or because we suspect they would be less than devoted to the black community, or for whatever reason.

Confronted with such a paradox, the options we are left with in any attempt to bring about greater equity are either: (1) the dismantling of the great and the medium-sized fortunes of America, which is a valid objective and one for which there is no shortage of white allies, although little prospect for success at this time, or (2) the development of some new type of collective black vehicle which would amass and manipulate vast quantities of wealth for the common benefit of the black community.

The questions of what form such a vehicle might take and how it could amass significant amounts of wealth are complex, and for the moment, unanswered. The cooperative form obviously comes to mind, but thus far the co-op has not been notably successful in the United States and probably is ideologically inappropriate for the task anyway, in that the co-op is designed to provide low-cost goods or services to its constituency or, in the case of a producers' co-op, to equalize bargaining strength between seller and buyer, but in all cases to return its profits to its members. It is not a vehicle for amassing wealth or for using its wealth to wield political power. (Which is not to say that the co-op is not a useful structure for many other purposes.) The newly emerging community development corporations such as Hough Development Corporation in Cleveland, Ohio, Inner City Business Improvement Forum (ICBIF) in Detroit, Michigan, United Durham, Inc., in Durham, North Carolina, and Bedford Stuyvesant Restoration Corp. in Brooklyn, New York, are structurally and philosophically more suited to the task of capital accumulation in that they are committed to utilizing their profits for the good of the community which they represent. They merit our serious attention and support, for they offer the prospect of becoming powerful vehicles for community expression combined with economic clout. By recycling the use of the community's money within the community they can plug up the disastrous leakage of black folk's money out of the community and raise income prospects of the residents. With expanding resources, they can go into manufacturing and other primary stages in the production and distribution cycle and begin to amass resources in the name of the black community. It is, however, too early to judge whether these novel experiments in expanded-participation organizational structures will prove to be administratively viable as well as economically successful.

Some variation on the Kelso "Second Income Plan" might also be developed as a means for expanded black participation in the capital-owning portion of the economy, although the promise which the Kelso plan offers is one of *raising* the incomes of the poor but not one of *redistributing* either income or power. Like the ill-starred Freedom Budget of four years ago (i.e., 1966–67), the Kelso plan proposes a means whereby poverty can allegedly be eliminated without in the least disturbing the wealth of the rich and the powerful. Such sophistry obviously reflects a certain political expediency, but its net effect may in the long run be inimical, because it promotes a false sense of national harmony. There *is* a class problem in America, and its political ramifications are extremely powerful. It serves no one to act as if it does not exist. However, as indicated earlier, I do not see that *blacks* can take on the enormous task of exposing and attacking the power structure and of refashioning the whole of American society along more equitable lines. We should certainly recognize the need for such change and should support white groups which are pursuing such programs. But our major thrust must be the herculean, but nevertheless considerably more modest, task of winning for ourselves a greater black equity within the existing, woefully inequitable total society. This more modest task can absorb all of our efforts for some time to come.

The achievement even of equality of earned incomes between blacks and whites promises to become ever more difficult in the coming years. The easier things have already been done; the more intransigent problems still lie before us. The hard-core unemployed remain, for the most part, unemployed. The training programs, in which so much hope was placed, have not proved too successful. Despite a noticeable influx of black faces into corporate management structures, the higher levels of management remain virtually impregnable to us. Nevertheless, current efforts to raise wage incomes of blacks via more and better educational training programs, expanded job opportunities, nondiscriminatory promotional policies, greater numbers of blacks in positions of management, etc., should be continued. At the same time, efforts to improve the welfare of the black community via health and housing programs and the full range of community-service activities, including enlarged welfare benefits, should be pushed vigorously. The efforts to expand black participation in petty capitalism merit continuance also, but hopefully free of some of the exaggerated expectations which have traditionally been attached to it.

Black entrepreneurship, as the term is presently used, is important to the black community principally for psychological reasons. From an economic point of view, most of the "black capitalism" presently being pursued is not capable of aiding more than an infinitesimal number of black people and therefore may be absorbing resources far out of proportion to the economic benefits which it bestows. A black capitalism approach at a really meaningful level requires the launching of medium-to-large economic ventures. On such a scale, even black ventures probably can be justified more on the basis of their wealth and power producing capabilities than on their labor income producing potential, although such predictions can hardly be made in isolation from some general view of the overall economy in which they are operating and the relationship of blacks to that economy. In any case, such ventures are far beyond the normal risk-capital capabilities of black people and require in addition a variety of government supports and subsidies, such as have traditionally been reserved for many large, sheltered industries. Thus, a precondition for meaningful black entrepreneurship is a substantial base of black wealth, which brings us back to our former focus.

The most direct means of seeking an equitable share of the wealth of America is obviously the one used by James Forman and the Black Manifesto—the demand for reparations. Essentially, this demand would state quite bluntly that white folks stole North America from the Indians and then stole our ancestors from Africa and forced them to build this nation, releasing us from slavery only after the booty was pretty well divided up. Now, a century later, we demand our fair share of the collectively produced product—not, of course, from the churches alone, but from the government. Despite the criticism made by some blacks regarding the reparations concept, its logic is unchallengeable. The sole problem with the reparations approach is our present inability to enforce the demand. How in fact this might be done is a matter to which we will need to devote increasing attention.

Despite the furor which some folks have raised over the injection of the emotive term "reparations" into the black struggle, the operational difference between the reparations concept and various other demands for massive aid for the black community, e.g., the domestic Marshall plan, is at best marginal. "Reparations" connotes a debt whose payment is being demanded and of course implies the existence of a criminal and a victim; most of the other proposals have been more in the nature of supplications based on an appeal to the white society's good will or self-interest. In a sense, Dr. King's famous speech at the 1963 March bridged this gap by referring to a "promissory note" which was falling due. Clearly it was a disguised demand for reparations. It ill behooves us to allow ourselves to become fragmented over questions of style when there is wide unity on the need for a massive transference of assets to the black community. Short of a revolutionary situation in which private property is overtly appropriated by force, these assets can only come from the public treasury, a fact which dramatizes the necessity of a black political/cultural thrust as a precondition to effective economic development for black America. Whether entitled "reparations" or disguised by another name, resources on a scale paralleling those dispersed in Vietnam will have to be transferred to the black community if we expect to correct existing inequities. A significant sum will be required merely to counter the enormous raids on the public treasury being perpetrated by white America's establishment in its own behalf. I refer here to oil depletion allowances, agriculture subsidies, public utility privileges, cost overruns and other financial shenanigans conspired in by big government and its favored defense contractors, political supporters, etc.—to say nothing of rectifying our exclusion from the 19th century welfare programs like the Homestead Act and the celebrated giveaways to the railroads and other establishment institutions of white America.

Our agenda for the seventies is fairly clear. By the force of our united power, used positively where possible and negatively where necessary, we must extract from white America a fair share of the nation's natural and manmade wealth for our own beloved black community. This is the agenda.

And concurrently, we must be about the task of creating some mechanism whereby we might begin creating a comprehensive national development plan for black people which would guide us in the use of whatever resources we have or can acquire.

Obviously, this latter undertaking is fraught with difficulty. We know that there are vast ideological differences within the black community, as well as many competing personal and institutional interests. It would be naïve to think that these could all be harmonized into a unified black economic development effort. Nevertheless, we at the Black Economic Research Center are convinced of the merit of at least exploring a concept of comprehensive national developmental planning for the black community, making whatever assumptions are necessary in order to proceed with that effort or perhaps developing alternative plans for alternative sets of assumptions. The crucial assumptions here, it seems to me, are concerned with the degree of racial integration or separatism which one envisions as necessary or desirable for the achievement of "the good life" for black people. With this all-important question undergoing such intensive debate within the black community it may be useful to develop plans based on assumptions appropriate to each of these ideologies.

Presently, such resources as are available for black economic development are allocated in a haphazard and uncoordinated fashion by various branches of government, by foundations, by the churches. No sense of priorities has ever been established; only minimal coordination exists among donors and even less among the recipients. For example, whether by design or by neglect, there has been virtually no effort to build mutually reinforcing linkages between various black development efforts. There is also clearly an urgent need for a black presence to be engaged in the monitoring of these efforts, in evaluating their actual contribution toward black economic development, and in shaping them into some coherent master program which can have maximum impact for black people. Although it is relatively easy to spend large sums of money, especially to help the disadvantaged, it is difficult to spend it well, and considerably more so when there is such a multiplicity of autonomous agencies doing the spending. A competent and credible team of independent black technicians charged with the overseeing and evaluation of the major black economic development efforts, although lacking any enforcement powers, could be a salutary influence toward ensuring rational allocation of available resources.

If a black community does in fact exist in America, if the concept of black economic development does have real validity, then we are ripe, if not long overdue, for such an effort at national black development planning. Without meaningful land reform and substantial redistribution of wealth, however, genuine black economic development will be unachievable whether we have a national development plan or not. But a plan will certainly help us to utilize our resources efficiently, and this is important.

There are related tasks to which we should be addressing ourselves as well. The Administration, under the increasing pressures of population growth and environmental considerations, as well as of more traditional economic stimuli, is avidly exploring new dimensions for a national growth policy, a concept which includes, among other facets, such matters as demographic control, regional growth nodes, and migration policy. I repeat: migration policy. It sounds innocent enough—and indeed it is a concept which I could support. I think we will all readily agree that this country's population is distributed very irrationally across this vast continent. But, like many other technical and social innovations, migration policy can have sinister implications for those who do not exercise control over its use. It is vital that there be a strong black input into such programs, or at least a black monitoring of them. If not, we may awaken one morning to find that the computers have programmed the black population into a configuration highly detrimental to our interests. I assure you, it can happen if we are not alert and united—and perhaps even if we are.

The hour is late, brothers and sisters. The forces of reaction are abroad in the land, and we must begin to look after ourselves, joining with allies when that is possible, but building our own strength and economic independence to the maximum extent which we can. A completely honest assessment of our position suggests to me that the prospects for our achieving an equitable portion of America's wealth and power are very dim indeed—virtually impossible. The numbers are too heavily against us and the obstacles too great. Conversely, as we enter this new decade one senses that the very survival, to say nothing of the growth and development, of the black community is being challenged by hostile elements within the white society to a degree which we have not seen for many years. During the sixties, a great deal was done *for* black people by various segments of the white community. During the seventies, however, black people must increasingly do for themselves most of what remains to be done. Financial and technical assistance from white America we will continue to need. But our goals, our objectives, our policies—we must select these for ourselves.

White Help for Black Business

Michael Brower and Doyle Little

In the past two years or so, most of the growing body of business literature dealing with the plight of America's disadvantaged groups has focused both on exhorting businessmen to assist in the development of black or other minority capitalism ventures, and on warning executives about the great difficulties and potential losses. Needed now is more knowledge, not further exhortations and warnings. Accordingly, we wish to report on a research study designed to find out:

▶ What are the actual attitudes and activities of business leaders with regard to promoting black capitalism?

▶ How much has been done by large white corporations to assist new black businesses?

▶ What are some of the methods and patterns which work best, and some of the missteps to avoid in this process?

Our research is based on a combination of two activities. One part of the input stems from the 281 responses to 679 mailed questionnaires sent to the presidents and/or chief executive officers of most of the 500 largest industrial corporations and to the business leaders of the top fifty companies in five other business categories. The other part is drawn from an analysis of our field interviews with black and white leaders in minority businesses and in business-promoting organizations.

Between us, we visited a dozen black manufacturing and service enterprises and a score of black and Puerto Rican economic and community development organizations. In so doing, we interviewed more than 100 black business and community leaders and "involved" white corporate and financial executives.

Major Findings

These are the observations and conclusions about white corporate support for minority economic development that have emerged from the responses to our questionnaire and from our field interviews.

1. *Executives of large corporations overwhelmingly endorse black capitalism.*

Many express an underlying assumption that black economic power (a) will lead to a fully integrated society with white and black people having equal opportunities, and (b) will not instead further polarize the races.

2. *The phrase "black capitalism" has a bad connotation to many people.*

Many whites and blacks take "black capitalism" to mean the promotion of small, marginal businesses, or exploitation of poor black workers by a few rich black capitalists. Because of this, a significant number of black community leaders prefer to work toward the development of sizable businesses owned, not by one man or a few, but widely by workers and residents of the community or by a broadly controlled community development corporation. Their goal is general economic and social development of the whole community.

This applies not just to blacks. Other nonwhite minority groups in our society face similar problems and needs for expansion of business ownership and community economic development.

Because we are reporting here on research about attitudes and activities of large corporations in supporting black capitalism, we shall continue to use this phrase at times in the remainder of the discussion, but we conclude that it would be better in the future to make the goal more broadly that of "minority community development" and "minority economic power" rather than the narrower "black capitalism."

3. *A growing number of large companies have established positive programs to support minority businesses.*

Almost one company out of four answering our questionnaire reported having one or more men assigned at least part-time to promoting black capitalism. One company reported having spent $300,000 in supporting black capitalism; fourteen reported costs of over $100,000; and three others from $10,000 to $100,000. A total of thirty-four companies indicated that they were making a special effort to buy products from black businesses, and that number is growing every month that passes.

4. *The total support for black capitalism offered by the largest corporations is still a tiny trickle.*

When we compare the resources the large corporations have available with the needs and opportunities that exist, we realize that only a small handful are putting forth a significant effort and making an important contribution.

The vast majority are still waiting on the sidelines, expressing support for the concept but doing nothing, or very little, as yet.

5. *Finding or developing competent black management is a crucial and difficult task.*

Perhaps not more than one half of the men placed in charge of the new black enterprises in the past two years or so have survived in their jobs as managers or will survive in the next two or three years.

The most successful managers of black businesses tend to be either those with previous managerial and technical experience in industry, or those who have previously started and managed their own small businesses. The least successful generally come from occupations such as teaching or government service, and lack experience as managers or owner-managers of small businesses.

With but a few exceptions, white corporations have not been too successful in choosing either black managers or temporary white managers for new black businesses.

Usually, better management has been selected when the white sponsoring corporation chose to work with a black community development organization and left the search, screening, and selection to that community organization.

Good results have also been obtained when black entrepreneurs sought out the white corporations, rather than waiting for the initiative to come from the latter.

White corporations can make major contributions toward assisting the development of black and other minority business skills. They can seek out, hire, train, and promote nonwhite managers. After a few years, the large corporation can encourage these men to choose between continuing with the white corporation and, if they are so motivated, striking out on their own in setting up new businesses, with the blessing and backing of the white corporations.

In at least three cases we know of, white sponsoring corporations have taken in and trained black managers for several months in preparation for the opening of their new black enterprises. And these and other corporations have provided continuing management support, with a number of functional specialists backstopping their counterparts in the new business.

6. *There is a need for marketing support.*

Certain sponsoring white corporations have guaranteed a particular level of contracts for one, two, or even three years to help new black businesses get started. This was done by General Electric for Progress Aerospace Enterprises, by Xerox for Fighton, by Kodak for both Camura and P.A. Plastics, Inc., and by the Container Corporation for the Community Paper Stock Corporation. We have also observed a number of other cases.

In fact, almost all of the new black manufacturing businesses encounter considerable trouble in finding experienced marketing men, and most of them could probably not have survived their first years without a sheltered market for a sizable part of their output offered either by a sponsoring corporation or by the government.

Aside from offering a guaranteed market, there are other ways in which corporations are assisting black businesses with marketing. In one case, the sponsoring corporation, Mattel, Inc., offered training, advice, and assistance to Shindana Toy in marketing products which are essentially competitive with its own.

Many corporations have either circulated lists of items that they are willing to purchase from new black suppliers, or in other ways made known their interest in increasing their purchases from black businesses. Some, such as Western Electric, have helped to sponsor fairs for black businesses to present their wares and to learn from white corporations' purchasing agents.

Services as well as goods are being purchased from black suppliers. S.S. Kresge has retained a black-owned insurance company to underwrite group life insurance for over half its employees.

7. Technical assistance is also needed.

White corporations, working with a black development organization, or directly sponsoring a black business, can provide a great deal of advice and informal training for black managers and technicians in a wide range of fields.

Other corporations, although not working directly with a given black business, have encouraged their employees to make their services available on company time as nonpaid consultants to black or other minority businesses through such organizations as the Interracial Council for Business Opportunity, the Urban Coalition, the TAP program in Chicago, Illinois, the black Inner City Business Improvement Forum (ICBIF) in Detroit, Michigan, and Capital Formation in New York City.

However, there are certain pitfalls to be avoided in lending technical assistance. For example, in two cases of direct assistance for a new black business, the sponsoring white company attempted to provide technical assistance in areas where it really did not have competent people. The black business suffered as a result, and the black workers and managers resented having to deal with white ''experts'' who added to their problems rather than resolved them.

In each situation, the white companies misjudged the amount of technology involved in producing ''simple'' products which they themselves had never produced.

Several black managers whom we interviewed said that they did not want white experts who merely get along well with black people; instead, they said, they would prefer a segregationist if he were able to solve problems efficiently and to pass along his knowledge to black employees.

In those cases where the sponsoring company had competent people, technical know-how was transmitted to black workers and managers more easily than expected. Several white advisers admitted privately that they were surprised at the high level of intelligence of some of the black workers hired off the street. The black workers who are interested in their jobs normally learn new skills rapidly, although many are of course not highly motivated by the prospect of a steady but dead-end job in a semiskilled assignment.

Another problem arising when personnel from a white corporation attempt to assist a new black business stems from the tremendous disparity in organizational size.

The managers and technicians who have had years of experience in large corporations have learned organizational patterns, management styles, and corporate policies which are only partly applicable to a small and struggling young business. Part of what they have learned, perhaps unconsciously, and try to pass on to the black business is at best irrelevant and at worst disastrous.

To cite just one example: the large organization will probably have well-developed specialization of jobs, departments, and personnel, but a small company needs a less structured and more fluid organization, with a small group of highly versatile managers who can handle a number of specialties from time to time as needs arise.

Another complaint we heard about technical assistance is that the rapid turnover of white advisers which sometimes occurs can be both frustrating and costly to the black manager, who must literally spend his time educating one after the ofter.

When there are separate advisers in different specialties, perhaps from a number of different white organizations, it is important that one generalist coordinate and oversee the whole advisory team. Otherwise, a lawyer, an accountant, a real estate expert, a personnel man, and a financial adviser may all be giving separate advice which, at least in part, conflicts with that offered by the others.

8. *Virtually every black business has a need for additional capital.*

The vast majority of black people in the United States have never been in a position to save very much, and capital is simply not available in significant amounts from either family or community sources. Some white sponsoring corporations have responded by putting up their own capital to help new business. For example:

▶ The Whirlpool Corporation has helped to set up Durable Products Company for the manufacture of wooden boxes and has put up about $80,000 to finance the plant.

▶ Mattel has spent more than $200,000 of its funds to provide plant, equipment, and working capital for Shindana Toy, which is owned and managed by Operation Bootstrap in Los Angeles.

▶ The Sun Ray Drug Company has funded two black franchises in the Philadelphia area, and plans to set up ten more. The black manager puts no money down and buys the store from Sun Ray at the actual cost of fixtures and inventory.

▶ Sparked by Van Heusen, the Menswear Retailers of America are establishing minority-owned clothing stores and arranging for a one-year credit on stock from suppliers.

Other corporations have indirectly aided in the financing of new black businesses by contributing to the Urban Coalition or to similar organizations, such as the Rochester Business Opportunities Corporation and the Chicago Economic Development Corporation.

In Detroit, funds raised by white corporations permitted a first-year grant of $850,000 to the ICBIF, leaving this black organization with full responsibility for the tough decisions on which ones of the black applicants should get the scarce funds. Unfortunately, donations for ICBIF are down this year despite its proven track record.

An increasing number of white corporations are indirectly assisting in the financing of black businesses by depositing some of the corporate liquid funds in the growing number of black-owned and black-managed banks throughout the country.

According to the New York biweekly, *Business and Society* (an excellent source of current information in this and related fields), Olin Corporation has $1,000,000 on deposit in black banks, as has Glen Alden Corporation; Sears Roebuck has had $530,000 in thirteen black banks; and Montgomery Ward has announced it would deposit $330,000 in eleven black banks. Prudential, with deposits in twenty-two black banks, and Aetna are among the insurance companies helping in this way. All told, more than fifty top corporations have begun this practice.

But the evidence is that the majority of white corporations sponsoring black businesses have been able to do so without any direct investment of their own corporate cash. This is possible, in part, thanks to the Small Business Administration's 90 percent loan guarantee program, and to the increased willingness on the part of many big city banks to make some minority-business loans which in previous years they would have refused.

Sometimes the sponsoring corporation has made bank financing possible by cosigning or guaranteeing a loan to the new black business. This was the case both when Hewlett-Packard guaranteed a $50,000 loan to help EPA Electronics get started, and when Container Corporation not only provided a long-term contract to the West Side Community Paper Stock Corporation but also guaranteed a $250,000 bank loan.

Even without a formal loan guarantee, however, an otherwise difficult-to-negotiate loan will often become bankable when the sponsoring white corporation makes a commitment of management assistance and/or a guarantee of purchases over the next few years. With General Electric committed to give management support and contracts worth over $2,500,000 over an 18-month period, a $350,000 First Pennsylvania Bank loan was made to the new Progress Aerospace Enterprises.

Despite these encouraging signs, it is still true that many a potential new business venture or expansion will be blocked for lack of as little as $2,000 for small projects (or as much as $100,000 or more for big projects) in basic seed capital—the 10 percent to 20 percent equity that the banks and the SBA normally require. Needed is some community organization, foundation, or sponsoring white corporation willing and able to make a grant, a noncontrolling equity investment, or a subordinated soft-term loan to provide the equity base for a bank loan.

And it is also still true that for every minority loan successfully processed, there are five or even as many as ten turned down for lack of funds committed to minority economic development loans.

9. *New black businesses can successfully hire and train the hard-core unemployed, preferably mixing them in with already experienced, productive employees.*

The experience of many new black businesses shows that the hard-core unemployed can be found, hired, trained, and motivated to do productive work in three to six months. Moreover, this can be done by the new black inner-city business with a capability at least as great as that of large white corporations under the National Alliance of Businessmen programs.

Where salary scales in the black business are above the national minimum of $1.60 an hour, where care is taken in the training, and where there are obvious opportunities for advancement, turnover may be less of a problem than in the large white corporation.

For the recently hard-core unemployed man, a fair wage and steady job that has promotion opportunities is a greater incentive than the possibility of participating in the ownership of shares in his company. Many black owners and organizations are planning to make stock available to employees, but they believe it prudent to postpone the action until the company is profitable and the stock has a positive value.

Experience suggests that a new minority business will find starting up easier if it does not attempt to staff itself completely from the hard-core unemployed. This is true even when some of the training costs are covered by Labor Department grants.

Black companies have proved that they are capable of manufacturing highly complicated and sophisticated products. The more complex the product, the more important it is to hire a solid base of the most qualified workmen available into which the newly trained, formerly hard-core unemployed can be merged.

10. *Black business needs assistance with purchasing.*

Several of the new black businesses we studied have had some difficulties in obtaining a regular flow of adequate raw materials. Trained black purchasing agents are scarce.

Sometimes suppliers are unwilling to extend normal suppliers' credit to the new business. At other times, competitors will put pressure on the suppliers to keep them from selling on equal terms to the new business.

In either case, the sponsoring white corporations can be, and are being, of great assistance. Their purchasing departments can handle purchases for the new business for a time. They can guarantee credit to be extended by a reluctant supplier.

11. *Profits should not be expected in the first year or two.*

It is almost (but not quite) universally true that new black manufacturing enterprises cannot be expected to make a profit in the first year or two.

This is in fact true of most new ventures, white or black. And new black businesses operating in the inner city often face additional hurdles which usually mean that they begin to produce profits even later than a comparable new venture in the same industry located elsewhere.

Thus, most of the new black businesses we studied are still losing money. Some have begun to make money toward the end of the second year, although that year as a whole still shows a deficit. (Often there are inputs, such as assistance from a sponsoring white corporation, which are not carried on the books.)

There are a few exceptions where one begins turning a profit late in the first year or early in the second. However, most ventures will fail to show a profitable full twelve months until the third year, if then.

Experience shows that it is far better to start with, and plan for, a realistic cash flow than to have overly optimistic projections which result in financial woes and shattered expectations.

12. *Black businesses should sell, and sometimes locate, outside the ghetto.*

When the need for promoting black capitalism and black community development began to be discussed several years ago, there was often a tendency to assume that the black business should sell solely or primarily to black people and that the business should always be located in the inner city.

With but few exceptions, if black businesses are to grow and generate significant income and employment, they must sell, not just to blacks, but to the national and international markets as well.

The second assumption is also challenged by many community leaders, white and black. And rightly so. For black-owned and black-managed businesses are badly needed inside the inner city. But it is also important that blacks be given assistance in establishing new businesses outside the inner city when such a location makes more economic sense.

13. *Whites should work with and through local black organizations.*

Corporations interested in helping to promote minority businesses are well advised to donate funds or management time to, or to sponsor a business in partnership with, an existing community or business development organization.

The minority community is in many respects like a foreign culture to the white professional and middle-class corporate executives. As is the case when they go overseas to begin business operations, when entering a minority community in this country such executives need help from, and if possible, the opportunity to work with, a local organization that understands the local situation.

Many of the mistakes and headaches that a sponsoring corporation might otherwise make are eliminated or at least reduced when it works not directly with an individual black business but with such a community organization.

Also, there is the additional benefit of helping to build that community organization's ability and strength to promote the development of other businesses and related activities. This gives a multiplier effect to the inputs of the white corporation.

Furthermore, increasing numbers of black community spokesmen and leaders around the country are saying that they and their followers must be involved in the important decisions affecting life in their communities.

For reasons such as these, and because they were impressed with the quality of the black leaders involved, General Electric, Xerox, Mattel, Container Corporation, McDowell-Wellman, and others chose to work with, respectively, the Zion Investment Associates in Philadelphia, FIGHT in Rochester, Operation Bootstrap in Los Angeles, the West Side Community Development Corporation in Chicago, and the Hough Development Corporation in Cleveland.

For similar reasons, many Detroit-area corporations have contributed funds and executives' time to the white-controlled Economic Development Corporation, which in turn supports the black ICBIF.

14. *There is a need for government pressure, assistance, and incentives.*

Whatever may be said in public, it is clear from many private conversations that most of the existing efforts by white corporate executives to assist black business came about as a result of fear engendered by the ghetto riots, threats and pressures from militants, and to some extent pressure or influence from government officials.

We grant that many corporations will make some contributions of corporate resources, including funds and executives' time, to promote something they believe to be morally right and important. But, in the long run, sizable commitments of resources from a wide variety of corporations will apparently come only because of (a) renewed and continued threats to corporate existence and to profits by militant groups, or (b) strong pressures from government, backed by economic incentives.

On the one hand, we cannot leave the promotion of corporate involvement in developing minority business solely to the conscience and moral views of corporate executives. On the other hand, we do not wish to leave it to continuing and increasing black militancy and further riots.

Therefore, we must look for a return to pressure from the government—which has lessened recently—and for the improvement of economic incentives by the government. Specifically, we need a great deal of improvement in SBA operation, and a larger volume of equity capital or subordinated loan funds throughout the country.

Perhaps the newly proposed system of Minority Enterprise Small Business Investment Companies, or MESBICs, will catch the imagination of enough white corporations to make a significant impact. However, original government funding levels are quite low, and there appears to be little prospect that a white corporation founding a MESBIC would get its money back, let alone make a profit, for a considerable length of time.

(Information on the MESBIC concept and on the 2-for-1 matching funds the government will provide can be obtained from the SBA or from the Office of Minority Business Enterprise, U.S. Department of Commerce.)

Most businessmen responding to a question in our survey about possible types of government incentive indicated a preference for an income-tax credit for part of the costs of sponsoring new black businesses. And they further emphasized that involvement in any activity like promoting black business will usually be directly related to the degree of economic incentives provided.

Perhaps income-tax credits are not the right road. But some things do seem clear:

▶ If the existing few score of black businesses of significant scope and size are to grow and multiply, they (and those still to be created) need a great deal more financial support than is now available, directly or through tax incentives.

▶ If the existing community development corporations and similar organizations which are working to promote business, economic, and social development in our minority communities are to survive—let alone grow and multiply—they need much more financial support than they are now getting from corporations, foundations, and the government. This must primarily be in the form of grants, for in their first five years or so these organizations are producing more in noneconomic social benefits than in cash income needed to repay loans.

▶ If the present trickle of white corporate support for building black minority businesses and minority community development is to grow and flourish into a broad stream of partnership sufficient to make a real impact on the inner-city, racial, and poverty problems, a variety of important new tax and other economic incentives must be offered by the federal government.

15. *Black capitalism is no substitute for integration.*

The point has been frequently stated, but our study underlines the importance of reiterating it: White corporations and executives should not support black capitalism or other minority economic development as their sole contribution toward solving racial, poverty, and inner-city problems. Such vital things as improvement in integration of the labor and management forces in their own companies and more integrated and low-income housing in their own communities also require their time and attention.

The vast majority of present and future minority-group job seekers must continue to find gainful employment in basically white organizations, even if minority business development succeeds beyond the wildest expectations and projections. Many corporations have made great strides in the past two years or so in employment of minority group members (or had, before the current economic downturn forced cutbacks), but many others still have a long way to go before the total number of their nonwhite employees matches the national or local proportion of non-whites in the population.

And most corporations, even those with major programs for hiring the hard-core in unskilled and semi-skilled jobs, still have a great deal to do to improve the promotion possibilities of their nonwhite employees. The percentage of nonwhites in upper managerial ranks of major corporations is far below one percent, while total nonwhite membership on major corporate boards of directors can probably still be counted on the fingers of one hand.

Black Capitalism

For the purposes of this article, black capitalism is defined as Negro ownership, management, and control of productive, profit-seeking organizations.

The black-controlled organization may sell any product or service in any local, national, or international market. Physical location of the organization is not important, and the employees may be black, white, or a mix of races.

The organization may be partially owned by nonblack people, but black people have, or will have, majority ownership and control. The top management is also predominantly black, or will be after an initial training period.

The benefits or profits from a black business may go to individual shareholders or to black community activities.

A company may support black capitalism by providing money, management know-how, technical assistance, raw materials, product markets, or other services. This support may be given directly to a black business or channeled through an organization which pools available resources and coordinates efforts to promote black capitalism.

If a white-controlled company organizes a subsidiary company with a legal or public commitment to convert that subsidiary to black ownership and control this is considered to be direct support of black capitalism.

Programs that provide better education, medical care, housing, or job opportunities for black people and do not establish or support black businesses are not black capitalism projects.

The Role of Residential Racial Segregation in Causing and Perpetuating Inferior Housing for Lower-Income Nonwhites

Garrett A. Vaughn

Residential racial segregation is an easily observed and widespread phenomenon in the United States.[1] Inspection of 1960 *Census of Housing* data reveals that in metropolitan areas of the United States lower-income nonwhites live in housing inferior to that of whites, even when socioeconomic factors such as age, education, sex, and occupation of household head are held constant.[2] The coexistence of residential racial segregation and inferior housing for lower-income nonwhites has often led observers to speculate that in some way separate housing markets are created for white and nonwhites.[3] Most housing economists agree that only a hypothesis of price discrimination can explain that portion of housing disparity unexplained by socioeconomic factors observed between whites and nonwhites in the United States.[4] Yet, the exact conditions under which residential racial segregation leads to a system of price discrimination, even in the context of a market that more nearly approximates pure competition than pure monopoly, have never been stated. This paper explains how and under what conditions residential racial segregation puts lower-income nonwhites at a disadvantage in the housing market.

The Model and Empirical Data

Housing data reveals an inverse correlation between age of housing unit and income of those dwelling in the unit. Such correlation has led to the formulation of a hypothesis commonly encountered in housing literature and known as "filtering," (i.e., new housing is purchased by higher-income people while lower-income people live in housing passed down to them by higher-income people).[5] It will be shown that a housing model based on the concept of filtering (in the form of Assumption 1 below) explains the growth of inferior lower-income nonwhite housing. The model to be discussed incorporates the following basic assumptions: (1) an inverse correlation exists between tenant income and age of housing units; (2) people prefer to live in neighborhoods homogeneous in terms of tenant income and race;[6] (3) costs of moving a housing unit from a first to a second unit of land are exceptionally high;[7] (4) whites and nonwhites of identical socioeconomic characteristics behave identically in their housing consumption when confronted with identical supply stimuli; (5) the total population can be completely subdivided into two income groups, the lower- and higher-income groups; (6) the total population can be completely subdivided into two racial categories, whites and nonwhites;[8] (7) nonwhites have a lesser percentage of their membership in the higher-income group than whites.[9]

The housing stock in total size and composition is directly related to the tenant income distribution (i.e., the higher the median income, the greater the total housing stock that will exist and the greater the percentage of the stock that is new housing). Lower-income people have two options in meeting their housing needs: purchase new housing in direct competition with higher-income people, or purchase used housing relinquished by higher-income people as, over time, higher-income people continue to purchase new housing. The first option is equally onerous for both lower-income whites and nonwhites. If the income distribution of nonwhites were identical to the income distribution of whites, then the second option would also be equivalent for lower-income nonwhites and whites because of Assumption 4, even if, as is assumed, neighborhoods are homogeneous at any point in time in terms of race. However, the income distribution of nonwhites is inferior to that of whites, and if positive costs of transferring units from white to nonwhite tenantry exist, then inferior housing for lower-income nonwhites vis-à-vis lower-income whites will result. New housing unit construction will occur in both white and nonwhite higher-income neighborhoods until the expected rate of return on any new unit, regardless of neighborhood, is equal, and also equal to the rate of return available from non-housing projects. A lower per capita rate of new housing construction will occur in nonwhite neighborhoods than in white neighborhoods because of the inferior income distribution of nonwhites. Lower-income nonwhites then face a more stringent second option than lower-income whites.

The question of whether or not lower-income nonwhites live in inferior housing can be answered only by examining the data. The model predicts that lower-income whites are definitely not at a disadvantage in the housing market so that, if the data show instances of lower-income whites living in worse housing than lower-income nonwhites, the model would be refuted. If the data show lower-income nonwhites living consistently in worse housing than lower-income whites, the model would be confirmed. Finally, if the data should not reveal any tendency for inferior housing to exist for nonwhites or for whites, the model's applicability would be uncertain.

The data sample is drawn from several urban centers rather than from a single or small number of urban centers for two reasons. First, it is possible that segregation over time exists in some but not all geographical areas of the United States. Choosing a single urban center for study results in an answer of either "yes" or "no" when the true answer is "sometimes." A large sample is better designed to reveal an answer of "sometimes." Second, housing data present unusual difficulties in interpretation since housing is a heterogeneous product: it differs by design, size, quality of construction, location, tax treatment, TV reception, etc. It is to be expected that the data will reveal several cases where whites pay, for example, $85 per month gross rental for a "superior" unit whereas nonwhites pay $81 per month for an "inferior" unit. Does the differential of $4 per month adequately compensate nonwhites for their inferior housing? Manipulating the data to answer this question is essential to create product homogeneity out of heterogeneity so that a comparison can be made. This is a task which the model is not designed to handle. A large sample helps to sidestep this difficulty, because, if a tendency toward inferior nonwhite housing does exist, it is likely that some cases will be so severe as to result in showing unambiguously inferior housing for nonwhites. A large sample increases the probability that these cases will be included. If there is no tendency for inferior housing to occur, no extreme cases will exist.

The U.S. *Census of Housing: 1960* was examined for comparative racial housing data of metropolitan areas: twenty-nine Standard Metropolitan Statistical Areas (SMSA's) and twenty-five central cities possess comparative racial housing data. The classification "Nonwhite" as used in the tables follows the Census definition of "Nonwhite."[10] The 1960 U.S. *Census of Housing* does not include a published racial category of "Whites" alone. Therefore, the "All" category which includes data on both whites and nonwhites in a single aggregate is substituted for a "White" classification on the rationalization that any difference in the data between the "All" and "Nonwhite" groups must be accounted for by differences in white and nonwhite housing. For example, if the median gross rent paid by "All" is $72 but $75 for "Nonwhite," it is concluded that nonwhites paid a higher median gross rent than whites, although it is not possible to say precisely how much more nonwhites paid than whites. In an attempt to control for family income, the tables include six income classifications.[11]

The 1960 Census does not publish the mean or median age of renter-occupied dwelling units. A proxy variable in place of a measurement of central tendency is required. The percentage (to the nearest percentage point) of renter-occupied units built on or before 1949 was calculated for both racial groups within each income level. The greater the percentage, the greater was the presumed age of housing. A proxy variable is also required in ranking housing stock by degree of crowding. The percentage (to the nearest full percentage point) of all renter-occupied units that had 1.01 or more persons per room was computed for each racial-income group. The greater the percentage, the greater was the degree of presumed crowding. Ranking the housing stock possessed by racial-income groups by degree of quality was done by accepting the Census definition and tabulation of "sound" units.[12] The percentage (to the nearest percentage point) of each racial-income category's renter-occupied units that were classified as "sound" by the Census was calculated; the greater the percentage the greater was the degree of presumed "quality."

The order of the ranking is shown in Tables 1 and 2. An "N" or "A" appears in the appropriate position depending on whether "Nonwhite" or "All" displays the less desirable ranking (i.e., higher rent, greater housing unit age, greater housing unit crowding, less housing unit quality); a "T" appears when the ranking does not differentiate between the two racial groups (i.e., the computed percentages are the same.) In general, Tables 1 and 2 indicate that "Nonwhite" may or may not pay higher median gross rents than "All" and usually, but by no means always, live in housing that is older than for "All." However, without exception people in "Nonwhite" live in housing of less quality than "All," and with but one exception (Los Angeles, California, Central City: $10,000 and over) "Nonwhite" exhibits more crowded housing than for "All." It will be impossible to find a single case of unambiguous price discrimination against whites if the quality criterion is retained, and it will be possible to examine but one case of price discrimination against whites if the quality criterion is jettisoned, but the rent, crowding, and age criteria are retained.

Cases of unambiguous price discrimination total sixteen in Table 1 and nineteen in Table 2. However, a great deal of double-counting is involved, for, if a particular SMSA displays unambiguous price discrimination, there is a very marked tendency for its Central City also to display unambiguous price discrimination. Each of these cases is denoted by an asterisk, and all occur against nonwhites. Even if the quality criterion is dropped and only the median gross rent, age, and crowding criteria are retained in the test for unambiguous price discrimination, the same results are obtained (i.e., the same sixteen cases in Table 1 and nineteen in Table 2).

There exist eighty-eight cases in Table 1 and fifty-three cases in Table 2 (marked by a "†" after the ranking), exclusive of the "$10,000 and over" income category, wherein nonwhites, while paying less median gross rent than whites, live in worse housing according to at least one of the three non-rent criteria while not exhibiting anything better than a "T" ranking for the remaining non-rent criteria. These cases may or may not involve price discrimination; the difficulty in ascertaining whether or not the differential in rent is sufficient to compensate for the less desirable housing prevents a definitive judgment. It would appear reasonable to suppose that at least some of these cases do involve price discrimination against lower-income nonwhites, particularly since twenty-three of the eighty-eight cases in Table 1 and twenty of the fifty-three cases in Table 2 involve a differential of three dollars or less in the reported median gross

TABLE 1
Rent, Age, Crowding, and Quality Rankings
for "All" and "Nonwhite" SMSA's

SMSA	Under $2,000	$2,000-2,999	$3,000-3,999	$4,000-4,999	$5,000-5,999	$10,000 & over
			Income Level			
Boston	AANN	ATNN†	ATNN†	ATNN†	ANNN†	ANNN†
Chicago	AANN	NANN	NANN	NANN	NTNN*	?NNN†
Cincinnati	ANNN†	ANNN†	ANNN†	ANNN†	ANNN†	ANNN†
Cleveland	NNNN*	NNNN*	TNNN*	NNNN*	NNNN*	ANNN†
Detroit	NTNN*	ANNN†	TNNN*	ANNN†	ANNN†	ANNN†
Honolulu	ANNN†	ANNN†	ANNN†	ANNN†	ANNN†	ANNN†
Indianapolis	ANNN†	ANNN†	ANNN†	ANNN†	ATNN†	ANNN†
Kansas City	ANNN†	ANNN†	ANNN†	ANNN†	ANNN†	uNNN
Los Angeles	TNNN*	ANNN†	ANNN†	ANNN†	ANNN†	ANNN†
Newark	ANNN†	ANNN†	ANNN†	ANNN†	ANNN†	ANNN†
New York	ATNN†	AANN	AANN	AANN	AANN	ANNN†
Philadelphia	ANNN†	ANNN†	ANNN†	ANNN†	ANNN†	ANNN†
Pittsburgh	NNNN*	TTNN*	TTNN*	ANNN†	ANNN†	ANNN†
St. Louis	AANN	AANN	ATNN†	ANNN†	ANNN†	ANNN†
San Francisco	ANNN†	ANNN†	ANNN†	ATNN†	ANNN†	ANNN†
Baltimore	ATNN†	NNNN*	NNNN*	NNNN*	NNNN*	ANNN†
Washington, D.C.	ANNN†	ANNN†	ANNN†	ANNN†	ANNN†	ANNN†
Memphis	AANN	AANN	AANN	ATNN†	ANNN†	ANNN†
Jacksonville	ANNN†	ANNN†	ANNN†	ANNN†	ANNN†	uNNN
Miami	AANN	AANN	AANN	AANN	AANN	uNNN
Dallas	AANN	AANN	ATNN†	ANNN†	ANNN†	uNNN
El Paso	ANNN†	ANNN†	ANNN†	ANNN†	ANNN†	uNNN
Houston	ATNN†	AANN	AANN	AANN	ANNN†	ANNN†
New Orleans	AANN	AANN	AANN	AANN	AANN	ANNN†
Norfolk-Portsmouth	ATNN†	AANN	ATNN†	AANN	AANN	uANN
Richmond	AANN	AANN	ANNN†	ANNN†	ANNN†	uNNN
San Antonio	AANN	ANNN†	ANNN†	AANN	ANNN†	uNNN
Atlanta	AANN	AANN	AANN	AANN	AANN	ANNN†
Birmingham	ANNN†	ATNN†	ANNN†	ANNN†	ANNN†	uNNN

Order of Rankings: Rent, Age, Crowding, Quality.

Notations are as follows:
A, "All" possesses the less desirable ranking.
N, "Nonwhite" possesses the less desirable ranking.
T, both racial groups possess equivalent housing for the criterion.
?, "Nonwhite" median gross rent is within the range of median gross rent reported for "All" (see note 10).
u, signifies that no data are provided by the *Census* for nonwhite median gross rent.
*, unambiguous price discrimination.
†, possible price discrimination.

TABLE 2

Rent, Age, Crowding, and Quality Rankings
for "All" and "Nonwhite" in Central Cities

| Central City | Income Level | | | | | |
	Under $2,000	$2,000-2,999	$3,000-3,999	$4,000-4,999	$5,000-5,999	$10,000 & over
Chicago	NANN	NANN	NANN	NANN	NANN	?NNN†
Cincinnati	ATNN†	ANNN†	ANNN†	ANNN†	ANNN†	ANNN†
Cleveland	NTNN*	NTNN*	NTNN*	NANN	NANN	?NNN†
Detroit	NANN	NANN	NTNN*	NNNN*	NNNN*	ANNN†
Honolulu	ANNN†	ANNN†	ANNN†	ANNN†	ANNN†	ANNN†
Indianapolis	ATNN†	AANN	AANN	AANN	AANN	ANNN†
Kansas City	ATNN†	ANNN†	ANNN†	ANNN†	ANNN†	uNNN
Los Angeles	NNNN*	ANNN†	ANNN†	ANNN†	ANNN†	ANAN
Newark	NNNN*	NTNN*	NNNN*	NTNN*	NANN	ANNN†
New York	ATNN†	AANN	AANN	AANN	AANN	ANNN†
Philadelphia	ANNN†	ATNN†	ATNN†	ANNN†	ANNN†	ANNN†
Pittsburgh	NTNN*	TANN	NANN	TTNN*	AANN	ANNN†
St. Louis	AANN	AANN	AANN	AANN	TTNN*	ANNN†
Oakland	ANNN†	ANNN†	ANNN†	ANNN†	ANNN†	ANNN†
San Francisco	AANN	AANN	AANN	AANN	AANN	ANNN†
Baltimore	ATNN†	TTNN*	NNNN*	NNNN*	NNNN*	ANNN†
Washington, D.C.	ATNN†	ATNN†	AANN	AANN	ANNN†	ANNN†
Memphis	ATNN†	AANN	AANN	AANN	ANNN†	ANNN†
Dallas	AANN	AANN	AANN	ANNN†	ATNN†	uNNN
El Paso	ANNN†	ANNN†	ANNN†	ANNN†	ANNN†	uNNN
Houston	ANNN†	TTNN*	AANN	AANN	ANNN†	ANNN†
New Orleans	AANN	AANN	AANN	AANN	AANN	ANNN†
San Antonio	AANN	ANNN†	ANNN†	ANNN†	ANNN†	ANNN†
Atlanta	AANN	AANN	AANN	AANN	AANN	ANNN†
Birmingham	ATNN†	AANN	AANN	ANNN†	ANNN†	ANNN†

For an explanation of the symbols used, see TABLE 1.

Source: Calculations done by the author using data from U.S., Bureau of
the Census, Division of Housing, *U.S. Census of Housing, 1960*, Vol. 2,
Parts 2–6 (Washington, D.C., 1963).

rents. Not a single case exists in either Table 1 or 2 wherein "All" reports
a lower gross rent but also reports housing less desirable in terms of at
least one non-rent criterion and no more desirable in the remaining non-
rent criteria. Not a single possibility of price discrimination against whites
can be found in Tables 1 and 2; yet Tables 1 and 2 do permit the location
of several unambiguous cases of price discrimination against nonwhites
and the identification of several other cases where price discrimination
against nonwhites may possibly exist.

Data analyzed by Rapkin present trends very similar to the trends reported here. Rapkin was able to obtain recent (Census) urban housing data covering three major U.S. geographical areas cross-classified by rental paid rather than by income level so that size of rental paid is cross-classified against dwelling unit "soundness." Moreover, Rapkin is able to hold constant the number of rooms per dwelling unit. Rapkin concludes, "Despite [a] major exception, it is more than evident that Negroes spending the same rent as whites to rent the same number of rooms obtain a substantially greater proportion of substandard units."[13]

An additional check on the views obtained from Tables 1 and 2 and the data reported by Rapkin can be made by reference to owner-occupied dwelling units. All the data in Tables 1 and 2 refer to renter-occupied housing; owner-occupied housing is seemingly ignored. Presumably owner-occupied housing bears a price to the owner in his consumer role similar in magnitude to the price charged the renter for similar housing. The price is the time and money spent performing the role of housing supplier to oneself, the interest forgone on invested equity, and capital loss (or gain) at time of resale. If the price of owner-occupied housing is significantly less or more than the price of renter-occupied housing, it can reasonably be expected that a switch between markets by consumers will occur until an equalization of price again exists. The problem here is that the price of owner-occupied housing is internalized and largely hidden from view.

Table 3 presents data for SMSA's on the median income of family units inhabiting dwelling units classified by owners' estimates of their units' market resale value. The data in Table 3 show that dwelling units of specified resale value owned by nonwhites have lower median income than "All." Of the 232 "cells" (resulting from the twenty-nine SMSA's times eight value classifications), 204 permit comparisons between the median income of "Nonwhite" and "All." In 176 of these 204 cells the median income of "Nonwhite" was less than the median income of "All," twelve cells display equal median incomes, and sixteen cells display the median income of "Nonwhite" exceeding the median income of "All." Six SMSA's (Chicago, Cincinnati, Cleveland, Honolulu, Los Angeles, San Francisco) account for all sixteen cells in which "Nonwhite" median income exceeds "All" median income. Adding three more SMSA's (Miami, El Paso, and San Antonio) provides a complete list of SMSA's that exhibit exceptions to the general tendency that the median income of "All" exceeds that of "Nonwhite" for dwelling units of specified value. In twenty of the twenty-nine SMSA's there is not a single exception to this general tendency; in nine of the twenty-nine SMSA's there are frequent exceptions. This is surprising behavior in view of Tables 1 and 2 wherein the gross monthly rental of whites so frequently exceeds that paid by nonwhites.

Value of Owner-Occupied Units for "All" and "Nonwhite" SMSA's

SMSA	Less than 5		5–7.4		7.5–9.9		10–12.4		12.5–14.9		15–19.9		20–24.0		25 or More	
	A	N	A	N	A	N	A	N	A	N	A	N	A	N	A	N
Boston	4.5	3.7	5.3	4.9	5.8	5.4	6.4	6.3	6.9	6.2	7.8	6.8	9.6	u	14.2	u
Chicago	4.5	4.9	5.2	5.4	6.0	6.0	6.6	6.6	7.1	7.1	7.9	8.0	9.1	9.0	12.5	11.3
Cincinnati	4.1	4.1	5.0	5.1	5.6	5.3	6.0	5.8	6.7	6.5	7.6	7.5	9.2	9.7	12.9	14.2
Cleveland	3.7	4.0	4.8	4.8	5.4	5.3	6.1	6.1	6.6	6.6	7.1	7.1	8.7	8.1	12.1	9.6
Detroit	4.1	3.3	5.2	4.5	5.8	5.1	6.6	5.5	7.3	5.8	8.4	6.7	9.9	8.4	13.4	8.3
Honolulu	4.8	5.0	6.1	6.2	5.9	6.1	6.6	6.6	7.2	7.5	7.5	7.7	8.4	8.6	10.8	10.0+
Indianapolis	3.9	3.3	5.2	5.2	6.0	5.1	6.8	5.8	7.5	6.5	8.5	6.4	10.2	u	14.3	u
Kansas City	3.7	2.8	4.9	4.0	5.7	4.8	6.4	5.2	7.0	6.0	8.1	5.9	10.0	u	14.2	u
Los Angeles	3.1	3.1	3.9	4.1	5.3	4.9	6.3	5.5	7.1	6.2	7.9	6.9	9.3	8.0	12.8	9.4
Newark	4.9	u	5.0	4.5	5.7	4.8	6.4	6.0	6.9	5.7	7.9	7.1	9.7	8.4	14.1	u
New York	5.7	4.1	5.0	4.5	5.5	4.8	6.2	5.4	6.9	6.6	7.9	6.6	9.4	7.1	14.1	7.8
Philadelphia	4.5	3.9	5.3	4.7	6.0	5.4	6.7	5.9	7.3	6.6	8.3	7.3	10.0	8.4	14.5	6.8
Pittsburgh	4.3	3.6	5.2	4.2	5.6	4.7	6.1	5.2	6.6	5.7	7.4	6.0	9.0	u	12.7	u
St. Louis	4.0	3.0	4.5	4.2	5.8	4.5	6.4	5.7	7.0	5.5	7.9	6.8	9.5	7.4	13.9	9.9
San Francisco	3.4	3.4	4.5	4.7	5.5	5.2	6.3	5.7	6.9	6.3	7.7	6.8	9.1	8.2	12.4	9.9
Baltimore	4.5	3.6	5.4	4.7	6.1	5.5	6.8	5.9	7.5	6.2	8.4	7.2	9.9	6.9	14.0	4.7
Wash., D.C.	4.5	3.1	5.0	4.4	5.8	4.6	6.6	5.6	7.3	6.4	8.7	7.4	10.7	8.2	13.5	9.9
Memphis	2.7	2.2	4.0	3.3	5.4	3.8	6.2	4.0	7.0	3.9	8.2	4.0	10.1	u	14.9	u
Jacksonville	3.1	2.3	4.5	3.5	5.4	3.8	6.1	4.1	6.6	4.3	7.8	4.5	9.7	u	12.7	u
Miami	2.8	2.6	3.5	3.3	4.5	4.0	5.3	4.6	5.8	4.4	6.6	4.7	7.8	u	10.9	u
Dallas	3.0	2.1	4.7	4.1	5.8	4.8	6.7	5.4	7.5	4.0	8.7	4.1	10.9	u	15.0	u
El Paso	3.0	2.9	4.1	3.5	5.1	4.2	5.9	4.7	6.9	6.2	8.8	7.6	10.8	7.7	14.0	9.3
Houston	3.5	2.6	4.9	3.1	6.0	3.7	6.9	3.9	7.7	5.2	8.8	5.4	11.0	5.5	14.6	7.4
New Orleans	2.8	2.4	3.6	3.1	4.3	4.3	5.2	3.9	6.6	4.6	6.9	5.1	8.1	5.3	11.3	4.7
Norfolk-Portsmouth	3.3	2.9	5.0	4.0	5.6	5.6	6.0	4.7	6.6	5.2	7.9	5.2	9.5	u	12.6	u
Richmond	3.5	3.1	4.9	3.9	5.9	4.4	6.6	5.6	7.1	5.7	8.4	7.7	10.2	u	15.0	u
San Antonio	3.0	3.0	4.1	4.0	5.3	5.0	5.9	5.4	6.9	6.7	8.2	6.8	9.9	u	13.7	u
Atlanta	3.2	2.6	4.5	3.3	5.5	3.8	6.3	4.2	7.2	4.9	8.3	4.8	10.0	6.3	14.2	8.7
Birmingham	3.0	2.3	4.5	3.4	5.6	4.0	6.2	4.4	7.2	4.6	8.5	5.2	10.2	u	15.0	u

Columns headed by A refer to "All;" columns headed by N refer to "Nonwhite;" u signifies data are unavailable in the source.

Source: U.S., Bureau of the Census, Division of Housing, *U.S. Census of Housing: 1960*, Vol. 2, Parts 2–6 (Washington, D.C., 1963).

The important point raised is why the resale values of nonwhite owner-occupied homes are so "inflated" relative to the resale values of white owner-occupied homes. As shown earlier, the model predicts that there will be greater "pressure" from lower-income whites for dwelling units than from lower-income whites if price discrimination exists. Thus, the price for housing offered by lower-income nonwhites is expected to exceed that of lower-income whites. Resale values reflect the present value stemming from the expected future price schedule and thus under the model one expects lower-income nonwhites to pay higher resale values than lower-income whites if price discrimination exists. The observed data offered in Table 3 would appear to bear out this prediction.

The model leads us to expect that price discrimination against lower-income nonwhites becomes more severe as the income level decreases, whereas higher-income nonwhites may actually exhibit a favored position in the housing market with respect to higher income whites. But Tables 1 and 2 indicate there is no marked tendency for price discrimination to become more severe as income level decreases. Nineteen SMSA's in Table 1 provide median gross rent data for both "All" and "Nonwhite" suitable for comparison between the two groups to be made for the "$10,000 and over" income category. In these nineteen SMSA's, "Nonwhite" in the "$10,000 and over" category live in worse housing than "All" by all three non-rent criteria, but also, in every case, median gross rent paid by "Nonwhite" is less than "All." In addition, the Chicago SMSA may or may not involve "Nonwhite" paying a lesser median gross rent than "All" (the data do not permit us to know) in the "$10,000 and over" category, but "Nonwhite" does exhibit inferior housing by all three non-rent criteria. This twentieth case may be as ambiguous as the other nineteen, or it may involve unambiguous price discrimination against higher-income nonwhites.

If the data were of suffcent quality to permit us to tell whether or not the lesser rent payment is insufficient to compensate for the reduction in housing consumed, we could examine each one of these cases for price discrimination against higher-income nonwhites (i.e., each of these cases involves possible price discrimination against higher-income nonwhites). It is reasonable to suppose that at least some of these cases do involve price discrimination against higher-income nonwhites. Not a single possibility of price discrimination against higher-income whites is to be found in either Table 1 or 2 (i.e., more refined data will not locate cases of price discrimination against higher-income whites). The cases that come closest to representing price discrimination against whites are located in the five lowest income categories. In Table 1 thirty-eight rankings from the lowest income categories have two or more "A's" in the overall ranking, but the "$10,000 and over" category does not contain a single such case. Rapkin notes from his evaluations that price discrimination against non-whites appears to "intensify" as income increases rather than as income decreases.[14]

How can this discrepancy between *a priori* expectation, nurtured by the model, and the data be accommodated? First, the model makes no allowance for government intervention in the housing market; but if the government does provide subsidies to lower-income groups with the goal of equalizing housing opportunities between whites and nonwhites as well as improving the overall housing position of lower-income people generally, then even an adherent of the model would predict that the degree of price discrimination suffered by lower-income nonwhites may be softened and perhaps even eradicated. The model assumes that housing inputs, such as land, are equally mobile in answering the demand of higher-income nonwhites and the demand of higher-income whites. There is no necessity that the real economic world does satisfy this assumption, but if the assumption is not met, the essential kernel of truth contained in the model is not necessarily jeopardized. Land may be relatively immobile toward higher-income nonwhites because land boundaries in the institutional framework of the United States so often define political boundaries and school districts. A certain plot of land coming into the possession of higher-income nonwhites implies that the previous political balance may be overturned. It might be surmised that political devices such as zoning (and other less subtle techniques) have been evolved by the existing political-social order with the purpose of creating such immobility. If we modify the model to incorporate an assumption to the effect that higher-income nonwhites face discrimination in the allocation of (i.e., increased costs of obtaining) land, it is not difficult to imagine that the result may be to produce price discrimination in housing for higher-income nonwhites vis-à-vis higher-income whites.

The question remains why the price discrimination faced by higher-income nonwhites is no less severe than that suffered by lower-income nonwhites if government subsidy practices do not fully account for this phenomenon. Even if certain housing inputs are relatively immobile with respect to higher-income nonwhites, this immobility serves only to restrict the flow of housing to lower-income nonwhites still further, and the expectation remains that price discrimination against nonwhites becomes more severe with lower income. The model is based on the assumption that segregation over time exists uniformly over the entire income spectrum, but again in the real economic world there is no reason that this assumption must be so. It is possible for segregation over time to exist in the higher-income strata, but once housing has been passed on to lower-income people, only segregation at a point in time remains. As appears more likely, segregation over time is more complete against higher-income nonwhites than lower-income nonwhites, but some segregation over time, although of varying degrees, confronts all nonwhites. If this is so, and if land is more immobile to higher-income nonwhite (rather than white) usage, the model modified to meet both of those conditions would predict a lesser degree of price discrimination suffered by lower-income nonwhites than by higher-income nonwhites. If it is assumed that the political system caters to the desires of middle- and higher-income whites more systematically than it does to lower-income whites so that more effective exclusionary zoning statutes are enacted and enforced for the benefit of the more affluent whites but not for the less affluent whites, this inequity would tend to result in segregation over time being preserved for the higher-income strata but not for the lower-income strata. Imagining under what conditions the model would survive the implications wrought by the data presented in Tables 1 through 3 is a much easier task than showing the model's applicability. The viability and acceptability of the model will depend on whether or not these adjustments, which the 1970 *Census of Housing* data hopefully will make possible, can in fact be made. The above data do indicate the following: an inverse correlation exists between income of family unit and age of dwelling unit;[15] the housing for nonwhites is less sound and tends to be older and more crowded than the housing of whites at a given income level; and certain nonwhites do pay equal or higher gross rents for less desirable housing. The data appear to show inflated home values for nonwhite owner-occupied dwelling units, and the data show the income distribution of nonwhites to be less favorable than that of whites.

Policy Implications

To be successful, policy intended to end price discrimination in the housing market must remove one or more of the conditions that permit the discrimination to exist. If the physical mobility costs of housing could be drastically reduced (e.g., mobile homes that are truly mobile), the discriminations would cease. Laws prohibiting the sale of housing on terms of race can be interpreted as an attempt to end racial segregation over time. Nothing in the model suggests that integration at a point in time must be adopted to end racial segregation. If Assumption 2 is an accurate description of the real world, "blockbusting" (i.e., promoting the transferral of neighborhoods from white to nonwhite tenantry until the price of housing between racial groups is equal) may be the only practical course in ending racial segregation over time. Finally, an attempt to end price discrimination can be made by creating similar income distributions for both whites and nonwhites. Direct housing subsidies (e.g., public housing) may be interpreted as an attempt to create similar income distributions through income in kind. More generally, the policy option seeks to equalize money income distribution, and the techniques of this equalization are beyond the scope of this article.

Attempts to end price discrimination by different forms of direct regulation of the market is a futile, and even counter-productive, exercise, since such measures do not alleviate the necessary conditions. For example, if the government successfully insists that lower-income nonwhites pay no more for housing than lower-income whites, a shortage in the nonwhite market will ensue since nothing will have been done to equalize the flow of units toward lower-income nonwhites. Furthermore, regulating the price level of lower-income housing to some point below the equilibrium level will, besides creating a shortage, also reduce resale price and hence reduce present value of new units. The flow of used units toward lower-income nonwhites will ultimately be reduced because of such price regulation. If the government through a building code insists that suppliers of lower-income nonwhite housing endow a minimum degree of "quality" in their housing, all that is accomplished, if the regulation has real effect, is to increase prices for lower-income nonwhites.

The 1970 *Census of Housing* Data

The 1970 *Census of Housing* data permit a second test of the above model. The basic determinants of inferior housing have remained essentially intact throughout the 1960s. The income distribution of nonwhites has remained inferior to that of whites, although in absolute terms both distributions improved throughout the last decade. Residential racial segregation over time, if it existed in the 1950s, was certainly in evidence in the 1960s, since residential location patterns (and the consumer preferences that lead to these patterns) are slow to change. According to the model, inferior housing for lower-income nonwhites is a long-run phenomenon and will not disappear as soon as certain short-run trends, such as the migration of lower-income blacks from rural to urban areas, diminish.

It was suggested that the model's failure to predict accurately the 1960 housing position of higher-income nonwhites relative to higher-income whites may have resulted from higher-income nonwhites' facing higher costs of obtaining land (and perhaps other) resources. To test this hypothesis, one could calculate the housing acreage one would expect higher-income nonwhites to possess on the sole basis of their being of higher-income, and then compare this amount to the housing acreage actually possessed. If land costs are higher for nonwhites, the actual amount should be less than the predicted amount. The testing could be done with both 1960 and 1970 data. A similar test could be done for lower-income nonwhites to see if segregation over time is more severe for higher-income nonwhites than it is for lower-income nonwhites. If the actual housing acreage possessed by lower-income nonwhites more closely approximates the predicted acreage than is the case for higher-income nonwhites, this finding would be consistent with the hypothesis that higher-income nonwhites face more complete segregation over time than lower-income nonwhites.

The numerous cross-tabulations, such as between race, income, rent, value of owner-occupied units, unit characteristics (i.e., number of rooms, age, etc.), and socioeconomic characteristics of the household head, that the 1970 *Census of Housing* will make available in the computer summary tapes should permit a frontal attack on the question of whether racial housing differences are attributable to demand differences, to supply differences, or to some combination of the two.[16] Failure to find strong indications of a difference in demand by race, assuming that the 1970 data again show inferior housing for lower-income nonwhites, would be implicit confirmation that, as the above model suggests, the problem is in the supply sector.

NOTES

1. Segregation over time of residential neighborhoods by race occurs if price discrimination by race exists in the housing market, but transfer of neighborhoods from white tenants to nonwhite tenants (or vice versa) which would eliminate the price discrimination if allowed to occur does not, in fact, occur. (Karl E. Taeuber and Alma F. Taeuber, *Negroes in Cities* [Chicago, Ill.: Aldine Publishing Co., 1965], pp. 28–68.)

2. This manuscript was completed before the 1970 Housing Census data were available.

3. Beverly Duncan and Phillip Hauser, *Housing a Metropolis: Chicago* (Glencoe, Ill.: The Free Press, 1960), pp. 203–4.

4. Price discrimination in housing by race occurs if whites face a market price for a (standardized) housing unit different from the market price faced by nonwhites. It is emphasized that a white living next to another white is judged to be equivalent to a nonwhite living next to another nonwhite; in other words, the existence of racial segregation in housing is not sufficient grounds to infer the existence of price discrimination.

5. "Filtering" is a term used extensively in real estate literature. William G. Grigsby gives an excellent discussion of this concept in *Housing Markets and Public Policy* (Philadelphia, Pa.: University of Pennsylvania Press, 1963), pp. 97, 129–30.

6. A "neighborhood" can be defined as a collection of housing units in contiguous physical proximity, which is homogeneous in terms of such factors as tenant income, race, and consumption habits. However, many neighborhoods are not completely homogeneous in terms of any characteristics, but the heterogeneous elements occur so rarely in comparison to the total population that these neighborhoods may be considered to display a significant degree of homogeneity. For empirical evidence of homogeneity of income and race (particularly race) occurring in the urban United States see Karl Taeuber and Alma Taeuber, *Negroes in Cities*, pp. 28–95.

7. "Exceptionally high" moving costs mean that it is impractical to move a housing unit to gratify one's desire for homogeneity of neighborhood.

8. Assumptions 5 and 6 are simplifying assumptions. One could construct a model with more than two income or racial classifications but at the cost of increased complexity in return for no significant change in ultimate conclusions.

9. Herman P. Miller presents data on the income distribution of the U.S. population by race in *Income Distribution in the United States* (Washington, D.C.: U.S. Government Printing Office, 1966), pp. 198–99.

10. I differ from the Census only in the instance of persons bearing Spanish or Mexican surnames residing in San Antonio (both the San Antonio SMSA and San Antonio city) and El Paso (both the El Paso SMSA and El Paso City). The Census publishes data on persons bearing Spanish or Mexican surnames for these two areas, but it would be inconvenient to establish a three-way racial classification (since the model is in terms of a two-way classification). In any case, there would be only two observations of the third classification. Therefore, these persons are included in the "Nonwhite" category for El Paso and San Antonio on the grounds that these individuals suffer discrimination from whites as do nonwhites in other areas of the United States. The Census includes persons with Spanish or Mexican surnames who are of Indian descent in the "Nonwhite" category for all SMSA's and cities other than San Antonio and El Paso. U.S., Bureau of Census, Division of Housing, *U.S. Census of Housing, 1960* (Washington, D.C., 1963), p. xviii.

11. These income categories refer to the 1959 income of either the principal family living in the dwelling unit, or, if there is but one wage earner in the family, the principal wage earner of the dwelling unit. The basic sampling unit utilized by the Census—the dwelling unit—is a serious source of heterogeneity. A dwelling unit is roughly the

physical space occupied by a collection of people, more or less recognizable as a family, with demographic factors differing. This morass of heterogeneity is modified to the extent that whites and nonwhites exhibit similar forms of heterogeneity at various income levels. Thus, for example, if for both whites and nonwhites of, say, $3,000–$3,999 income, education, form of employment, and other characteristics of the household head are essentially similar, the housing data will be comparable; but whites and nonwhites are not always similar. There is not much recourse but to (unhappily) coexist with this state of affairs.

Data are available for higher-income nonwhites in the form of a "$10,000 and over" classification, but data for "All" are available in two classifications for incomes $10,000 and above ($10,000–14,999) and $15,000 and over. To make the data comparable between the two racial groups, the two income categories of "All" were compressed into a single "$10,000 and over" category. But because a median gross rent figure is given by the census for both "All" income categories, it is impossible to determine what the true median figures is for "All" in the entire "$10,000 and over" category. This lack of precision did not cause problems too often, since the median rent figure for "Nonwhite" was more often than not below the lower of the two median rent figures for "All." It could still be determined in these cases that nonwhites paid a lesser median gross rent than whites. (See Table 1 footnotes.)

12. Ranking by quality the housing stock racial-income groups possess poses problems above and beyond the type already encountered in ranking by age and degree of crowding. The "ideal" measurement of housing quality is much more difficult to conceptualize than housing age or crowding, and even if successfully conceptualized, more difficult to put into statistical operation. The *U.S. Census of Housing, 1960* definition can be (and has been) criticized on the grounds that it does not really contain the essence of what is "sound" housing. Even if it does contain this essence, the manner of collecting the data by an army of nonprofessional census takers inadequately drilled in the execution of the definition has led to a high degree of measurement error. *U.S. Census of Housing, 1960*, p. xx.

13. Chester Rapkin, "Price Discrimination Against Negroes in the Rental Housing Market," *Essays in Urban Economics* (Los Angeles, Calif.: University of California Press, 1966), p. 338.

14. *Ibid.*, p. 343.

15. This correlation is not as strong for nonwhites as for the rest of the population since higher-income nonwhites live in housing only marginally less old than housing lived in by lower-income nonwhites. This circumstance, however, implies that nonwhites are more, rather than less, dependent on the resale housing market, making the question of whether or not nonwhite access to the housing resale market is as free as for the rest of the population all the more pertinent.

6. Housing demand and supply are not unrelated and are in fact intertwined. For example, suppose higher-income nonwhites have a lesser per capita housing demand than higher-income whites but lower-income nonwhites have the same per capita housing demand as lower-income whites. With segregation over time, lower-income nonwhites will be at a relative disadvantage in the housing market since their higher-income brethren are constricting the flow of used units in comparison to higher-income whites; i.e., a difference in demand at one income level can create a difference in housing supply for another income level.

An Eclectic Approach to the Problem of Black Economic Development

Courtney N. Blackman

The theory of black economic development in the United States is a fledgling discipline. Before such conflagrations as Watts and Newark in the mid-1960s, the economic condition of blacks, with a few exceptions, was not viewed as an important economic problem that demanded a substantial allocation of scholarship. White scholars who did write on the problem of discrimination against blacks frequently adopted an apologetic stance. As late as 1962, Milton Friedman, although deploring racial discrimination, scolded the black community for its failure to recognize that the free market had been the major factor enabling the restrictions upon them "to be as small as they are."[1] In more recent years, however, with the remarkable rise of black consciousness and the persistent demands of black students across the nation for black studies, a modest attempt to study the problem of black economic development is underway.

Unfortunately, there has been very little useful theoretical analysis of the problem of black economic development. As a matter of fact, the most useful theoretical insights on the problem of black economic development are to be found in comments sprinkled throughout Lester Thurow's econometric study *Poverty and Discrimination*.[2] The only theoretical study by a major American academician remotely associated with the problem of black economic development is Gary Becker's *The Economics of Discrimination*.[3] As we shall see, Becker's work is designed not so much to illuminate the phenomenon of discrimination as to fit it into the traditional framework of marginal utility theory. At the other end of the spectrum, writings by black intellectuals are emerging from the category of polemic.

It has been a misfortune for the black community that its economic problem has attracted attention at a time when the economics profession is firmly under the stranglehold of the econometric fad. Nowadays, an economic problem is no longer the occasion for reflection but an opportunity to build an econometric model. Econometric models are useful in predicting the behavior of a relatively stable system. However, the problem facing the black community today is one of breaking out of a system which has proven to be disastrously stable for them. It is the existing parameters of the system, not so much the variables, which distress them. The need now is more for bold and imaginative new theory than econometric models. In short, the study of black economic development has yet to move into its Keynesian phase.

Because of the lack of an adequate theory of black economic development, there has been a tendency to perceive hasty analogies between the black situation and some other and to apply to the problem of black economic development models conceived for other purposes. There has also been a proliferation of strategies which focus upon a single aspect of the problem to the neglect of the others. For example, there is currently a sharp debate as to which is the more appropriate strategy for black economic development—black ownership of business enterprise or black participation in the white-owned corporation. In fact, these two strategies are not mutually exclusive; both are required.

This paper is a modest attempt at an integrative approach toward a theory of black economic development in the United States. I will begin with an examination of the nature of the economic problem facing the black community. Secondly I will discuss the most significant literature on the subject. Thirdly I will conduct an economic analysis which will be rooted in empirically observable features of the black economy. Finally I will set out the policy implications of our analysis.

The Problem of Black Economic Development

Ironically blacks' impatience with their economic condition has been rising in spite of a decade of impressive economic gains for the black community. Nonwhites have raised their median family income from $3,794 in 1960 to $6,279 in 1970. This rate of increase was, in fact, slightly better than that of white families. In 1960 more than half of all black families fell below the poverty line (basically a poor household is defined as one which has to spend more than one-third of its income on a minimum diet); by 1970 the proportion had fallen below one-third.[4]

Employment gains for the minority groups averaged as high as 200,000 in the past few years. At most times in 1960, 13 percent of the nonwhite labor force was out of work. During 1969 the proportion fell below 6 percent, the lowest level since the Korean War. In 1970 the unemployment level for nonwhites did rise as high as 10.5 percent; but this is still far short of the 17 percent for the recession of 1957.

Over this decade, blacks also substantially improved their occupational status. In 1960 only 11 percent of employed nonwhites were professionals, technicians or managers. By 1969 the proportion had risen to 14 percent. Meanwhile, the percentage of unskilled nonwhites in the labor force had declined from 15 to 7.

But blacks are much less impressed by their recent economic gains than by the fact that their economic position relative to that of whites has not altered significantly, and this has been a major source of frustration. Although they enjoy much higher incomes than they did formerly, their median family income is still only 61 percent of that for whites, and the average black family needs an additional earner in order to earn substantially more than half the income of the comparable white family.[5]

The occupational status of blacks has improved but whites still dominate the top-level jobs, from which formal or informal practices have excluded nonwhites. Of whites in the labor force, 27 percent hold technical, managerial, and professional positions, as against 14 percent for blacks. Results of a survey released by the Race Relations Information Center in September 1970 showed that of 3,182 senior officers and directors of the nation's top 50 firms only three were black. Another survey sponsored less than two years ago [i.e., since 1969] by the Ford Foundation revealed that of the nation's 100,000 certified public accountants 150, at most, were black, while the proportions of lawyers, physicians and dentists who were black were found to be 1, 2, and 2.5 percent respectively.

Moreover, blacks remain rooted on the lower rungs of the occupational ladder, with a larger than proportionate share of the lower-paid, less-skilled jobs. In 1969 18 percent of the male black labor force fell into the category of nonfarm laborers as against 6 percent for whites, and 20 percent of the female black labor force worked as domestics as opposed to 3 percent of the white females employed. In spite of the gains in employment made by blacks, their rate of unemployment over the past ten years has remained steady at about twice that for whites.

The most glaring discrepancy is in the relative wealth positions of whites and blacks. In 1966 black families, comprising 10 percent of the population, owned less than 2 percent of the nation's net household asset accumulation of $942 billion. Fewer than 2 percent of all business enterprises were owned by blacks.[6] Thus, neither as asset holders nor as highly placed managers have blacks been in a position to influence the major economic decisions in the nation.

The problem, then, is not simply one of increasing the economic welfare of the blacks as measured by percentage increases in jobs, income, etc., but it is also a question of improvement in their situation relative to whites. Progress is to be measured by the rate at which statistics of black welfare approach parity with the white sector's. In other words, the problem is primarily one of structural rather than of absolute growth. Kenneth Boulding defines structural growth as a situation "in which the aggregate which 'grows' consists of a complex structure of interrelated parts and in which the growth process involves change in the relation of the parts."[7]

Many white liberal economists do not understand this need for structural change and continue to place great faith in full employment as a solution to the problem of black economic development. It is true that tight labor markets will benefit marginal black workers. It is also true that white resistance to black employment, especially from the white craft unions, is less adamant when there are plenty of jobs around. However, full employment, although desirable, is not a sufficient condition for the structural growth about which we are talking. In addition to economic expansions, certain fundamental changes must occur in the social and the political as well as economic relationships between whites and blacks in American society. At the same time, of course, the black community must also initiate a major drive to disturb the low-productivity syndrome with which it has for too long been afflicted.

Review of the Literature

It is now almost a convention to begin any study connected with discrimination against blacks in this country with a reference to Gary Becker's *The Economics of Discrimination*. This is a reflection not so much of its usefulness as of its uniqueness. Although mathematically quite elegant, Becker's analysis is static and neglects the historical and institutional determinants of discrimination.

The first weakness of Becker's study is its transparently apologetic tone:

> Although discrimination against negroes in the United States receives world-wide publicity, the extent of discrimination in the market place in this country is probably much less than in any other country in the world.[8]

This is a remarkably sweeping generalization to appear in a scientific work, but it tells us where the wind is blowing.

Our suspicions are further aroused by Becker's disingenuous attempt to equate the discriminatory taste of an admiring male for a glamorous Hollywood star with discrimination met by a black trying to integrate a white neighborhood.[9] Certainly there is an important difference in taste as determined by the social, political and historical institutions of a nation. From a policy standpoint, it is of significant importance whether tastes are institutionally determined or occur randomly in individuals throughout the society. If the former is the case, public policy can be most useful; if the latter, there is little we can do, as Becker would presumably have us, but try to persuade individuals to give up their individual tastes for discrimination. In fact, one logical policy implication of Becker's theory is the government subsidization of the white discriminators so that they may be persuaded to trade with blacks.

A second difficulty with Becker's study is his failure to root the *a priori* assumptions of his theory in the empirically observable features of black-white economic relations. Nowhere, for example, does Becker face the implications of the fact that in "international" trade between whites and blacks, whites in fact determine the terms of trade and do not simply express their taste. As Thurow points out:

> The dominant group controls much more than its willingness to trade or not to trade with the minority. Physical, social or economic pressures may

enable the dominant group to trade with the subservient group as a discriminating monopolist or monopsonist.[10]

But Thurow also demonstrates that even with Becker's assumptions, whites may derive gains from discrimination depending on the scope of the supply schedule for black labor. The white society gains if the supply schedule is perfectly inelastic and loses if the supply schedule is perfectly elastic. In intermediate situations white gains/losses depend upon the degree of the elasticity of the supply schedule for black labor.[11]

Much more serious is Becker's attempt to identify the determinants of market discrimination. At the outset of his analysis, he is careful to treat the "taste for discrimination" as a theoretical construct for the purpose of analysis, treating the co-efficient of discrimination as a quantitative measure of the presence of this taste:

> If an individual has "a taste for discrimination," he must act *as if* he were willing to pay something either directly or in the form of reduced income, to be associated with some persons instead of others.[12] [Italics are Becker's.]

This "as if" approach permits him to measure the effects of discrimination without reference to the true causes of discrimination. As a matter of fact, Becker concedes in another part of his work that, although the coefficients of discrimination of consumers and employers "are the proximate determinant of choices, they are in turn like other tastes influenced by more fundamental variables."[13] In yet another part of the analysis we find Becker arguing as if the taste for discrimination was in fact the empirically observed fundamental cause of market discrimination and not merely a theoretical construct:

> Monopolies, political discrimination, are at most secondary determinants of market discrimination and . . . individual tastes operating within a competitive framework constitute the primary determinant.[14]

But, certainly, whites do not emerge from the womb with a "taste for discrimination." This taste is instructed and sustained in the United States by an awesome complex of institutional arrangements. It seems clear that institutional factors must be the fundamental variables and the "taste for discrimination" the secondary determinant. At any rate Becker cannot have his cake and eat it too. His "taste for discrimination" is either a theoretical construct or a fundamental determinant; it cannot be both.

One approach, made popular among white liberals by Nathan Glazer's and Daniel P. Moynihan's *Beyond the Melting Pot,* treated the blacks as one of a long line of ethnic groups who had arrived in the urban centers, especially New York. Although burdened by somewhat greater disadvantages, they would in their turn "become part of the game of accommodation politics . . . and in this . . . would not do so badly."[15]

In fact, blacks are not the last in a long line of immigrants. They have been among the first to reach American cities. The error of Glazer and

Moynihan is their failure to investigate why, although the black was one of the first migrants, he has been one of the last to enter the mainstream of American economic life. Harold Sheppard and Herbert Striner effectively dispose of this spurious analogy between blacks and other European ethnic groups:

> The Jews, Irish, Italians, Poles, or Scandinavians who see no difference between their former plight and that of Negroes today are either grossly uninformed or are enjoying an unforgivable false pride . . . . A background of emancipation, mocked by a hundred years with the aid of legal loopholes is different from a history free from the need for emancipation . . . . And finally, the color of the skin is not only different but unchangeable.[16]

Andrew Brimmer and Henry Terrell utilize the international trade model to analyze the relative positions of the black and white sectors of the economy. Because their assumptions are rooted in historical realities, their analysis yields some useful insights. The economic effects of racial discrimination over the centuries, they observe, are "similar to those produced in international trade when a high tariff wall is erected between two countires: separate markets prevail in the two areas for items subject to tariff control."[17] These separate markets prevail especially in personal services, since it was in this area that the refusal of whites to service blacks was most adamant. Residential segregation also provided a wall of protection for black professionals and entrepreneurs operating within the black community. "In occupations which were dependent upon national markets," Brimmer and Terrell observe, "Negroes were conspicuously absent."[18]

This analysis explains convincingly the plight of the black community in terms of narrow markets, the low income of black consumers, and the low productivity of black productive units. Although this model is useful in the analytical description of the situation of black business enterprise, it remains essentially static. It therefore does not represent a contribution to the theory of black economic development, which, of course, is an exercise in dynamics. Brimmer never asks the question, "How can black enterprise break out of its low-productivity syndrome?" He seems to assume that black business is forever doomed to its present condition. Indeed, he actually discourages blacks from business entrepreneurship, urging them instead to enter the white-owned corporation. He is especially harsh on the black banks:

> From this assessment of the performance of black banks, I am convinced that the multiplication of such institutions should not be encouraged in the belief that they can make a major contribution to the financing of economic development in the black community.[19]

Brimmer's preoccupation with the probability of business failure among black entrepreneurs and his impatience with the black banks betrays unfamiliarity with the process of economic growth. Societies, like individuals, learn by doing, and some business failure is the price of economic progress. In the 1930s many of the commercial banks in this country failed; it was the price of today's sound banking system.

Brimmer also fails to recognize that the development of independent black businessmen could provide the foundations of political power in numerous communities across the nation—political power which could be parlayed into economic gains. It will be decades before black executives in the white corporation reach the point where they exercise significant economic power.

Brimmer also neglects the psychological aspects of economic development. "Being an economist," he writes, "I must analyze the black experience in economic terms."[20] Yet the study of underdeveloped countries suggests that "non-economic" and psychological factors, such as cultural awareness and racial pride, which Brimmer downgrades, can in fact, if properly channeled, contribute significantly to economic growth. An economist who restricts himself to "economic" factors in the study of economic growth will certainly fall into error. It is interesting that Irma Adelman and Cynthia T. Morris in their study, "An Econometric Model of Socio-Economic and Political Change," write:

> It is indeed a striking feature of the model that 66 percent of the causal relationships of economic variables involve partially or totally non-economic traits of society.[21]

An analytical approach especially popular among black economists and intellectuals involves the use of the model of an underdeveloped and/or ex-colonial country. It is observed that the characteristics of low levels of education, health, and income apply to both black neighborhoods and underdeveloped countries. Roy Innis writes:

> There is a very striking similarity between the so-called underdeveloped countries and our underdeveloped black communities. Both have always been oppressed; almost always there is an unfavorable balance of trade with the oppressors or exploiters; both suffer from high unemployment, low income, scarce capital, and we can point to a series of other similarities.[22]

D. S. McLaurin and C. D. Tyson push the analogy of the developing country to its logical conclusion in their "Ghediplan":

> The Ghediplan views the ghetto an an underdeveloped nation . . . . When the United States helps underdeveloped nations, it concentrates on extending the free enterprise system . . . . A central banking system, insurance networks, and other instruments of capital accumulation are established . . . . To eliminate Wattses, Newarks, and Detroits, the cities' underdeveloped ghetto-nations must be given the economic tools with which to build stable and sound economies.[23]

The "Ghediplan" falls down because of its failure to recognize that the factor of sovereignty is central to development planning. As Robert S. Browne points out, a comprehensive economic plan "assumes the existence of a nation which has title to a cluster of contiguous resources and which exercises sovereignty over both itself as a community and over its members, who must feel themselves to be part of this community."[24] To be fair to Innis, he does recognize the important qualifications of sovereignty: "Let me point to at least one vital difference. In every so-called underdeveloped country, the people have a measure of sovereignty."[25] It is to meet this limitation that he makes political control of the ghetto—self-determination—his goal:

> You cannot have economic development unless you have certain supportive political realities, one of which is some degree of self-determination.[26]

Innis gave strong support to the Community Self-Determination bill which was introduced into the Congress in 1968, and which would have promoted broadly owned community development corporations in areas defined through a referendum process.

Another approach treating the ghetto as a separate economic entity focuses on the ghetto's "balance of payments" problem. Robert Browne writes:

> It has become fairly generally understood . . .that one source of the (ghetto) community's poverty lies in the fact that money too often only "passes through" their community without lingering long enough to "turn over" several times and thereby generate incomes for other of the community's residents.[27]

This approach implies a strategy of maintaining profits within the ghetto—halting the "balance of payments" drain—thus leading to increased investment within the ghetto.

The balance-of-payments approach, as Thomas Sowell points out, confuses money with wealth. At any rate, there is no conceivable institutional arrangement for preventing the flight of capital from the ghetto. "Capital," Sowell observes, "is the most fluid of all resources. It goes wherever the rate of profit is highest, allowing for risk."[28]

More importantly this approach neglects the fact that the economic weakness of the ghetto derives from factors whose roots lie outside the urban center and over which the ghetto has no control. John Neidercorn, who presents a mathematical model of balance-of-payments approach, admits that a strategy of keeping money within the ghetto would be difficult: "The problems associated with low levels of skill, shortages of capital, lack of business experience, irregular work habits, and finding markets are not easily overcome."[29] Yet he omits all of these crucial variables from consideration in his model.

The fact is that black neighborhoods are open economies. Their inhabitants are free to move their resources in and out as they please. In fact, the evidence is that as their income rises blacks do opt to flee the ghetto for suburbia whenever they can overcome patterns of residential discrimination. Innis's dream of politically autonomous black neighborhoods also seems chimerical. The problem of black economic development cannot be treated within the confines of the urban center but must address itself to the varied and stubborn obstacles which militate against the black community throughout American society.

By far the most useful work on the subject of discrimination against blacks is Thurow's work *Poverty and Discrimination,*[30] which by the use of econometric models explores the quantitative relationships of the phenomena of discrimination and poverty, using the empirical data at hand. It is true, as John Handy points out, that Thurow's analysis does not really establish the causal roots of black poverty,[31] but Thurow is much more cognizant of the structural determinants of poverty than Handy gives him credit for and is, in fact, quite mindful of the difficulties which Handy raises. His findings deserve our attention if only because his work forms the most reasoned and exhaustive quantitative analysis of the subject to date:

1. Equal rights for Negroes, and the push to full employment can make significant reductions in the number of families living in poverty.[32]
2. Although...unbalanced (i.e., tight) labor markets alone are not a sufficient answer to the problems of poverty and discrimination, they present strong evidence that such markets can lead very quickly to a substantial reduction in both.[33]
3. Education and on-the-job experience do not completely explain the distribution of earnings, but they are important ingredients.[34]
4. Negroes have less human capital and receive less remuneration for what they have....Without eliminating discrimination, Negro poverty cannot be eliminated and the Negro and white income distributions cannot be equalized.[35]
5. Attacking human capital discrimination will not raise Negro incomes by itself, since wage, employment, and occupational discrimination would make the enforcement of these other types difficult in the absence of government discrimination.[36]
6. Programs to eliminate poverty will not work for Negroes unless they operate on racial discrimination. Programs to put an end to racial inequality will not work unless they act on the causes of poverty which affect black and white alike.[37]

The Theory of Black Economic Development

The uniqueness of the situation of the black man in the United States makes the problem of black economic development especially difficult to resolve. Unlike the black in Africa, he is in a minority; unlike the European ethnic, he is highly visible; unlike the Jew, he lacks cultural cohesiveness; unlike the citizen of a developing country, he lacks sovereign control over his community. He is like all these people in some respects, and yet in each case he is significantly different. Furthermore, since the black community is not concentrated in one region, we cannot speak of the black economy in aggregative terms, as we can of a nation or even a region, and use a macroeconomic approach. We can, however, use the institutional and psychological insights from the theory of economic development since institutions and attitudes are not confined by geographical or national boundaries. Because of the uniqueness of the problem we must use, not a single, but an eclectic, approach. We must choose carefully the relevant elements of various bodies of theory for application to the problem. In our analysis we will utilize the conventional price theory to examine the situation of the black firms in the setting of a market structure defined in terms of Brimmer's international trade model. We shall also use elements of the theory of economic growth developed since World War II to cope with the dynamics of development in the black community.

An examination of black business enterprise shows that it is concentrated heavily in the personal service sector, catering to sheltered and narrow local markets. Johnson Products, which deals in cosmetics specially prepared for black women and which was the first black-owned firm traded on the American Exchange, is one of the few black firms catering to the black community on a national basis. Forty-two percent of all black businesses are engaged in the provision of personal and other services as opposed to 27 percent for white establishments. A survey of Washington, D.C., showed that of all the black businesses classified as services 44 percent were barber shops, beauty salons, or beauty schools, while 12 percent were drycleaning establishments. The proportion of black firms engaged in manufacturing is less than 4 percent compared with 7 percent for whites. However, black firms represent but 1.2 percent of all manufacturing firms, and are concentrated among the smallest establishments.

The sales volume of the typical black firm is also very low relative to the national average. A survey by the National Business League revealed that the average receipts of a black firm engaged in the service and retail industries were less than $20,000 per year compared to the national average of over $100,000.

Finally, the productivity of the average black firm, when measured in terms of receipts per employee, is low relative to the national standard. In service and retail industries the receipts per employee for the average black firm in 1968 were under $6,000, compared to an average of more than $24,000 for the nation as a whole.

The situation of the black firm described above is consistent with the Brimmer international trade model, in which the black firm operates in protected markets caused by patterns of segregation. The cost of this protection is restriction to a narrow market of low-income consumers.

The combined effects of small markets and low-income customers is illustrated in Figure 1, in which the "black" industry demand curve is drawn significantly to the left of the "white" industry demand curve. It can be seen that even if P_b (the price of goods sold by black firms to black customers), is greater than P_w (the price of goods sold by white firms) the total income of black firms P_b Q_b (Q_b is the quantity of goods sold by black firms) is much smaller than the total income of white firms P_w Q_w

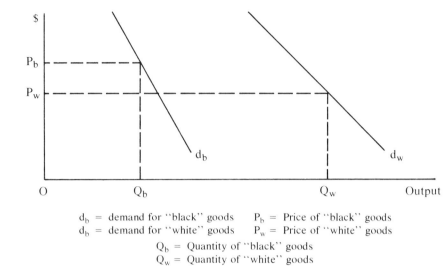

d_b = demand for "black" goods   P_b = Price of "black" goods
d_b = demand for "white" goods   P_w = Price of "white" goods
Q_b = Quantity of "black" goods
Q_w = Quantity of "white" goods

Fig. 1. Industry demand curves in "black" and "white" markets assuming identical production functions. $

(Q_w is the quantity of goods sold by white firms). There may be cases where a black entrepreneur is able to enjoy monopoly profits within the protected "black" market (i.e., where he faces a relatively inelastic demand curve). Even so, the narrowness of the market imposes a lower ceiling on potential earnings than in the case of the white entrepreneur. This is why the vast majority of blacks who are wealthy by national standards have made their wealth by selling their services in the national market and in such fields as entertainment and sports after discrimination against them was alleviated.

Narrow and poor markets also contribute to higher costs for black industry than for white industry. Because of lower sales, black firms are unable to benefit from the economies of scale. Figure 2 illustrates how the lower levels of production lead to higher prices in black industry than in white. In cases where a higher price cannot be asked, the quality of the black industry will tend to be lower.

White firms also enjoy an absolute cost advantage over black firms. That is, even where the scale of production for both black and white firms is similar, black industry costs tend to be higher. In the first place, the fixed costs of doing business in black neighborhoods, where most black firms operate, are much higher than in white neighborhoods, where the majority of white firms operate. Police protection, sanitation, and general utility services are notoriously deficient in black neighborhoods, sometimes to the extent that insurance becomes unavailable at any price to the black businessman. In such an unfavorable environment bank loans are scarce and costly when obtainable.

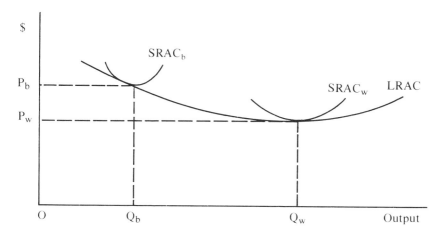

SRAC_b = Short run average cost curve for black industry
SRAC_w = Short run average cost curve for white industry
LRAC   = Industry long run average cost curve

Fig. 2.   Industry demand and cost curves in "white" and "black" markets assuming identical production

The variable costs of black enterprises are also likely to be higher for black firms than for white. In Figures 1 and 2 we assumed, as does Becker, that white and black inputs of labor and capital are homogeneous. This assumption is, of course, wildly unrealistic. The quality of the labor force available in the black neighborhood is most inferior to that available in the white, especially because educated blacks can earn more in the national labor markets. Besides, superior capital and managerial resources make it possible for white industry to employ more advanced technology and higher productivity.

Figure 3 illustrates the effects of the absolute cost advantage of a white firm over the black firm which tries to produce for the national integrated market. Note that the long-run cost curve of the black firm is substantially higher than that of the white.

Since the experience of blacks in the management of large corporations is minimal, the efficiency of the black firm relative to the white decreases as the scale of operations increases. This is also illustrated in Figure 3, where the gap between the white and black long-run average costs curves widens as the scale of operation increases.

There are two main inferences which we may readily draw from the above analysis. The first is that black enterprise must increase its productivity—i.e., lower its costs of production—if it is to compete successfully with white enterprise. The second inference is that any serious attempt at black economic development must contemplate the entry of black firms into the national markets. Brimmer is entirely right to stress

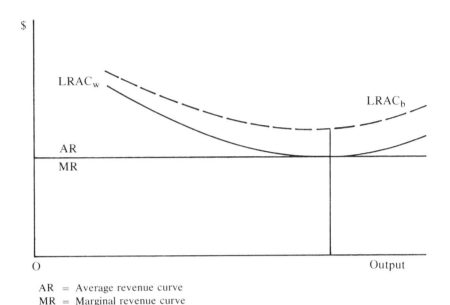

Fig. 3.   Cost functions for black and white firms in an integrated market.

this point: "Entrepreneurs who limit themselves to these segregated markets will be denied the economies of scale which are a precondition of long-run economic development."[38]

Capital—the source of productivity

The central lesson of economic-growth theory is that increased productivity results from the greater use of capital relative to labor inputs, providing, of course, that the capital inputs are available in the appropriate form. Black firms are less efficient than white firms because they employ relatively fewer inputs of capital. Furthermore, because "black" capital inputs are quantitatively and qualitatively inferior to "white" capital inputs, black firms are not able to utilize the most advanced technology available. For this reason models such as Becker's which posit that blacks have a comparative advantage in labor are not very useful. To say that a firm has a comparative advantage in labor is to say that its productivity is low. A firm whose productivity is low cannot in any useful sense be said to have an advantage. To have a comparative advantage in labor is to be poor.

A strategy for black economic development must seek to increase both quality and quantity of capital inputs. A brief exploration of capital is therefore essential. We may break capital into three categories: financial capital, human capital, and social capital. In each of these categories the black community is at a serious disadvantage vis-à-vis the white.

By financial capital we mean the funds required for the purchase of plant and equipment and the provision of working capital. Financial capital is generated out of income, and, since the income accruing to black families is substantially less than that of white families, it is not surprising that the financial capital available to black firms is less than that available to white firms. Financial capital may also be borrowed, but creditors usually require collateral in the form of their existing asset holdings. This makes whites better credit risks than blacks. Because blacks find financial capital difficult to obtain, they cannot get control of assets. Because they lack control of assets their income is low and they are unable to generate capital—an excellent example of the familiar vicious cycle.

Human capital represents the investment in individuals which leads to an increase in skills and to an increase in productivity. This would include expenditures on education, on-the-job training, and medical care. Human capital is now recognized as a crucial factor in economic growth. Becker shows that private rates of return on college education exceed those on business capital.[39]

The inadequate level of investment in black human capital is reflected in the low level of education among blacks relative to whites. In spite of tremendous gains made by nonwhites over the last decade, nearly 30 percent of the black civilian labor force has only an elementary education as compared with less than 20 percent for whites. Fewer than 50 percent of the nonwhites have graduated from high school as opposed to almost 70 percent for whites, and about 15 percent of employed whites are college graduates compared to fewer than 10 percent for nonwhites. Besides, because of segregation and lower investment per child, achievement levels for black children are lower than for whites.

The lower rate of investment in blacks is also reflected in the statistics on health. In 1968 a white person aged 25 had a life expectancy of 5.3 years more than a black of the same age. In the same year the mortality rate for nonwhite infants less than one month old was 23.0 per thousand live births, versus 14.7 for white infants, and 11.6 for nonwhite infants between one and twelve months old as against 4.5 for white infants in the same age group.[40] Barbara Bergman, in a study for the Joint Economic Committee, estimates at $50 billion the accumulated deficiency in capital investment in blacks.[41]

Unfortunately, the accumulation of human capital is a painful and time-consuming process. It cannot be borrowed or readily transferred from one person to another. Lawrence Cooper, President of the Management Council in Los Angeles, insists that management ability, not financing, "is the missing ingredient from most minority business."[42] Managerial skill is but one return to investment in human capital. The acquisition of human capital is extremely difficult for those who lack access to the use of social capital.

Social capital represents the collective savings of a society and manifests itself in highways, airports, hospitals, universities, parks, swimming pools, playgrounds, museums, libraries, schools, etc. Access to educational and health facilities reduces the cost to the individual of acquiring human capital; access to public services, such as police protection, transportation, and justice, greatly reduces the fixed costs of doing business. Throughout much of America and for over two centuries, black Americans have been denied equal access to the use of much of the nation's social capital. The inadequacy of social services has become even more desperate as wealthier whites have fled to the suburbs, leading to an erosion of the tax base of the central cities where the black population is concentrated.

A crucial form of social capital is the "stock of knowledge" which society holds collectively, and which, although not necessarily passed on through formal educational channels, enables citizens to function effectively within the given society. For example, it would be difficult to survive among the Eskimos unless you learned their way of life. The most distinctive stock of knowledge in the American society is business management. This includes not only managerial and technical skills, but positive attitudes towards work, knowledge of business routines, and an understanding of the techniques of economic advancement which, for want of a better word, we might call "sophistication." This is the kind of knowledge transmitted from father to son, gathered in the board rooms, across the negotiation table, at the business luncheon, etc. Not all of it can be learned in business schools.

Unequal access to the society's stock of business knowledge is an important contributing factor to the economic backwardness of the black community. Indeed, economist Thomas Sowell makes explicit reference to the economic value of "particular situations and individuals":

> Knowledge of specifically who, where and how to get things done is very unequally distributed, and constitutes a tremendous handicap to the poor in a highly complex society. A ghetto youth with a knack for mathematics and a potential for engineering or chemistry probably does not know a single engineer or chemist who could give him some idea of what his avenues and alternatives are.[43]

The lack of sophistication has forced firms employing hard-core black unemployed to provide complementary counseling services which are normally unnecessary in industrialized societies.

Demand and productivity

An increase in the quality and quantity of black capital is but half the battle. Effective demand is required to transform increased productivity into value. Blacks cannot benefit fully from their increased productivity unless they are permitted to sell their products on the national markets. There still remain substantial barriers to full entry into national markets by blacks. They are still in many instances paid less for the same work. Quantitative controls still limit black entry into some professions, especially the building trades. Black returns to investment in education are still very much lower than for whites, although the gap seems to be closing at the upper levels. Besides, on the national business scene there is an intricate complex of business alliances and informal relationships into which it is extremely difficult for black businessmen to break. It is in this area that white cooperation and good-will are most needed.

Even if discrimination against blacks were to cease dramatically, the problem of the capital deficit would still remain. Again, white cooperation is critical if this deficit is to be rapidly wiped out. Europe also suffered from a severe capital shortage in the 1940s and 1950s as a result of wartime destruction. The Americans moved massively under the Marshall Plan to correct the situation. But that rescue operation was relatively simple. Although the Europeans were short of financial capital, their human capital and the most important elements of their social capital, i.e., technical and organizational know-how, were still intact.

Although much financial capital is required, the mere transfer of money, then, will not cure the capital deficit in the black community. In addition to cash transfers, extensive programs must be developed to increase the educational level and technical skills of the black community and to bring to bear on the problem the tremendous resources of American national institutions, such as government, corporations, and universities. In many instances, however, the largely white-controlled national institutions, through lack of familiarity, will not be able to deal effectively with some problems. In such cases, the black community will be forced to develop specialized institutions for themselves.

It is an illusion on the part of black separatists to think that the black community can make significant economic progress in the face of solid white hostility or even intransigence. The black community can and must do a lot on its initiative; the white community also has a grave responsibility to remove barriers to black entry into the national market and to come up with measures for closing, in as short a time as possible, the gap between capital resources of the black and white communities.

The role of institutions

In the above analysis we have identified a shortage of capital—financial, human, and social—as the root cause of the poor economic performance of the black community. We have traced this shortage ultimately to black exclusion from the use of the nation's social capital. Social capital is the key variable in any attempt to correct the over-all deficit, since, as we have seen, access to social capital reduces the cost of the acquisition of human capital, which, in turn, increases the earning power of individuals. Transfers of financial capital from the white community are necessary to maintain the black poor who, because of past deprivation, are unable to make a living. Funds from the white financial institutions are also needed for the initiation of black businesses. In the long run, the broadening of social capital available to the black community is crucial to the solution of the problem of black economic backwardness.

Institutions are the main repository of social capital. However, the full black participation in national institutions is not enough. Such participation would immediately increase the income of the relatively few blacks who are fully equipped to benefit from these institutions but would be of little assistance to those most affected by the capital deficit. For this reason, special institutions must be designed to repair the capital deficit in as short a time as possible.

Because the black population in the United States is so heterogeneous and diffuse, we cannot establish a master plan for such institutions. They must be encouraged whenever and wherever they seem useful. Three criteria of usefulness suggest themselves. First, they should be economical—affecting the lives of a maximum number of people at minimum costs. Second, the output of the institutions—information, training, etc.—should be keyed primarily to the needs of the national economy. Third, the operation of the institutions themselves should provide a training ground in the arts of management for a significant cadre of blacks.

The emotional factor in economic development

The third criterion leads us to a consideration of the composition of these institutions, and here the examples of developing countries yield useful insights. The first observation to be made is that societies must develop themselves; they cannot be developed from the outside. As W. W. Rostow puts it:

> A new elite—a new leadership—must emerge and be given scope to begin the building of a modern industrial society.[44]

To adapt this observation to the black situation, new black leaders must be given scope to develop the institutions necessary for black economic development. Black economic development cannot be programmed from Washington. Moreover, the long years of separation from the black community have rendered a majority of whites quite insensitive to the problems of the black community, not least among them the white economists. This makes it imperative that blacks themselves take the initiative in establishing special institutions.

The second observation is that economic development has usually been accompanied by some powerful emotional manifestation. Again we quote Rostow:

> As a matter of historical fact a reactive nationalism . . . reacting against intrusion from more advanced nations . . . has been a most important and powerful motive force in the transition from traditional to modern societies, at least as important as the profit motive.[45]

The lesson from this observation is that developmental institutions require an emotional input to provide the internal dynamic. Without this emotional energy institutions degenerate into bureaucracies. The prospects for black economic development are enhanced by the heightened sense of humiliation among blacks in recent years. In fact the current drive for economic development is directly traceable to this emotional upheaval. The rate of growth in the future will depend on how effectively this emotion can be harnessed and channeled into productive activities.

Policy Implications of the Theory

The integrative approach outlined above implies the adoption of the following policy measures for the achievement of black economic development:

1. The efforts of the traditional Civil Rights movement to gain access to the social capital of the American society must be maintained. The black man must never again allow himself to be excluded from the economies of full participation in the world's largest and most dynamic economy.

2. As blacks assert their right to participation in the national institutions, specialized institutions must be established to repair the capital deficit of the black community.

3. The initiative for establishing specialized institutions must come from the black community itself.

4. The economic value of the recent surge in black consciousness must be exploited. The emotion of present black revolutionary movements must be channeled towards the creation of a dynamic for developmental institutions.

5. The active cooperation of the white society must be encouraged, especially toward the entry of black individuals and enterprises into the national markets.

NOTES

1. Milton Friedman, *Capitalism and Freedom* (Chicago, Ill.: University of Chicago Press, 1962), p. 109.

2. Lester C. Thurow, *Poverty and Discrimination* (Washington. D.C.: The Brookings Institution, 1969).

3. Gary S. Becker, *The Economics of Discrimination* (Chicago, Ill.: University of Chicago Press, 1957).

4. "The Social and Economic Status of Negroes in the United States." U.S., Dept. of Labor, Bureau of Labor Statistics, Report 394 (1970).

5. *Ibid.*, p. 32.

6. Andrew Brimmer, "Education, Income, and Wealth Accumulation in the Negro Com-

munity." Remarks at Booker T. Washington Business College, Birmingham, Alabama, 1970.

7. Kenneth Boulding, *Beyond Economics* (Ann Arbor, Mich.: University of Michigan Press, 1968), p. 65.

8. Becker, *Economics of Discrimination*, p. 1.

9. *Ibid.*, p. 5.

10. Thurow, *Poverty and Discrimination*, p. 117.

11. *Ibid.*, pp. 113–15.

12. Becker, *Economics* . . . , p. 6.

13. *Ibid.*, p. 123.

14. *Ibid.*, p. 123.

15. Nathan Glazer and Daniel P. Moynihan, *Beyond the Melting Pot* (2d ed.; Cambridge, Mass.: M.I.T. Press, 1970), p. x.

16. H. Shepherd and H. Striner, "Civil Rights, Employment, and the Social Status of American Negroes," *Studies in Employment and Unemployment* (Kalamazoo, Mich.: W.E. Upjohn Institute for Employment Research, June 1966), p. 48.

17. Andrew Brimmer, "The Economic Potential of Black Capitalism" (paper presented, with Henry S. Terrell, before 82nd Annual Meeting of the American Economic Association, Dec. 29, 1969).

18. *Ibid.*

19. Andrew Brimmer, "The Black Banks: An Assessment of Performance and Prospects" (paper presented to the American Economic Association, Detroit, Mich., Dec. 28, 1970).

20. Andrew Brimmer, "Economic Integration and the Progress of the Negro Community," *Ebony*, August 1970, p. 118.

21. Irma Adelman and Cynthia Taft Morris, "An Econometric Model of Socio-Economic and Political Change in Underdeveloped Countries," *American Economic Review*, Dec. 1968, p. 1202.

22. Roy Innis, "Separatist Economics: A New Social Contract," in *Black Economic Development*, ed. by William F. Haddad and G. Douglas Pugh (Englewood Cliffs, N.J.: Prentice-Hall, 1969), p. 53.

23. D.S. McLaurin and C. D. Tyson, "The Ghediplan for Economic Development," *ibid.*, p. 131.

24. R.S. Browne, "Toward an Overall Assessment of Our Alternatives," *Review of Black Political Economy*, Spring/Summer 1970, p. 19.

25. Roy Innis, "Separatist Economics," p. 53.

26. *Ibid.*, p. 54.

27. R. S. Browne, "Cash Flows in a Ghetto Community," *Review of Black Political Economy*, Winter/Spring 1971, p. 28.

28. Thomas Sowell, "Economics and Black People," *Review of Black Political Economy*, Winter/Spring 1971, p. 16.

29. John Neidercorn, "A Neo-Mercantilist Model for Maximizing Ghetto Income," *Review of Black Political Economy*, Winter/Spring 1971, p. 26.

30. Lester Thurow, *Poverty and Discrimination*.

31. John Handy, " 'Poverty and Discrimination,' " *Review of Black Political Economy*, Spring/Summer 1970, pp. 103–9.

32.. Lester Thurow, *Poverty and Discrimination*, p. 44.

33. *Ibid.*, p. 64.

34. *Ibid.*, p. 94.

35. *Ibid.*, p. 110.

36. *Ibid.*, p. 138.

37. *Ibid.*, p. 160.

38. Andrew Brimmer, "Small Business and Economic Development in the Negro Community," in *Black Americans and White Business*, ed. by E.W. Epstein and David R. Hampton (Encino, Calif.: Dickenson Pub. Co., Inc., 1971).

39. Gary S. Becker, *Human Capital* (New York: National Bureau of Economic Research, 1964), p. 120.

40. "The Social and Economic Status of Negroes in the United States," pp. 97–8.

41. Barbara R. Bergman, "Investment in the Human Resources of Negroes," U.S., Congress, Joint Economic Committeee, *Federal Programs for the Development of Human Resources*, Vol. 1, Part 11: *Manpower and Education* (Washington, D.C., 1968), p. 263.

42. Lawrence Cooper, as quoted in *U.S. News and World Report*, Nov. 23, 1970, p. 40.

43. Thomas Sowell, "Economics and Black People," pp. 6–7.

44. W. W. Rostow, *The Stages of Economic Growth* (Cambridge: Cambridge University Press, 1969), p. 26.

45. *Ibid.*

Problems of Economic Growth in the Black Community: Some Alternative Hypotheses

Frank G. Davis

The persistence of black ghetto poverty,[1] high rates of unemployment of black workers even during periods of prosperity,[2] and the general maladjustment of blacks with respect to the resources of the economy have all led to a great deal of social engineering in the black community.[3] While it is recognized that the obvious need of black ghettos consists of jobs and income,[4] no economist to this writer's knowledge has yet presented a systematic and integrated analytical approach to the solution of the problem of ghetto development. To be sure, there has been a great deal of statistical output on the social and economic conditions of Negroes,[5] but the use of this data by economists has followed the conventional wisdom that the poverty of blacks (looked at in terms of black/white income differentials) can be approached in terms of the concept of individual supply and demand analysis for Negro labor,[6] where discrimination is taken to be reflected in both supply and demand forces. In the case of education, for example, quality and/or quantity educational job standards make discrimination a supply phenomenon: blacks and whites are supplied different education (in terms of quality or quantity) at the same price.

In the job market, discrimination is conceived of as a demand phenomenon: two racial groups are demanded at a different price (alternatively, fewer services are demanded from one group than from another at the same price).

This individual supply and demand approach to Negro development places economic analysis in the position of chasing the rainbow of nondiscriminatory markets in a highly complex system of industrial concentration. This raises some fundamental questions of just what analytical tools the economist should use in approaching the phenomenon of poor blacks. Is the phenomenon of poor blacks different from that of poor whites, except for discrimination? If the answer is yes, does the phenomenon of black ghetto poverty come within the purview of economics by way of the theory of individual supply and demand analysis, with all of the attendant assumptions of the pure competitive model, modified only by racial barriers? If so, does not the logic of the racially modified competitive model lead to the view that the black ghetto is merely a residential area, similar to any other residential area, even, say, white suburbia, except that the individual inhabitants of the ghetto happen to be black and also happen to be poor by virtue of the unfortunate circumstances of present racial discrimination? Does the logic of such a competitive model, adjusted for racial factors, constitute a fruitful economic abstraction in analyzing the incidence of poverty among black people and in planning the future course for their economic development? My answer is no. My basic hypothesis is that the economic forces generating black poverty are different from those which generate white poverty;[7] and in this respect black poverty differs from white poverty, racial discrimination in the job market notwithstanding. My plan is:

1. To demonstrate that the approach to the problem of black community development by means of a microeconomic model of supply and demand analysis, within racial constraints, sheds no light on the problem of black community development but leads only to some point of supply and demand equilibrium in the Negro job market, short of full employment and at some wage rates which yield incomes below the poverty level ($3,553 for a family of four).
2. To test a new agenda of hypotheses on the problem of the utilization of black labor in terms of certain exogenous factors which restrict the economic development of the black ghetto economy.
3. To analyze the problem of ghetto development in terms of factors endogenous to the ghetto community as a subeconomy rather than as a residential area.
4. To show the economic implications of our hypotheses with respect to factors which are exogenous as well as endogenous to the ghetto economy, in terms of the nature of a solution to the problem of ghetto development.

I shall now turn to conventional approaches to the problem, which are mainly in terms of the microeconomic model of supply and demand analysis, where discrimination on both the supply and demand site represents the impediment to black community development.

The Demand Phenomenon of Discrimination

In analyzing the demand phenomenon of discrimination, some economists, for example Gwartney,[8] have undertaken to measure discrimination (on the demand side) by adjusting for differences in income in terms of productivity factors, (quantity of education, level of scholastic achievement, regional, age, and city-size distributions). It has been concluded by

Gwartney that while the unadjusted income of nonwhites was only 58.3 percent as great as whites', the income of nonwhite urban males is estimated between 81 and 87 percent of white income after adjustment for the five factors of productivity. An income differential of between 13 and 19 percent remains unexplained. Gwartney attributes this residual difference largely to discrimination.

There are two major difficulties with viewing black/white income differentials in terms of discrimination in the job market, even after adjusting for productivity factors. The first difficulty is methodological; the other is in the assumptions implicit in the black/white income analysis. Methodologically, summary measures such as black/white median income are quite misleading if the attempt is to measure (at least by implication) the relative well-being of blacks compared with whites, if there were no discrimination. Data on black median income as a percentage of white does not really measure changes in ghetto poverty (with or without discrimination), because factors affecting poverty in the black ghetto areas are different from factors which alter the income level of the higher income blacks. For example, inflation leads to more unequal black incomes.[9] That is, there is greater income dispersion.[10] This occurs because the bulk of ghetto residents are low-paid unskilled workers, experiencing high rates of unemployment and receiving limited raises above the legal minimum wage during periods of inflation, as will be shown later. Thus, the impact of factors, such as inflation, have one effect upon the median income of blacks as a whole; they have quite a different effect upon the fixed incomes (legal minimum) of a large mass of unskilled ghetto labor, on the one hand, and the higher income blacks on the other hand.

The assumption underlying the demand phenomenon of market discrimination is that over time the demand for black ghetto labor will be made to shift upward to the right if somehow, through antipoverty and legal measures, job discrimination is eliminated. But this assumption is not applicable to the large mass of unskilled ghetto labor where unemployment rates are high, come boom or depression. For example, unemployment rates of 20 percent[11] among adult Negro men in central city ghettos of six large cities during 1968 and 1969 could hardly be directly attributable to individual employer discrimination. Thus, the poverty results of this inordinate unemployment rate in central city ghettos appear to be only indirectly related to individual employer discrimination, at least on the demand side. This suggests that perhaps a growing number of these unskilled workers are redundant to the requirements for unskilled labor in manufacturing industries where technological changes are occurring. If this is so, the demand for unskilled black labor in high-paying industry will shift downward accumulatively, the shift becoming quite large over time. The result, of course, would be a perpetuation of low wages and poverty in the black ghetto together with a continuous rise in income inequality between lower income ghetto blacks and higher income nonghetto blacks during periods of prosperity. In this case, changes over time in the over-all income differentials between black and white may have little or no effect upon the poverty of unskilled ghetto blacks.

The Supply Phenomenon of Discrimination

With respect to education as a major factor on the supply side, some economists have approached the problem of personal income distribution in terms of the rate of returns on a "varied mixture of human resources."[12] The objective is to determine the rate of return to schooling as an investment in human capital (raw labor). Thomas Johnson has developed a model which will predict life-time earnings.[13] The model is "formulated such that parameters can be estimated simultaneously and hypotheses tested for several types of investment in human capital, as a function of race and region."

If we assume that employer demand for blacks is a function of the relative rates of return on educating and training blacks, compared with whites, we may test the validity of this hypothesis by observing the level of investment in the education and training of blacks where the rate of return on educating and training for blacks is higher than for whites. This hypothesis implies that the employer follows the profit motive and will hire blacks if the supply cost (on-the-job training) is less than for whites.

In testing this hypothesis, my analysis of Thomas Johnson's data and computations reveals the following: (1) At all levels of schooling, net schooling investment for blacks is substantially less than for whites in both the North and the South. (2) At all levels of schooling, total lifetime earnings of whites rise progressively and significantly up through graduate school; the lifetime earnings of blacks reach a peak for those whose schooling is between the ninth and twelfth grade and falls thereafter until a year of graduate work is completed.

For a given unit of supply of raw black labor seeking schooling as an investment, the data show it does not pay (in terms of observed life earnings) for the individual black to go beyond the 9th grade unless he plans to complete college and go to graduate school. Except for the black who goes to graduate school, the total observed income from the end of schooling until retirement (at age 65) is maximized; beginning with schooling at the eighth or ninth grade level it is $155,000 in the North and $101,437 in the South, and these earnings stay within the range of schooling between the ninth and twelfth grades. After the twelfth grade, further investment in education among blacks is accompanied by a fall in total earnings between school and retirement until the graduate level is reached. Since the lifetime earnings of the black worker go down with additional schooling beyond the twelfth grade, the black worker earns his highest rate of return on his investment in education with schooling between the ninth and twelfth grade.

On the basis of the foregoing data, it is observed that, except for graduate work, it pays the black worker both in terms of his total lifetime earnings and the rate of return on his investment in education, to drop out of high school and take low-paying jobs.[14] This implies that the supply schedule for the individual black is infinitely elastic at some low wage rate which maximizes his rate of return on his investment in education. From the employer's side (demand for labor) it is observed that at all levels of schooling from the fifth grade upward the employer pays the individual black substantially less than he pays the individual white. Also, at all levels of schooling, the gross on-the-job investment in blacks is substantially less than gross on-the-job investment for whites. In other words, the employer pays the individual black less than the individual white and invests less in the black's on-the-job training (OJT). This implies that both the employer's schedule of demand for black labor and his schedule of investment in blacks are quite different from those for white labor. The crucial question is: in this separate black labor market, where is the point of equilibrium between the employer's demand schedule for black labor at lower levels of OJT and rates of pay and the black worker's supply schedule in terms of the wage rate which will maximize the rate of return on his education over his working life? As previously mentioned, the supply schedule of the individual black worker is logically infinitely elastic at some wage rate which will maximize his total lifetime earnings and yield the highest rate of return on his schooling investment. We may now observe what the employer is willing to do at the point where the employer's demand schedule is assumed to cut an infinitely elastic labor supply schedule. This is shown in the following table.

TABLE 1

Quantities Derived from Parameter Estimates

Race/ Region	Lower Level Schooling (Grade)	Upper Level Schooling (Grade)	Rate of Returns	Gross O-J-T Investment	Net Positive Investment	Net Positive O-J-T Investment	Total Lifetime Earnings (to age 65)
Nonwhite/	3	9-11	.3187	$28,359	$1,671	$7,322	$138,410
North	8	12	.2841	33,442	-1,392	6,857	155,129
	9-11	12	.3926	24,286	-402	5,158	155,092
	12	13-15	.1747	46,396	-6,406	6,793	146,937
White/	8	9-11	.2456	$68,335	$ 902	$15,316	$220,025
North	8	12	.2146	67,664	-690	14,704	245,433
	9-11	12	.2521	57,951	453	13,235	245,399
	12	13-15	.1752	93,916	-6,598	17,170	278,323

Source: Thomas Johnson, "Returns from Investment in Human Capital," *American Economic Review*, Sept. 1970, p. 558.

It is observed that the quantities in the above table, representing nonwhite/North and white/North,[15] indicate that [at] a schooling level (grades 9-11 to 12) where the rate of return on educating blacks (.3926) is highest, the net positive on-the-job training investment[16] is lowest, and net OJT is negative by $402. And any value above or below -$402 gives a larger negative net OJT investment; and a larger net positive OJT investment.

Beyond this equilibrium point of supply and demand for black labor, which occurs at a low wage rate, the employer prefers investing in white labor whose total lifetime earnings rise for those with some college training (12 to 13-15 years of schooling) while the total lifetime earnings of blacks with some college training fall.

We conclude that the competitive model of individual supply and demand analysis where discrimination is assumed to be reflected on both the supply and demand side does not shed any light on why there are high rates of unemployment among black workers, especially under conditions where the individual, when employed, can maximize the rate of return on his education at low wage levels. The model does help us to see that on the supply side the supply curve of the individual black laborer is probably infinitely elastic at some low wage where the rate of return on his education is maximized when schooling is between ninth and twelfth grades. At this low poverty wage, returns on educating and training the individual black are higher than for individual whites. But this micro-observation does not help us approach the poverty problem, especially when the individual employer finds it most profitable to hire and train the individual black worker just at the point where the worker's rate of return on education is highest. This condition of equilibrium at a low wage suggests that it is profitable to both the individual black worker and the individual employer to perpetuate low wages and poverty. That is, if the black individual worker seeks more education, he will forfeit a part of his lifetime earnings; and if the individual employer hires a black with above-average education, his net positive OJT investment will rise. This net positive OJT will also rise if he hires a white worker with above average education. Apparently, the employer thinks that it is more profitable in the long run to invest in the white worker because there are no racial barriers to his upward mobility in the firm. The competitive model assumes, of course, that the individual employer will not make unprofitable investments even if the law says he must not discriminate in the hiring and training of blacks.

We conclude here that the microeconomic approach to the training and employment of the individual black worker results in a condition of supply-and-demand equilibrium in the Negro job market at wage rates below the poverty level and leaves high rates of unemployment in central city ghettos unaccounted for; except to say that the employer finds it unprofitable in the long run to invest in blacks beyond a point of supply and demand equilibrium at some low wage.

Alternative Hypotheses

Let us now consider some alternative hypotheses with respect to the problem of utilizing a large mass of unemployed, unskilled black labor residing in the ghettos of the central city. Here our approach to black economic development is mainly macro in the sense that we wish to focus upon the functioning of the market system as a whole vis-à-vis the utilization of the labor resources of the black population.

In this connection, we drop the competitive individual supply-and-demand model where discrimination is taken to be reflected in both supply and demand forces, and where the objective of public policy is to track down individual employer discrimination and to seek to educate and train individual blacks to take jobs with apparently nondiscriminatory individual employers. We will take discrimination as given, systemic, and ineradicable in the market system as a whole, and certainly not eradicable on an employer-by-employer basis.

Our point of departure is that the black economic development problem is the central problem of urban development. It is mainly in the urban slums, inhabited mostly by blacks, where poverty and property deterioration are greatest. The rebuilding of the slums is a necessary, but not a sufficient, condition of urban economic development, for urban economic development is entwined with the problem of poverty and the efficient utilization of a growing proportion of black workers in the central city of metropolitan areas where over half of all Negro families live.[17] And urban renewal will not make the problem of poverty and the efficient utilization of Negro labor go away.

Some indication of the magnitude of the problem is shown in Table 2 by the location of all nonwhite families in 1965, and the percent of those below the poverty level in each location.

TABLE 2

Percentage Distribution of Nonwhite Families
and Percentage Below Poverty Level

Area	Percentage Distribution of Nonwhite Families	Percentage in Each Location below the Poverty Level
United States	100	39
Farm	5	68
Nonfarm	95	35
Small town rural area	21	56
Metropolitan areas	74	30
1,000,000 or more	45	25
250,000 to 1,000,000	21	34
Under 250,000	8	41

Source: U.S., Department of Commerce, Bureau of the Census

It will be noted that in the largest metropolitan areas (1,000,000 population or more) where 45 percent of nonwhite families live, a fourth of such families were below the poverty level. This large percentage of poor families suggests that the general nature of the problem of Negro development is to counteract the economic forces outside and within the ghetto—discrimination notwithstanding—which generate poverty by restricting the full and efficient utilization of black labor. Outside the ghetto, the economic forces which impinge upon the ghetto are mainly rapid technological changes under conditions of oligopoly. And within the ghetto these economic forces are generated mainly by the enclave nature of the ghetto's economic structure. I shall analyze in turn these two sets of forces and point to the nature of a solution to the problem of ghetto economic development.

The effects of exogenous forces on ghetto development

My purpose at this point is to show that the outside forces which generate poverty in central city ghettos are mainly rapid technological changes in manufacturing under conditions of oligopolistic pricing. The way in which these outside technological forces generate poverty in central city ghettos may be summarized as follows:

1. An expansion of investment in manufacturing industries depends heavily upon technological changes which lower production costs.
2. Under oligopoly pricing, the price level is rigid (downward) but shows remarkable upward flexibility.
3. Technological changes in manufacturing, together with a condition of oligopolistic price maintenance, reduce the demand in manufacturing for black ghetto labor, which is predominantly unskilled, and the supply of black labor as a whole becomes redundant to high productivity and high-paying manufacturing industries.
4. The redundant supply of unskilled black labor, no longer needed in manufacturing, must compete for jobs in low-productivity employment and low-paying service industries where black workers are already concentrated.
5. Low-paying trade and service industries with fixed labor/capital ratios can expand during periods of prosperity without raising the real wages of unskilled labor substantially above the real-wage equivalent of the legal money wage for unskilled workers.
6. Black workers employed in low-productivity service industries and jobs suffer a loss in real income and employment as the total output of the economy expands. That is, given oligopolistic industries as the center of prosperity in the economy, the expansion of output under conditions of oligopolistic pricing results in the following:

   (a) Demand for unskilled labor in manufacturing is reduced,[18] particularly for ghetto labor, which becomes a special case, because black labor is already over-represented in low productivity service industries with fixed labor/capital ratios where expansion of output can occur without raising real wages for unskilled labor.

   (b) White workers, who are already employed in substantially greater proportions than black workers in high-productivity and higher-paying industries (notwithstanding unionization) can share in the increase in industrial productivity through higher real wages.

(c) Black ghetto labor with fixed wages (the legal minimum) can share in the increased productivity only if industrial prices are reduced in accordance with the increase in industrial productivity. But oligopolistic pricing prevents significant price reduction even under conditions of a recession.

(d) The difference in industrial affiliation between white and black labor, accompanied by basic changes in the industrial composition of the labor force (rise in the proportion of the labor force in service employment), together with oligopolistic pricing, reduces the real income of the black ghetto mass of unskilled labor vis-à-vis the real income of white labor.

(e) If the economy were perfectly competitive in the final product market, workers who are concentrated in low productivity and low-paying industries with limited industrial mobility could share in the increase in productivity of high-productivity and higher-paying industries. Increases in productivity would pass to the consumer in the form of lower prices, thereby raising the real income of all workers.

The tendency of real wages rates among ghetto dwellers as a whole to fall or not to rise far above the real wage equivalent of the minimum legal rate is shown empirically in Table 3. It is noted that although hourly rates in current prices increased from $1.38 in 1959 to $1.55 in 1967 (an increase of 12.3 percent), real hourly rates fell by 0.6 percent. Also, the legal

TABLE 3

Median Gross Weekly and Hourly Earnings of All Ghetto Workers
in Central Cities, 1959–1967

Year	Current Prices			1957–59 Prices*		
	Actual Weekly	Hourly	Legal Minimum† Hourly	Actual Weekly	Hourly	Legal Hourly
1959	54.31	1.38	1.25	53.50	1.34	1.23
1967	61.84	1.55	1.40‡	53.17	1.33	1.20

*   Earnings in current prices divided by the consumer price index.
†   Workers in private employment subject to a minimum wage under the Fair Labor Standards Act.
‡   For workers already covered, the 1966 amendments raised the specified minimum from the previous $1.25 an hour to $1.40, effective Feb. 1, 1967, and $1.60 on Feb. 1, 1968.

Source: Computed from median earnings of Negro workers in Central Cities, in U.S., Department of Commerce, *Trends in Social and Economic Conditions in Metropolitan Areas*, Series P-23, No. 27. (Feb. 7, 1969), p. 47.

hourly rates rose in money terms by 12 percent over the period; but there was a fall of 2.4 percent in the real wage equivalent of the legal money wage. Thus, there was a fall in both the actual hourly real rates of ghetto dwellers and the hourly real wage equivalent of the legal minimum. The difference between the actual hourly real wage and the hourly real-wage equivalent of legal money wage was 11 cents in 1959 and 13 cents in 1967.

The large and growing supply of unskilled black labor in the face of a falling demand for the unskilled in manufacturing will continue to depress the money wage rates of ghetto workers. As employment opportunities for unskilled manual labor in manufacturing shrink, black workers must seek jobs in lower paying, service-producing jobs and industries (trade and service industries).

In short, my argument is that black workers are primarily unskilled and are paid to a great extent the legal minimum wage. In a period of prosperity and rising prices their real income falls, because product prices are rising. In the long run, technological change reduces the demand for unskilled labor in high-productivity manufacturing employment, and thus black workers are faced with declining economic opportunity. If the economy were perfectly competitive, rising productivity would lead to falling product prices rather than rising wages for the skilled and organized.

This argument implies the following supporting hypotheses:

1. That the real income of black workers in central city ghettos has fallen as a result of the failure of product prices to fall as productivity rises.

2. That real wages of unskilled black workers fall during business expansion.

3. That technological change in manufacturing has reduced the demand for unskilled black workers in manufacturing.

The effects of oligopolistic pricing upon the real income of black ghetto workers in low-productivity employment is shown in Table 4.

In terms of price level changes over the eight year period 1959–67 the median ghetto workers income should have risen by 15 percent to maintain the same real income, but the ghetto workers real income fell by 0.6 percent. However, productivity in manufacturing rose over the period (1957–59=100 percent) from 103.7 percent in 1959 to 133.5 percent, a net rise of 29.8 percent. If the economy were perfectly competitive, the rise in productivity of 30 percent over the period would have led to a fall in product prices instead of a rise in real wage of the skilled and organized by 13.6 percent.

Now, if industrial prices over the period had been cut, say 24 percent, in terms of the rise in productivity by 30 percent, the real income of all workers could have risen by 30 percent by way of price reductions. In the case of ghetto earners, a 30 percent rise in real wages by price reductions would have meant an increase in the median real wage of ghetto workers from $2,782 in 1959 to $3,616.60 in 1967; instead it fell to $2,765, a real loss of $834.60 in ghetto worker median income between 1959 and 1967 due to the absence of a perfectly competitive economy.

TABLE 4

Index of Change in Productivity in Manufacturing and in Real Wages
of All Workers in Manufacturing and of Black Workers in Central City,
with Percentage Change in Real Wages 1959–1967

Year	Output per Manhour in Manufacturing* (index) 1957–59=100% (In Percentage)	All Workers in Manufacturing (Weekly)	Black Workers in Central City Ghettos‡ (Weekly)	Percentage Change 1959–67 All Workers in Manufac.	Black Ghetto Workers
		Real Wages† in 1957–59 Prices			
1959	103.7	$86.96	$53.50		
1967	133.5	98.80	53.17	113.6	99.4

* Establishment basis.
† Earnings in current prices divided by consumer price index.
‡ Includes median earnings of non-farm laborers and all service workers.

Source: *Economic Report of the President*, Feb. 1968, pp. 247 and 248; and U.S., Department of Commerce, Current Population Reports, Special Studies, Series P-23, No. 27 (Feb. 7, 1969), pp. 47 and 48.

But since the economy is oligopolistic, prices do rise, notwithstanding rises in productivity. Thus, the median ghetto worker between 1959 and 1967 lost $17.00 in real income over the period due to price-level changes and $834.60 in terms of the failure of industrial prices to fall proportionately to the rise in industrial productivity. The total lost was $851.60.

7. The operation of economic forces within the economy is such that the black ghettos become worse off as total output expands; and the crucial political issue of the black community is *one of group survival in a sea of economic forces with strong ruling currents of racism.* This is evident in Table 5 where it is shown industrial output rose by 51.8 percent between 1959 and 1967, and the real income of ghetto workers fell by 0.6 percent over the period.

TABLE 5

Comparison of Changes in Industrial Output with Changes
in Real Wages of Ghetto Workers, 1959–1967

Year	Index of Industrial Production 1957–1959=100%	Percentage Change in Ghetto Worker Real Wages, 1959–1967 in 1957–1959 Prices
1959	106.0	100.0
1967	157.8	99.4

Source: Board of Governors of Federal Reserve System, Industrial Production, 1957–59 Base, and *Federal Reserve Bulletin;* and U.S., Department of Commerce, *Trends in Social and Economic Conditions of Negroes,* Series P-23, No. 27, Feb. 7, 1969.

8. The economic problem of low productivity jobs and industries where ghetto labor is over-represented is beyond the reach of monetary and fiscal policies, whether under conditions of prosperity or recession. Under both sets of conditions, the black ghettos will show high rates of unemployment and low wages. In these low-productivity jobs, a high proportion of black workers employed therein earned less than $3,000 in 1966. This is shown in Table 6.

TABLE 6

Year Round, Full-Time Employed Men Who Earned below $3,000,
by Color, for Selected Industries, 1966 (in Thousands)

Industry	Number of White Low Earners	As Percentage of All Whites Employed	Number of Nonwhite Low Earners	As Percentage of All Nonwhites Employed
Manufacturing	348	3	160	16
Service-producing Industries:				
Trade	300	7	160	36
Service industries	322	7	147	25

Source: U.S., *Manpower Report of the President,* Apr. 1968, p. 33.

It is observed from Table 6 that in trade and service industries 36 percent and 25 percent, respectively, of black men were employed at a wage below $3,000, compared with 16 percent in manufacturing.

TABLE 7

Percentage Distribution of Employment of Nonwhite Workers, and Index
of Change in Employment by Broad Occupation Groups, 1954–65

Year	Agriculture		Blue Collar		White Collar		Service	
	Percentage	Index 1954 = 100%	Percentage	Index 1954 = 100%	Percentage	Index 1954 = 100%	Percentage	Index 1954 = 100%
1954	15.5	100	41.8	100	11.8	100	30.8	100
1955	14.5	93.5	42.0	100.4	12.0	101.6	31.6	102.5
1956	14.5	93.5	41.7	99.7	11.5	97.4	32.2	104.5
1957	13.8	89.0	41.4	99.0	12.8	108.4	32.0	103.8
1958	12.7	81.9	40.5	96.8	13.7	116.1	33.1	107.4
1959	12.9	83.2	40.9	97.8	14.7	124.5	31.9	103.5
1960	12.4	80.0	39.8	95.2	16.0	135.5	31.8	103.2
1961	11.7	75.4	39.1	93.5	16.4	138.9	33.2	107.7
1962	11.0	70.9	39.5	94.4	16.7	141.5	32.8	106.4
1963	9.7	62.5	39.8	95.2	17.7	150.0	32.8	106.4
1964	8.7	56.1	40.3	96.4	18.7	158.4	32.2	104.5
1965	8.1	52.2	40.7	97.3	19.5	165.2	31.7	102.9

Source: U.S., Department of Labor, *The Negroes in the United States, Their Economic and Social Situations,* Bulletin No. 1511.

The impact of economic forces upon the industrial affiliation of black workers in high-paying and high productivity blue collar employment is shown in Table 7.

It will be observed that while the downward trend in the proportion of black workers in agriculture has been most dramatic between 1954 and 1965, there has been also a steady, though less dramatic, downward trend in the proportion of all black workers in blue-collar employment. And along with this trend, we observe in these blue-collar jobs that blacks are heavily concentrated in the lowest-paid categories.[19]

The relatively smaller decline, between 1954 and 1965, in the proportion of all black workers in blue-collar production work, along with their continuous concentration in the lowest-paid categories of a blue-collar employment, has a much greater economic significance than appears on the surface. It means a *reversal* of a possible shift of unskilled black labor from lower-paid service and blue-collar employment, where black workers in general are over-represented, to higher-buying industrial jobs where black workers are under-represented. But the trend of employment of black workers is toward further concentration in industries with the highest proportions of low-wage black workers. This is shown in Table 8 where it is observed that between 1960 and 1969, Negroes employed in service-producing industries rose to a third of their total employment while those employed as semi-skilled rose to roughly a fourth. And those employed as skilled (craftsmen) increased from 7.4 percent to 8.4 percent, representing a 1 percent increase over a nine-year period.

TABLE 8

Changes in the Proportion of Total Negroes Employed, by Selected Occupations, 1960–1969

Segment of Work Force	1960	1969
Total Employed Negroes[1]	6,927	8,369
Number in service-producing industry	1,918	2,766
Percent of total employed	27.7	33.0
Number employed as semi-skilled[2]	1,414	1,998
Percent of total employed	20.4	23.9
Number employed as skilled	515	704
Percent of total employed	7.4	8.4

[1] Includes other nonwhite races.
[2] Operatives.

Source: U.S., Department of Labor, *The Social and Economic Status of Negroes in U.S.*, 1969, p. 41.

The nature and scope of the imbalance in the industrial affiliations of black workers, which is now being affected adversely by technological trends, is shown in Table 9.

TABLE 9

Percentage Distribution of Nonwhite Male Employment
by Industry and Index of Industrial Affiliation, 1964

Industry	Percentage of Total Male Work Force	Index of Industrial Affiliation of National Nonwhite Index = 100%
Construction	10.7	111.45
Manufacturing	7.8	82.97
Furniture and fixtures	7.5	79.78
Stone-clay glass products	9.6	100.00
Fabricated metal products	7.1	73.95
Electrical machinery	4.8	50.00
Transportation equipment	8.8	91.66
Miscellaneous manufacturing	6.2	64.58
Food and kindred products	10.6	110.41
Textile mill products	6.8	70.83
Apparel	8.3	86.45
Printing & publishing ind.	4.7	48.95
Chemical and allied products	7.1	73.95
Other nondurable goods	6.5	67.70
Trans. and public utilities	10.1	105.20
Trade	9.1	94.79
Finance, ins., and real estate	5.8	60.41
Business and repair services	9.4	97.91
Personal services	19.4	201.04
Entertainment and recreation	13.0	135.41
Professional services	10.4	108.33
Hospital	22.9	238.54
Public administration	10.3	107.29

Source: U.S., Department of Labor, *The Negro in the U.S.*, Bulletin No. 1151.

It is observed, for example, than in 1964, the male nonwhite percentage of total male was 22.9 in hospital work as compared with only 4.8 percent in electrical machinery; 19.4 percent in personal service as compared with 7.8 percent in manufacturing.

The reversal of the possibility of the movement of unskilled black labor into higher-paying production work in manufacturing is, of course, a reflection of a general change in the industrial distribution of civilian employment. This is shown in Figure 1 which indicates a relative decline in blue-collar production workers since 1920, as shown by the dotted line.

The special problem of black workers is that the change in the occupational structure of labor is shifting in the direction of service-producing industries, including those lower-paying service-producing jobs where unskilled black workers are already concentrated. The extent of this concentration by occupation is shown in Table 10, which indicates that the proportion of black nonfarm laborers and service workers is almost

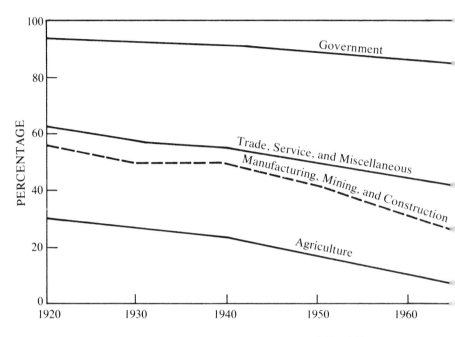

Fig. 1. Industrial distribution of civilian employment, 1920–1966.

Source: U.S., Department of Labor taken from Samuelson, *Economics,* (New York: McGraw-Hill, 1967), p. 137.

three and one-half times the proportion of whites; while the proportion of black craftsmen and foremen is only three-fifths the proportion of white in this higher-paying occupation.

The existence of an almost 4:1 ratio of nonfarm black laborers to white, as shown in Table 10, is occurring at a time when the supply of unskilled black labor is likely to increase rather than diminish. That is, by

TABLE 10

Occupational Distribution of Year-round, Full-time Employed Men, by Color

Occupation	Percentage of White Workers	Distribution Nonwhite Workers	Index White = 100%
Total Employed	100.0	100.0	100.0
Service workers	5.4	17.1	316.7
Nonfarm laborers	3.8	14.8	389.5
Total	9.2	31.9	346.7
Craftsmen and foremen	21.5	12.9	60.0
All others	70.3	44.8	63.7

Source: U.S., *Manpower Report of the President,* Apr. 1968, p. 32.

1975 nonwhites in the labor force will have increased much faster than whites. This increase will occur in workers between the age of 16 and 24 years; and this nonwhite age group, where unemployment rates among blacks are highest, will account for more than one-fourth of the total nonwhite labor force, as compared with about one-fifth of the total a decade earlier. Thus, by 1975 we may expect a high increase in the proportion of unskilled and inexperienced nonwhite workers, while the most experienced nonwhites (age 25–44 years) will represent a smaller proportion in the labor force in 1975 as compared with 1965.[20]

The fall in demand for unskilled labor in manufacturing

Between 1950 and 1960, as previously mentioned, the number of men's laboring jobs in manufacturing fell 20 percent.[21] The fall in demand in manufacturing industries for the growing supply of unskilled black labor since 1960 is shown in Table 11, which indicates that between 1960 and 1968, productivity increased 33.7 percent, (1957–59 = 100%), thereby causing a fall in the proportion of total employment in manufacturing. The nonfarm labor percentage of total employment (1960 = 100%) is projected to drop to 67.2 by 1975, while the number of Negroes employed as laborers shows a projected drop of roughly 97,000, or 10 percent by 1975.

TABLE 11

Changes in Manhour Productivity; Proportion of Manufacturing Employment; Nonfarm Labor Proportion of Total Employment; and Changes in Employment of Nonfarm Negro Labor, 1960–1975

	Actual			Projected	
Item	1960	1965	1968	1970	1975
Index of Total Private Output per Manhour (Labor Force Basis) 1957–59 = 100%	104.5	125.0	138.2		
Percent manufacturing employment of total	31.0	29.7			25.9
Percent change (1960 = 100)	100.0	95.8			83.5
Percent nonfarm labor of total employment	5.5	5.3		3.7	3.7
Percent change (1960 = 100)	100.0	96.3		67.2	67.2
Number of Negroes employed as nonfarm laborers	951,000		876,000*	868,000	860,000
Percent change (1960 = 100)	100.0		92.1	91.3	90.4

*Figure is for 1969

Source: *Economic Report of the President*, Jan. 1969, p. 266; *Manpower Report of the President*, Apr. 1967, p. 274; and Apr. 1968, p. 304. U.S., Department of Labor, *The Social and Economic Conditions of Negroes in the U.S., 1969*, p. 41.

This drop in demand for unskilled black labor in manufacturing is reflected in the inordinate rates of unemployment in the black labor force of central city ghettos. This is shown in Table 12. It is noted that for six cities combined, at any time during the year (July 1968–June 1969) unemployed adult Negro men represented 20 percent of the black ghetto labor force and Negro teenagers represented 49 percent.

TABLE 12

Percentage of Unemployment of Negro Men, Women, and Teenagers
Central City Ghettos of Six Large Cities* Combined, July 1968–June 1969

Black Ghetto Labor Force	Unemployed at Any Time during the Year†
Adult Negro men	20%
Adult Negro women	17%
Negro teenagers	49%

* Atlanta, Chicago, Detroit, Houston, Los Angeles, and New York City.
† Unemployment was not confined strictly to the time period of July 1968–June 1969. Depending on the actual week of interview "any time during the year" could extend as far back as late 1967.

Source: U.S., Dept. of Labor, Bureau of Labor Statistics, Report No. 375, Current Population reports, series P-23, No. 29, p. 93.

We have observed that, given a large mass of predominantly unskilled black workers in central city ghettos, heavily unemployed and heavily concentrated in low-productivity service producing jobs and industries, the effect of prosperity and rising prices is to reduce their real income, because product prices are rising. The long-run effect of technological change in manufacturing is to reduce their economic opportunity, because technological change in manufacturing reduces the demand for unskilled labor in high-productivity and high-paying manufacturing employment. And the effect of rising productivity would lead to falling product prices, rather than rising wages for the skilled and organized, if the economy were perfectly competitive rather than oligopolistic. So, given black labor as predominantly unskilled, we conclude that a major factor in central city ghetto poverty is the unique way in which economic forces (technological and oligopolistic) restrict the rise in real income of the black ghetto community as a whole. This suggests that the approach to ghetto economic development must be in terms of macroeconomic analysis, with attention focused on the ghetto community as an economic aggregate representing a phenomenon apart from the rest of the economy. That is, from the standpoint of economic analysis, we cannot profitably view the black ghetto community as simply a residential area having a spatial dimension, where poverty is viewed in individualistic terms and where welfare measures and policies concerning poverty are tied to this microeconomic view. Such a view not only omits the unique effects of exogenous forces upon continued ghetto poverty but also fails to consider how forces endogenous to the economic structure of the ghetto economy generate a permanent condition of poverty.

We will now consider the problem of ghetto development in terms of the effects of endogenous factors upon ghetto poverty. Our frame of reference is the present flow of ghetto resources where we observe that the economic structure of the ghetto is a result of the allocational processes of the ghetto market mechanism, albeit market forces are constrained by racial factors. That is, in both consumer and producer markets of the ghetto, economic choices with respect to the mobility and utilization of ghetto resources are limited by economic as well as racial factors. I am assuming, for example, that Negro population density in a well-defined spatial area with poor-quality housing and low incomes are concomitant variables, reflecting economic as well as racial factors. In this connection, I will consider first the effects of the land/population ratio in the ghetto and, second, the effects of the enclave sector of the ghetto economy.

Effects of the land/population ratio

The absence of economic and social mobility on the part of black ghetto residents makes the ghetto community a unique case of high economic and social cost relative to the rest of the economy. This is shown in the very nature of the economic and demographic structure of the black community. As a result of technological forces in southern agricultural regions where Negroes have formerly lived, the trend has been toward increasing concentration of Negroes in more or less all-black areas situated in the heart of the largest metropolitan areas.

The trend of this concentration of population toward the largest metropolitan area, as shown by Figure 2, has increased the ratio of population to land in the urban ghetto,[22] along with a rise in the proportion below the poverty level.

In other words, the very movement of the black migrants to the most heavily populated areas, under conditions of housing and economic discrimination, has: (1) created a problem of land scarcity in urban ghettos; and (2) raised ghetto land values relative to the productivity of the labor and capital employed there.[23] That is, the population pressure has caused the land values to rise disproportionately to the rise, if any, in the productivity of the unskilled labor and obsolete capital with which the land is combined.

The rise in land values is caused by the relatively high rent for slum dwelling units whose rents remain up while the quality of the housing deteriorates. Thus, the effect of the rise in ghetto population pressure on a restricted land area is to raise the economic rent, which, of course, is reflected in the high institutional rents, thereby reflecting higher land values—that is, site values, not the value of the often or more frequently found dilapidated buildings and tenements for which ghetto residents pay dearly. We, therefore, have the phenomenon of poor people and poor business resources[24] being combined with high-cost land, where the cost of living on the land (economic rent) gives a larger share of ghetto output to the landlord. That is, the decrease in the land/population ratio causes

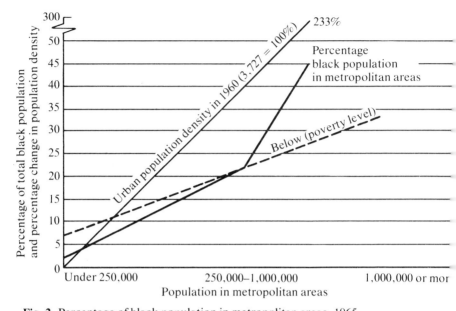

Fig. 2. Percentage of black population in metropolitan areas, 1965.

Source: BLS Report No. 332, Current Population Reports Series P-23, No. 24. 1960 Population, U.S. Census, Vol. I, p. xiii.

economic rent to rise relative to the returns to labor and capital. Institutional rents then also rise, even with rent ceilings, the rise occuring when the landlord neglects the costs of maintenance and upkeep and continues to receive constant or fixed rental rates. Consumers are, then, paying the same price (rent) for less and less housing service—an example of the poor paying more for housing. And in the case of the black ghetto the poor are locked into this situation by both economic and racial factors. Economic and racial factors are involved in the sense that being poor and black, one is forced to live in the black ghetto where more is paid for housing; and when more is paid for housing in the ghetto, both the quantity and quality of housing remains restricted. This results in a further rise in housing costs and economic rent as the black population expands.

If we view the site value of ghetto land in terms of its relatively high economic rent, we must at the same time view the actual and potential productivity of labor on this land. The most abundant productive factor of the ghetto is unskilled black labor, which is combined with high cost land by the inhabitants, as laborers as well as residents. In terms of the present industry mix of the ghetto, consisting primarily of mercantile business operations requiring a small and fixed amount of labor per business unit, the growth of the ghetto population reduces the marginal value of productivity of labor employed in the ghetto. So that, as time goes on, wage rates in the ghetto will remain low while ghetto employers will find it unprofitable to put ghetto labor to work even at low wage rates.

The rise in ghetto economic rent due to population pressure means that the price of land per unit of capital in the ghetto rises relative to the land cost per unit of capital in less densely populated metropolitan areas. That is, for the individual entrepreneur, the rise in economic rent reduces the marginal-value productivity of land relative to its prices; and the

$$\frac{\text{marginal-value productivity of land}}{\text{price of land}}$$

is less in the ghetto than in the outlying suburbs.

The effects of differentials in returns to labor and capital because of differences in the land cost per unit of capital in ghetto and suburban areas is shown in Figure 3.

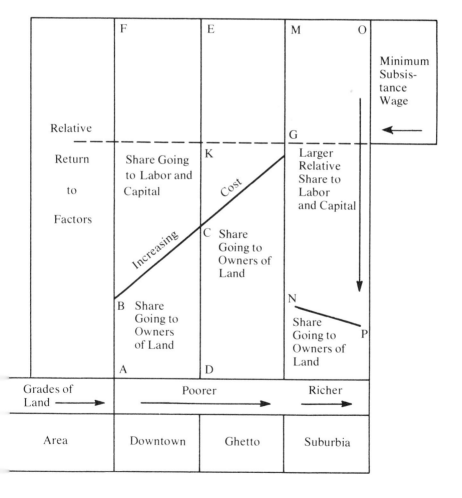

Fig. 3. Relative factor share by area, downtown, ghetto, and suburbia.

Increasing the ratio of population (labor) to land in the ghetto has caused the marginal-value productivity of land per dollar of capital to fall. If the marginal-value productivity of land per dollar of capital falls, the land cost per unit of capital rises; and, assuming no change in technology, a larger share of the community's product goes to the landlord; and, of course, a smaller share goes to labor and capital. This is shown in Figure 3, where the area DCGN shows that when recourse is taken by the ghetto population (labor) to higher-cost land per unit of capital (defined as poorer-grade land), diminishing returns to both labor and capital occur. Therefore, the ghetto area under its existing technology becomes a high-cost subsistence area. Returns to labor and capital fall from EC in downtown to as low as MG in the ghetto. At this level, if labor is to be paid its subsistence wage, the return to capital shrinks to zero in the ghetto.

Under the circumstances, assuming no change in ghetto technology, the capitalist seeks a larger return per unit of capital by moving to suburban areas where the land cost per unit of capital is cheaper. This is shown in the chart by area MNPO where a larger relative share of the output goes to labor and capital compared with the smaller share of the product going to the landlord. The same basic force also operates for the relocation of existing industry outside central cities, as well as the location of new industry outside central cities. As can be seen from the diagram, return on the marginal unit of land of EC in the downtown area leaves a margin of KC in excess of subsistence wage, in contrast to a zero surplus over subsistence in the ghetto. Thus, the black ghetto is left with declining or negative capital investment, increasing cost of production, decreasing return to labor and capital, and a growing supply of underemployed black labor because of a shift of industries both from the ghetto and the central cities.

Effects of the enclave sector of the ghetto economy

My recent study of the present flow of ghetto resources indicates that the production pattern (industry mix) of the ghetto economy is generated by the enclave sector of the ghetto economy, which owns and controls the bulk of private capital resources employed in the ghetto. This is shown in Table 13, which indicates the proportion of the produced income out of aggregate ghetto purchases going to the black-owned domestic sector.

Table 13 shows that only 1.8 percent of $215.7 million in gross sales in Newark ghetto[25] goes to the black-owned sector, while 25.6 percent of gross sales goes to the white-owned enclave sector; and 71.3 percent represents returns to productive factors employed outside the ghetto economy.

Figure 4 shows the same data in terms of the end results of the enclave structure of resource allocation when going from the concept of

TABLE 13

Yearly Average of Aggregate Ghetto Sales Receipts, by Factor Payments
and Other Costs, Newark Ghetto, 1965–67

Item	Amount (in Dollars)	Percentage
Gross sales	$215,749,915	100.0
Depreciation	3,055,140	1.3
Factor payments to enclave sector	55,828,000	25.6
Factor payments to black sector	3,867,500	1.8
Other costs and expenses	153,999,275	71.3

gross sales to income allocation among the factors of production within the ghetto economy. First, it is noted that gross investment represents 1.3 percent of gross sales, which is enough to cover depreciation but possibly insufficient for significant net positive investment.

Secondly, it is observed from Figure 4 that out of the total value added in the ghetto economy, after depreciation, 25.6 percent goes to the white enclave sector. And, as already indicated, 71.3 percent of total factor returns go to business purchases, representing the returns to the factors of production employed in the rest of the economy. This indicates that, in terms of factor payments and returns, the returns to the enclave sector factors and to factors of production employed in the rest of the economy supplying goods to the ghetto economy reduce the black-owned domestic sector to a marginal position in the ghetto economy. That is, the present ghetto system of market organization provides the present black-owned sector with only marginal opportunities with respect to capitalizing upon the aggregate flow of ghetto economy business payments and factor returns.

Implications of a macroview
of black ghetto development problems

Our macroview of the problems endogenous to the ghetto community leads us to observe an economic distinction between black and white communities. We have observed that the economic structure of the black ghetto consists of a high-cost residential-commercial operation. We can, therefore, make an economic distinction between the black ghetto community and non-ghetto white communities where residential and commercial operations are spatially or economically separated. Zoning laws, which provide for this separation, are based upon the principle of efficiency in land use. High-cost commercial land is efficiently combined with high-productivity capital; instead of being combined with low-productivity capital in the form of uneconomic business units or in the

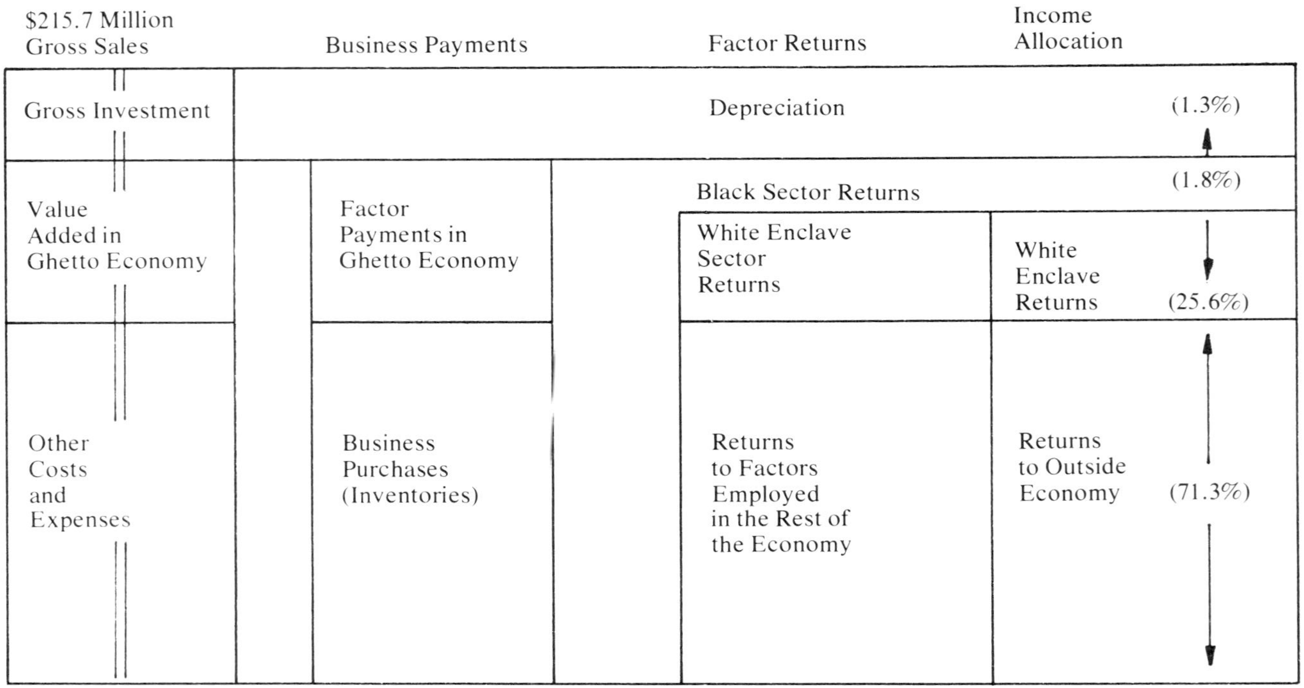

Fig. 4. The relationship between the yearly average of aggregate sales, business payments, and factor returns, Newark Ghetto, 1965–1967.

form of deteriorating dwelling units. To combine an efficient factor of production with an inefficient factor of production raises the opportunity cost to the producer and the social cost to the community. Since the existing form of residential-commercial operations of the ghetto represents an inefficient combination of land and capital (the combination of uneconomic business units and poor housing units with high-cost land), we may say that a the black community has a higher economic and social cost in the employment of resources than the rest of the economy.

If we define an economy as consisting of the economic processes of production, consumption, and distribution, we can say that a sub-economy, such as the black economy, may develop within the geographic confines of a larger economy to the extent that economic processes in the larger economy generate significant economic and social differentials which represent the factorial conditions of economic separateness between the black and white communities. That is, significant differentials between these two communities may occur in the production function, the levels of employment and income, the industry mix, the consumption function, and the entire pattern and level of consumption, where all differentials in these economic processes are occurring within a well-defined sector of the larger economy. For wherever these differentials in economic processes exist there will inevitably follow differentials in economic and opportunity costs between the designated sub-economy and the rest of the economy. And these differentials may be taken as criteria of the separateness between the general U.S. economy and the sub-economy of the black ghetto.

The rise of cost differences between the black economy and the rest of the economy are illustrative of Gunnar Myrdal's "backwash effect," where, in this case, the growing capital-intensive white community has exerted a "strong, agglomerative pull, accelerating their rate of growth, and bringing increasing stagnation" to the labor-intensive ghetto economy. In this respect, we may say that this conditon of economic stagnation and decay in the black ghettos of America is not self-correcting within the price system. Rather, the pull of economic forces sets up a permanent condition of inequality between a low-income labor-intensive black economy and the rest of the economy. For example, incomes may rise in the white community as national output expands while at the same time, as we have shown, the real income of the black ghetto may fall. Also, there are substantial differentials in the rates of unemployment between the black ghetto community and the rest of the economy for any given level of national output.

In short, the movement of capital and the allocation of resources in the price system vis-à-vis the black ghetto economy and the rest of the economy constitute a difference to a degree of such extremity as to represent a real difference in the kind of capital employed, the kind of production organization, the kind of employment, the kind of income received in the community, the kind of prices paid[26] for goods and services, and the kind of consumption and the nature of consumer demand.[27]

And since the ghetto community has only low-paid labor to sell, the ghetto community has no way, under its present structure, of acquiring ownership of capital resources as a means of raising its income.

Conclusion

Our hypotheses on the development problem of the black economy, lead to the following conclusions:

1. *The problem* of the development of the black economy is the problem of restructuring (change in the system of resource organization and control) a system of market organization of economic processes which is delineated from the rest of the economy on the demand side for consumer goods by spatial, cultural, and economic factors but functions on the supply side, within the general economy, as a labor-intensive, one-sector export economy with nothing to sell to the rest of the economy but low-priced unskilled labor. Unskilled labor is traded for goods from the capital-intensive sector of the rest of the economy under conditions where: (1) prices of imports to the ghetto economy from the rest of the economy are fixed and rigid (downward); (2) prices of ghetto labor (wages) are fixed and rigid (upward); and (3) where the effects of technological change in the manufacturing industries of the capital-intensive sector is to reduce over time the economic opportunity for high-paid, unskilled labor exports from the labor-intensive ghetto sector. The combination of the foregoing conditions results in deteriorating terms of trade (falling real income) between the black ghetto economy and the rest of the economy, together with high rates of unemployment of unskilled black labor, the demand for which in high-paying manufacturing industries becomes increasingly income-inelastic relative to the growth rate of the national income.

2. *The economics* of development of the black economy, is the economics of the conditions of growth and development of a labor-intensive economy (the black ghetto) functioning as an enclave sector of a capital-intensive economy (white community) characterized by oligopoly and rapid changes in the production function; where rapid changes in the production function generate downward shifts in demand for high-paid, unskilled labor from the labor-intensive black economy under oligopolistic conditions of rigid (downward) changes in prices.

3. The development of the appropriate economic strategy must deal with this tendency toward a fall in real-wage income of ghetto dwellers, as a whole, as the national income rises. The basic questions to be answered in this connection are: What is the possibility of a more productive role (rise in black worker productivity and employment) for the black ghetto community as a whole in the economic system? If there is a more productive role for the black ghetto community, what is this role? What is likely to be the optimum productivity (black community income divided by total manhours worked) of these workers? What is likely to be the optimum

growth rate in their per capita real income (growth rate in the black community's aggregate income divided by growth rate in black population)? How can the black community be restructured (change in the industry mix and resource control) so as to counteract to some extent the effects of its low rate of productivity and limited income class mobility as national income rises? How can even the low rate of income class mobility among ghetto workers employed outside the ghetto be made to generate capital growth within the ghetto? If a rise in the aggregate wage bill paid to ghetto residents employed outside the ghetto economy (through employment of unemployed ghetto residents or movement of some ghetto residents to higher-paying jobs) can be made to generate capital growth within the ghetto, what is likely to be the capital/output ratio (dollar amount of output per dollar of capital investment) within the ghetto economy? How much of the total output will go to ghetto labor? All of these questions ultimately boil down to one basic question: What is the optimum economic relationship between the ghetto economy and the rest of the economy?

That is, as the national income rises, and assuming the continued existence of a rising proportion of black people in central cities,[28] what would be the maximized share of the national income going to black-community residents (ghetto households) in the form of factor payments (wages and salaries, dividends, rent, and profits) based upon the earnings of ghetto production factors employed inside the ghetto economy and outside the ghetto economy? In order to achieve this optimum condition of income flow between the black and white communities, what would be the economics of restructuring the ghetto economy so as to optimize the distribution of a rising national income among ghetto residents?

The answers[29] to the foregoing questions, constitute the crux of the solution to the problem of the economic development of black people.

NOTES

1. Some recent estimates show that nonwhites enter poverty at more than twice the rate at which whites enter and that the probability of a nonwhite family's escaping poverty is about three-fourths that of a white family. In general, almost twice as many families remain poor as become nonpoor. See President's Commission on Income Maintenance Programs, *Technical Studies*, p. 24 and 26.

2. Between 1965 and 1966, when real private gross national product rose 5.6 percent and employment in the private economy rose 3.0 percent, the ratio of the nonwhite unemployment rate to white unemployment rate actually *rose*. In 1966, the ratio was at its highest point since 1962, indicating that nonwhites entered poverty at a higher rate than whites and escaped at a slower rate. See President's Commission on Income Maintenance Programs, *Technical Studies*, p. 10.

3. A series of economic nostrums to help individual black workers under the cover of OEO, other palliatives such as "black capitalism," and more recently the proposed Income Maintenance Program.

4. Charles C. Killingsworth, *Jobs and Income for Negroes*, Policy Papers in Human Resources and Industrial Relations, No. 6. (Ann Arbor, Mich.: Institute of Labor and Industrial Relations, May 1968).

5. For more recent and comprehensive data, see President's Commission on Income Maintenance Programs, *Technical Studies*, and Background Papers by the Commission.

6. Terrence F. Kelly, "Factors Affecting Poverty: A Gross Flow Analysis," in the President's Commission on Income Maintenance Programs, *Technical Studies*, p. 32.

7. Alan Batchelder, "Poverty: The Special Case of the Negro," *American Economic Review*, Papers and Proceedings May 1965, p. 530. In this paper Batchelder identified five economic considerations which distinguish Negro from white poverty.

8. James Gwartney, "Discrimination and Income Differentials," *American Economic Review*, June 1970, p. 396.

9. Lester C. Thurow, "Analyzing the American Income Distribution," *American Economic Review*, Papers and Proceedings May 1970, p. 262.

10. *Ibid.* Thurow reports that the income distribution for blacks is much more dispersed than it is for whites. The Gini Coefficient for blacks is substantially higher than it is for whites.

11. In six large cities (Atlanta, Georgia, Chicago, Illinois, Detroit, Michigan, Houston, Texas, Los Angeles, California, and New York City) at any time during the year, July 1968 to June 1969. See U.S., Dept. of Labor, Bureau of Labor Statistics, Report No. 375, *Current Population Reports*, series P-23, No. 29, p. 93.

12. Becker and others. Gary Becker, *The Politics of Discrimination* (Chicago, Ill.: University of Chicago Press, 1957).

13. Thomas Johnson, "Returns from Investment in Human Capital," *American Economic Review*, Sept. 1970, p. 546.

14. Jobs which pay below the poverty level. Lifetime earnings of $155,000, starting at age 16 and ending at age 65, would yield average annual earnings below the poverty level.

15. Quantities for nonwhite and white South differ mostly in the order of magnitude of quantities (lower) but show generally the same relationship between nonwhite and white.

16. Net positive OJT investment is defined as the integral of net OJT investment from the end of schooling to the time at which net investment is zero.

17. Fifty-four percent in 1968. The number of Negroes in central cities rose from 9.5 million in 1960 to 11.9 million in 1968.

18. Alan Batchelder, "Poverty: The Special Case of the Negro," points out that between 1950 and 1960 men's laboring jobs in manufacturing fell 20 percent (by 200,000).

19. An analysis of official reports filed by employers covered under Title VII of the 1964 Civil Rights Act, which bans discrimination in employment, shows that "Negroes generally are heavily concentrated in the lowest paying blue collar jobs." *Nine City Minority Group Employment Profile*, Research Report 1967—19—A, Aug. 6, 1967, p. 21.

20. U.S., President, *Manpower Report of the President*, Washington, D.C., Apr. 1968.

21. U.S., Census of Population, 1960, Detailed Characteristics, U.S. Summary (Washington, D.C., 1963).

22. In 1960 the population density in three central cities in the northern New Jersey-New York, urbanized area was 24,537. In general the density of central cities was more than double that of the urban fringe area: 7,788 as against 3,200.

23. Between 1956 and 1966, the average annual increase in land prices was estimated between 5.0 to 6.0 percent. Residential and multifamily land increases most rapidly. See Grace Milgram, *U.S. Land Prices–Directions and Dynamics* (Washington, D.C.: U.S. Government Printing Office, 1968), p. 38.

24. For example, the Office of Economic Development, City of Newark, New Jersey points out that downtown Newark, "a highly commercial area, is surrounded by a ring of marginal business establishments and some industry and residential areas which are obsolete." City of Newark, Office of Economic Development, *Economic Blueprint for Newark*, July 1968.

25. An area covering 303 blocks with a population 95 percent black. Data collected by the writer under a grant from the Economic Policy Council of New Jersey.

26. David Caplovitz, *The Poor Pay More* (New York: Free Press, 1967).

27. The author's forthcoming book, *The Economics of Black Community Development*, chapter 3, "The Ghetto Market System and Economic Structure," (Chicago, Ill.: Markham Publishing Co.). [Published 1972—eds.]

28. Between 1960 and 1968, the proportion of Negroes residing in central cities increased from 52 percent to 54 percent, whereas the proportion of whites within central cities dropped from 30 percent to 26 percent. The Negro percentage of the population in central cities rose from 9.5 percent in 1960 to 11.9 percent in 1968, an increase of 25 percent. U.S. Department of Commerce, Series P-23, No. 27, Feb. 7, 1969.

29. See Frank G. Davis, *The Economics of Black Community Development*.

REFERENCES

President's Commission on Income Maintenance Programs, *Technical Studies*, also Background Papers by the Commission (Washington, D.C.: U.S. Government Printing Office, 1970).

Killingsworth, Charles C., *Jobs and Income for Negroes*, Policy Papers in Human Resources and Industrial Relations, No. 6 (Ann Arbor, Mich.: Institute of Labor and Industrial Relations, May 1968).

Kelly, Terrence F., "Factors Affecting Poverty: A Gross Flow Analysis," in President's Commission on Income Maintenance Programs, *Technical Studies*, 1970.

Batchelder, Alan, "Poverty: The Special Case of the Negro," *American Economic Review*, 60 (May 1965).

Gwartney, James. "Discrimination and Income Differentials," *American Economic Review*, May 1970.

Thurow, Lester C. "Analyzing the American Income Distribution," *The American Economic Review*, May 1970.

BLS Report No. 375, *Current Population Reports*, series P-23, No. 29.

Johnson, Thomas. "Returns from Investment in Human Capital," *American Economic Review*, Sept. 1970.

Nine City Minority Group Employment Profile, Research Report 1967—19—A, Aug. 6, 1967.

Manpower Report of the President, Apr. 1968.

U.S., Census of Population, 1960. Detailed Characteristics, U.S., Summary (Washington, D.C., 1963).

Becker, G. *The Economics of Discrimination*, Chicago, Ill.: University of Chicago Press, 1957.

Trends in Social and Economic Conditions in Metropolitan Areas, Series P.-23, No. 27. Feb. 7, 1969.

Economic Report of President, Feb. 1968.

Current Population Reports, Special Studies, Series P-23, No. 27, Feb. 7, 1969, U.S. Department of Commerce.

U.S., Board of Governors of Federal Reserve System, Industrial Production, 1957–59 Base, and *Federal Reserve Bulletin*, Feb. 7, 1969.

U.S., Department of Labor. *The Negroes in the U.S., Their Economic and Social Situation*, Bulletin No. 1511, 1969.

Samuelson, Paul A. *Economics*, New York City: McGraw-Hill, 1967.

Economic Report of President, Jan. 1969.

Manpower Report of President, Apr. 1967 and Apr. 1968.

Milgram, Grace. *U.S. Land Prices–Directions and Dynamics*, Washington, D.C.: U.S. Government Printing Office, 1968.

BLS Report No. 332, *Current Population Reports*, Series P-23, No. 24. 1960 Population, U.S. Census, Vol. 1.

Economic Blueprint for Newark, N.J., Office of Economic Development, City of Newark, July 1968.

Caplovitz, David. *The Poor Pay More*, New York: Free Press, 1967.

Davis, Frank G. *The Economics of Black Community Development*, Chicago, Ill.: Markham Publishing Company, 1972.

Topics for Discussion

1. Explain the relationship between black political power and black economic development. What is the impact of one on the other? How is one aided by or limited by the strength or limitations of the other? What does this imply about the relationship between, or the roles of, black economists and black political leaders? What does this imply about the training of black businessmen and black economists to identify and find solutions to the problems of black economic development with respect to policy decisions?

2. What is the impact of the inequality of income and wealth distribution in America on the problems of black economic development? What does this imply about having a few blacks (or success stories) in corporate structures versus the economic situation of the masses of black people? How do the class (based on income) problems in the United States and the identification of black people as a low-income class of people interact with the problems of racial discrimination?

3. A. Discuss individual income mobility versus community economic development. What do the contrasts and comparisons imply for the prospects of overall black economic development?
   B. What is meant by "institutionalized discrimination"? How does this concept limit the analysis of black economic development with respect to the generally accepted conceptual and analytical tools of traditional business and economic theory?

4. Discuss the circular effect of black and social immobility in terms of (1) residential segregation, (2) segregation of black business from national or otherwise unbounded markets, (3) lower per-pupil expenditures in schools, and (4) lack of adequate transportation, sanitation, police protection, and other social services necessary for an economic and social environment conducive to growth.

5. Why is urban renewal a necessary condition but *not* a sufficient condition of urban economic development?

Suggested Readings

Allen, Robert L. *Black Awakening in Capitalistic America: An Analytic History.* Garden City, N.Y.: Anchor Books, Doubleday & Company, Inc., 1970.

Bergman, B.R., and Atkinson, L.C. "The Prospect of Equality of Incomes between Black and White Families under Varying Rates of Unemployment: A Comment." *Journal of Human Resources,* Fall 1972.

"Black—Capitalism. Point of Conflict." *Black Business Digest,* March 1971 (special section).

Booms, B.H., and Ward, J.E., Jr., "The Cons of Black Capitalism, Will This Policy Cure Urban Ills?" *Business Horizons,* October 1969.

Browne, Robert S. "Cash Flows in a Ghetto Community." *Review of Black Political Economy,* Winter/Spring 1971.

Coleman, J., Berry, C., and Blum, Z. *White and Black Careers during the First Ten Years of Work Experience: A Simultaneous Consideration of Occupational Status and Income Changes.* Report No. 123. Baltimore, Md.: Johns Hopkins University, Center for the Social Organization of Schools, December 1971.

Cross, Theodore L. *Black Capitalism.* New York City: Atheneum Press, 1969.

Farmer, Richard N. "The Pros of Black Capitalism." *Business Horizons,* February 1970.

Haddad, W.F. and Pugh, G. Douglas, editors. *Black Economic Development.* Englewood Cliffs, N.J.: Prentice-Hall, Inc., 1969.

Hund, J.M. *Black Entrepreneurship.* Belmont, Calif.: Wadsworth Publishing Company, Inc., 1970.

Lapham, V. "Do Blacks Pay More for Housing?" *Journal of Political Economy,* November-December 1971.

Ribich, T.I. "The Problem of Equal Opportunity: A Review Article." *Journal of Human Resources,* Fall 1972.

Sackrey, Charles M., Jr. "Economics and Black Poverty." *Review of Black Political Economy,* Winter/Spring 1971.

Tabb, W.K. "Decreasing Black-White Income Differentials: Evaluating the Evidence and a Linear Programming Framework for Urban Policy Choice." *Journal of Regional Science,* December 1972.

Tabb, W.K. "Viewing Minority Economic Development as a Problem in Political Economy" *American Economic Review,* May 1972.

Tabb, W.K., *The Political Economy of the Black Ghetto*. New York: W. W. Norton, 1970.

Timmins, Jeffry A. "Black is Beautiful—Is It Bountiful?" *Howard Business Review*, November-December 1971.

von Furstenberg, G.M.; Horowitz, A. and Harrison, B., editors. *Patterns of Racial Discrimination*.

III
Programs

Programs for the Economic Development of the American Negro Community: The Moderate Approach

William L. Henderson and Larry C. Ledebur

In 1967 Bayard Rustin noted that the civil rights movement had entered a new phase. The new strategy and priority is the economic advancement of the Negro. In 1968, economic development programs advocated by black militants were the significant events reinforcing the new "economic direction" of the black leaders. Black militants, particularly in CORE, have been innovative in program design and resourceful in marshalling support and enthusiasm for broad-gauged economic development programs. Nonmilitant or moderate blacks also renewed their earlier interest in an economics focus to solve basic Negro problems. Nonmilitant national Negro organizations have recognized the need for economic development and improvement but have concentrated their resources on legal issues. The nonmilitant civil rights groups created the necessary and sufficient conditions within the system that permitted the current economic thrust to occur.

The proposals for action in economic programs of the Negro moderates are the subjects of this article. There is an evolving emphasis on economic-development and entrepreneurship programs as opposed to skills training and the creation of more employment opportunities. These embryonic programs are structured and developed well enough now to permit evaluation of their viability to meet the urgent needs of black Americans who remain ouside of the "mainstream" of the American economic system.

The Moderate Position

Questioning the staff of the National Business League (NBL) on the organization's economic ideas and historical influences, an interviewer received this reply from one staff member: "We are pure Adam Smith."[1] This statement provides a basis for understanding the difference in the

169

economic orientation of black militants and moderates. The Negro moderates or non-militants have tied their own economic development to already established capitalistic institutions, rather than the establishment of separate, unique black economic entities.

The concept that guides the nonmilitant Negro is essentially an individualistic evolutionary development through private enterprise institutions. Basic to this process is the idea of an "economic man" motivated by his material self-interest. The economic man is driven to improve his material condition. The 19th century classical orientation suggests that material acquisitiveness is a universal trait that identifies and unites all men. For the individual Negro, this orientation implies specialization in a productive skill, or job, or operation of a business. The acquisitive activity related to the skill or job and business operation permits personal and economic growth.

Booker Washington's legacy. Emphasis on entrepreneurship is well grounded in Booker T. Washington's ideas and philosophy. Washington was a vigorous advocate of the Negro effort to "make it" within the system. He stressed thrift, self-respect, and persistent striving. Negro artisans, businessmen, and property owners were the product of education and industrial training. His ideas and efforts constitute a legacy for modern Negro conservatives.

Washington's basic position was forcefully stated at the opening of the Cotton States Exposition in Atlanta in September, 1895.

> To those of my race who depend upon bettering their condition in a foreign land, or who underestimate the importance of cultivating friendly relations with the Southern white man who is his next door neighbor, I would say: "Cast down your bucket where you are"—cast it down in making friends, in every manly way, of the people of all races by whom we are surrounded.
>
> Cast it down in agriculture, mechanics, in commerce, in domestic service and in the professions. And in this connection it is well to bear in mind that whatever other sins the South may be called to bear when it comes to business, pure and simple, it is in the South that the Negro is given a man's chance in the commercial world. . . . We shall prosper in proportion as we learn to dignify and glorify common labor, and put brains and skill into the common occupations of life; . . . No race can prosper till it learns that there is as much dignity in tilling a field as in writing a poem. It is at the bottom of life we must begin, and not at the top.[2]

Five years after this speech Washington aided in founding the Negro Business League to promote Negro businesses, the predecessor of the NBL.

The National Business League. Washington's recurring theme that the "black man who was succeeding in business, who was a taxpayer, and who possessed intelligence and high character. . .was treated with the highest respect by members of the white race"[3]—pervades the programs advocated and implemented by the modern National Business League.

The following is a restatement of Booker Washington's early ideas by

B. G. Burrell, president of the National Business League, to community leaders of Memphis in June, 1968:

> This is a dollar society. A business world. A profit-making culture that places the highest premium on success in business and profit making. Every man in this country is measured by his peers on the basis of his relative economic success.
> The news vendors on the street corners are respected and looked up to by their peers because they are 'in business for themselves.' The captains of industry, the high and the mighty of the world of business enjoy the greatest degree of admiration—indeed—adulation—as a result of their profit making skill.
> . . .Each and every businessman is revered by the small sample population that knows him primarily because he is in 'business.' Every strata of our society holds the business functionary in great high regard and accords him an inordinate amount of respect.
> In the light of these facts it would seem that only elementary common sense would be required to point up the need for an entrepreneurial class of indigenous citizens.

The NBL is dedicated to the development of the economic base and Negro business leadership to achieve economic, political, and social equality. The NBL seeks (a) an acknowledgement of the right of all Americans to enter business, (b) equal access to capital, and (c) the partnership of government and private enterprise in providing technical assistance to supplement the initiative of potential successful businessmen.

The NBL does not advocate a separate black economy.

> We hold the opinion that a concentrated effort to develop an area of significant Negro participation as employers in the aggregate economy of the nation is essential to meeting both the grievances of Black Americans and the requirements for maximum economic growth by the national economy.[4]

The NBL is the pre-eminent advocate of minority entrepreneurships. NBL activities are designed to aid the Negro in becoming a self-sufficient businessman and entrepreneur. Skills training and more jobs are subsidiary concerns of the NBL.

> It is an article of faith with us that the free entrepreneurship system that is an American trademark is directly and indirectly responsible for all of the good things that have inured to our citizenry. *We want to become a truly meaningful part of the system. . . !* We do not want a *hand out* but we need and seek the warm right hand of fellowship that only our White contemporaries can provide us. Give us nothing but *loan us* what we need. Money, guidance, counseling, know-how, are all professional commodities that should be available for a price. We ask only that the price be reasonable and equitable.[5]

The organization's programs are professionally developed and formally structured. Entrepreneurship opportunities of Negroes are currently enhanced by the NBL's Mainstream and Outreach projects. These interlocking projects underwrite the NBL philosophy of self-help and "the partnership not plantationship" doctrine.

Project *Mainstream* is a composite five-point program that coordinates existing government programs in a cohesive manner to achieve economic growth and development. The program is designed to make local citizens an integral part of the urban development process through (1) the creation of small business investment companies to provide equity capital resources for indigenous businesses; (2) the creation of "local" or "state" development companies to facilitate the development of the physical plants and equipment for the local enterprises; (3) establishment of urban development foundations that seek participation by community organizations in the development process; (4) providing basic training for entrepreneurship as a prerequisite for more advanced training; and (5) setting up and operating data-processing business reporting and accounting control systems to bring to the local businessman services of this type that he could not afford.

The NBL brochure describing Project *Mainstream* notes:

> The principle of self-help is and always must be paramount in all our efforts. While the deprived entrepreneur must receive reasonable assistance from the total community it must be clearly understood and fully appreciated that neither *Mainstream* nor any other NBL program aims at replacing individual's own initiative, diligence, physical exertion and financial sacrifice.[6]

The self-help, individual idea permeates all NBL projects. Project Outreach, for example, is primarily directed toward the most disadvantaged owners of small businesses. Services of management training, business counseling, and the preparation of basic financial records are provided for the owners of small businesses. The management assistance program is the most important feature of the Outreach effort. ". . . The major problem confronting small business operators is their own management deficiencies."[7] The management assistance program is designed to attack this basic deficiency by developing and implementing orderly and rational approaches to small business problem-solving. The NBL hopes to organize more small businesses, to set up alternative forms of business organization, and to foster cooperative activities for small inefficient firms.

The NBL also is engaged in twelve cities under a federal government contract in a pilot program of basic business education, management training, guidance, and counseling. The modest goal is to provide 40 persons capable of successfully holding management training jobs, 250 persons who will open sound new businesses, and 500 entrepreneurs whose business activities will show measurable improvement. Outreach is taking the first step in identifying persons interested in going into business and is providing preliminary training and technical assistance and advice to get them into business. Outreach also sets up the basic mechanics for providing business training and technical advice so that these Negro businessmen can meet competition and experience normal growth of their businesses. The NBL also provides other services for budding Negro entrepreneurs. One current program is the development of franchises. The Franchise and Business Opportunity analyst of the NBL is responsible for locating and identifying viable franchise opportunities and establishing the reputability of the originators. Work has been done with A. W. Willis and others to develop a franchise package on a national basis for Mahalia Jackson-Glori-Fried Chicken. The franchise concept is, of course, particularly constructive because it can provide complete advice and guidance on all of the services and skills necessary to establish and operate the enterprise. There is standardization of physical facilities, inventory control, accounting, and other functions.

The scope of the programs offered by NBL is extensive and includes housing and urban development as well as economic development and entrepreneurship assistance. The "modular core" concept is a $75 million housing and business development plan advocated for every ghetto in the NBL's 50 chapter cities. This plan is an overall blueprint for the revitalization of blighted urban areas. The "core" contains a housing, business, and public-service mix. The major elements are a new housing environment, shopping center, and a community center. On the periphery of these modular cores, provision is made for light manufacturing and warehousing.

> Within this new core we would create a new economically stratified housing environment, a new diversified shopping environment and a new governmental services or civic environment. During the process of physically erecting the core, we would involve every element in our moving vibrant community. We would train the able-bodied in skills that are marketable as they rebuild an area they can identify as their own. We would create a class of entrepreneurs by the merging of White resources with minority capability. We would maximize the benefits of government social programs by making them productive of meaningful social benefits.[8]

The modular core approach attacks many of the basic problems of the inner city, i.e., overpopulation, shortage of housing, high rates of unemployment, increasing cost of crime prevention, and the exodus of industries, and thus jobs, to the nearby suburbs. The NBL believes that social amenities and community protection must be provided so that the central cities will be a desirable place for employers to locate, employees to work, and everyone to live.[9]

Small Business Development Center. Another small organization which directs its efforts to providing practical advice, counseling, and training for the small Negro entrepreneur is the Small Business Development and Guidance Center (SBDGC) at Howard University. Wilford White, although not Negro, is the director; the assistant director, French Stone, is a very successful businessman; the chairman of the advisory group for the SBDGC, F. Naylor Fitzhugh, is a former Howard University professor and now a vice-president of Pepsi-Cola.

Fitzhugh characterizes the essential orientation of the advisers of the SBDGC as "economic development within the system."

> We have definitely accepted American standards, American goals. We wanted to achieve within the American frame of reference. It has been my experience that as far as Black businessmen are concerned, they had a great deal more faith in business as a philosophy of life and as a means to salvation. As a matter of fact, I used to criticize businessmen's associations. I used to say if you would stop trying to save the Negro race and start saving your businesses, the association would make more sense. . . . They were 110 percent committed.
> . . . I have had several people say to me, keep talking about the Negro middle class. Why stay middle class. There's nothing wrong with our getting wealthy. If we have 10 percent of the population, let's have 10 percent of the multi-millionaires.[10]

In discussing the programs of the Small Business Development and Guidance Center, A. S. Venable underscored the Washington-Burrell-Fitzhugh development orientation. "We strongly believe that economic organization of minority group owned businesses represents an effective means of setting in motion self-perpetuating machinery which will allow the Negro community, eventually, to function and grow on its own as a vital part of the total business community."[11]

The purpose of the Center is to expand employment in small business firms by providing management assistance to small businessmen located in metropolitan Washington, Baltimore, and Richmond. Since 1964 the Center's assistance has been offered through individual and group counseling and training programs. Emphasis has been placed on administrative and operating problems, such as record keeping, marketing, personnel, housekeeping, location, and relations with taxing and regulatory agencies. Financing and loans are not emphasized unless the needs of a business call for a loan and the owner is qualified to manage the money successfully.

In 1966 the Economic Development Administration funded a program organizing dry cleaners into a self-help group. Other services such as automotive repair, day nurseries, rug and upholstery cleaners have also been organized in similar groups. The counseling effort involves a few entrepreneurs and a leader meeting to discuss problems of the owner, employees, markets, money, and methods. But the scope of the program is limited by facilities and funds. During the 1967 fiscal year classes were held for 17 organized groups with about 260 people enrolled. The number of people affected is relatively small when compared with other national organizations.

Urban League programs. Whitney Young as a spokesman for the Urban League reflects the "within the system, jobs-oriented, upward mobility" commitment of that large organization. The work of the Urban League since its incorporation in 1913 has been primarily concerned with the Negro's advancement in business and industry. The purpose of many Urban League programs has been to improve training and productivity and thus improve the Negro's opportunity to find jobs, to increase his chances of being promoted to higher paying jobs, and to assure him equal pay for equal work. Although the League has a general policy of improving urban conditions, it has emphasized skills training and job placement.[12] The Urban League has carried out a major role in program development and planning of on-the-job training programs implemented by Urban League affiliates and funded by the Department of Labor. In terms of the number of people participating in funded programs, the Urban League's activities are the most significant of all Negro groups'. For example, in 1966, 4,000 people received training and job placement, while over 40,000 people took advantage of its job placement services.

The Urban League has relied on the federal government for financial aid, as have all organizations with working programs. Mr. Young has advocated a guaranteed annual wage and the use of the government as an employer of the last resort. He has also supported the A. Philip Randolph proposal called the "Freedom Budget" as a source of funds to finance massive programs in housing, education, health, and employment improvement.[13]

Improvement in employment conditions, higher pay, and emulation of the white privileged group in economic acquisitiveness are advocated in the programs and administrative policies of most of the national Negro organizations.

The NAACP approach. Although the NAACP does not have a well-developed economic program, upward economic development of the Negro is a functional aspect of the long-term drive for civil rights. William Morris, who is director of housing programs of the NAACP, states:

> Economic development to me means the development of Negro entrepreneurship, the development of Negro businesses where they can have some degree of economic independence, and opening up the upward mobility of Negroes into the general level of management and sub-management positions where they can participate fully in the mainstream of business and economic life.[14]

Mr. Morris prefers the private-business sector as a source of aid and advice for the evolving Negro entrepreneurial group. "The role of private industry in this would be one I would first pursue because I think they are able to move much faster; they are not complicated by the bureaucracy, the tight regulations of federal operations, they can move more freely, make their own decisions, and they could be very instrumental in getting any program off the ground."[15]

The Southern Christian Leadership Council. A moderate civil rights organization that until recently offered inspired leadership to a large segment of the black community is the Southern Christian Leadership Conference (SCLC). In the six months before his death, Martin Luther King had begun to implement a generalized economic program to direct attention to the "poor people." Dr. King's successor carried through the plans for the "Poor People's Campaign" in Washington to attract national attention to the plight of minorities. It is difficult to determine the economic goals and objectives of the SCLC, other than focusing the national attention.

In testifying before the Subcommittee on Equal Opportunity in an Urban Society at the Republican National Convention (1968), Dr. Ralph Abernathy noted the need to expand numerous government programs, such as the food stamp plan, Head Start and summer jobs under OEO, welfare programs, and other income maintenance programs, model cities, low-income housing, and economic development programs in rural areas. The SCLC has originated no specific programs. It is difficult to evaluate the omnibus thrust advocated by Dr. Abernathy. There are elements of the older skills-training and employment-opportunities approach, as well as an elementary concept of economic development applied to rural areas.

Recent pronouncements from this group add little substantive information as to the manner appropriate to dealing with the problems of the SCLC constituency. In a United Press International dispatch of January 9, 1969, Dr. Abernathy is reported to have said that he was not interested in making black individuals rich, but in helping groups. "We need to organize community owned development corporations where profits will be returned to the building of the community. . . . We want to share in the public sector of the economy through publicly controlled non-profit institutions. . . . I don't believe in Black capitalism. I believe in Black socialism." Although considered a moderate, Dr. Abernathy has made recent statements which appear inconsistent with the ideas and programs of other nonmilitant organizations.

The Capital Dimension of the Programs

One characteristic of all of the programs noted in this review is newness. With the exception of selected "jobs-oriented" programs of the Urban League and selected NBL activities, the programs are in the planning or formulation phases. A secondary characteristic of all of the programs is the need for financing. Raising the money capital necessary for successful implementation of the programs becomes the principal impediment to getting the programs moving. Money or the control of purchasing power over resources is a fundamental prerequisite in all capital development programs, whether in the American ghetto or in other areas of the world.

Capital accumulation is inexorably entwined in the folklore and formal analysis of economic development. The process of raising income and speeding wealth accumulation is a function of the capacity of the individual and the system to exert economic power to substitute machinery for human motive power or to increase purchasing power over resources. The capital scarcity syndrome with its inherent restriction on economic accretion and expansion has been applied to Negro economic problems in the United States.

The vicious cycle of poverty income is a generalized explanation of the fate of many individual blacks. If incomes are low, all of the income is committed to subsistence purchases or to debt retirement. No economic accretion occurs. In the entrepreneurship cases, the black businessman is typically in the services and his sales volume is relatively low. The business organization is invariably a proprietorship or partnership. The small volume, labor-intensive, limited market, and high risk elements have created credit limitations to supplement others already at work in the money market.

Attempts to isolate and identify problems of capital formation or financing as the fundamental causal factor in the failure of the black community to develop are problematical. Capital sources are, however, a salient factor in the pattern of permissive factors which would aid in current and future economic development. Problems such as skills training, discrimination, limited markets acquisitive motivation, management acuity, geographic mobility, and entry barriers other than capital interact with capital problems in black development. The capital problem is selective and should not be viewed as a panacea even if the concept of black development has been defended satisfactorily. It is interesting to note the amount and sources of funds currently available or being sought for programs formally structured by blacks with an economics focus.

Conservative organizations have sought funds from both the private and public sectors and continue to do so. Funds for the National Business League's Project Mainstream illustrate the public-private cooperative emphasis. In the 12 regions where NBL's Small Investment Companies are being organized, funds are being sought from the white "majority business community." The NBL has solicited outright grants from large corporations and has offered a variety of equity and debt instruments for sale to any interested party. The local and state Development Companies of the project were created to utilize Section 502 of the Small Business Act, which provides financial support for plant and equipment for shopping centers and small industrial parks that employ the urban hard-core unemployed. Private funds are being sought to finance the data-processing centers.

The pilot project for management training Outreach activated by the NBL is financed by the Department of Commerce, Economic Development Administration, and the Office of Economic Opportunity. The franchise and other similar projects are funded by private and public sources with emphasis placed on local sources of funds.

The massive "modular core" program of NBL, which is really a broad-gauged urban development program, must also look to the "majority white business community" and the federal government for funds for various components.

The individual and group counseling activities of the Small Business Development and Guidance Center have been provided by the EDA. The modest funding, about $150,000 per year, has been used for actual operations. The current constraints on the expansion of the SBDGC activities are physical facilities and staff. The SBDGC needs more space and more facilities than are currently available in the temporary buildings at Howard University.

The Urban League has been tapping private-sector personal and corporate funds as well as government resources. Its highly successful job placement and training programs have been funded by the Department of Labor. The Urban League's larger community development interest in housing, education, and health care requires extremely large amounts of capital. As noted earlier in this review, Mr. Young has argued for "A Freedom Budget" before the Senate Subcommittee on Executive Reorganization (Committee on Government Operations).

A Freedom Budget

The Freedom Budget was developed under the auspices of the A. Philip Randolph Institute with professional advice from Leon Keyserling and others. This program is of particular interest because it, like most of those noted in this paper, is a product of black origin and is advocated by blacks as consistent with their views on economic development. It is important because of the black estimates of the magnitude of funds needed for an omnibus approach to the overall development. The Freedom Budget provides for seven basic objectives: (1) to provide full employment for all willing to work; (2) to assure decent and adequate wages to all who work; (3) to assure a decent standard of living to those who cannot or should not work; (4) to wipe out the slum ghettos and provide decent homes for all Americans; (5) to provide decent medical care and adequate educational opportunities for all at a cost they can afford; (6) to purify our air and water and develop our transportation and natural resources on a scale suitable to overall economic growth, and (7) to unite sustained full employment with sustained full production and high economic growth.

These goals must be implemented through national programs with the federal government exercising the leadership role. The Freedom Budget assumes that if the federal authorities exercise prudent monetary and fiscal policies the national output should rise to between $1,085 and $1,120 billion by 1975. For the ten years used in the Freedom budget, "a level of total national production averaging annually $2.315–2.442 million higher, and aggregating over the ten years $2.315–2.442 billion higher, than if total production remained during these ten years at the 1965 rate."[16] This aggregate ten-year figure of $2.3 to 2.4 billion is the "economic growth dividend" upon which the Freedom Budget draws to fulfill its purposes.

The programs of the Freedom Budget would be specified in a new section of the President's Economic Report. The allocation of the economic growth dividend would be for existing but expanded programs and for new programs not now included in the federal budget. For example, the funds for the Economic Opportunity Program should rise from $1.4 billion in 1967 to 3.0 billion in 1970 and then to $4.0 billion in 1975. Housing and community development programs should rise from $0.1

billion to $3.3 billion and then to $3.8 billion; for agriculture and natural resources combined outlays should increase from $5.9 billion to $10.5 billion and then to $12.0 billion; for education the increase should be from $2.6 billion to $7.0 billion to $9.5 billion; health services should rise to $7.0 billion in 1975; public assistance, labor and manpower, and other welfare services total budget expenditures should be at the $7.5 billion mark in 1975.

Total federal budget outlays with the Freedom Budget allocation would not increase as a percentage of GNP over the ten-year period. Stated in different terms, at the time the Freedom Budget was developed, average GNP per capita was $3,500. ''We grant to the federal government a slice equal to roughly $500 in the form of taxes, leaving us an average of about $3,000 to spend on our other needs.''[17]

> If our nation's productivity continues growing at the same rate as in recent years—and it will if the Freedom Budget is adopted—each share will grow at about $5,000. Thus the federal government's slice will grow to $700, . . . and we will still have $4,300 left for our other needs.
>
> What the Freedom Budget proposes is this: Budget a fraction of this $200 increase in federal tax revenues to provide jobs for all who can work and adequate income of other types for those who cannot.[18]

In commenting on the Freedom Budget, A. Philip Randolph points to the necessity for government channeled resources to eradicate poverty.

> But the very nature of a total war against unemployment and poverty and all their manifestations calls for greatly increased emphasis upon adequate federal programs and huge increases in federal expenditures. Increases in private incomes alone, while necessary, cannot themselves at appreciable speed channel a large enough part of our resource into clearance of slums, the rebuilding of our cities, the construction of schools and hospitals, the recruitment and adequate pay of teachers and nurses.[19]

Mr. Randolph expects the federal government to serve as the catalyst in developing full employment and estimates that a financial commitment of at least $185 billion is necessary. It is interesting to note that Mr. Randolph's budget would also directly alter the economic well-being of white Americans in similar poverty conditions.

The Ghediplan

Sources of government funds are the principal concern of another capital funding program suggested by Dr. Dunbar S. McLaurin. Dr. McLaurin's program, called the ''Ghetto Economic Development and Industrialization Plan,'' was prepared for the Human Resources Administration of the City of New York. The *Ghediplan* has two basic components: a source of funds for business in the ghettos, and a guaranteed market for the ghetto businesses once established.

Of the $200 million potentially available under this plan, half would represent guaranteed financing for businesses and half would be in guaranteed markets for products and services of the businesses. The plan has elements of an approach to the restructure of New York slums similar to those found for developing nations on an international basis. In the particular plan proposed, the City of New York would provide the financing by depositing a portion of city funds in slum-area banks on the condition that the banks make development loans to ten newly founded corporations created to funnel the monies into local businesses. Five of these corporations would be nonprofit Local Development Corporations to attract new industry and to otherwise stimulate the ghetto community. The remaining corporations would be Small Business Investment Companies which would help convert the local government deposits into venture capital and loans.[20]

The Ghetto Economic Development and Industrialization Plan would increase the productivity of the ghetto's private sector and employ the city's under-utilized fiscal and purchasing resources.

> By encouraging guaranteed markets for the program from the resources of the city, the federal government and private business corporations would be formed within the ghettos in an effort to reclaim some of the ghetto income and put it to work there.[21]

Although no action has been taken by the City of New York to implement the development concept, Cyril Tyson, Commissioner of the City Manpower and Career Development Agency, has noted that,

> the use of government procurement to provide a guaranteed market for ghetto businessmen to start a business, or to expand one or put a floor down is clearly a dynamic new use of our resources. We in New York City believe it can work nationwide as well as locally.[22]

The magnitude of the estimates of the capital resources necessary to revitalize the ghettos and to eradicate poverty throughout the nation should be noted. The Freedom Budget makes reference to $185 billion over a ten-year period, the local *Ghediplan* project estimates the use of $200 million for New York City alone, while the National Business League's initial and single modular core costs are set at $75 million. A nonblack estimate of the capital cost of urban development was made for Goodbody and Company, a brokerage, investment banker, and financial services organization, by economist Lawrence Ritter of New York University. Ritter estimates that the cost of a domestic "Marshall Plan" is "likely to range between $150 billion and $250 billion over a ten-year period, or about $15 billion to $25 billion annually at current prices."[23]

Each of the programs noted is directed at total or fractional economic development of the black community and requires the large outlay of money and resources. At issue in the potential success of this myriad system of programs is the adequacy of financing, the administration of the programs, and, more fundamentally, the appropriate design of a scheme to alleviate the root causes of the poverty and discrimination problems.

Nonblack Programs

Government agencies have also established a series of black economic development programs. In almost all cases the programs have been guided by advice from segments of the black community. Legislation affecting the Small Business Administration's lending and financing policies has been directed to meeting some of the financial constraints facing minority businesses. The SBA's new Project Own is designed to establish 10,000 new minority businesses by the end of fiscal 1969 and 20,000 by the end of fiscal 1970. This expansion of minority ownership will require investment at the rate of $250 million by the end of the first year and $500 million during the second year. The SBA's "Sec. 502" local development company program is another recent example of the legislative sponsorship of developmental financing for indigenous community groups.

The Department of Commerce through its "Affirmative Action Programs" has developed and implemented a variety of specific projects designed to aid disadvantaged minority businesses. These elements of the Economic Development Administration's activities include credit pools and loan guarantees, the development of additional leadership in the Negro business community (Youth Enterprises, Inc.), franchise opportunities, aid to Negro construction companies in urban, and housing development projects.[24]

Numerous other "developmental" programs affecting the ghetto communities are administered by the Department of Housing and Urban Development. An encyclopedic listing of these and other agency programs would only reinforce the idea that development thrust and large outlays are required for the private and public sector activities advocated by or for both the black and white communities.

The Issues—Summary and Evaluation

Programs advocated by nonmilitant blacks are designed to help the Negro "make it" within the existing economic framework. There are no suggestions for a separate black state or other forms of economic segregation. All of these proposals are aimed at raising income, expanding business opportunities, and improving the economic well-being of the Negro.

Any evaluation of the economic development programs advocated must include social, financial, and conceptual issues, as well as an assessment of the emphasis and format of economic programs.

Three elements of concern are noted about the implications of the present thrust vis-à-vis the Negro economic programs and the direction of overall social policy in this country: (1) For the Negro, economic development is not an end in itself, but a technique to achieve other social and political priorities. The viability of economic development as a vehicle for obtaining these other non-material goals needs to be carefully evaluated. (2) If it can be argued that economic development is an appropriate device for obtaining these ends, then it is necessary to evaluate the techniques that are being employed to augment development. (3) The drive for economic development is being undertaken to achieve social goals for the Negro. The consequences of the present orientation for overall social policy and priorities in the United States should be investigated.

Studies in the sociology and economics of development indicate that cultural and institutional changes are prerequisites for successful initiation of the development process in both the social and economic dimensions. One precondition for development is an emerging sense of cultural pride or identity, such as nationalism, which can overcome the traditional cultural constraints to high achievement and motivation in the populace. Viewed in this perspective, the current emphases of the Negro movement on "black power" and "black pride" are coherent steps in establishing the preconditions for the social and economic development of the Negro. In the current focus on black capitalism it is assumed that a direct relationship exists between the acquisition of control over economic means and the acquisition of social and political leverage. This is an unsubstantiated assumption. Economic development alone has not been the panacea by which other minority groups have achieved social and political power or gained admittance to the institutional structure of American society. Even if economic integration into American society is not the goal, the assumption that self-determination for the black populace can be achieved through economic power is critical and should be reexamined. There are international examples of countries whose weight in world politics is disproportionate to their economic base. If this assumption of a relationship between economic wealth and political power is valid within the United States, the economic focus of the Negro movement can be interpreted as a pragmatic adjustment to the reality of a serious defect in American democracy.

There is also a serious issue arising from the differences in the business forms and their relationship to power. The simplest form of black businesses which could be successfully established would be small retail or service proprietorships. However, the economic power derived from this type of activity cannot be great unless it represents an overall increase in individual economic welfare with an aggregate increase in economic power. The presence of black retail firms in ghetto areas would challenge the contention that white retail firms in these areas cause all surplus and investible funds to flow out of the ghetto, excluding them from use in local economic development. This is an unexamined premise. The share of these funds retained in the ghetto may or may not be greater if these firms were black owned and operated. Only comparative analysis of actual cases would substantiate this. It is quite probable that the increase in the share of funds retained within the ghetto would be only the owner's profit (in the area of a 2 to 4 percent increase). These black owners must be willing to spend and invest within the black community. The remainder of the income of these firms would flow out for inventory purchases, advertising expenditures, taxes, labor costs, etc. Only the wage payments would remain in the ghetto. This usually occurs whether the firm is white or black owned (assuming that white businessmen hire Negro employees).

The alternate course of action would be to concentrate on black ownership of industrial firms. The size of these undertakings and the associated economic power would be significant. The capitalization for industrial activities of this size is usually obtained by the dispersal of ownership through sales of shares of stock. There has been a tendency, particularly in the postwar period, for ownership to be separated from effective control. The actual economic power represented by ownership may not be very significant. Thus two interesting alternative possibilities for action are implied.

A more effective way for the Negro to obtain economic power might be through the development of management and executive personnel to infiltrate the practical sources of economic power in the industrial establishment and the government. The economic costs to the Negro community of achieving economic power through the management route would be significantly lower than through attempting to establish new industrial concerns, and the risks involved are fewer. The contemporary evolution of the American industry structure is characterized by the horizontal expansion of established industries into new enterprises, rather than by the successful creation of new industries. Negroes have not traditionally chosen education or professional careers in management, in part because of the inaccessibility of both management training and job opportunities. The constraints upon Negro participation in this occupational field seem to be eroding in the contemporary social and business environment.

Another possibility suggested by the difficulties of obtaining economic power through the creation of black-owned large-scale industrial enterprises is the creation of smaller industrial firms using the cooperative form of organization. In cooperatives ownership and control are more closely aligned because of the communal nature of the decision-making processes. Cooperative activities on a significant scale have proved successful in many activities such as banking, milling, real estate, factories, and mills. The possibilities for cooperatives have been noted in the Negro community. One Negro writer argues:

> Now after years and years of procrastination, we need to become attuned to the cooperative business line which has already brought security and protection to millions of White families around the world. We need to face up to the current economic revolution initiated by the development of automation and unite in cooperative action to insure us a solid foundation to build and live the good life.[25]

The assumption of correspondence between acquisition of economic power and political and social leverage is critical. If this relationship can be verified, then the successful development of economic power is essential to the aspirations of both militants and nonmilitants. It is imperative that the modes of economic development undertaken have the greatest possibility for success. It is important that the assumptions under which economic development is undertaken be verified and the means chosen be effective.

Kain and Persky of Harvard have made several careful studies of the programs designed to attack the sources of economic deprivation of the Negro. Their comments are illuminating and potentially helpful:

> Despite the urgency of the current situation, alternative policies must be evaluated in terms of their long run impact. The selection of specific program tools should be governed by a careful definition of the underlying problems. Few existing programs have such a legitimate birth.[26]
>
> . . . .
>
> The Negro in this country clearly faces a broad range of pressing problems, problems that challenge the basic structure of our social and physical environment. While there are many proposals and counterproposals aimed at the ultimate solution, it is clear now that no easy way out exists.[27]

NOTES

1. Interview.

2. Roy L. Hill, *Rhetoric of Racial Revolt* (Denver, Colo.: Golden Bell Press, 1964), p. 39.

3. See Proceedings of the National Negro Business League, 1900, and Earl E. Thorpe, *The Mind of the Negro: An Intellectual History of Afro-American* (Baton Rouge, La.: Ortlieb Press, 1961), p. 422.

4. *Operations Manual* for Project Outreach of the National Business League, p. 4.

5. Speech by Berkeley G. Burrell, "If Not Now, When? If Not Us, Who?" before the Mount Vernon Avenue Improvement Association, Columbus, Feb. 8, 1968.

6. Project *Mainstream,* brochure by the National Business League, 3418 Georgia Ave., N.W., Washington, DC 20010.

7. *Operations Manual* for Project *Outreach,* p. 14.

8. B. G. Burrell, statement presented to the Joint Economic Committee, Congress of the U.S., Washington, D. C., June 5, 1968.

9. Statement on Inner City Economic Development, Project *Outreach,* 4324 Georgia Ave., N.W., Washington, D. C., p. 1.

10. Interview with F. Naylor Fitzhugh, Vice-President, Pepsi-Cola, Inc., New York City, July 18, 1968.

11. Abraham S. Venable, "Mobilizing Dormant Resources: Negro Entrepreneurs," remarks made available by the Business and Defense Services Administration, May 1967.

12. See Benjamin Mays, *The Negro's God* (Boston: Chapman and Grimes, 1939). Statements by Whitney Young in *Federal Role in Urban Affairs,* U.S., Senate, Committee on Government Operations, 89th Congress, Dec. 14 and 15, 1966, pp. 2921*ff.* (Part 14).

13. See *Federal Role in Urban Affairs,* Part 14, pp. 2932–40.

14. Interview with William Morris, NAACP Offices, New York City, July 17, 1968.

15. *Ibid.*

16. *A 'Freedom Budget' for All Americans* (New York: A. Philip Randolph Institute, Oct. 1966), p. 5.

17. *Federal Role in Urban Affairs,* Part 9, p. 1993.

18. A *'Freedom Budget' for All Americans, A Summary* (New York City: A. Philip Randolph Institute, Jan. 1967), p. 11.

19. A. Philip Randolph, "Toward a Freedom Budget," *Dissent* 13 (Mar.–Apr. 1966): 125.

20. See article by Charles G. Bennett, "City Development Plan Seeks to Aid Slum-Area Businesses," *New York Times,* Apr. 11, 1968.

21. "McLaurin Offers Plan to Aid Slum Sections," *Daily Argus,* Mount Vernon, N. Y., Apr. 12, 1968.

22. "Asks Building, Business for Ghetto," *Amsterdam News,* New York, Apr. 13, 1968.

23. Lawrence S. Ritter, *A Capital Market Plan for the Urban Areas* (New York: Goodbody and Co., undated), p. 12.

24. See Projects No. 200–1, 300–1, 400–1, 500–1, published by the Business and Defense Services Administration, United States Department of Commerce.

25. Theora Makeda, "A Challenge for Black Leadership," *Liberator* 7 (June 1967): 11.

26. John F. Kain and Joseph J. Persky, *Alternatives to the Gilded Ghetto,* Program of Regional and Urban Economics, Discussion Paper No. 21, Harvard University, Feb. 1968, p. 1.

27. *Ibid.,* pp. 31–32.

Programs for the Economic Development of the American Negro Community: The Militant Approach

William L. Henderson and Larry C. Ledebur

American culture has demonstrated a capacity to assimilate people from diverse national minorities. However, the Negro has not been integrated successfully into our social, political, or economic structure. Earlier patterns of action to move the Negro into the institutional structure of American society have achieved limited objectives. Recent programs legislated by governments and those undertaken by civil rights organizations have progressed slowly in achieving social, political, and economic equality for the Negro.

The Focus on Economic Development

Bayard Rustin argues that, in view of the existing social situation and current phase of the civil rights movement, the Negro effort must focus on the problem of economic advancement for the Negro.

> The problem before us in this . . . period is basically an economic one. It is economic in that the objectives of the first two periods, while not completed, are completed enough that a dynamic cannot be created around them.
> It is not possible for Negroes to gain economic independence unless the problem of poverty is dealt with. If the civil rights movement does not concentrate basically on economic issues, freedom for Negroes in our time will never be achieved.
> . . . true freedom must be conceived in economic categories. The economy is the bone, the social institutions are the flesh, the political institutions the skin which grows on that bone and flesh. Ultimately, all human freedom is determined by the economic structure of the institution.[1]

The strategy that is now receiving priority among most Negro leaders of national organizations is black economic development or black capitalism. The Negro has identified the economic system with its capitalistic elements as a major source of power—power from which they believe they have been systematically excluded. Thus economic institutions and related ideological bases may be viewed as a central obstacle to emancipation of the Negro:

> . . . Ten years ago when the militants criticized the system, they were talking about the political system. Today when they are talking about the system, they are talking about the economic system. They have seen through the controls that the economic system exerts over the political.[2]

From the conservative National Urban League and National Business League to the militant Congress of Racial Equality, members and leaders now assume that the Negro must participate in the ownership, control, management, and operation of the economic enterprises of this country and that, if he is blocked in his efforts by the present institutional structure, then the economic system must be restructured. Many organizations are already prepared to achieve economic power outside of our existing economic institutions.

Some civil rights organizations (National Association for the Advancement of Colored People and Urban League) retain the older and traditional interest in jobs and skills training, but most organizations have adopted fresh approaches. New directions are found in current policies of most conservative Negro organizations as well as of the black militants. Berkeley G. Burrell of the National Business League maintains that:

> Certainly jobs are an essential part of the cure for our urban ills, but they must not be considered the sole palliative to the sickness. We had full employment of the hard core under slavery. Today we want a piece of the action in the mainstream business system. The jobs now being provided by sincere and well- meaning white businesses serve only to provide a sense of "slave security" that will only result in greater frustration, bitterness and rancor, destruction, and retribution in the days that lie ahead.[3]

A similar view is presented by William Morris, director of housing programs for the NAACP:

> It is not enough simply to provide jobs, jobs, jobs, where people are being employed by someone else; and perhaps limited as to how far they can go in the upward path. . . .[4]

The position of the Congress of Racial Equality also illustrates the prevalent attitude of militant organizations:

> Economic development takes priority over jobs per se at this point. A number of years ago our basic drive was for jobs. We have looked upon this as a way of solving the problem. We thought that was the answer. Based on the economic reality of our situtation, jobs and that kind of income cannot reduce the gap, or cannot even keep it from getting any broader. We must have part of the kind of income that comes from the possession of the tools. And the kind of income that comes from being the one who receives the

dividends. Our goal is economic development based upon this rationalization. That is the only answer to keeping Black people from becoming a
totally dependent population.[5]

Economic integration through jobs and skills training is no longer
receiving priority in the Negro actions for economic and social equality.
The primary and current orientation in the quest for economic participation is the drive for black ownership and control of economic resources or
for black capitalism.[6] Given this economic goal of establishing a viable
black economic base, the choice of strategy becomes dominant. What is
the most effective means of establishing black entreprenurial ability and
black businesses?

Strategy for Development

In attempting to get the power associated with the control of economic resources, the Negro faces an ideological dilemma when he tries to
discover effective approaches. This dilemma is illustrated by the polar
case options that seem to be available to the black. The black must push
either for integration within the existing economic institutions or for some
form of economic separatism. The choice of strategy depends upon the
alternatives available. One course of action would institute black businesses within the established economic community. Here fledgling Negro
businesses and entrepreneurs would face the competition across the color
line. The risk to new black businesses in attempting to establish a biracial
economy is extremely great.

The alternate course is to establish a black economic substructure.
Black businesses would cater to a market composed of black consumers
or to the ghetto areas of the inner city. The risks involved in this line of
attack are also extremely high. The Negro market is limited by the low
level of its purchasing power. The attempt to establish black business of
any large scale is constrained by inadequate demand for the product or
services being marketed. It is difficult to establish a self-sufficient black
economy in the midst of a highly integrated white economic system. It is
necessary to maintain linkages with the established economic system,
particularly to supply needed capital funds and raw materials.

In extreme form the separate economic system alternative has a
geographical dimension. Where should the separate and self-sufficient
black society and supporting economic structure be established? The
separatist alternative is advocated by black nationalist organizations such
as Black Muslims, Black Panthers, and others.

Economic Separatists—The Militant Approach

These organizations have continued a well-established pattern of
emphasizing separation by a minority of blacks. The historical precedents
for black separatist movements can be found in the Niagra Movement,

Marcus Garvey's undertakings, recommendations by Frederick Douglass, and the more recent pronouncements of the Black Muslims. The older and more modern separatist concepts, however, are not homogeneous and differ as to the geographical focus, the time span for implementation, and, of course, the strategy for achieving the separate-entity status.

The modern separatist movements are more relevant in their reflection of the root economic causes that motivate separation. Many of these modern concepts are, however, no more complete than older concepts in regard to the manner in which a separate black economy can be operated and sustained.

Black Panthers and Black Muslims. The Black Muslims believe that the Western world is deteriorating, arguing that immorality is widespread within it. They feel that the only alternative open to the black, since he should not be integrated into a corrupt society, is to separate. The separate system would be one in which the life and liberty of the black would not be controlled or regulated by nonblacks. The economic element of this rejection of Western society is reflected in the criticism of capitalism as a tool for exploitation of the black man. For example, Malcolm X, a former Black Muslim and an early interpreter of some current Black Panther philosophy, noted in 1965 that,

> It is impossible for capitalism to survive, primarily because the system needs some blood to suck. Capitalism used to be like an eagle, but now it is more like a vulture. . . . As the nations of the world free themselves, then capitalism has less victims, less to suck, and it becomes weaker and weaker. It is only a matter of time in my opinion before it will collapse completely.[7]

The contemporary economic emphasis in the Black Panther organization is difficult to describe in detail. What is apparent, however, is that this organization wants "freedom" and the "power" to determine the destiny of the black community. Other economic elements of their wants are decent housing, educational programs uniquely designed for blacks, and full employment. They maintain that the government is responsible for this full employment plus a guaranteed annual income and that if full employment cannot be provided by the white business community, the means of production should be taken from the business men and placed in the community. The population of the community would then organize the business structure in such a way as to employ everyone in positions that assure a decent standard of living. Since white landlords do not provide decent housing, property should be expropriated and cooperatives set up with government help to provide acceptable standards of housing. The Black Panthers also ask for a cash indemnity from the government as "compensation" for the "genocide" of 50 million blacks by "racist" America. The total sought is based upon a contention that forty acres and two mules were promised the blacks as retribution for slavery and is an overdue debt.

The Panthers "reserve" the "right" to alter and abolish the system of government and institute a new form of government they say will be more consistent with the safety and happiness of indigenous peoples. It is assumed that military and other associated means could be used to overthrow the system.[8]

Related militant views on the relationship between black economic power and black political power were expressed in the publication *Black Power*.

> In the final analysis, we prefer cooperative black business ventures to private enterprise. . . . . Finally within the Afroamerican's struggle for survival and national liberation, black business must be viewed as an aid to that struggle, and not an end in itself. There is no way to achieve liberation inside the framework of Chuck's economic system; we can achieve a certain degree of autonomy in the economic sphere, but in the final analysis, **black political independence must precede black economic independence! Black power!**[9]

The time span of implementation and the method of operating a separate black economy are not detailed. Other than the references to expropriation and the cooperative movement, it may be assumed that a central government would be responsible for selected resource allocation decisions in the autonomous black community. The revolutionary overthrow of the existing economic institutions is a unique emphasis of the Black Power group.

The Black Panthers' program seems to contain certain secular and substantive, but no operational, elements of the Black Muslim concepts for economic autonomy.

The need to establish a Black Muslim nation is predicated on a conglomerate of religious, social, racial, and economic factors. The Muslims have adopted a nonrevolutionary approach in the early stages of establishing black economic autonomy. Through "normal" church channels of cash contributions, plus sales of equity ownership, the Muslims have established a black restaurant and supermarket in Chicago. They continue to plan for the regular establishment of those services needed by the indigenous black community. The time span for implementing the separate black economy is not firm nor are the details of location, form of industrial organization, or the structure of the system clear. The Muslims have, from time to time, espoused the concept that several southern states should be set aside for their use and occupancy. The implication is that the economy would be basically agricultural, located in the United States, and probably reflect stages of growth similar to those described by Rostow.[10]

The Republic of New Africa movement. In the spring of 1968 two hundred black persons met in Detroit to organize the Republic of New Africa, a new nation within the United States with a separate government and its own elected officials. At this organizational meeting the delegates approved a Declaration of Independence which stated that the black people of America were "forever free and independent of the jurisdiction of the United States."[11]

The reasoning behind the complete separation from the United States is clearly delineated.

> We cannot exist side by side with White America, with her huge military, unless she changes. Therefore we will have to depend upon internationalism for protection. But so long as we remain citizens of the United States of America no foreign government will come to our aid or even introduce our case to the U.N.[12]

This new "republic" proposes to establish a provisional capital in the state of Mississippi governed by its president, Robert F. Williams. The first goal of the new "government" is to hold a "plebiscite" among the Negro population of the United States. The results of this poll will be presented to the United Nations in an effort to persuade this international body to establish a legal base for the state in accordance with international law.

The Republic of New Africa has also requested "reparation payments" and land from the United States government.

> Reparations have never been paid to Black people for the admitted wrongs of slavery (or since slavery) inflicted upon our ancestors with the sanction of the United States Constitution. . . . . The principle of reparations for national wrongs, as for personal wrongs, is well established in international law. The West German government, for instance, has paid $850 million in equipment and credits in reparations to Israel for wrongs committed by the Nazis against the Jews of Europe. Demands for reparations, funnelled through a united Black power congress must include not only the demand for money and goods such as machinery, factories and laboratories, but a demand for land. And the land we want is the land where we are: Mississippi population, 42 percent Black; Louisiana, 32 percent; Alabama, 30 percent; Georgia, 29 percent; and South Carolina, 35 percent.[13]

Other than the demand for "reparations," the Republic of New Africa movement appears to be mainly political in nature with little specification of the economic form or mode of the new state.

The Core approach. Another evolutionary, separatist movement is led by the Congress of Racial Equality.

> The key idea . . . is the realization on the part of the present leadership of CORE that we are in fact two separate nations, two individual people. There are black people and there are white people. . . . If you look at yourself as a separate people, then you can view yourself as a nation-like entity. There are historical parallels. There were a number of peoples who didn't have any land for years, but who viewed themselves as a nation. And the nation State might, of course, be in the future, but the nations could co-exist. . . . Black nationalism would be the motivating factor behind the economic development. . . .[14]

The time span for the CORE program is as long or "at least equal to he number of years that one has been held back or one has been held in :heck and could not make any economic breakthrough."[15]

Although the evolutionary, as opposed to revolutionary, emphasis dominates the CORE programs, the sense of urgency to provide immediate relief to the black is apparent. ''Anytime you are in mortal danger, and we conceive ourselves to be in mortal danger, . . . the confrontation between black and white is on in this country and can be an awesome kind of potentiality for us, and probably for the greater society, too.''[16]

Roy Innis, national director of CORE, added form and substance to the organization's position in testifying before the resolutions committee at the 1968 Republican National Convention:

> Blacks must manage and control the institutions that service their areas, as it has always been for other interest groups. There is an essential need in such institutions as educational, health, social service, sanitation, protection, fire, housing, etc.
>
> Large and densely populated black areas, especially in urban centers, must have a change in status. They must become political sub-divisions of the state, instead of sub-colonial appendages of the cities. They must become more autonomous of the existing urban centers. In short, black people must be able to control basic societal instruments in the social, political, and economic areas.[17]

CORE's push for economic independence, at least in the short run, is directed toward the implementation of the CORE Development Corporation and the passage of the Community Self-Development Act and the Rural Development Incentive Act of 1968.

The goal of the CORE development program is to establish the power to produce wealth for low-income individuals by financing a second or ghetto economy in which ownership can be acquired by indigenous black families. CORE has proposed that corporations join with them in partnership arrangements. The corporation would first determine plant locations and then establish industries in the ghetto. CORE would determine the space and plant requirements and negotiate a lease on the property with this partner firm. The corporation would then provide the capital for plant construction. Rental income paid to CORE by the corporation would be used to repay indebtedness and to return to the firm its initial capital contribution. CORE would eventually assume full ownership after the corporation's equity investment was retired. The CORE interests would be held in a development corporation which would be owned by ghetto residents whose incomes were below some specified minimum.

An alternate technique for economic development has also been proposed by CORE. The corporation would pay a portion of its wage bill through an equity sharing or bonus program which would eventually transfer the ownership of the firm to the community

In 1968 a concept developed by CORE for establishing community self-development and rural-development corporations was introduced in the House of Representatives. This legislation represents the first attempt by a major black organization to initiate and develop federal participation of this type and magnitude. The Community Self-Development Act is an extensive package designed to attack all basic problem elements in low-income communities. The purpose of the legislation is to establish a new institutional structure in communities so that the indigenous population can achieve economic development and the ownership of resources through their own efforts and under their own control.

The basic elements of the program are the Community Development Corporation and the Community Development Bank. The CDC would own and manage subsidiary business and conduct a range of social services. For practical purposes, the CDC has features of a modern conglomerate corporation and a charitable foundation. The CDC Banks would serve the same general functions as the existing National Land Bank Association and as a secondary liquidity financial institution similar to the Federal Home Loan Banks. Tax incentives for large corporations are also built into the program. The incentives are designed to spur large corporations to establish plants in the local community, train local people as managers, and then pass ownership to the CDC. Other programs are designed to mobilize the talents and resources of the people left behind. The programs would require $1 billion funding in 1970 and additional private and public subscription of hundreds of millions of dollars.

The companion Rural Development Incentive Act of 1968 is designed to provide incentives for industries to establish job-producing industrial and commercial facilities in rural poverty areas through a system of tax rebates and incentives.

What is most significant about the CORE program is that it is the *only* well-formulated and carefully designed program for economic development advocated by the black militants. No other militant organization has gone as far as CORE in setting forth the operational aspects of the steps necessary to establish ghetto autonomy.

The Self-Development Act is the economic phase of the total drive for black autonomy. Mr. Innis noted in his testimony at the Republican National Convention in July, 1968 that "The constitution of the United States of America, which is a national contract for this nation, was never meant for Black people. . . . The obvious solution then is a new social contract (constitution). This contract will redefine the relationship between Blacks and Whites."[18]

The Black Power Elements of Development

James Boggs, a writer from Detroit, is currently working to develop the political elements of the establishment of a unique autonomous and separate black community. His work on the writing and development of a new social contract will add to the substantive understanding of the structure required by independent black communities. Boggs has written extensively on the subject of revolution, cybernetics, capitalism, and black power. Insight into his approach on the development of the economic elements of the social contract can be obtained from the following commentary:

> The organization for Black Power must concentrate on the issue of political power and refuse to redefine and explain away Black Power as

black everything except black political power. The development of technology in the United States has made it impossible for blacks to achieve economic power in the U.S.A. by the old means of capitalist development. The ability of U.S. capitalists today to produce an abundance not only makes competition with them on an economic capitalistic basis absurd but has already brought the U.S.A. technologically to the threshold of [a] society where each can have according to his needs. Thus black political power, coming at this juncture in the economically advanced U.S.A., is the key not only to black liberation but to the introduction of a new society to emancipate economically the masses of the people in general. For black political power will have to decide on the kind of economy and the aims and directions of the economy for the people.[19]

Black political control inexorably tied to the concept of black economic development is an accepted premise among many leaders of black militants.

For the Reverend Albert Cleague, Jr., the emergence of a well-defined philosophy on self-determination is significant:

Self-determination means seeking an escape from the powerlessness which is the basic problem in the black community, both in the areas of economics and in the area of politics. In the area of economics, the escape from powerlessness is a struggle for Black Power. It has to do with securing economic control of black ghetto communities. . . .
Essentially during the last year we have tried to change from the position of being completely powerless, economically. It's been really white businesses controlling black ghetto life with no sense of accountability to the Black community and no sense of participation by the Black community. The businesses, industry, anything that comes in, just set up in the community and exploit it and do whatever they like without any participation or accountability.[20]

In practical terms Cleague is moving toward a form of local political control over schools and other public services as well as over employment and control by blacks of businesses in the ghetto areas. This well-defined pattern of action is merely a stage in the evolutionary process of political and economic control until the blacks can be made more powerful economically. Cleague has also criticized the basic concepts of black capitalism because "it just continues an exploitive pattern." The "cooperative economy" is looked upon as a logical and acceptable alternative to the structure of black economies. Cleague noted "that there doesn't seem to be any other way to avoid the exploitation that is going to creep in just by the sheer preponderance of the control of the money. Even on the basis of the community corporation, it's the same thing." The cooperative economy would prevent the drain of economic power to selected groups, make inroads into the basic capital shortage problem, and permit the form of organization to be used in economic and noneconomic activities to assure local control. In the development process it is assumed that black cooperatives would first be substituted for existing retail and services outlays and then be extended to manufacturing, then back to the farm or agriculture, and then through the entire economic system. Cleague knows and has made use of Sweden's experiments in cooperatives. The interest in that country's experience continues to be a source of knowledge and motivation for those militants following Rev. Cleague. The cooperative thrust is consistent with the militant concept that "black people, more and more, recognize the fact that their identification with the total structure has been broken. Most black people are willing to do the sacrificial thing necessary in order to help black people to build some kind of economic position in American life."[21]

Support for this separatist approach among black nationalists is based on new dimensions of being black. For example, Rolland Snelling writing in the *Liberator* indicated that ". . . before we can free our people from White America, we must first free outselves! This can be accomplished by what is called the Internal Revolution of the psyche. We must search ourselves through and through to thoroughly examine our outlooks and goals, comparing them with the realities of present-day White America with its technical barbarism which is strangling our race." Snelling is an outspoken critic of capitalism, black or white. The economic and its related political system, he holds, perpetuate a system of exploitation through a master-and-slave relationship.[22]

Daniel Watts, the editor of the *Liberator,* a black militant monthly, eloquently phrases the black dilemma:

... do we want to save America, is America worth saving? It seems to me that this is the fundamental question, given the violent nature of American society today, the apparently increasing emphasis on violence as a way of life and this impenetrable wall of hate that emanates from the white community. I think one of the fundamental questions that the black people must answer is do we want in? I think this leads to a great deal of confusion in the black community. So despite the fact that you have many militants screaming 'Black Power' and talking about the ecomonic viability of the black community and things like that, there is still a great deal of ambivalence among ourselves as to whether or not we want into [to] the American scene. So let's assume for purposes of this discussion that we want into the American scene, into the mainstream of America.

It seems to me that our interest in the mainstream would mean a fundamental change in the economic, political, and social structure of America . . . we have to constitutionally find a way in which the races can coexist together. . . . If there is any tacit admission that the black people have a right to live in this world, there we may have the basis for a new social, political, and economic order in this country.[23]

Despite the fact that Watts illustrates the dilemma and points the way to the embryonic steps of accommodation between the separatists and the moderates, he believes that whites with economic and political power will not give up that power. The issue for Watts is whether or not the white community is willing to sit down with black leaders and discuss the meaningful transfer and sharing of power and coexistence. If the whites do not, "we are going to have to fight white America at the barricades."[24]

Given the attitudes concerning the alternatives faced by the blacks in gaining some limited degree of economic development, it is important to note that the bases for a separate economy and political system are fairly well established in the ethos of the black-white confrontation. The political elements of the separatist concept are intertwined with the economic aspects. The separate political and economic entity concept has been illustrated here without reference to the actual viability of separate black nations or economies. Regardless of the validity of the thesis of viability of black autonomies, widespread evidence exists that able black leadership would prefer to "make it" economically outside the system, and represent one polar case strategy to improve the economic conditions of the black.

The Issues—Summary and Conclusions

The dichotomy confronting the American Negro has been whether to attempt to achieve meaningful integration into a social and institutional structure resistant to this effort or to separate from the society and thus from the controls and the constraints exercised through its institutions. Because of exhaustion of alternatives other than the economic and because of the evolving nature of the movement for equal rights, present activities of that movement must focus upon problems of economic advancement of the Negro within the black community. This ideological dilemma in the choice of effective action is now transferred into an economic context.

Within this context, militant leaders of national organizations have by-passed the historical emphasis of civil-rights organizations on attempting to achieve economic integration through jobs and skills training. They argue that economic development for the Negro can only come through black ownership and black control of productive resources. The tactical dilemma facing the Negro is whether to attempt to build viable black economic institutions within the existing and largely white economic structure or to establish these institutions within a separate, all-black environment. The militants have resolved this tactical dilemma in favor of separation.

Within the separate black economy alternative, another choice of strategy has yet to be made. One option is a semiseparate state in which economic institutions would be established in the racial ghettos of the cities. Another option would be the establishment of a geographically separate state with no political ties with the existing national structure.

This paper has surveyed and briefly catalogued the alternatives advocated by militant leaders of national organizations and the techniques for implementing these goals. It is not feasible in this paper to give a careful evaluation of these programs. But the correspondence between the development alternatives currently advocated by militants and pervasive social policies may be assessed. The report of the National Advisory Commission on Civil Disorders concluded that three basic future choices confront the United States in the attempt to provide socially viable answers to the problems of our cities. Under the first alternative, the "present policies choice," the share of national resources presently allocated to welfare efforts would be maintained. The absolute amount of welfare allocations should increase through time with the growth of federal revenues. Since the present share of federal revenues allocated to antipoverty programs is insufficient even to carry out a holding action against the social and economic deterioration of the inner-city, the Commission argues that the "present-policies choice" is not a realistic solution.

The second alternative, "the enrichment choice," would attempt to offset the adverse effects of continued segregation and deprivation of the ghetto and generate significant improvements in the environmental quality of these areas. This effort would not be designed to affect appreciably the pattern of segregation in the inner-city, but make the ghetto areas more habitable.

The third alternative, "the integration choice," would improve the quality of life in racial enclaves, but with the concomitant emphasis of creating incentives for out-migration from inner-city ghettos and integration into the social, economic, and political fabric of American life.

The integration alternative, under which every citizen can exercise free choice without confronting racial barriers, corresponds most closely to the idealism which American social philosophy has historically expressed. But it is now evident that economic programs are formulated in government agencies, in industry, and in the black community without consideration of their long-run social consequences, which may lead inadvertently to the "enrichment choice." For example, the present emphasis on ghetto economic development and black capitalism implies that the ghetto can serve as a viable unit for economic development. Attempts are being made to bring industry into the inner-city to provide sources of income for ghetto residents and to make available capital funds to assist Negro entrepreneurs in establishing black businesses which cater to a market composed of Negro consumers. Policies of this nature may result in increasing rigidity of the segregated pattern of life in metropolitan areas.

The crucial decision to be made in the black community is whether the "integration choice" is feasible and desirable at the economic level. In terms of productive capacity and the potential to provide an acceptable level of economic welfare for all members of the society, the capitalistic system is worth attempting to integrate. Daniel Watts, a militant, has recognized this.

   Which now leads us to the whole question of whether black people accept capitalism. This question was asked of me at a university by one of the white students who took the position that capitalism was intrinsically bad, it was exploitive, etc., etc. I take the position that we, the black community, would bring a new dimension in terms of human wealth, human values into the white capitalist system in terms of how we view human life and the value that we place on it as opposed to the whites who, I think, look upon human life as something secondary, something to be bargained for with dollars. I don't think that coming out of the black experience that black people would view human beings in the same light as whites do. So I think that it is still possible for black people to get involved in the capitalistic structure, and whether you like it or not, the basic fact of life is that the capitalistic system in America does produce. There is no question about it, the system works, it produces.[25]

If, however, it is true that elements of racial constraint are built into all American institutions, it may not be possible to achieve economic integration into our capitalistic system as presently constituted. The Reverend Albert Cleague militantly argues that this is the case:

. . . I think as far as the black community is concerned, the capitalistic economy doesn't work for us because we don't have any stake in it. It just happens that when we got to a place where we were able to do something, we were outside and the concentration of wealth in the white capitalistic set up is so complete now that you can't break into that. And with all the other racist elements in American society, we are not only outside of it, but we are frozen outside of it.[26]

NOTES

1. Bayard Rustin, "Funding Full Citizenship," *Council Journal* 6 (Dec. 1967), p. 7. The two periods referred to are (1) the period of legal action in the courts which culminated with the 1954 decision, and (2) that of the civil-rights marches and sit-ins to obtain compliance with the law.

2. F. Naylor Fitzhugh, vice-president, Pepsi-Cola, Inc., personal interview, New York City, July 18, 1968.

3. Berkeley G. Burrell in a speech presented at the Business Opportunity Workshop for Industrial Procurement, Bethpage, New York, May 24, 1968, p. 5.

4. William Morris, personal interview on July 17, 1968 at the NAACP national headquarters in New York City.

5. Kermit Scott, program director for CORE, personal interview at the CORE National Convention in Columbus, Ohio, on July 8, 1968.

6. President Richard M. Nixon endorsed the concept of "Black Capitalism." In "Bridges to Human Dignity," an address on the CBS Radio Network, Apr. 25, 1968, he said: "For too long, White America has sought to buy off the Negro—and to buy off its own sense of guilt—with ever more programs of welfare, of public housing, of payments to the poor, but not for anything except for keeping out of sight: payments that perpetuated poverty, and that kept the endless, dismal cycle of dependency spinning for generation to generation," (p. 2). "It's no longer enough that White-owned enterprises employ greater numbers of Negroes, whether as laborers or as middle management personnel. This is needed, yes—but it has to be accompanied by an expansion of Black ownership, of Black capitalism. We need more Black employers, more Black businesses," (p. 9). "If our urban ghettos are to be rebuilt from within, one of the first requirements is the development of Black-owned and Black-run business. The need is more than economic. Black ownership—of homes, of land, and especially of productive enterprise—is both symbol and evidence of opportunity, and this is central to the spirit of independence on which orderly progress rests," (p. 16).

7. From interview, "Malcolm X Speaks: Last Answers and Interviews," *Young Socialist*, Mar.–Apr. 1965.

8. See the *Black Panther*, No. 23, 1967, p. 7. (Published by the Black Panther organization in California.)

9. "Black Business: Its Role in the Liberation Struggle," *Black Power*, Mar. 1967, p. 10.

10. W. W. Rostow, *Stages of Economic Growth* (Cambridge, Mass.: Harvard University Press, 1960).

11. David Llorens, "Black Separatism in Perspective," *Ebony* 33 (Oct. 1968): 88.

12. Richard B. Henry, Minister of Information of The Republic of New Africa, quoted in Llorens, *Ebony*, 33:95.

13. *Ibid.*

14. Interview with Kermitt Scott, project director, CORE, Columbus, Ohio, July 1968.

15. *Ibid.*

16. *Ibid.*

17. Statement, before the Subcommittee on Equal Opportunity in an Urban Society for the Resolutions Committee, Republican National Convention, Miami Beach, Fla., July 30, 1968, pp. 6–7.

18. *Ibid.*, p. 6.

19. James Bogges, "Black Power," *Liberator*, May, 1967, part II, p. 9.

20. Interview with the Rev. Albert Cleague (Central United Church of Christ), Detroit, Mich., July 24, 1968.

21. *Ibid.*

22. Rolland Snelling, "Toward Repudiating Western Values," *Liberator*, Nov. 1964, pp. 11–12.

23. Interview with Daniel Watts, New York City, July 18, 1968.

24. *Ibid.*

5. *Ibid.*

26. The Reverend Albert Cleague, personal interview, Detroit, July 24, 1968.

The Prospects for
Minority-owned Commercial Banks:
A Comparative Performance Analysis

John T. Boorman

The ownership of commercial banks and other financial institutions by members of minority groups has expanded rapidly in the past ten years. In December 1962, only ten commercial banks with total assets of $87 million were listed as minority controlled. By December 1972, the number of such institutions had increased to 41 and their total assets had grown to over $675 million.[1] The most rapid expansion in the number of these institutions has occurred within the past three years and the pace is still quickening. No fewer than 33 minority groups (blacks, American Indians and Mexican Americans) are currently at some stage of the bank-formation process.

While most of the older minority institutions were located in small or medium-sized southern cities, almost all of the institutions chartered more recently are found in the nation's largest metropolitan areas.[2] These urban areas are often characterized by low income, high unemployment, and sometimes by chronic physical deterioration. This fact alone has raised serious questions about the potential profitability of these banks and about the role they may be expected to play in community economic development. These issues have previously been discussed by Brimmer [1971, 1972, 1968], Irons [1971] and by Boorman and Kwast [1972]. However, the very rapid growth of some of these banks, together with the failure of one of the newer ones and the special assistance required by another, as well as the intense interest demonstrated by a large number of minority groups in applying for new charters, all suggest the need for additional analysis. The purpose of this paper, then, is to review the evidence on the recent performance of minority-owned banks. These banks are first compared with a sample of nonminority banks by updating and expanding the work of Brimmer and Irons. Next, the hypothesis that the performance of the newer minority-owned banks differs not only from that of nonminority banks but also from that of the older minority-owned institutions is tested. The evidence indicates that significant differences do exist between the older and newer minority-owned banks. This result, together with the apparent improvement in the relative performance of the minority-owned banks between the time of Brimmer's study and our own, suggests the desirability of examining the performance of the newer minority-owned banks with that of a sample of new nonminority banks on a time series basis. This comparison is presented in the last section. The additional information content of the disaggregated time series study leads to more optimistic conclusions about the prospects for successful operation of minority-owned institutions than would be suggested by the single-period data alone.

Brief Look at Studies by Andrew Brimmer and Edward Irons

The essential conclusions presented in the studies by Brimmer and Irons indicate that the current earnings potential of the average black-owned commercial bank is substantially below that of an average nonminority institution. Some of the causal factors cited in these papers to explain the observed performance of these banks include the following:

▶ Inefficient operations due to the lack of experienced management and banking expertise in the black community
▶ High costs caused both by poor management and by the fact that black banks attract a large number of small, highly active deposit accounts
▶ Large loan losses due to the employment and income characteristics of the markets served
▶ Lower gross earnings resulting from the banks' greater need to diversify into lower yielding, more secure assets

Brimmer analyzed the operating performance of black-owned banks both on a limited time-series basis [Brimmer, 1968] and, more recently, in a detailed single-period extension of that work [Brimmer, 1971]. In his earlier paper, because almost half of his black-bank sample was chartered after 1962, Brimmer hypothesized that the poor average performance of the entire sample reflected the especially poor showing of the newer banks. His evidence seems to support this hypothesis. Comparing the profitability of new black banks during their first several years of operation with that of other newly chartered banks in the country, he concludes that " . . . new Negro-owned banks do face a much more difficult task than do new banks generally" [Brimmer, 1968, p. 21].[3]

In his later paper, Brimmer presents more detail on the operations of his sample banks but limits the analysis to one year, 1969, and aggregates over all black banks. He presents comparative data on operating costs, profitability, and management performance for the black banks and for several samples of nonminority-owned banks. Brimmer's pessimistic conclusions from the analysis of these papers leads him to propose that we focus on alternative means of financing community development.

The data in Irons's study generally support Brimmer's assessment of the relatively poor performance of the black banks (in terms of management capacity, earnings and return on capital).[4] However, Irons injects a strong sociological element to conclude that "potentially . . . [black banks are] . . . as sound as any group in the United States" [Irons, 1971, p. 424]. The current performance of black banks, he concludes, is a reflection of " . . . all the past constraints imposed by society . . . " Therefore, their potential for success is a "societal contingency" dependent upon active programs instituted by the community to bring about the economic equality of the black banks' primary customers—the black family and the black businessman—and to bolster the function of these banks as depositories for government and corporate funds. Most importantly, Irons contends that even at a cost these institutions are necessary to provide the community leadership essential to reversing the increasing deterioration of black areas.

The Current Performance of Minority-owned Banks

This section reports on the results of a single-period analysis similar to those presented by Brimmer and Irons for 1969. Employing the December 1971 Reports of Income and Reports of Condition, the performance of a sample of minority-owned commercial banks has been compared with that of all insured commercial banks with less than $50 million in deposits.[5] The minority bank sample consists of the 17 banks founded before 1968 and owned and controlled by members of minority groups (mostly black Americans). The banks included in this sample are indicated in Table 1. The nonminority bank sample consists of 11,758 institutions and includes all insured commercial banks founded before 1968.[6]

The data in Tables 2 to 4 indicate that there are important and obvious differences between the minority and nonminority sample banks with regard to the sources of their deposits, their asset portfolio and their sources and uses of income. In addition, the evidence in Figure 5 shows that when judged on the basis of loan-portfolio management and overall profitability, the minority banks as a group do not appear to perform as well as the nonminority banks. These various elements of minority bank performance will now be examined in more detail.

Asset and liability composition of minority-owned commercial banks

The most important differences evident in the composition of deposit liabilities of the sample banks involve the very large proportion of U.S. Government deposits attracted by the minority banks and the structure of private time and savings deposit accounts at these banks.

TABLE 1
Minority Banks in Existence as of June 1972

Bank	SMSA or County	Date Estab-lished	Total Assets* ($ Thou-sands)
Citizens Trust Company B, I, C	Atlanta	6/21	40,745
Unity Bank B	Boston	6/68	14,218
Highland Community	Chicago	11/70	12,156
Independence B, I, C	Chicago	12/64	46,633
†Seaway National B, I, C	Chicago	1/65	48,708
†Victory Savings Bank B, I, C	Columbia, S.C.	10/21	5,044
First State Bank B, I	(Danville, Va.)	9/19	7,796
Unity State Bank	Dayton	8/70	7,204
First Independence	Detroit	5/70	27,305
Mechanics & Farmers B, I, C	Durham	3/08	37,694
†Riverside National B, I, C	Houston	8/63	18,788
Swope Parkway National B	Kansas City (Mo.)	7/68	12,188
Douglas State B, I, C	Kansas City (Kan.)	8/47	18,806
†Bank of Finance B, I, C	Los Angeles	11/64	28,433
Tri-State B, I, C	Memphis	12/46	19,627
First Plymouth B	Minneapolis	2/69	12,364
Citizens Savings Bank & Trust B, I, C	Nashville	1/04	8,423
†Freedom National B, I, C	New York	12/64	47,111
Freedom Bank of Finance B	Portland, Ore.	8/69	4,413
Consolidated B, I, C	Richmond, Va.	7/03	19,621
†Gateway National B, I, C	Saint Louis	6/65	16,701
Carver State B, I, C	Savannah	1/27	7,370
Liberty Bank B	Seattle	5/68	6,415
Peoples Bank	Springfield	9/70	5,246
†United Community B, I, C	Washington, D.C.	8/64	21,039
Industrial B, I, C	Washington, D.C.	8/34	34,479
Atlantic National	Norfolk, Va.	9/71	8,762
North Milwaukee State Bank	Milwaukee, Wis.	2/71	9,022
Skyline National**	Denver, Colo.	12/71	6,399
Vanguard National Bank	(Nassau, N.Y.)	5/72	10,923
Greensboro National Bank	Greensboro, N.C.	11/71	3,579
First Enterprise	San Francisco-Oakland	6/72	8,404
American State Bank	Tulsa, Okla.	11/70	4,128
†Pan American National Bank B, C	Los Angeles	4/65	21,014
Pan American National Bank	Union City, N.J.	7/71	12,021
Centinel Bank of Taos	Taos, N.M.	3/69	8,858
Bank of Commerce of Laredo	Laredo, Texas	9/66	23,516
Banco del Pueblo	Santa Ana, Calif.	7/71	8,695
Pan American National Bank	Houston, Texas	8/70	7,592
Gateway National Bank of Chicago***	Chicago	12/72	10,195
Guaranty Bank & Trust Company***	Chicago	12/72	5,298
			676,933

*Total Assets as of Dec. 1972.
**Closed, Mar. 26, 1973.
***Purchase of existing bank.
B—Bank included in study by Andrew Brimmer (1970).
I—Bank included in study by Edward Irons (1970).
C—Bank included in single period comparison in part II of this paper.
*—Bank included in Time Series Study of new minority-owned banks.
Source: Federal Deposit Insurance Corporation.

TABLE 2
Deposit Liabilities of Insured Commercial Banks* and
Seventeen Sample Minority-Owned Banks, December 1971

Classification of Deposit Liability	Minority-Owned Banks	Nonminority-Owned Banks
A. *Deposits as a Percentage of Total Liabilities*		
1. Demand, IPC	30.7	36.2
2. Time and savings, IPC	44.6	49.9
3. U.S. government, total	8.7	1.4
4. State and political subdivision	9.8	9.1
5. Certified and officers checks	3.8	0.8
B. *Demand Deposits as Percentage of Total Demand Deposits*		
1. IPC	69.4	82.9
2. U.S. government	18.1	3.2
3. State and political subdivision	5.9	11.0
4. Deposits of commercial banks	0.05	0.77
5. Certified and officers checks	6.4	1.9
C. *Time and Savings Deposits as Percentage of Total Time and Savings Deposits*		
1. Savings deposits, IPC	53.3	35.7
2. Time deposits, IPC	32.1	54.6
3. U.S. government	1.36	0.08
4. State and political subdivision	13.1	8.5
D. *Deposits as a Percentage of Total IPC Deposits*		
1. Demand, IPC	40.77	42.04
2. Time and savings, IPC	59.24	57.96

*Less than $50 million in deposits; established before 1968.
Source: Federal Deposit Insurance Corporation.

During 1971, federal government deposits at the minority-owned banks in this sample increased by over $10 million to $44.9 million. This new balance represents more than 18 percent of their demand deposit liabilities and over 10 percent of their total deposit liabilities. In contrast, federal government deposits generally account for only about 2 percent of total deposits at nonminority banks.[7] This increase in deposits results primarily from the U.S. Treasury's Minority Bank Deposit Program. Announced in October, 1970 by Charles Walker, this program committed

the Nixon Administration to " . . . increasing deposits in minority banks
by $100 million during the coming year" [Walker, 1970, p. 7]. In addition
to a direct increase in its own deposits of $35 million, the government
promised to launch a solicitation effort to encourage corporations,
unions, foundations and others to channel funds to these institutions.s
    While the immediate goal of increasing minority bank deposits would
seem to have been achieved, the concomitant goal of stimulating additional lending by these banks to minority business enterprises in inner city
areas may not yet have been accomplished. Black bankers have com-
plained that they are unable to make loans on the basis of the government
deposits, because these deposits are too volatile. While it was hoped that
the volatility of these accounts would be lower than average, thereby
reducing the overall liquidity needs of minority banks and releasing funds
for commercial lending, it appears that this has not been the result. In his
examination of this question, Brimmer pointed to the large volume of
government securities held by minority banks, and noted that " . . . it
appears that black banks may be in the anomalous position of campaigning for U.S. government funds which they then use to finance a disproportionate share of the Federal debt" [Brimmer, 1972, p. 9]. His data suggest
the need for additional analysis to determine the true benefits of the
government's deposit program for the minority banks and for the areas
which they serve.
    In addition to these differences in government accounts, examination
of the FDIC collected Summary of Deposits reveals significant differences between the minority and nonminority banks in the structure and
composition of private time and savings deposit accounts. Whereas only
35 percent (by value) of all time and savings accounts at nonminority
banks are classified as "savings" accounts with no fixed maturity, this
figure is over 53 percent at the minority banks. In addition, the average
number of such accounts at the minority-owned banks is extremely large,
ranging from two and one-half to three times the number at the nonminority banks. However, the average balance in such accounts at minority
banks is less than 60 percent as large as that at the nonminority banks.
These figures reflect both the lack of financial sophistication and the
lower-than-average income and wealth levels of minority-bank customers. It has been found that these customers often employ their savings
accounts as very short-term repositories of funds in much the same way
that higher-income individuals employ their checking accounts. This
leads to frequent withdrawals of funds causing unusually high teller expenses. Failure to induce customers to use demand deposit accounts for
regular bill payments has led many of the minority-owned banks to
impose a service charge structure on savings accounts to cover the costs
of this activity. In some cases, this has been explained as an inducement
to encourage customers to open demand deposit accounts and to become
familiar with the use of checking facilities; in other instances, it was
recognized as a simple device for recouping the cost of teller activity. In
either case, however, it has been the source of sizable revenue at many of
the minority banks.

TABLE 3
Asset Allocation of Insured Commercial Banks* and
Seventeen Sample Minority-Owned Banks, December 1971

Asset Category	Minority-Owned Banks	Nonminority-Owned Banks
As percentage of total assets		
1. Cash and Due from Banks	11.10	11.38
2. Securities	36.58	35.35
a) U.S. Treasury	16.38	17.67
b) U.S. agencies and corporations	11.16	5.82
c) States and political subdivisions	7.77	11.19
d) Other	1.27	0.67
3. Federal Funds sold	8.20	4.02
4. Loans	40.31	47.32
5. Other	3.80	1.83
As percentage of total loans		
1. Real Estate		
a) Secured by Farmland	0.19	6.24
b) Secured by 1-4 Family Properties-FHA	4.05	0.92
c) Secured by 1-4 Family Properties-VA	1.02	0.28
d) Secured by 1-4 Family Properties-Conventional	29.00	15.98
e) Secured by Multifamily Properties-FHA	1.17	0.04
f) Secured by Multifamily Properties-Conventional	1.76	0.33
g) Secured by Nonfarm, Nonresidential prop.	8.80	6.32
Total (nonfarm), (b) to (g)	(45.80)	(23.87)
2. Loans to Farmers	0.02	20.84
3. Commercial and Industrial Loans	18.76	17.76
4. Auto Instalment Loans	11.23	11.93
5. Other Consumer Loans	0.06	1.96
6. Repair and Modernization-Instalment	4.79	1.12
7. Other Instalment Loans	7.64	4.13
8. Single Payment Loans	4.06	6.81

*Less than $50 million in Deposits; established before 1968.
Source: Federal Deposit Insurance Corporation.

Significant differences in asset management are also evident in the portfolios of our sample banks. The comparative figures presented in Table 3 indicate that the minority banks tend to be more liquid than the nonminority banks, concentrating more heavily on government securities, and trading more actively in Federal Funds. Concomitantly, the minority banks generally devote a smaller proportion of total assets to loans and allocate their loan funds to different uses than do the nonminority banks. The most important differences in the loan portfolios involve the relatively heavy concentration on residential mortgages and the virtual absence of any loans to farmers by the minority-owned banks. The nonminority banks allocate less than 25 percent of all loans to residential mortgages as compared with over 45 percent at the minority banks. These and other figures in Table 3, such as the relative proportion of loans in the instalment loan category, may reflect the general urban orientation of most of the minority banks.

TABLE 4
Costs and Revenues of Insured Commercial Banks* and
Seventeen Sample Minority-Owned Banks, 1971

Asset Category	Minority-Owned Banks	Nonminority-Owned Banks
As a percentage of total operating income		
1. Interest and fees on loans	51.01	59.07
2. Income on Federal Funds sold	4.78	2.97
3. Interest and dividends on securities	14.14	17.14
4. Service charges on deposits	9.56	3.97
5. Other service charges	2.91	1.95
Total Service Charges	12.47	5.92
6. Other operating income	1.38	1.26
Total operating income/total assets	5.72	5.96
As a percentage of total operating expenses		
1. Employee salaries and wages	28.14	26.03
2. Pensions and other benefits	2.50	3.14
3. Interest paid on deposits	34.50	45.87
4. Interest on capital notes and debentures	0.24	0.08
5. Premises and equipment	8.30	6.71
6. Provision for loan losses	6.92**	2.55
7. Other operating expense	19.30	15.35
Total operating expense/total assets	5.35	4.79
Net current operating earnings/total assets	0.37	1.17
Net current operating earnings—exclusive of provision for loan losses/total assets	0.74	1.29

* Less than $50 million in Deposits; established before 1968.
** If we exclude the minority-owned bank which has suffered unusually high loan losses in recent years, this figure is 5.79.
Source: Federal Deposit Insurance Corporation.

Cost and revenue at minority-owned commercial banks

In Table 4, comparative figures are presented on the major income and expense items for the sample banks. Many of the differences reflect the portfolio compositions noted above. However, there are important differences which require additional examination. On the revenue side, for example, service charge income resulting, in part at least, from the special charges imposed on low-balance, high-activity savings deposits, account for more than twice the proportion of total operating income for the minority banks as for the nonminority institutions. On the basis of this single-period evidence, this factor appears to represent a significant structural difference imposed on the minority banks by the characteristics of the market areas which they service.

On the cost side, the minority banks have slightly higher employee expenses, lower interest costs, and much larger loan losses than do the nonminority banks. In 1971, employee salaries and wages measured as a percent of total operating expenses were 28.14 percent for the minority banks and 26.03 percent for the nonminority banks—a 2.11 percent differential. This represents substantial improvement over the performance reported for 1969 by Brimmer [1971] and Irons [1971].[8] This decline in the minority bank ratio relative to that for the nonminority banks over this two-year period may be the result of increasing efficiency on the part of the minority banks. This conclusion is supported by the trend in the ratio of total assets to the number of employees at the sample banks. In Brimmer's 1969 data, this ratio was $586,600/employee for the nonminority banks and only $310,300/employee for the minority banks. This compares with 1971 figures of $605,915/employee for the nonminority banks (an increase of 3.4 percent over the 1969 figure) and $434,800/employee for the minority banks (an increase of 40 percent over the 1969 figure).

The lower interest expenses of minority-owned banks reflects both the lower proportion of higher-yielding time deposits in the time and savings deposit category at these banks and the higher-activity, lower-average balances of savings deposits. These latter characteristics reduce the claim of their owners to interest payments on such accounts.[9]

By far the largest proportionate differential between expense items at the minority and nonminority banks occurs in the provision for loan loss account. This represents the amount set aside to cover loan losses and, since 1969, is counted as an expense by commercial banks.[10] In 1971, this figure, as a percent of total expenses, was almost three times as large for the minority as for the nonminority banks and accounted for some of the differential in net current operating earnings between these banks. As shown in Table 4, net current operating earnings relative to total assets was 0.37 percent for the minority banks and 1.17 percent, or almost three times as high, for the nonminority banks. However, excluding provision for loan losses from current operating expenses and recalculating net operating income on this adjusted basis increases the minority bank figure to 0.74 percent and the nonminority bank figure to 1.29 percent. The differential, thus, drops from 80 to 55 basis points. In short, the performance of minority-owned banks compares substantially more favorably with that of the nonminority banks if loan loss experience is kept separate from the other operating statistics of these banks.

Profitability of minority-owned commercial banks

Data on profitability, loan loss charge-offs and capital accumulation

TABLE 5
Profitability of Insured Commercial Banks* and
Seventeen Sample Minority-Owned Banks, December 1971

	Minority-Owned Banks	Nonminority-Owned Banks
1. Net current operating income/current operating income	6.51	19.67
2. Net securities gains and losses/securities†	0.39	0.19
3. Net income as percentage of:		
a) Current operating income	7.11	15.42
b) Total assets†	0.41	0.91
c) Total capital accounts†	5.16	11.46
Addendum:		
A. Loan losses		
1. Provision for loan losses/total operating expense†	6.92	2.55
2. Gross loan losses charged off/total loans†	1.01	0.38
3. Net loan losses charged off/total loans†	0.73	0.24
4. Reserves for loan losses/total loans†	0.80	1.51
B. Accumulated capital accounts		
1. Total capital accounts/total assets	0.055	0.076
2. Dollars of assets per dollar of capital	18.08	13.10
3. Category as a percentage of total capital:		
a) Notes and debentures†	5.97	1.12
b) Equity capital	94.03	98.87
c) Common stock†	41.50	24.77
d) Surplus	36.16	39.60
e) Undivided profit	14.59	31.76

* Less than $50 million in deposits; established before 1968.
† Difference is significant at the 5% level.
Source: Federal Deposit Insurance Corporation.

are presented in Table 5. Measuring net income as a return on either total assets or total capital, the minority banks are less than one-half as profitable as the nonminority sample banks. As with the data of the previous section, actual losses charged off against loan loss reserves show that this single item is the source of a large portion of this differential in sample bank profitability.

The cumulative effect of the past performance of the sample banks is reflected in the current position of their capital accounts. The minority banks are undercapitalized relative to the nonminority banks, having about $18 of assets for each dollar of capital compared to only about $13 of assets per dollar of capital at the nonminority banks. However, these figures probably tend to understate the capital problem of the minority banks. Examining the sources of total capital shows that minority banks have had to rely on stock issues and even on the issuance of notes and debentures to bolster their capital position. Nonminority banks, on the other hand, have been able to generate a much larger proportion of their total capital "internally" through retained earnings. On a current basis, this reflects the historical difficulty the minority banks have had in generating after-tax profit. Once again, however, this probably understates the divergence between minority and nonminority bank profitability inasmuch as it does not take account of paid-out dividends. These have been extremely small at the newer minority banks.

The data above seem to confirm several important conclusions presented by Irons and Brimmer. Minority-owned banks are, on the average, substantially less profitable than nonminority banks. Furthermore, much of this differential may be attributed to the very high loan losses suffered at the minority banks. At the same time, however, the data on employee expenses and deposit structure indicate that it would be hard to argue both that the minority banks are still substantially less efficient than the nonminority banks and that substantial improvement has not occurred at the former. At least in some aspects of their operation, then, the minority banks as a group seem to be performing relatively better in 1971 than they were when examined by Irons and Brimmer in 1969.

Maturity and the Performance of Minority-Owned Commercial Banks

While the data presented above provide a rough indication of the performance of minority-owned banks relative to other banks in the country, the confidence one may place in the conclusions derived from that analysis is weakened by several important factors. First of all, these data were derived from the December 1971 Reports of Income and Reports of Condition. The former records the experience of the banks for only a single period; the latter contains balance sheet figures for only a single date. It is impossible to determine from these data alone, for example, whether the differences found in sample bank performance will persist or, if they are likely to change, whether they will change for the better or the worse. Even more basically, it may be argued that the concept of "minority bank" itself does not provide us with a homogeneous sample of banks which has any real economic meaning. Within the group of seventeen banks identified as minority-owned, nine are 25 years old or older and located primarily in small cities in the Southeastern part of the country. The remaining eight banks, which have all been established since 1963, tend to be oriented towards large, urban markets populated primarily by members of minority groups.

Therefore, because of differences in both age and location, it is plausible to expect the performance of the newer banks to differ significantly from that of the older minority-owned institutions. To bring some evidence to bear on this hypothesis, the minority bank sample was disaggregated into two groups: Those founded before 1948 and those that are part of the new movement which began in 1963. Several significant differences between the older and newer minority-owned banks regarding their sources of funds and the allocation of those funds for investment purposes are revealed in the disaggregated data. While the proportion of IPC deposits[11] held in various categories is nearly equal at the two classes of banks, the older banks have a significantly higher proportion of state and local government deposits among their total deposits (11.88 percent versus 7.56 percent), and the newer banks have a larger share of federal government deposits (11.25 percent versus 6.39 percent).[12] These differences are reflected in the investment policies of the minority banks. The newer banks have invested 40.3 percent of their assets in highly liquid U.S. government securities (including the securities of U.S. agencies and corporations) and 3.9 percent of their assets in municipal securities. At the older banks, these figures are 25.1 percent and 11.2 percent, respectively. The relatively high activity of the newer banks in the Federal Funds market further demonstrates their desire to maintain a highly liquid position.

The major difference in lending policy between the older and newer banks derives from the heavy concentration by the former in residential and nonresidential mortgages. In December 1971, for example, the older banks had more than 58 percent of their loans committed to this type of investment. The 31 percent of loans in these categories at the newer banks was very much closer to the 23 percent figure for all insured banks. The bulk of these investments at the older banks are in 1–4 family residential mortgages. Specialization in this area seems to be a hallmark of the older minority banks located in the small southeastern cities. In many cases, it is matched by an equally high concentration of deposits in rather stable time and savings accounts. The 50 percent of total liabilities in this category at the older banks is significantly higher than the 40 percent figure at the newer minority banks. Deposit source may be an important explanation of the differential in investment policy at the sample banks.

Besides these portfolio differences, there are important differences between the profitability and current capital positions of the older and newer minority banks. In Table 6, the data on nonminority banks from Table 5 is reproduced and comparative figures for the minority banks are presented on a disaggregated basis. Since one of the newer minority banks had extremely large losses in 1971, averages for the newer banks are presented both inclusive and exclusive of that bank's data.[13] The exclusive averages will be employed in most of the comparisons below.

In general, the data support the original hypothesis of this section: Several of the important operating statistics and capital account ratios differ significantly between the older and newer minority-owned banks. Almost every current performance measure for the older minority-owned banks lies between the averages for the newer minority banks and the nonminority banks. As items (3a) and (3b) indicate, the newer minority banks are less profitable than the older banks, though the difference is not as great as that between the older minority-owned banks and the nonminority institutions.

TABLE 6
Comparative Performance of Nine Older and Eight Newer
Minority-Owned Commercial Banks, December 1971

	Older Minority Banks	Minority Banks Established 1963–1965*		Nonminority-Owned Banks Established before 1968
		(1)	(2)	
1. Net Current Operating Income/ Current Operating Income	9.12	3.57	7.59	19.67
2. Net Securities Gains and Losses/Securities	0.39	0.41	0.45	0.19
3. Net Income as Percentage of:				
a) Current Operating Income	9.38	4.57	8.63	15.42
b) Total Assets	0.55	0.25	0.48	0.91
c) Total Capital Accounts	9.16	0.66**	8.25	11.46

ADDENDUM:

A. Loan Losses

1. Provision for Loan Losses/Total Operating Expense†	4.22	9.95	8.47	2.55
2. Gross Loan Losses Charged Off/Total Loans	0.69	1.37	0.82	0.38
3. Net Loan Losses Charged Off/Total Loans†	0.40	1.10	0.57	0.24
4. Reserves for Loan Losses/Total Loans	0.78	0.82	0.94	1.51

B. Accumulated Capital Accounts

1. Total Capital Accounts/Total Assets	0.063	0.049	0.056	0.076
2. Dollars of Assets per Dollar of Capital	15.87	20.41	17.76	13.10
3. Category as a Percentage of Total Capital:				
a) Notes and Debentures†	1.17	11.36	8.71	1.12
b) Equity Capital†	98.83	88.64	91.29	98.87
c) Common Stock†	35.54	48.21	45.74	24.77
d) Surplus†	45.75	25.36	28.45	39.60
e) Undivided Profit†	14.48	14.72	16.70	31.76

† Difference between older and new minority banks (both including and excluding the high-loss bank) significant at the 5% level.
†† Less than $50 million in deposits.
* The figures in column 2 are calculated exclusive of the high-loss minority-owned bank.
** This extremely low figure results from the fact that the high-loss minority-owned bank has negative Net Income equal to 95% of the combined Net Income figures for the other seven newer minority-owned banks. As is evident from line 13, much of this loss resulted from loss write-offs in the loan portfolio.
Source: Federal Deposit Insurance Corporation.

Interestingly, the major performance difference between the older and newer minority-owned banks involves their loan-loss experience. For example, in the case of net losses charged against reserves—perhaps the best measure of a bank's recent loan-loss experience—the figure for the older minority banks is about midway between the very high figure for the newer minority banks and the figure for nonminority institutions. Current loan-loss experience is also reflected in the "provision for loan losses" figure. These data suggest that the newer banks are allocating more than twice the proportion of their total current expenditures for loan losses as compared with the older minority banks and more than three times the proportion set aside by the nonminority banks.

The relatively low net income of the newer minority banks resulting from this loan-loss experience influences the current capital position of these banks. In general, the newer banks rely much more heavily upon debt financing than either the older minority banks or the nonminority banks and they have generated far less capital into the "internal" accounts represented by surplus and undivided profit. Again, since these figures are not adjusted for the dividend payments made by the banks, they probably understate the historical difficulty the newer banks have had in generating funds internally. Dividends at the newer banks have been extremely small relative to customary dividend payments by commercial banks.

These figures suggest several things. First, there are important and significant differences between the operating statistics and capital positions of older and newer minority-owned banks. These differences ought to be taken into consideration when analyzing the performance of these banks as a group, since averages derived from aggregation of overall minority-owned banks may be misleading. Second, these data point up again that much of the difference in the profitability of minority and nonminority-owned banks derives from the poor loan-loss experience of the former.

Time Series Comparison of the Performance of New Minority-Owned Commercial Banks

The relative improvement in some of the minority banks' operating statistics presented in the second section of this paper over the performance measures presented by Brimmer and Irons suggest that it may be worthwhile to examine the performance of these banks on a time series basis. At the same time, the significant differences between the older and newer minority banks noted above suggest that disaggregation by maturity is desirable if inferences are to be made about the expected performance of the new minority banks currently being organized. Consequently, in Tables 7 to 10 we present a limited time series comparison between the operating performance of the eight minority-owned banks established between 1963–1965 and a forty-six-bank sample of nonminority institutions founded in the same years and located in the same SMSAs as these minority banks.[14] Time series data are presented on only those operating measures which appeared to differ significantly between the minority and nonminority banks in the single-period comparison presented above.[15]

In Table 7 the tendency of the minority banks to concentrate relatively more resources in the liquid asset accounts is clearly documented. In addition to their relatively large holdings of U.S. government securities, in recent years these banks have turned to the Federal Funds market as an outlet for their short-term funds to a much greater extent than the new nonminority banks.

This tendency on the part of minority-owned banks to hold an increasing proportion of their total assets in liquid investments reflects (and may, in part, be the result of) the declining proportion of total resources devoted to lending operations. There appears to have been a conscious attempt on the part of the newer minority-owned banks to reduce loan losses by modifying their credit evaluation and loan-approval procedures. In the process of modifying these procedures, the rate of growth of the banks' loan portfolios has decreased sharply and, in some cases, the total volume of loans outstanding has been reduced. By 1971, the proportions of total assets held as loans at the new minority-owned banks was more than thirteen basis points below the proportion at the nonminority sample banks. In conversations with officers of these banks, this retrenchment has been explained as a temporary readjustment which will allow better servicing of credit-worthy local-loan applicants in the future. In some cases, this represents a substantial change in attitude on the part of these bankers as to their role in the local community and reflects a turn to a more conservative (and, sometimes, a more business-oriented) loan policy. In the meantime, however, this policy has reduced the lending of these institutions to inner city minorities—one of the bases of the minority bankers' claim to special treatment by the government and one of the goals of the government's Minority Bank Deposit Program.

The direct effect of the government's assistance to the minority banks under that program is clearly demonstrated in the government deposit figures in column (4) of Table 7. The increasing ratio of government deposits to total deposits suggest that this form of assistance may have begun even before the special program was announced in 1970.

Data on net current operating earnings and on some of the most important components of total income and total expenses are presented in Table 8. The trends in these figures demonstrate clearly the important additional information content of time series data. In each of the years 1964–1971, differentials similar to those presented in the single period studies by Irons and Brimmer and in the analysis of the 1971 data above are evident. However, there is a striking convergence in the minority and nonminority series which may have important implications for the future comparative performance of the minority banks. Consider, for example, net current operating earnings of the sample banks (column 4).[16] The earnings figure for the minority banks is continually lower than the earnings figure for the nonminority banks. The differential declines from 78 basis points in 1966—the first full year of operation for all banks in the

TABLE 7

Portfolio Ratios—Weighted Averages at Eight New
Minority and 46 Nonminority Banks

Year	Percentage of Total Assets									Percentage of Total Deposits		
	(1) Cash and Due from Banks + U.S. Gov. Sec.			(2) Federal Funds Sold			(3) Total Loans			(4) Deposits of U.S. Government		
	M′	NM′	M′−NM′	M′	NM′	M′−NM′	M′	NM′	M′−NM′	M′	NM′	M′−NM′
1964	53.77	39.64	14.13	0.0	0.0	0.0	36.43	54.16	−17.73	2.21	2.33	−0.12
1965	34.42	40.46	−6.04	0.83	0.37	0.46	59.57	52.87	6.70	5.43	2.50	2.93
1966	34.24	38.09	−3.85	0.0	0.72	−0.72	60.01	55.12	4.89	1.52	2.10	−0.58
1967	46.04	35.29	10.75	1.63	0.49	1.14	47.00	56.35	−9.35	2.95	1.42	1.53
1968	43.79	32.25	11.54	2.16	1.35	0.81	49.84	56.22	−6.38	3.26	1.33	1.93
1969	40.15	26.55	13.60	7.84	3.16	4.68	46.08	57.47	−11.39	5.64	1.70	3.94
1970	44.31	27.65	16.66	5.39	3.54	1.85	43.30	52.95	−9.65	8.27	2.08	6.19
1971	44.07	27.45	16.62	8.58	1.98	6.60	39.33	52.42	−13.09	11.0	1.97	9.13

M′ = New minority-owned banks.
NM′ = New nonminority-owned banks.
Source: Federal Deposit Insurance Corporation, December Reports of Condition.

TABLE 8

Income and Expenses of Eight New Minority
and 46 New Nonminority Banks

Year	Percentage of Total Operating Income (1) Total Service Charges			Percentage of Total Operating Expense (2) Total Employee Expense			(3) Int. Paid on Deposits			Percentage of Total Assets (4) Net Current Oper. Earnings		
	M'	NM'	M'−NM'	M'	NM'	M'−NM'	M'	NM'	M'−NM'	M'	NM'	M'−NM'
1964	22.6	13.7	8.9	44.2	37.6	6.6	11.1	15.7	− 4.6	−1.63	−0.38	−1.25
1965	21.2	10.3	10.9	41.2	35.3	5.9	15.0	27.6	−12.6	− .74	.27	−1.01
1966	23.2	11.1	12.1	40.0	34.2	5.8	21.9	30.4	− 8.5	− .18	.60	−0.78
1967	23.5	11.1	12.4	39.4	31.7	7.7	25.6	36.1	−10.5	.17	.79	−0.62
1968	21.2	10.7	10.5	37.4	30.8	6.6	27.9	36.8	− 8.9	.39	1.05	−0.66
1969	17.6	10.0	7.6	37.0	31.3	5.7	27.4	36.1	− 8.7	.97	1.55	−0.58
1970	17.1	9.6	7.5	35.6	31.0	4.6	31.4	36.6	− 5.2	.83	1.47	−0.64
1971	14.8	9.6	5.2	33.9	29.8	4.1	34.1	38.4	− 4.3	.61	.97	−0.36

M' = New minority-owned banks.
NM' = New nonminority-owned banks.
Source: Federal Deposit Insurance Corporation, December Reports of Condition.

sample—to less than half that figure by 1971. To some extent, this results from the relative decrease in the employee-expense figures in column (2). Additional information on the factors generating declining employee expenses is contained in Table 9. The implication of these data seems clear: The efficiency of minority banks as measured by the number of employees (or employee expenses) required to service a minority bank of a given size has declined continually as the minority banks have matured. Interestingly, the nonminority banks, with large pools of trained talent to draw upon, immediately establish an average ratio of number of employees to total assets which remains relatively constant as they mature. It appears that it is this ratio towards which the minority banks—unable to draw upon a stock of trained personnel and forced to do a great deal more of their own training—are moving. One conclusion which may be inferred from these data is that many of the operational problems faced by new minority banks are indeed solvable and have, in fact, been overcome by many of the sample banks.[17]

TABLE 9
Number of Employees Per Million Dollars of Assets for Eight New Minority and
46 New Nonminority Banks

Year	M'	NM'	M'−NM'
1964	6.4	2.7	3.7
1965	5.3	2.7	2.6
1966	4.4	2.6	1.8
1967	3.4	2.4	1.0
1968	3.4	2.2	1.2
1969	2.9	2.4	.5
1970	2.9	2.4	.5
1971	2.3	2.1	.2
1964–71 Mean	3.9	2.4	
1969–Mean	2.7	2.3	

M' = New minority-owned banks.
NM' = New nonminority-owned banks.
Source: Federal Deposit Insurance Corporation, December Reports of Income and Reports of Condition.

The implications of these figures are confirmed to some extent by perusal of the examination reports for the minority banks. In many cases these banks have been able to decrease their total number of employees as they mature—even as they grow larger. Furthermore, examiners' comments seem to imply some progress in improving the daily routine of bank operations as the banks mature, such as, for example, more efficient use of part-time employees.

The data presented in Table 8 suggest more optimism for the potential of minority-owned banks for successful operation than is suggested by the single period comparisons above. This does not mean that the convergence in these ratios implies that all minority bank performance ratios will continue to approach the norm established by the nonminority institutions. Indeed, the character of the markets served by these banks and the personnel problems they are likely to encounter for a long time to come suggest that there may be a permanent differential which will be established between the average performance of these institutions and that of nonminority banks which do not suffer these same difficulties. However, with that differential decreasing to the levels reached by 1971, it may well be that there is a tolerable range in which these banks may operate—a range not so far below the performance of the average nonminority bank that they would cease to be useful and productive economic enterprises.[18]

There may be one important qualification to this position. The primary business of commercial banking remains local lending. As noted above, however, minority banks have substantially decreased the proportion of their assets devoted to loans in an attempt to reduce their default losses. Yearly data on the loss experience of the sample banks and of all insured commercial banks is presented in Table 10. Examination of the data in column (3) on net loss experience suggests several interesting conclusions. First, all new banks, both minority and nonminority-owned, suffer substantially greater loan losses than those incurred by all insured commercial banks. Between 1966 and 1971 the new nonminority banks had average yearly losses equal to 0.52 percent of total loans. This same figure for all insured commercial banks was about 0.22 percent or less than half as large. Minority banks charged-off an average of about 1.10 percent of their loan portfolio to losses each year. These figures reflect the magnitudes evident in the data in Section I: Minority bank losses average between two and four times the losses of nonminority banks.

There is information in this disaggregated time series data not available in the statistics previously presented on this issue. By far the worst performance of any bank in the sample was that of the minority bank excluded from the calculations in Table 6.[19] Recognizing the danger of removing extreme values from a small number of observations, loss rates for the other seven minority banks in the sample have been calculated for 1970 and 1971 and included in Table 10. Although these figures remain about twice as large as the loss rates for all insured commercial banks, they are very close to the rates calculated for the new nonminority banks. This is the first piece of evidence suggesting that even this aspect of minority bank operation may be approaching the performance criteria established by the nonminority sample banks.[20] The decrease in the minority bank loss rates comes at a time when many of these banks have cut back their loan activities. This suggests that retrenching to avoid high risk loans has been successful. However, it sheds no light on the more important question: Will the minority banks continue to operate at these more acceptable loss rates when they again expand their loan operations?

The high employee expenses and large loan losses of previous years have adversely affected the ability of the new minority banks to generate additions to capital internally through retained earnings. As shown in

TABLE 10

Gross and Net Loan Loss Charge-offs Measured as a Percentage of Total Loans (Weighted Average over Eight New Minority-Owned and 46 New Nonminority-Owned Banks)

Year	(1) Gross Loss*			(2) Recovery*			(3) Net Loss*		
	M'	46 New Nonminority	All Insured Commercial Banks	M'	46 New Nonminority	All Insured Commercial Banks	M'	46 New Nonminority	All Insured Commercial Banks
1964	0.0	.16	.23	0.0	.02	.09	0.0	.14	.14
1965	0.48	.48	.21	0.29	.05	.06	0.19	.43	.15
1966	1.75	.90	.24	0.32	.26	.06	1.43	.64	.18
1967	1.89	.62	.25	0.27	.16	.07	1.62	.46	.18
1968	1.26	.40	.23	0.22	.11	.08	1.04	.29	.15
1969	.59	.48	.24	0.35	.12	.07	0.24	.36	.17
1970	1.13	.94	.41	0.27	.16	.08	0.86	.78	.33
	(0.98)†			(0.26)†			(0.72)†		
1971	1.64	.81	.42	0.26	.22	.09	1.38	.59	.33
	(0.82)†			(0.24)†			(0.58)†		

† Figure excludes data on high-loss minority bank.

* Gross Loss = Losses charged to Reserves for Bad Debts and Other Reserves exclusive of Reserves on Securities.
  Net Loss = Losses charged to reserves less recoveries credited to reserves for Bad Debt losses.

Source: Federal Deposit Insurance Corporation, December Reports of Income and Reports of Condition.

Table 6, the new minority banks have had to rely on external financing—new issues of stock and the sale of capital notes and debentures—to a much larger degree than either the older minority banks or the nonminority banks. Even without the payment of any significant dividends, the new minority banks have been unable to accumulate sufficient capital to maintain an acceptable capital/asset ratio. This problem results primarily from the inability of these banks to generate net income, but it has been exacerbated by the very rapid growth in assets they have experienced—encouraged to some degree by the special programs instituted by the federal government, corporations, and other private groups to channel deposits to these institutions. While these programs obviously stimulate growth and provide funds for expanded lending, it is not clear that they have stimulated income to the extent required to help maintain the new minority banks' capital position. Certainly programs such as the American Bankers Association Minbanc program designed to provide additional capital to the minority banks are most welcome additions to the list of special efforts directed at these institutions.

Summary and Conclusions

The single-period analysis of minority-bank performance presented in the second section of this paper indicates that there has been significant improvement in some aspects of minority-bank operations since the presentation of the studies by Brimmer and Irons in 1970. The decrease in the (sample) performance differentials unfavorable to minority-owned banks, evident only in the time series data, suggests the desirability of time series analysis to track the relative performance of these banks. At the same time, however, other factors indicate that there may be significant differences in performance between the minority banks themselves. In particular, the unique nature of the markets served by the newer minority banks as well as the character of the problems faced by all newly-founded financial institutions suggests disaggregating the minority bank sample by maturity and examining the performance of the older and newer institutions separately. The initial tests indicate that there are indeed significant differences in the behavior of these groups.

The results of the time series analysis are perhaps more encouraging than any of the results presented in the other studies of minority-owned banks. In particular, on an operating basis, the decline in one of the major performance differentials between the minority and non-minority banks—the cost of employee services—suggests that some of the initial inefficiencies of the minority banks may have been corrected. The current status of other problems, especially loan loss charge-offs, is very difficult to interpret, however. The variance between individual bank performances is large enough to make any generalization on the basis of such a small sample very tenuous. Although some of the newer minority-owned banks have reduced losses to the levels characteristic of nonminority banks, many have accomplished this only by severely cutting back their lending operations. Furthermore, two of the black banks—one in the eight-bank sample and another founded in 1968—have suffered extreme difficulties from loan defaults. Only additional analysis of the problems specific to these individual banks and of the particular policies they have followed relative to the more successful institutions will reveal the kind of information most useful to those groups now in the bank-formation process. In general, however, the convergence evident in many of the data series suggests some optimism about the operating viability of the new minority-owned commercial banks is warranted.

In this paper, the related problem of the potential of the minority-owned banks to play an active role in community economic development has not been examined. The analysis has focused instead on the simpler question of the economic viability of these institutions. The problem of integrating these institutions into the community development process in a fundamental way is much more difficult and can be examined properly only by examining the individual loan portfolios of these banks. However, one thing can be said on this issue: If the minority banks can maintain tolerable loan losses only by severely restricting their local lending activity, they are certainly not going to provide the immediate stimulus to community development for which they were initially begun. Other means must be found to arrest the deterioration of some of the country's inner city areas.[21] However, this by no means implies that the formation of these institutions should be discouraged. They may continue to serve several important tasks. They continue to be useful as financial depositories in their communities; they can still take some role in lending to new business enterprises through SBA guaranteed loans and other such mechanisms; they can be an important source of new financing to minority-owned businesses which have demonstrated some initial success; and, finally, they can develop as the inner city develops and take on additional responsibility for continued development as the income and employment characteristics of their markets improve. There is, in addition, the obviously important sociological role to be played by these institutions in dispelling the idea that there are certain areas of commerce, such as banking, from which minority groups will continue to be excluded.

NOTES

1. Assets as of December 1972.

2. A list of minority-owned institutions, together with their locations, dates of establishment, and total assets is presented in Table 1.

3. The analysis upon which this conclusion is based includes a comparison of only net current operating earnings and of net income for these banks and is, unfortunately, never extended to more detailed portfolio and performance measures. Consequently, the specific source of difficulty confronting the black banks in generating acceptable levels of net income is impossible to detail from these data alone.

4. See Table 1 for the names of the minority-owned banks included in the samples examined by Brimmer and Irons.

5. The Report of Income is a detailed profit and loss statement submitted to the federal bank regulatory agencies each December 31 by all commercial banks in the country. The December Report of Condition is a detailed balance sheet submitted as of the close of business for the last day of the year.

6. Newer nonminority banks and banks with more than $50 million in deposits are excluded to improve comparability with the minority-bank sample. The largest minority-owned bank is Freedom National, New York. It had total deposits of $47.1 million (Dec. 1972). All banks founded since 1968 have been excluded to avoid the distortion that would be introduced in operating ratios and in earnings and capital account ratios by the inclusion of newly formed institutions. See Boorman, 1973.

7. This factor accounts for much of the difference in the composition of private accounts suggested by the figures on lines A1 and A2 of Table 2. Relative to total private deposits (deposits of individuals, partnerships, and corporations) the percentages of demand and time deposits were 40.8 and 59.2, respectively, at the minority banks and 42.0 and 58.0 at the nonminority banks.

8. The same figures for all black-owned banks and all member banks of the Federal Reserve System reported from the December, 1969 data by Brimmer were 30.8% and 24.0%, respectively—a 6.8% differential. Irons, measuring the same expense item relative to total operating revenue, found the figure for black banks to be 27.3% and that for all insured commercial banks to be 19.4%—a 7.9% differential.

9. In some cases banks will not credit an interest payment below some minimum—$1.00, for instance—to a customer's account. Since the average savings account balance at minority-owned banks—in accounts with less than $1000 deposited—is only about $160, compared with about $450 at nonminority banks, it is likely that a larger proportion of these accounts would fail to earn this minimum interest payment at the former than at the latter. (Source of data: Federal Deposit Insurance Corporation, Summary of Deposits, June 1972).

10. In fact, the figures in Table 4 may actually understate the loan loss problem of the minority banks. These banks generally hold proportionately more participations than nonminority banks and we would expect that portion of their loan portfolio to be relatively secure.

11. Deposits of individuals, partnerships and corporations.

12. The growth rates of federal government deposits have been very different at these two classes of banks. As noted previously, federal government deposits at the 17 banks in the original sample increased by just over $10 million in 1971. Of this amount, $8.65 million was accounted for by the eight newer banks and only $1.43 million by the nine older institutions. The growth rate at the former was over 40 percent compared with about 11 percent at the latter.

13. Confidentiality of individual bank income data prohibits identification of that bank.

14. The minority banks included in this sample are indicated in Table 1. The 46 nonminority banks are located in six SMSAs: Houston, Washington, D.C., Los Angeles, Chicago, New York and St. Louis.

15. A more complete evaluation of the performance of new minority-owned commercial banks is presented in *New Minority-Owned Commercial Banks: A Comparative Analysis,* by John T. Boorman, Federal Deposit Insurance Corporation, 1973.

16. Changes in tax laws affecting commercial banks (the Tax Reform Act of 1969) and in the reporting forms submitted to the regulatory agencies (1968) make time series comparisons of Net Income over this period very tenuous. Modifications in the treatment of gains and losses on securities, the accounting conventions employed to determine transfers to various reserve accounts, and the regulations related to reserve balances make Net Income after 1969 conceptually different from the figure presented before that date. To avoid these difficulties, this analysis focuses on three comparable elements in the income generating process: Net current operating earnings, loan losses and the ability of banks over the entire period to pay dividends and to generate increases in their capital accounts.

17. See *New Minority-Owned Commercial Banks: A Comparative Analysis,* for additional information on this issue.

18. This is not to say that all minority-owned banks perform below the norm established by the nonminority bank averages in the sample. There is substantial variation within the minority bank sample and there are several instances in which the minority bank clearly outperforms its nonminority SMSA sample counterparts.

19. Loan losses incurred by this bank in the years 1970–1971 ran more than 75% higher than the losses suffered by the next worst performing minority-owned bank. In 1971, its loss rate was more than 6.5 standard deviations above the mean loss rates for the other seven new minority-owned banks.

20. The loss rates for the new minority banks may understate their loan default problem because of the relatively large volume of participations in their portfolio.

21. See Brimmer [1971, 1968].

REFERENCES

Bates, Timothy. *An Econometric Study of Black Capitalism: Feasibility, Profitability and Financial Soundness.* University of Wisconsin, Madison, 1972. Unpublished dissertation.

Boorman, John T. *New Minority-Owned Commercial Banks: A Comparative Analysis.* Washington, D.C.: Federal Deposit Insurance Corporation, 1973.

———, and Myron Kwast. "The Start-up Experience of Minority-Owned Commercial Banks: A Comparative Analysis." Working Paper No. 72–11, Division of Research, Federal Deposit Insurance Corporation, Washington, D.C., 1972. Forthcoming, *Journal of Finance.*

Brimmer, Andrew F. "The Black Banks: An Assessment of Performance and Prospects." *Journal of Finance,* 26 (May, 1971): 379–405.

———. "Recent Developments in Black Banking: 1970–1971." Washington, D.C., July 31, 1972, unpublished.

———. "The Banking System and Urban Economic Development," presented before a joint session of the 1968 Annual Meetings of the American Real Estate and Urban Economics Association and the American Finance Association in Chicago, Ill., Dec. 1968.

———. "The Negro in the National Economy." In *The American Negro Reference Book,* ed. by John P. Davis. Englewood Cliffs, N.J.: Prentice Hall, Inc., 1966, pp. 251–336.

Harris, Abram. *The Negro as Capitalist: A Study of Banking and Business Among American Negroes.* Gloucester, Mass.: Peter Smith, 1968.

Irons, Edward D. *Organizing a New Community Bank.* Studies in Banking and Finance No. 5, Austin, Tex.: Bureau of Business Research, The University of Texas, 1965.

———. "Black Banking: Problems and Prospects." *Journal of Finance* 26 (May 1971): 407–25.

Leavitt, Brenton C. "Black Banks: A Review of Earnings Performance." An address before the First Annual Director—Senior Management Seminar of the National Bankers Association, Inc., Atlanta, Ga., July 21, 1972.

Thieblot, Armand J., and Linda Pickthorne Fletcher. *Negro Employment in Finance: A Study of Racial Policies in Banking and Insurance.* Philadelphia, Pa.: Industrial Research Unit, Wharton School of Finance and Commerce, University of Pennsylvania, 1970.

Walker, Charles E. Address before the 43rd Annual Convention of the National Bankers Association, St. Louis, Missouri, Oct. 16, 1970. Reprinted in the Department of the Treasury *News,* Washington, D.C.

Black Banking:
A Comment on the
Andrew Brimmer Bias

Rawle Farley

Quick Ratio[1] published a brief summary of Andrew Brimmer's views on black banks as expressed at the American Economic Association Convention held at Detroit in December, 1970.[2] Essentially, Dr. Brimmer regarded black banks as "ornaments." By implication, the Brimmer view was tantamount to saying that the big metropolitan banks were enough and that black-owned banks were economically useless. Dr. Edward Irons, then Executive Director of the National Bankers Association, made a dissenting comment vis-à-vis the Brimmer bias in the *Washington Post* of Sunday, January 17, 1971. Dr. Brimmer may have had cause to modify his views since then. His original views were so instantly electrifying, however, that the impact of any change of views is likely to remain limited for a long time to come. *Black Enterprise* records the sharp reaction of prominent black bankers against Dr. Brimmer's bias.[3]

Black Banking in an Enterprise System

Black banking is clearly not a new exercise. The brief but important chronicle set out in *Black Enterprise* suggests that in 1888 there were at least 135 black-owned banks. On evidence, the history of black banking is certainly seismographic. Seventy-five of these banks failed before 1936. Until then the average life span of the black bank was a brief nine years. By 1967, there were only seventeen black-owned banks, most of these being post World War II foundations. By 1971, however, the number of black banks in existence had increased again to 33. This number is expected to grow over the next few years.

A history of this kind is interesting in itself. The Brimmer remarks may certainly stimulate further historical research. But even without the fascination of history, black banking assumes priority as one of the key determinants of the course and character of black economic development. The role of black-owned banking in changing existing economic conditions in the ghetto has so far not been a prominent focus of research in the search for a general theory of development relevant to black America. In fact, the role of black-owned banking is largely ignored in the plethora of new texts on the economics of poverty and the economics of black America. This indifference to the importance of black-owned banking, as well as the position of national distinction which Andrew Brimmer holds in the banking sector of the American economy, justifies this brief reconsideration of the Brimmer perspective.

The emergence of black-owned banks can, in the first instance, be looked upon as a victory for black private enterprise in America. The mass of black poor may of course see no immediate gain in a few blacks' emerging as banking entrepreneurs, for their emergence may be looked upon as a purely private matter, making no difference whatever to the immediate and massive dimensions of American black poverty. Again, the black intellectual wedded ideologically to a complete command economy may be equally contemptuous—but from a political perspective exactly opposite to that of Brimmer. The substitution of a complete command economy, however, does not produce evidence that *ipso facto* the problem of national or group poverty is immediately eradicated. Neither Russia nor China has achieved any such sudden transformation.

At the other extreme, *laissez-faire,* if it ever existed, obviously cannot produce the kind of change required in the economic status of black America. The market system under which the American economy operates is a mixed enterprise system. The free price mechanism is undoubtedly defective.[4] The issues to which these defects give rise center not on replacing the system by a command economy but on the extent to which the government must intervene to counteract the inequitable results thrown up by the skewed working of the system. For clearly the system confronts us with an agonizing paradox, in that poverty continues to exist in the midst of the unprecedented affluence of modern America, yet economic transformation is impossible without the emergence and contribution of entrepreneurship.

The command economy cannot solve the problem. *Laissez-faire* cannot solve the problem and the remaining alternative—the mixed-enterprise system—cannot continue to work without entrepreneurship as a key strategic determinant of changes in the behavior and structure of the economy. The emergence of black entrepreneurship is therefore an initial expectation if initial conditions are to be changed. The argument is not that entrepreneurship is a sufficient condition. But it is an unavoidable condition. In the context of black economic development, the greater the emergence of black entrepreneurs, the greater the chances, other things being equal, of securing the endogenous economic transformation which black communities idealistically espouse.[5] The emergence of black-owned banks therefore fulfills an essential principle of development. This immensely vital principle seems to have become externalized by the Brimmer bias.

Modifying Entrepreneurial Disequilibrium

The matter goes beyond this. Even if the linkages of the black-owned banks were external to the ghetto—looking outward rather than inward—the psychological impact of their emergence cannot be ignored in that they make the seemingly impossible a practical and attainable reality. In the black mind banking remains by and large an unattainable area of operation. The emergence of black-owned banks emphasizes the important point that it can be done—as Jackie Robinson showed in baseball, Jesse Owens in track, and Andrew Brimmer, in his preeminence, in the world of American banking. A continuing gap in entrepreneurial capacity—as between groups in any nation—serves only to make more permanent both the inequalities in the division of the national cake and the historically rooted hiatus between the groups. The emergence of black-owned banks is at least a beginning, however small, towards modifying a preexisting entrepreneurial disequilibrium between the black community and the rest of American society.

A parallel international model exists in the astonishing emergence of Japanese entrepreneurship, which contributed to ending a state of entrepreneurial disequilibrium between America and Japan. Entrepreneurship in the broadest sense accounts for the Japanese penetration of the American market. Black America is part and parcel of the American market. The American market is national territory for black Americans. Black Americans therefore enjoy advantages over Japanese entrepreneurs in that their transport costs are less; they face no tariff barriers; they have no language problems; they need no psychological cram courses to learn the American market; and they face no legal inhibitions to the lawful development of entrepreneurial activities. The Japanese survive through business development. Canadians, like West Germans, survive similarly. For black America, concentration on politics is not enough. Nor can economic separation do the job. No country can opt out of the international economy and survive. The Russians, for political and economic reasons, have abandoned their original idealistic proclamation that they can go it alone. The Chinese have recently done so—dramatically. Internationally, the poor try to do business with the rich because that way they make more money to buy the capital and consumer goods they need to improve their own economic well-being. Likewise, no poor group can opt out of the national economy and hope to survive. The poor in America must therefore do business with the rest of America. But the poor cannot do this unless they produce entrepreneurs from their own group. The emergence or reemergence of black-owned banks is the beginning of the recognition of this reality.

This is not to say that entrepreneurship is the single condition for bridging the economic gap. Public action at federal, state, county, city, and village levels, private community and corporate action, and effective institutionalization are all essentials. The bridging of the economic gap calls for upgrading, to a level of equality, skills in public and business administration, in technology, economics, and science, and in the whole range of qualities which make for an equal or superior competitive capacity to survive. This is entrepreneurship in the broadest sense of the term. Any achievement in these terms counts toward achieving the great end. Whatever the overall conditions for black economic development, the emergence, expansion, and survival of black-owned banking conforms in part to the necessities for black economic survival into a better state of affairs.

Development: Active and Passive Banking

We have asserted that even if the operations of black-owned banks are external to the ghetto—that is, outward-looking, noncommunicating, or without linkages to the black community as such—there are still advantages in terms of a psychological lift to the black community in the sense that a black breakthrough into a hitherto monopolized area of economic activity is seen to be possible. Others may be encouraged to follow.

The impact on black economic development of black-owned banks which have no linkages with the black community is, however, likely to be negligible. Externally linked activity of this kind would certainly contribute to an increase in national welfare, to personal net welfare, and to ethnic psychic pleasure of blacks who keep account of the economic achievements of their brothers. But externally linked black banking activity would not, given this circumstance, contribute to the necessary increase of black group welfare. Since black economic development is a matter of emergency, the relation between this problem and black-owned banking becomes a matter for urgent consideration. Any decline in black-owned banking linked to the black economic development would mean a deceleration in the prospects for more rapid economic change in the ghetto, for black-owned banking directly linked to ghetto development is part of the essential institutionalization for changing the existing economic conditions of the ghetto. Any such innovation is unavoidable from the evidence of economic experience. This principle is as true for black economic development in America as for the development of poor countries outside of America.[6]

Given this principle, further differentiation becomes possible. Black-owned banks located in the ghetto can be regarded as merely service-oriented banks and therefore *passive* rather than *active* banks if, in their operations, they simply pursue the traditional paths of the larger non-ghetto commercial banks.[7] Yet the indirect contribution of the passive traditional black bank may not be insignificant if it supplies working capital to clients who in turn invest their entrepreneurial capacities in ghetto development. Firm evaluations are impossible on the basis of limited data.

The Peculiar Role of the Black Bank

Black-owned, ghetto-linked banking activity is clearly not the single, key solution to the problems of the ghetto. The solution to the problems of the ghetto involves the manipulation of a whole range of complex quantitative and qualitative variables. However, the problem can be simply stated so that the role of black-owned, ghetto-linked banking activity becomes immediately clarified. The ghetto is an island of underdevelopment within and shut out from an otherwise affluent society. The ghetto stands out as a startling contrast to a level of affluence unequalled in the history of the world. The problem, therefore, is to transform these stagnating sectors of despair so that all Americans share in the ongoing prosperity of the world's most highly developed economy. Such a conquest of poverty would represent the true culmination of the American dream and usher in what I have called elsewhere *the sixth stage of economic growth*.[8] This is the stage at which poverty is obliterated—a necessary analytical sequence since Rostow's stages of growth analysis culminating at the fifth stage, "the age of high mass consumption" occupied by the United States, ignores the continuing phenomenon, even at this stage, of poverty amid affluence in the United States and the equally corporate condition of poverty among two-thirds of the world's peoples.[9]

What cannot be ignored are the differences in the functions of banking institutions in a developed context as against a developing context. Perspectives can be easily improved through consulting the experience of the Government Development Bank of Puerto Rico,[10] the Banco Obrero of Venezuela, the Nacional Financiera, S.A., or other banking and credit institutions in Mexico and other successful developing countries. These reference points are far more relevant than, and can usefully supplement, experience gained in a particular traditional bank or at the level of the Federal Reserve Board.

We have argued that institutional innovation is essential to the initiation and promotion of economic development—along with other quantitative and qualitative changes in the variables determining the rate and character of economic change. Banking institutions, though not a sufficient condition for development, are critical to any change in existing economic conditions.[11] The initial choice in the ghetto lies between attracting the large, solidly ongoing corporate banks (the Brimmer bias) and establishing new banking institutions (the black banks) specifically geared to meet the unique needs of the ghetto. The Brimmer bias overlooks the constraints to the entrenchment of his bias.

Development in the ghetto takes place in an atmosphere of risk and uncertainty—risks that are new to the large banks but risks and uncertainties which are more manageable to those who are familiar with the attitudes, personnel, atmosphere, and economic opportunities of the ghetto. For exactly these reasons, the large banks did not go to the ghetto. The risks appeared too great. The personnel of the large banks remain largely unfamiliar with the socioeconomic conditions in the ghetto. Because of this unfamiliarity, the risks remain magnified. Besides these discouraging factors, the large banks have comparatively safer areas of operation and profit outside of the ghetto. Above all this, despite the revolution in the range of banking activities, large bank operations remain normally limited by the conventional constraints of commercial bank activities—constraints which would paralyze their operation in the ghetto right from the beginning just as, say, in the uncharted rural areas of Brazil.

Black banks in the ghetto therefore represent an unavoidable attempt (already successfully carried out in the world of development overseas) to counteract the limitations and hesitancies of the large commercial bank. These hesitancies are far from being irrational. As economic reasoning goes, if the risks were not unusual in the ghetto, the large commercial bank would have been there long ago. Presumably, it calculates the risks in the ghetto to be higher than in traditional areas of operation in North America or Puerto Rico or Guiana or Venezuela, for instance, where large commercial banks have established long-standing and successful branches. The black bank therefore fills the gap in the ghetto, operating as a commercial bank and as a development bank simultaneously.

The black bank is essential to the performance of new functions necessary for initiating changes in the development status of the ghetto. The black bank takes risks which are greater than the traditional risks. Black banking operations give banking experience to black Americans, enabling them to carve out new economic pathways and gain the experience needed to hold their own within the American economic system. The black bank in the ghetto aids the discovery of and supplies support to new enterprises—which remain out of reach of the tradition-oriented, large, established bank. The black bank can pump-prime and stimulate and influence desirable development directions because it is there. But beyond this, it is more than likely that if the black bank does not take the risk in the ghetto, more business is not likely to be attracted from within the ghetto or from without the ghetto. For if banks are in the ghetto, and if they are successful because they know the area, new business would tend to be attracted, adding to the forces attempting to shift the economic status of the ghetto away from present stagnation.

The black bank is an essential instrument in rescuing the ghetto from economic isolation. It has the potential to establish backward and forward linkages and so bring to black ghettoland the development of a capacity and of instruments to take advantages of the *whole* American market. There is the additional possibility that black banks can command the leverage to secure a considerable share of the foreign business done in the United States by African, Caribbean and other developing countries.

The limitations Brimmer ascribes to black banks are to be put in proper perspective. They are the inevitable limitations of what is still a beginning stage. Banks have failed in America before; banks will no doubt continue to fail. Past failure is not confined to black banks, and it will be senseless to presume that future failures will occur only in the case of black-owned banks. But failure itself is an experience which can be a source of future profit. Bank failures did not factor out banks as essential institutions in America. New banks developed, led by wiser people who had learned the lessons of failure.

Business survival calls for ingenuities—to reduce costs, increase efficiency, and to expand—which might come better from the experience of being in the business. There is no reason to doubt that the ingenuities required for the black bank to survive would be forthcoming as the experience of the black bank accumulates. Andrew Brimmer, for instance, might very well be persuaded to establish large areas of cooperation and exchange of experience between black banks and the traditional banks in which he holds so prominent a place. General Motors has commendably shown the kind of faith which is essential to give the new institutions initial momentum.

The Brimmer Bias: Constructive Aspects

The Brimmer bias is not altogether negative, however. One aspect of vital importance can be factored out. It is that competitive efficiency matters for the survival of all banks—black and traditional—and at all times. Black banks therefore may not, without the penalty of failure, allow emotional blockage or chauvinistic 'nativism' to prevent them from adopting firm policies to achieve a minimum efficiency *no less than equal* to that of the large traditional bank. A beginning step in this direction could very well be a study of the organization and business procedures of the large bank aided by a willingness of the black bank to change its operational character without changing its development commitment.

The Brimmer bias comes into its own in the long run. If competitive efficiency triumphs as a tenet among black-owned banks, it can safely be forecast that as the black banks succeed the conventional commercial banks will become more attracted by the new and more attractive climate for business. Their branches will become established in the ghetto. Competition, cooperation, and partnership will develop. Internal ghetto capital and external capital—financial and human—will be more rapidly mobilized within the ghetto. A new and broader development stimulus will spread and the old economic inertia will begin to disappear under the impact of the new forces. Linkages will have developed with the wider American market and the ghetto will have begun to exploit the advantages it enjoys over Japan and West Germany, over Ghana and Mexico, in being constitutionally an integral part of the biggest economic market in the world, namely, the United States.

New issues will of course have emerged; but then, given a shift from the initial economic conditions, the resolutions of issues will be taking place at a different level of economic existence. If the path of development we have described takes place, the black-owned banks would then be firmly entrenched and well able to contribute to healthy bargaining leverages over the control of the new ghetto economy.

Conclusion

The Brimmer bias may embody constructive aspects in that black owned banks must be as competitively efficient as the established traditional banks operating outside of the ghetto. The argument, however goes further than this. Black-owned development-oriented banks located in the ghetto—what I have called active banks—are, in terms of economic theory and practical experience, an essential part of the institutionalization necessary for changing the existing economic conditions of the ghetto. They represent the necessary emergence of black private enterprise. They contribute toward and modify the entrepreneurial gap between the black and nonblack groups of America. They exercise peculiar functions not performed by the traditional nonghetto banks. As the black-owned banks contribute to the emergence of the sixth stage of economic growth, forgotten by Rostow, they would be there to exercise some effective influence in determining issues of social control over the new, profitable levels of economic activity.

NOTES

1. *Quick Ratio,* 2 (Mar. 1971): 2. This is the organ of the National Bankers Association, Washington, D.C. Dr. Edward Irons was the Executive Secretary.

2. Andrew Brimmer is the only black member of the Board of Governors of the Federal Reserve System.

3. *Black Enterprise,* 2 (Oct. 1971): 30–33. This periodical is published monthly by the Earl G. Graves Publishing Company, Inc., 295 Madison Avenue, New York City, New York 10017.

4. The general reader may wish to consult the following: Paul N. Rosenstein-Rodan, "The Flaw in the Mechanism of Market Forces," and Harry G. Johnson, "The Market Mechanism as an Instrument of Development," in *Leading Issues in Economic Development: Studies in International Poverty,* ed. by Gerald M. Meier (2d ed.; New York: Oxford University Press, 1970), pp. 679–86; cf. Keith B. Griffin and John L. Enos, *Planning Development* (Reading, Mass.: Addison-Wesley Publishing Company, 1970), pp. 20–29; and W. Arthur Lewis, *The Principles of Economic Planning* (New York City: Harper & Row, 1969), pp. 12–14.

5. *Cf.* Frank G. Davis, *The Economics of Black Community Development* (Chicago: Markham Publishing Co., 1972), pp. 12–21.

6. *Cf.* Stephen Enke, *Economics for Development* (Englewood Cliffs, N.J.: Prentice-Hall, 1963), esp. pp. 261–76. This is one of the few texts on economic development which includes a chapter on banking and economic development; *cf.* also Rawle Farley, *Planning for Development in Libya: The Exceptional Economy in the Developing World* (New York: Praeger, 1972), pp. 226–42.

7. See, for instance, statement of black banker David Harper, president of the First Independence Bank of Detroit, in *Black Enterprise,* 2 (Oct. 1971): 30; also Thomas W. McMahon, Jr., "Minority Banks," *Black Enterprise,* 2:34.

8. See Rawle Farley, "Poverty and Enterprise in America and Overseas—Towards the Sixth Stage of Economic Growth," New York State Economic Association 1968 *Proceedings* (Dec. 1968), pp. 79–118.

9. W. W. Rostow, *Stages of Economic Growth* (Cambridge [England]: The University Press, 1960).

10. See Rawle Farley, "Puerto Rico: Development, Urbanization and Integration" in International Institute of Differing Civilizations (INCIDI), *Urban Agglomerations in the States of the Third World: Their Political, Economic, and Social Role* (Brussels, Belgium: Editions de l'Institut de Sociologie Université Libre de Bruxelles, 1971), pp. 610–35.

11. *Cf.* Shirley Boskey, *Problems and Practices of Development Banks* (Baltimore, Md.: Johns Hopkins Press, 1959), pp. 3–10.

The Small Business Capital Gap: The Special Case of Minority Enterprise

W. J. Garvin

This paper discusses the "capital gap" presumption underlying federal programs of financial assistance to small business and the conflicting views as to the the gap's existence and measurement. It also presents evidence developed in a study of the performance of borrowers who had received business loans from the Small Business Administration (SBA) which appears to support the view that a capital gap does in fact exist for small business as a whole. If this is so, an even wider gap may be assumed for minority persons confronted with additional bars to entry into or survival in business.

The paper examines the position of minority-owned businesses both in the inner city—where the largest concentrations of minority-owned firms are now found—and without regard to location. The capital gap in the inner city is all-pervasive, extending to consumer, home mortgage, and business credit. It is aggravated by a high incidence of crime against business and the availability of crime insurance at several multiples of standard rates, if at all. The cost of doing business is further increased by usurious interest rates and losses on credit customers.

That businesses survive at all under these conditions argues for a high potential return on investment in efficient firms, if the noneconomic barriers to business growth can be lowered. For minority persons as a whole, the dearth of capital needed to participate in business appears both as an objective fact and as perceived by them. These observations are supported by an opinion survey of black heads of households and an analysis of recent experience with bank participation in Small Business Administration minority enterprise loans.

The paper visualizes an accelerated rate of growth in the minority business population as a result both of public assistance and the continued advance of minority persons into the more desired occupations. Its underlying thesis is that this development is not only a measure of social justice but that it will also, in the end, further strengthen the free enterprise system and improve the allocation of scarce capital resources.

Is There a Small Business Capital Gap?

The case usually made for special financial assistance programs for small business rests upon a presumption that imperfections in the nation's capital markets result in allocating to the small business sector of the economy less capital than would be allocated by a properly functioning financial system operating solely on the basis of the potential profitability of its use. This concept was embodied in the statement of policy of the Small Business Act, which authorized assistance to small firms only when financing is not elsewhere available "on reasonable terms," yet also requires a reasonable expectation of repayment.

The most comprehensive study of the financial needs and problems of small business was that conducted by the Federal Reserve System in 1958.[1] Its report to the House and Senate Banking and Currency and Small Business Committees found " . . . some evidence in the background studies . . . that there is an unfilled margin, perhaps a rather thin one, between the volume of funds available to small concerns in general, and to new firms in particular, and the volume that could be put to use without prohibitive risk."

On the other hand, the two background studies treating specifically the adequacy of small business financing reached diametrically opposite conclusions. One study reached the following conclusions: "First, our banking institutions do satisfy borrower demands for short-term loans. As length of term increases, inadequacies in our financing structure become more apparent."[2] The other study reached contrary conclusions:

> One measure of the adequacy of financing is the health and ability to grow of small business. By this test, financing appears to have been adequate for the sector as a whole in the post-war period . . . A second measure of the adequacy of financing is a fair and equitable division of funds . . . On this basis, it can be said that in the post-war period, credit has become more readily available to small business, for more extended periods, and at a cost that has differed less and less from that of large business. In fact, the tremendous post-war increases in indebtedness of small businesses might raise the contrary question of whether credit had become too readily available and at too low a price relative to the cost of equity.[3]

Among the reasons for wide differences of opinion as to a small-business capital gap is that a rigorous definition of the gap virtually defies demonstration of its existence or measurement of its dimensions. A gap may be said to exist if one or both of two criteria are satisfied. First, a gap exists if the marginal return on funds invested in small business exceeds the marginal cost of capital; in other words, if opportunities to improve the allocation of scarce financial resources are being lost due to inadequate financing of small concerns. Second, a gap exists if the cost of money to small concerns (the riskless rate of interest plus allowances for differentials in risk and loan administration costs) exceeds the cost of money to large concerns. A recent study concerned with the second criterion reached the conclusion that there is no small business equity gap.[4]

A study made by my office applying the first criterion has developed significant evidence of a small business capital gap with respect to intermediate and long-term credit.[5] This study reviewed the Agency's [SBA's] business loan program from the time of its inception through December 1967. Using the financial reports of some 22,000 borrowers, it assessed their achievements year-by-year after receiving a loan with respect to the principal measures of economic growth: profits, sales, assets, and net worth. The results indicated that the borrowers, in the aggregate, experienced a markedly more rapid growth in profits than industry averages over the same time period. The other growth indicators—sales, assets, and net worth—also revealed generally superior performance on the part of the borrowers included in the study.

The study also undertook a benefit/cost analysis of the program. The stream of annual benefits associated with each loan was made up of changes in profits and officer withdrawals (over the base year) plus interest payments and loan repayments to the Government. A parallel stream of costs was comprised of the amount disbursed, interest payments to the Treasury, liquidation losses, and the cost (including overhead) of making and servicing the loan. Both streams were discounted at a 10 percent annual rate to derive their respective present values and a benefit/cost ratio. The ratio which was obtained from this computation was 1.7, ranging from 0.8 in retailing to 2.5 in manufacturing. This equated to an approximate 15 percent internal rate of return. These results suggest that these borrowers, who, by definition, had been unable to obtain financing elsewhere "on reasonable terms," nonetheless yielded returns on invested capital which equalled or surpassed the returns which might have been expected from alternative uses.

These results, together with firsthand observations of the financial problems of many small business concerns, have confirmed the Agency's belief that a small business capital gap does exist, especially with respect to intermediate and long-term credit. Small firms rely largely on the commercial banking system, rather than on the organized national capital markets, to satisfy their needs. One authority has, in fact, defined small business as " . . . any business whose needs for equity and loan capital are too small to interest the investment banker to to be marketed in the national capital and credit markets."[6]

The reluctance of commercial banks to satisfy the capital needs of small concerns is attributable primarily to the liquidity problems associated with intermediate and long-term paper. Some efforts have been made to cope with this problem by establishing secondary markets for such paper, but the results have not yet been sufficient to make a significant contribution toward narrowing the gap. The Federal Reserve Board, in a recent reappraisal of its rediscount practices, dealt with the problem but concluded that its solution lay outside the scope of the Federal Reserve System's mission. According to the Board:

A possible type of credit accommodation not provided for in the redesigned window is long-term credit to meet the needs of banks servicing perennial credit-deficit areas or sectors. It was concluded that the solution to this problem does not properly lie within the scope of discount-window operations. . . . More direct and fundamental answers to the credit-deficit problem are believed to lie in the improvement of secondary markets for bank assets and liabilities.[7]

It seems clear that some form of capital bank to create the needed secondary market would be highly beneficial to small business in general and, as we shall see later, to minority enterprise in particular.

Minority Enterprise

Nature and dimensions of the minority enterprise capital gap

If we accept the existence of a capital gap for small business as a whole, it follows that an even greater gap must prevail for minority enterprise. The minority person seeking to establish or expand a business and competing for an economically justifiable share of scarce capital resources labors under two sets of disadvantages—those common to small business in general and those stemming from discrimination based on race or national origin.

A study directed by my office [Planning, Research and Analysis for the Small Business Administration at this writing] revealed that as of 1968, the number of minority-owned businesses accounted for only 3.7 percent of the U.S. business population, as contrasted with their 15 percent share of the human population.[8] The ownership gap amounts to roughly 600,000 enterprises in terms of numbers of businesses. There is a qualitative gap as well. Minority-owned businesses, on the average, are half as large as other businesses in employment, sales, and assets. We estimate that it would require in excess of $40 billion to raise the number of minority-owned businesses to the level representative of their share of the U.S. population and to change their industry distribution, location, and size to conform with like characteristics of the total business community.

Minority enterprise in the ghetto environment

While minority persons own less than 30 percent of the businesses in urban ghettos, almost one-third of all minority-owned businesses are located in these areas.[9] Further, there is a clear need for increased resident ownership of those businesses as well as for an upgrading of their efficiency. It is important, then, to examine the need for and availability of funds to finance these ventures.

As pointed out by numerous witnesses at the 1968 hearings of the Financial Institutions Subcommittee of the Senate Banking and Currency Committee, there is an all-pervading credit and capital gap in our inner cities—consumer credit, mortgage credit, and business credit.[10] Explanations for this are not hard to come by. The low-income population served by ghetto businesses is highly sensitive to changes in employment levels. Neighborhood stores must accept the high risk of consumer credit. These businesses are generally found in high-crime areas. This was brought out in the SBA crime study, which found that the 4 percent of all U.S. businesses which are in ghettos accounted for 2 percent of sales but for 8 percent of all dollar losses due to crime.[11] Denials and cancellations of crime insurance have been growing steadily. What insurance is available can be purchased only at several times standard rates. With no or inadequate insurance, eligibility for business loans evaporates. Creditors in the ghetto are being progressively abandoned to the loan shark. Finally, urban banks—until recently—have shown little inclination to understand the special problems of ghetto business and little interest in bringing their services to the ghetto or in attracting ghetto businessmen into their remote downtown offices.

Yet, there is a market in the ghetto which could sustain prosperous businesses. For example, in a 1968 study of business practices in low-income areas of Washington, D.C., the Federal Trade Commission found that retailers of furniture and appliances realized an average gross profit margin on sales of 62.2 percent as compared with 35.5 percent for their counterparts in the general market. Net profit returns on sales were 3.9 percent and 2.3 percent, respectively.[12] The higher prices charged by the stores in the low-income areas reflect the higher cost of doing business in the ghetto environment. It is not too much to expect that a concerted attack on the environment's problems would result in a largely resident-owned set of commercial facilities serving their communities with better quality merchandise at lower cost.

Minority enterprise in the business mainstream

While social and economic gains can be expected to accrue from an increased minority ownership of businesses in the communities in which they reside, especially in the ghettos, no significant minority enterprise program can be confined to the ghettos. Only 4 percent of the nation's businesses are in ghettos. Even if all were minority owned, minorities would still be grossly underrepresented in the business community. The minority-enterprise program must reach beyond the ghetto into the nation's business mainstream to upgrade both the location and industry distribution of minority-owned enterprises. The balance of this paper views the program in this broader perspective.

Adequacy of finance as perceived by minority persons

It was pointed out in the Federal Reserve Study that a small business-man is unlikely even to express a need for additional capital when experience has taught him that it is not available.[13] We should expect an even greater sense of futility among minority persons in business or persons who might enter if they believed that adequate financial assistance would be available.

We have been able to shed some light on this question as a result of interviews of a sample of black households in thirty-three U.S. cities. The "Black Buyer Survey," conducted a year ago by the Resource Management Corporation, included several questions proposed by the Small Business Administration. Responses revealed that, of all the heads of household interviewed, 5 percent were in business. Thirty-seven percent had never considered entering business. Of the 58 percent who were not in business but had considered entering, 72 percent cited lack of financing as the principal impediment.

This pattern of response was by no means confined to persons with low incomes or little education. Those with incomes of $15,000 and above had the highest percentage (17 percent) in business. Thirty-nine percent had not considered entering. Of the 44 percent who were not in business but had considered entering, 64 percent cited lack of financing as the principal impediment. A similar response pattern emerged when respondents were classified by years of education. Of these, persons with one to three years of college were most likely to be in business. Briefly, the results showed: 15 percent in business; 39 percent had not considered entering; 46 percent had considered entering, of whom 74 percent cited finance as the principal deterrent.[14] The results are summarized in Table 1.

TABLE 1
The Capital Gap as Perceived by Nonwhite Heads of Households

Employment Category of Respondent	Percentage of All Heads of Households	Percentage with Income $15,000 and over	Percentage with 1–3 Yrs. College
Already in business	5	17	15
Had not considered entering business	37	39	39
Had considered	58	44	46
Reasons for not entering:			
Finance	72	64	74
Other	28	36	26

Clearly, a very large proportion of black persons with better-than-average achievement records perceive a capital gap as a reason for not seeking to enter business. Having this perception, they are unlikely to take the trouble to seek assistance from financial institutions.

Bank participation in the Small Business Administration minority enterprise program

We sorely need information as to the amount of investment which is being placed in minority enterprise by commercial banks, investment banks, insurance companies, suppliers and other creditors. Since this information is not now available, the best information we now have relates to the degree of private financial institutions' participation in Small Business Administration financial assistance programs.

We have recently completed the initial phase of an evaluation of the Small Business Administration's minority enterprise program in which success achieved in securing private sector participation in lending programs has been a major factor. Our initial analysis has been confined to very general conclusions which can be drawn from data available from central office files. We intend to proceed in the second and final phase of the evaluation to an on-site review of the status and prospects of a representative sample of minority borrowers.

The most important single conclusion drawn from the first phase of the study is that there is an extremely wide geographic variation in performance. Since each district office has a different ratio of minority persons to its total population, we had to devise a measure of performance which would take these differences into account. To this end, we devised a bank participation loan index. This index was so constructed that a district which contained the same percentage of the national minority population as its share of all loans to minority persons would be assigned an index of 100. That is, it would be performing at the national norm. Indexes above or below 100 would reveal the degree to which a district exceeded or fell short of the national norm.

After Puerto Rico, Hawaii, and districts accounting for less than one-half of 1 percent of the total minority population were excluded, a total of forty districts remained.

The results of this analysis revealed that the rate of bank participation in minority loan programs varied from a high of 792, about eight times the national norm, in Boston, Massachusetts, to a low of 16, about one-sixth of the national norm, in New Orleans, Louisiana.

After a thorough review of all the factors about which we could develop information as to the relative volume of loans granted by banks, we concluded that the most important single factor was the ratio of the minority to the total population in each district. In general, the relative performance of a district is inversely proportional to the ratio that its minority population bears to its total population. There are exceptions to this generalization: San Francisco, California; Miami, Florida; Phoenix, Arizona; and San Diego, California, had higher-than-average loan densities, as well as higher-than-average minority population ratios. On the other hand, of the twenty districts with the lowest density indexes, only one—Oklahoma City, Oklahoma—had a slightly lower-than-average minority population ratio.

The conclusions we have drawn from the loan data are supported by Table 2. In this table, each SBA district with more than one-half percent of the total minority population (Puerto Rico and Hawaii are excluded for other reasons) is ranked according to its bank participation loan density index. Related to this is its minority population ratio.

TABLE 2
Loan Density Index and Minority Population Ratio by SBA District,
Fiscal Year 1970

	Highest-Scoring			Lowest-Scoring	
District	Density Index	Percentage Minority Population	District	Density Index	Percentage Minority Population
Boston	792	3.4	Marshall	84	37.6
Syracuse	551	3.4	Houston	78	27.6
Denver	446	14.8	Los Angeles	70	20.9
Pittsburgh	349	4.2	New York City	67	20.9
Indianapolis	242	6.7	Oklahoma City	55	11.9
Seattle	226	6.4	Jacksonville	53	19.6
Kansas City	216	8.1	Albuquerque	52	49.9
Newark	214	12.4	Richmond	51	23.0
Detroit	205	11.7	Birmingham	51	29.4
Hartford	193	8.3	Charlotte	50	25.1
Chicago	169	14.6	San Antonio	47	59.2
San Francisco	158	18.3	Baltimore	45	19.0
Cleveland	147	8.3	Atlanta	43	27.6
Louisville	139	7.3	Nashville	43	16.7
Miami	114	19.4	Dallas	42	18.0
San Diego	110	29.3	Washington, D.C.	33	27.1
Columbus	98	8.8	Jackson	25	41.3
Phoenix	97	28.2	Little Rock	23	20.5
Philadelphia	97	11.8	Columbia	19	33.4
St. Louis	92	14.4	New Orleans	16	31.9

Each district is named for the principal city in which it is found. In the majority of cases, district is contiguous with the state in which it is located.

The twenty districts with the highest participation loan density indexes are shown in the two columns at the left. The density indexes ranged from a low of 92 percent of the national norm to a high of 792. The minority population ratios ranged from a low of 3.4 percent of the district population to a high of 29.3 percent. The weighted average index for a twenty regions was 186, with an average minority population ratio of 11. percent. Data for the twenty lowest-scoring districts are arrayed in the last two columns. Among these, the participation loan density index ranged from a low of 16 to a high of 84. Minority-population ratios range from a low of 11.9 percent to a high of 59.2 percent. The weighted averag index was 50 and the average minority population ratio 25.2 percent.

It is clear from these data that, except in a few already noted district the probability that a minority person would receive a loan with bar participation is significantly greater where the minority population small relative to the total population. Some distance factors—both spati and social—appear to be at work where minority populations are rel tively large and these factors appear to make bridging the capital gap mo difficult than elsewhere.

We next sought to test the hypothesis that the variations among the districts might be due to timing. If that were the case, we ought to be able to develop evidence that the low-scoring districts were beginning to accelerate their rates of growth in participation loans and that the high-scoring districts were showing evidence of tapering off.

To test this hypothesis, we developed data showing the rate of change in the number of bank participation loans for the same forty districts between Fiscal Year 1969 and 1970. Here, again, we found a very wide range of variation from a low of −64 percent in Baltimore, Maryland, to a high of +300 percent in Oklahoma City. These data with the districts arrayed as before according to their participation indices appear in Table 3.

TABLE 3
Loan Density Index and Bank Participation Growth Rate by SBA District,
Fiscal Year 1969 to Fiscal Year 1970

	Highest-Scoring			Lowest-Scoring	
District	Loan Density Index	Participation Growth Rate (%)	District	Loan Density Index	Participation Growth Rate (%)
Boston	792	42	Marshall	84	267
Syracuse	551	15	Houston	78	41
Denver	446	68	Los Angeles	70	98
Pittsburgh	349	9	N.Y. City	67	−46
Indianapolis	242	8	Oklahoma City	55	300
Seattle	226	71	Jacksonville	53	6
Kansas City	216	−10	Albuquerque	52	36
Newark	214	86	Richmond	51	−6
Detroit	205	79	Birmingham	51	14
Hartford	193	−14	Charlotte	50	34
Chicago	169	92	San Antonio	47	130
San Francisco	158	77	Baltimore	45	−64
Cleveland	147	7	Atlanta	43	−14
Louisville	139	64	Nashville	43	40
Miami	114	−8	Dallas	42	36
San Diego	110	108	Wash.,D.C.	33	6
Columbus	98	−45	Jackson	25	5
Phoenix	97	38	Little Rock	23	0
Philadelphia	97	− 8	Columbia	19	−19
St. Louis	92	14	New Orleans	16	140

It will be noted that some of twenty lowest-scoring districts—Marshall, Los Angeles, California, Oklahoma City, San Antonio, Texas, and New Orleans—had exceptionally large increases in the number of bank participation loans. On the other hand, half of the districts which experienced reductions in loans—New York City, Atlanta, Georgia; Baltimore, Richmond, Virginia; and Columbia, South Carolina—were also in the low-scoring group.

On the whole, we found no clear evidence to sustain the hypothesis that any consistent relationship exists between the relative volume of participation loans and the rate of change of loan volumes.

A definitive explanation of these wide geographic variations in performance will require in-depth analyses of individual communities and their institutions. The summary data developed thus far suggest that we still have a long way to go to get adequate private financial resouces placed at the disposal of minority-owned businesses. This is especially true of such places as New York, Washington, Baltimore, and Atlanta where some of the largest concentrations of the minority population are found and where loan volumes have been relatively low and are either falling off or growing at a very slow rate. Atlanta, it should be said, may be an exception. It has a long tradition of black business ownership and of acceptance of black persons by the banking community. It is possible, if not probable, that the private sector is serving black business without benefit of our guarantees. We are seeking to determine whether there may be a relationship between district loan volumes and their growth rates and the quality of loans. To this end, we are testing the hypothesis that relatively high loan densities and growth rates may be associated with abnormally high risks. In other words, we wish to know whether districts with high loan densities and growth rates are bringing in high proportions of borrowers who have little chance of survival in business. A definitive answer to this question will require a survey of a representative sample of borrowers and case studies in a number of different locations. Our preliminary probings in this area, however, suggest that the reverse relationship may exist. For example, we have found indications that the highest expected survival rate among minority borrowers may occur in such districts as Boston, Newark, New Jersey, Denver, Colorado, and Chicago. These districts all scored high in relative loan density and rate of growth in loan volumes.

Nationwide private participation in minority enterprise loans reached almost $100 million—an all-time high—in fiscal year 1970. This contrasts with approximately $1 million and $2 million in fiscal years 1967 and 1968 respectively. While this reflects a highly encouraging growth rate, the amount remains extremely small in comparison with the investmen needed to ensure significant representation in the business mainstream New measures are needed to bring about a further sharp increase ir participation by private financial institutions and other sources of funds ir the immediate future. Proposals now before the Congress, for the mos part applicable to all small businesses, include tax incentives, interes subsidies, and a variety of measures to expand secondary markets fo SBA-guaranteed paper. The last mentioned appears to me to promise th greatest long-term benefit. It would be better still if these were pressed t their logical conclusion through the establishment of a capital bank.

The supply of ownership candidates

No examination of the problem of financing minority enterprise woul be complete without some treatment of the supply of minority busines ownership candidates. We frequently encounter the assertion, especially among our friends in the financial community, that money is not the problem. Those who hold to this view maintain that wherever a candidate with the necessary qualifications and capabilities can be matched with a promising business opportunity, adequate financing will be promptly available. Whether this is true or not is a moot question. There may have been a shortage of candidates in the past, but this is changing and can be expected to change further as we proceed through the 1970s. Those who assert that adequate financing will be available should soon have their assumptions tested in the marketplace.

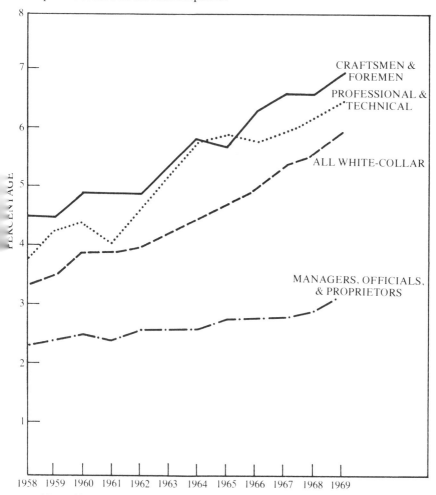

ig. 1. Nonwhite employment as percentage of total employment by occupational ategories.

ource: Data were furnished by the Bureau of Labor Statistics to update an article entitled, Changing Patterns in the Employment of Non-White Workers," *Monthly Labor Review*, ar. 1966.

I have already touched upon the reluctance of actual and potential small businessmen in general, and minority persons in particular, to seek financing from private financial institutions. Those who do not see financing as a problem must realize that the minority enterprise capital gap may be due in part to a credibility gap. The latter appears to be in the process of being bridged, at least in a number of locations.

Additional evidence to support an expectation of significant increases in the supply of minority ownership candidates may be deduced from a review of the past achievements of minority persons in the more attractive occupations, and their prospects for the future. The former is displayed in Figure 1.

The broken line on the chart depicts nonwhite workers (almost 80 percent of all those we define as minority persons) as a percentage of the total number of white-collar workers. It will be noted that the ratio of nonwhite persons (who currently account for 11 percent of total employment) in these occupations rose from 3.2 percent to 6.0 percent between 1958 and 1969.

The dotted line shows the comparable ratio for professional and technical workers, among the most highly skilled and highly paid white-collar occupations. The nonwhite share of this employment category rose from 3.8 percent in 1958 to 6.5 percent in 1968. The upper solid line shows an expansion in the nonwhite percentage of employment among craftsmen and foremen, the most highly skilled and highly paid of the blue collar occupations from 4.5 to 7.0 percent between 1958 and 1969.

In contrast with these, nonwhite employment in the managers, officials and proprietors category rose only from 2.3 percent in 1958 to 3.2 percent in 1969. Further, the nonwhite ratio rose by only 5/10 of one percentage point between 1958 and 1967. It increased an additional 4/10 of one percentage point between 1967 and 1969. (Absolute numbers for this occupational category may be misleading as indicators of nonwhite participation in business, since they include some persons who are no businessmen and do not include some businessmen who are picked up in other occupational classes. We have found, however, that the percentage figures of the type cited are reasonably good indicators of the *relative* position of nonwhites in the nation's business population and of their distribution by industry.)

In terms of absolute numbers, total nonwhite employment in all categories under consideration (all white collar plus craftsmen and foremen) rose from 1.2 million to 2.9 million between 1958 and 1969, a increase of 1.7 million. In the three high-skill categories (craftsmen and foremen; professional and technical workers; and managers, officials, and proprietors), the rise was from 800,000 to 1.7 million, an increase of 900,000.

The Bureau of Labor Statistics forecasts an increase of 13.5 million in total employment in the occupations under consideration between 1968 and 1980.[15] By that time, nonwhites will account for approximately 12 percent of the labor force. To achieve a representation in all the occupations under consideration equal to their population percentage, nonwhites employment in these occupations would have to increase by an additional 4.3 million by 1980. The corresponding increase required in the three selected occupations is 2.6 million. Assuming continued emphasis on training programs and continued progressive improvement in nonwhite educational achievements, such gains cannot be ruled out. As the total gap is narrowed, two results can reasonably be expected:

1. The rate of increase in the percentage of nonwhites in those occupations where they are are currently best represented (craftsmen and foremen, and professional and technical workers) will slow down as parity is approached.
2. The pool of candidates for manager, official, and proprietor occupations will grow at a more rapid rate than the total nonwhite labor force in all the occupations we have reviewed.

Accordingly, any dearth in the supply of candidates for business ownership should soon disappear, if it does in fact exist.

Conclusion

Data presented in this paper warrant a measured optimism with respect to the outlook for minority enterprise in the years ahead. Evidence has been cited to support the conclusion that a capital gap exists for small business in general, at least for other than short-term funds. A much broader gap exists in the special case of minority enterprise. It is especially acute in urban ghettos but exists as well in a broad spectrum of geographic locations.

The evidence presented as to the performance of Small Business Administration borrowers suggests that satisfying the capital needs of small business can result in an improved allocation of scarce financial resources. There are, of course, important considerations of equity which argue for special efforts to satisfy the financial needs of minority enterprise. I believe that a significant increase in the number and quality of minority-owned businesses will reap economic rewards as well. Secretary Stans described these rewards most succinctly in a recent report to the President:

First, the United States cannot afford to continue wasting the potential contribution to economic progress which rests within those who have in effect been excluded from ''the system.'' Productive capitalism thrives on broad competition. Increasing our base of entrepreneurs will not exhaust a limited marketplace. On the contrary, it can increase both the size and the quality of the enterprise economy. In that process, all can benefit.[16]

NOTES

1. Federal Reserve System, *Financing Small Business*, Report to the Committee on Banking and Currency and the Select Committees on Small Business, United States Congress (Washington, D.C., Government Printing Office, 1958), p. 102.

2. Kaplan and Banner, "Adequacy of Small Business Financing; One View," *Financing Small Business*, p. 122.

3. Schweiger, Irving, "Adequacy of Small Business Financing: Another View," *Financing Small Business*, p. 148.

4. Stoll and Curley, "Small Business and the New Issue Market for Equities," *Journal of Financial and Quantitative Analysis*, June 1970, pp. 309–22.

5. The results of this study are set forth in a paper presented by the author to the Institute of Management Sciences entitled, "An Economic Evaluation of the Business Loan Program of the Small Business Administration," in Sept. 1968. The detailed data have not been published.

6. Harold T. Smith, *Equity and Loan Capital for New and Small Business* (Kalamazoo, Mich.: The W. E. Upjohn Institute for Employment Research, 1959).

7. Federal Reserve System, *Reappraisal of the Federal Reserve Discount Mechanism*, Report of a Systems Committee (Washington, D.C.: Board of Governors of the Federal Reserve System, 1968).

8. Albert J. Reiss, "Minority Entrepreneurship," reprinted in *Review of Small Business Administration's Programs and Policies–1969;* Hearings before the Select Committee on Small Business, United States Senate, 91st Cong., 1st Sess. (Washington, D.C.: Government Printing Office, 1969).

9. *Ibid.*

10. *Financial Institutions and the Urban Crisis*, Hearings before the Subcommittee on Financial Institutions of the Committee on Banking and Currency, United States Senate, 90th Cong., 2nd Sess. (Washington, D.C.: Government Printing Office, 1968), *passim*.

11. Small Business Administration, *Crime against Small Business*, A Report to the President and the Congress (Washington, D.C.: Government Printing Office, 1969).

12. Arthur T. Anderson, "Installment Credit and the Low Income Consumer: A Case Study," *Small Business Administration Quarterly Economic Digest*, June 1968, pp. 11–30.

13. Kaplan and Banner, "Adequacy of Small Business Financing."

14. Alice F. Hansen, "The Black Businessman and the Black Buyer," *Small Business Administration Economic Review*, Fall 1970, pp. 18–35.

15. U.S., Bureau of Labor Statistics, *The U.S. Economy in 1980*, Bulletin 1673 (Washington, D.C.: Government Printing Office, 1970), p. 57.

16. Maurice H. Stans, Secretary of Commerce, *Report to the President on Minority Business Enterprise* (Washington, D.C.: Department of Commerce, June 1970).

Profit Motivation and Management Assistance in Community Economic Development

John E. Oxendine and Alvin N. Puryear

In July 1968 a community development corporation (CDC) in one of New York City's depressed minority communities initiated an economic development program which was designed to encourage local residents to initiate business ventures. After two years it had provided financial and management assistance to over thirty minority entrepreneurs. The purpose of this paper is to present the findings of a study which examined the importance of profit motivation and management assistance in determining the success or failure of twelve of these businesses.

The Assistance Program

The CDC in this study is a nonprofit, community-based corporation which supplemented its economic development activities with housing, community-development, and employment projects. Its economic development program emphasized the establishment and expansion of business enterprises owned and operated by local residents. With respect to financial aid, the CDC gave loans of approximately $2 million, which, in turn, stimulated banks and private investors to provide a nearly equal amount of capital to these businesses.

The CDC felt that the creation and expansion of locally owned businesses was not a unique feature of community economic development. It believed that the more challenging task was to provide the means for ensuring that local businesses would maintain their existence and grow into financially sound firms capable of generating economic returns for the community. While the CDC recognized that there was a need for management assistance, its approach in meeting this need differed from that of many other organizations. The dominant view in other assistance programs was that management assistance could best be accomplished through a system of volunteers, usually from outside the affected community. While recognizing that volunteers can play a very effective role in assisting local business development, the CDC questioned whether volunteers should be the primary instrument of assistance. As a consequence, the CDC decided not to use a "canned" program which might have worked for others, adopting, instead, a "contact man" system for its management assistance effort.

Under this system each businessman was designated the client of a CDC contact man, who was given full responsibility for helping that client until a successful business operation was established. The contact man was expected to provide a wide range of services to the client. Initial assistance was often in the form of guidance to the client in his preparation of a request for funds. Typically, the contact man then assisted the client in negotiating with a bank, obtaining a business location, and selecting equipment and machinery. In effect, he provided all services which were needed to help an entrepreneur who was starting or expanding a business. Once the doors of the business were open, the contact man increased his efforts. It was then his responsibility to insure that the enterprise would be a success and add to the economic growth of the community. Obviously, the contact man, regardless of his skills, could not solve all problems and often had to go outside of the CDC to seek specialized skills. However, under this approach even outside assistance, whether from volunteers or paid consultants, was secured under the direction of the contact man.

The Determinants of Success

In order to determine the ingredients necessary to insure a successful small business operation in a depressed community, we examined thirty-two firms assisted by the CDC and then selected twelve for an intensive study. Of the twelve, two were franchise operations, six were retail and service firms, and four were manufacturing companies. In the first category were a transmission franchise and a fried-chicken franchise. The retail and service firms included a uniform guard service, a photo studio, a radio and television service store, an electonics store, a men's shoe store, and a moving company. The manufacturing concerns included a plastics manufacturer, a metal fabricator, a dress manufacturer, and a handbag manufacturer.

The twelve cases suggested that many factors influence the ultimate success or failure of a new business. In order to focus on the primary determinants of successful business development, we isolated five key factors which the case studies indicated were most important. The five were: (1) the technical competence or experience of the entrepreneur; (2) the capitalization of the business; (3) the amount of risk incurred by each entrepreneur; (4) the motivation of the entrepreneur; and (5) the ability and willingness of the entrepreneur to accept management assistance.

Technical Competence: A Panacea

At the beginning of its economic development program, the CDC believed that one key to successful community economic development was to assist individuals possessing technical competence or experience. The following factors supported this rationale: (1) The entrepreneur would know how to provide the products or services; (2) the entrepreneur would have a working knowledge of the industry's problems and practices; (3) the entrepreneur would know the sources of supply for raw materials and methods of distribution; and (4) the entrepreneur would be able to work out start-up problems in a shorter period of time. Consequently, the majority of the persons assisted by the CDC possessed a relatively high degree of technical competence. Many of these entrepreneurs had acquired their technical experience through employment in similar enterprises or through operating marginal businesses. All six of the service and retail trade entrepreneurs had some experience in their respective fields. Of the four manufacturers, only the plastics manufacturer lacked extensive experience before receiving CDC assistance.

While the CDC believed that technical competence was essential, it also made loans to a few persons who did not have experience in their new business fields. For example, it assisted the operators of the transmission and fried-chicken franchises because it felt that these were standardized operations and that the franchiser management support greatly increased chances for success. Its loan to the plastics manufacturer was to continue the business that his cousin had started. In this instance, it felt that he would be able to hire persons possessing the necessary technical competence.

If the CDC's theory about technical competence were correct, one would expect that the businesses having owners with this competence would be more successful than those without. That is, the nine businesses in which the owners had technical experience would be successful, while those three in which the owners did not have experience would be less successful. Yet, the case examples did not allow us to draw such a conclusion about the value of technical experience. We saw that only four of the businesses in which the owners had technical competence were successful. These were the uniform guard service, the radio and TV service store, the metal fabricator, and the handbag manufacturer. At the same time, the other five—the photo studio, the electronics store, the men's shoe store, the moving company, and the dress manufacturer—were failures. Looking at the businesses in which the owners lacked technical proficiency, we found that two of the three—the transmission franchise and the plastics manufacturer—were failures, while the third—the fried-chicken franchise—was entrenched solidly in success. Thus, while the CDC believed that technical competence was the key to creating successful businesses, the facts did not support this belief. Instead, the experiences of these entrepreneurs showed that technical competence was not a panacea and that certain other ingredients would have to be present if success was to be achieved. In this regard, we examined the role of capital investment, since many persons theorize that adequate capital is a necessary supplement to or substitute for technical competence.

Money: An Enigmatic Experience

Studies of community economic development indicate that minority entrepreneurs can seldom marshal enough capital to start a business. Our analysis of owner's equity showed that twenty-seven of the thirty-two CDC-assisted businesses had owner's equity of less than $5,000. More important, the average capital invested by the owners of the twenty-seven was $1,750, or only 3.6 percent of the $48,000 average capital required. While three of the thirty-two businesses had owner's equity between $5,000 and $15,000, the owner's average capital contribution was $9,500 or only 5.3 percent of the average capital required of $179,500. Finally, the CDC assisted two businesses which had capital contributions greater than $15,000 and whose stockholders raised amounts which represented a relatively high 16 and 33 percent of the total capitalization required. Except for these two, however, it is significant that the entrepreneurs of the other thirty businesses were able to contribute less than 5 percent of the total capitalization their businesses required.

It should come as no surprise to the reader that depressed minority communities have a severe shortage of internal capital. While one might expect outside capital to be available for ventures which show good economic promise, this has not been the case. In fact, the absence of external capital is as acute as the absence of internal capital. So the ghetto businessman must turn to the Shylock for financing or, if he is lucky, to a community development corporation.

As indicated earlier, the CDC in our study has approximately $2 million which is utilized with the owners' small equity investments to partially capitalize the businesses. At the same time, it leveraged its funds by pursuing bank participation on each venture. Consequently its $2 million, coupled with the owner's investment and bank loans, provided sufficient capital for the thirty-two businesses. The initial capital positions of the twelve case studies indicate the distribution and importance of this funding.

The two franchises had a total capitalization of $97,400, $36,400 of which came from the CDC, $57,500 from other lending institutions, and only $3,500 from the owners. In both cases this was ample funding for the two operations. Yet one failed while the other succeeded. The six retail and service firms also had adequate capitalization, although primarily because of assistance from the CDC and lending institutions. Of the total funding of $232,352 for the six firms, the CDC provided $172,000, lending institutions $51,252, and the owners but $8,200. In three cases—the uniform guard service, the photo studio, and the radio and TV service store—the CDC provided $89,500 or 96 percent of the total capitalization, a very high figure. Regardless of the "funding mix," the fact remains that each of the six was financed adequately and that four of the six failed while only two succeeded. Finally, a similar pattern existed with the manufacturing operations. While the lending institutions provided $162,338 to the four operations, the CDC was the primary financier supplying $594,530 or about 75 percent of their total funds. Again two of the four were unsuccessful despite the fact that they received adequate funding from the CDC and the lending institutions.

Thus, although the CDC had limited funds, it was able to generate sufficient funds for all of the businesses it assisted. Yet, of the twelve businesses, seven failed, including five of the nine in which the owners were also technically competent. While the CDC, the community, and the entrepreneurs believed that money could solve almost all problems, they learned that money and technical competence are not enough in themselves to guarantee success.

Risk: The Unconscious Persuader

In deciding among business alternatives in which to invest, it is important that funds not be given too freely, lest they defeat their primary purpose—to generate profits. Economists argue that the level of profits should be commensurate with the level of risk. In the absence of risk, one may no longer be concerned with profitability and funds may be used injudiciously for noneconomic goals, thereby decreasing scarce pockets of capital. However, despite acceptance of this principle, the CDC did not include a risk factor in its financial assistance program. The evidence indicated clearly that most of its financial assistance was given consciously on a risk-free basis.

So far we have seen that the entrepreneurs of the six service and retail firms possessed a relatively high degree of technical competence and had sufficient funds to create profitable businesses. Furthermore, three of the four owners of manufacturing firms also had technical experience and sufficient funding. Finally, though the owners of the two franchises and one of the manufacturing companies did not possess this same degree of technical competence, they, too received sufficient financial resources. Therefore, the question remains, Why did seven of twelve fail? Moreover what accounts for five failures in cases where the entrepreneurs received sufficient financial assistance *and* had technical competence? Perhaps the failures of both the technically proficient and nonproficient can be explained by an *absence* of financial risk.

The case studies showed that only two of the nine entrepreneurs who had technical competence assumed any measurable amount of financial risk in starting their businesses. In this regard, it should be pointed out that all of the CDC loans were made to corporate entities, with the owners of the corporations having no legal obligations for the loan repayment. The best examples of absence of risk are found in the owners of the uniform guard service, the photo studio, and the radio and TV service store, all of whom not only received interest-free CDC loans, but in addition, had no bank financing for which they were liable personally. Equally important, they all had marketable skills which guaranteed them employment in the event that their businesses failed.

A step removed from these with respect to degree of risk were the partners of the moving company, the handbag manufacturer, the dress manufacturer, and the metal fabricator. Although they were liable personally for bank loans, there was little risk since each of the four firms had collateralized loans secured by equipment, the value of which more than offset the owners' personal liabilities. Finally, only two of the technically proficient entrepreneurs were vulnerable in that their bank loans were not covered fully by capital assets. The owner of the electronics store had borrowed from a commercial bank to supplement his CDC loan. Though he had repaid some of this obligation before his store closed, the equipment which remained did not offset fully his liability to the bank. Similarly, the men's shoe store owner did not have sufficient assets to offset his $21,500 bank loan. As a matter of fact, the store's fixtures and inventory were valued at only $5,000, thereby placing a relatively large amount of risk on the owner.

Of the three entrepreneurs who did not possess technical competence at the outset, only one—the plastics manufacturer—was completely free of risk. While he received $29,500 from lending institutions, it was more than offset by $100,000 in plant machinery. The other two owners in this category—the transmission franchisee and the fried-chicken franchisee—both had risk. Because the bank loan to the former was not offset fully by the value of the machinery and equipment remaining in his transmission shop, he stood to suffer from a business failure. The latter, because of heavy debt financing, was also in a very vulnerable position. Not only was he personally liable to lending institutions for $40,000, but in addition, his chicken shop had little in capital assets as an offsetting security. Thus, only three of the twelve owners faced a degree of risk likely to cause them to sustain personal financial losses.

In several of the cases we found that lack of risk permitted or even *encouraged* the entrepreneurs to be unconcerned about the futures of their enterprises. Such cases illustrate clearly what happens to entrepreneurs who have sufficient money and technical competence, but who have nothing at stake in the event of failure. Had these entrepreneurs been liable for their investments to the extent of their personal and future assets, they might have exercised more protection for the assets of the business. Or they might have chosen not to go into business at all, in which case the risk factor would have served to select individuals committed totally to running successful ventures.

The case study revealed, however, several instances in which owners *did not* neglect their entrepreneurial duties even though they made small investments and had no personal risks. Do such cases indicate that in lieu of risk, entrepreneurs will be successful if, for example, they are willing to work long hours as did the handbag manufacturer and fried-chicken franchisee? Certainly long hours are laudable, but do they explain success? Probably not, since is seems unreasonable to define *risk-free, but successful*, entrepreneurs in terms of hard work alone.

The Roles of Motivation and Management Assistance

Motivation: mover of men

Motivation is an intangible quality which makes an individual want to succeed no matter what the cost. One might view it as a creative dissatisfaction which forces a man not to accept his lot but to seek new levels of achievement. Regardless of a definition of motivation, it became clear from the twelve cases that it was a key ingredient in business success. Unanswered was how motivation is translated into successful business operations. Wanting to succeed, wanting to go into business, or seeking levels of achievement does not insure success. The evidence in the cases suggested that if the entrepreneur were to be successful, his motivation had to be directed toward business goals, and the most basic of all business goals is profitability. Therefore, essential for the successful development of a business are entrepreneurs characterized by a high degree of *profit motivation*. The twelve cases illustrated that profit motivation was present in the operators of the successful ventures, and absent in the operators of the failures.

The contrast in the two franchisees, for example, was most evident in their respective views of the ultimate objectives of their businesses which accounted largely for the success of the fried-chicken franchise and the failure of the transmission franchise. While the owner of the former committed himself totally to making his business a financial success, the owner of the latter spent insufficient time at his enterprise, did not utilize the management advice he received, and demonstrated that he was not interested in making his enterprise financially successful. The case for profit motivation was also evident in the experiences of the six service and retail firms. Although all of these entrepreneurs possessed sufficient experience and capitalization, only two of the six were successful. As with the franchise operations, it was clear that an essential element in determining the success of each was their owners' high motivations toward the goal of profits. The importance of profit motivation was made clear again in the case studies of the manufacturers assisted by the CDC. The metal fabricator and the handbag manufacturer possessed a high degree of profit motivation, while the unsuccessful owners reached their goals by "being in business," not by showing a profit. The divergence between these two views is wide enough to show that the profitability goal was a key determinant of success.

Thus a significant difference between the two groups—the successful and the unsuccessful—was the level of their commitment to the goal of profitability. This was reflected in the entrepreneurs' willingness to put forth the effort necessary to guide their firms to profitable positions, regardless of other—often personal—considerations. The cases illustrated that while technical proficiency, money, and risks contributed toward success, they had to be supplemented by profit motivation. Yet all of these were useless without a vehicle to give them proper direction. This vehicle was managerial skill.

Management: The Essential Ingredient

In the twelve case studies we found that a variety of conditions existed with respect to each business and each entrepreneur. This was especially true in correlating success to technical ability, financing, and risk. Though all twelve firms were funded adequately, the degree of success of each was not related directly to the experience of the entrepreneur or his potential for a personal loss. In fact, the only consistent ingredient with respect to success was that the five successful entrepreneurs had a high degree of motivation toward achievement of profitability which was absent in the seven unsuccessful owners. Implicit in the cases was the notion that, in addition to profit motivation, the successful firms were also characterized by a pattern of good business management.

The CDC's experience showed that management may take one of two forms: enlightened or unenlightened. The unenlightened manager was incapable of giving overall direction and coordination to his business. Moreover, he was unable to see the necessity of supplementing his abilities with the skills needed to develop a profitable enterprise. Of even greater significance, the unsuccessful manager was not even *motivated* sufficiently to accept the management assistance provided through the CDC's contact man system. Thus, the unenlightened manager did not recognize the need to supplement his skills even when the assistance was available and given within an organized structure.

In this regard, an analysis of the twelve cases indicated clearly that the seven unsuccessful owners, in addition to lacking profit motivation, were also unenlightened. In looking at the management experiences of the five technically proficient owners who failed, one might have argued that their prior experiences should have prepared them to operate a business. This was not the case since their technical experiences could not overcome their management deficiencies. More important, these entrepreneurs also refused to accept any management assistance from the CDC. And the refusal to accept management advice does not limit itself to entrepreneurs who possess technical proficiency. Unfortunately, the owners of companies without the technical experience were also unreceptive. The transmission franchisee and the plastics manufacturer failed because they were deficient in both technical competence and management skills. In both cases the entrepreneurs did not accept the free management assistance made available by the CDC and others.

Despite such instances, there are cases—including the five successful firms in this study—where the CDC management assistance effort bore fruit. However, it should be recognized that in such cases, the owners were *motivated* to accept and fully use such assistance. Thus, the *enlightened* manager's capacity to give overall direction and coordination to the business resulted because he supplemented his management skills with the management assistance of an outsider who provided council.

If a businessman practices good management skills, or if he is willing to utilize fully a good management assistance program, it matters little that he might not possess the optimum amount of technical expertise. This fact is borne out in this study where the five owners who were motivated toward profit achievement did well regardless of their prior experiences. Of greater significance, these five cases also demonstrated that the entrepreneurs with this profit motivation were willing to accept, and, indeed, often sought CDC assistance in solving management problems.

Conclusion

Our analysis of the twelve case studies indicates that a variety of complex variables are important in determining how successful community development corporations will be in introducing economic development programs in this country's depressed areas. While one cannot say that these twelve examples are illustrative of all such minority business enterprises, it should be clear that—at the very least—they do introduce several factors which must be considered relevant for successful community economic development.

The analysis shows that while technical experience is useful, it does not insure success. This point is especially pertinent when the experience is not related directly to the management aspects of business. Also apparent is the fact that adequate capital investment is a necessary ingredient to successful community economic development. However, the familiar cry for dollars must be offset with the knowledge that funds invested without adequate direction will bring no return. Even the widely accepted view that investment capital must be accompanied by a reasonable degree of risk is not sacred. For as our study shows, risk does not guarantee that the entrepreneur will direct himself toward the business goal of increased profits. Finally, at least two other ingredients must be present if the CDC is to promote successful economic development programs. First, the entrepreneur must have a high degree of profit motivation. That is, he must see profits, and not "going into business," as *his* primary goal. Second, good management is essential. However, because most businessmen assisted by CDC's do not possess management backgrounds and training, they must be exposed to a good program of management assistance. We have seen that the profit-motivated entrepreneur will avail himself of such management assistance.

Black Business Development

Fred C. Allvine

The demands and objectives of Afro-Americans have continually changed during the last fifteen years. When signs indicated conditions relating to one problem were improving, new objectives were formulated. Gradually social problems, such as the right to vote, poor and restricted housing, and substandard education, were supplemented with economic programs. More jobs and improved advancement opportunities were the central economic objectives.

The economic goals of blacks have been enlarged within the last two years. A new objective was presented at the meeting of the Urban Coalition in Washington, D.C., during the summer of 1968. Employment was no longer the number one priority issue. It was displaced with the need to create opportunities for blacks to *own* and *manage their own businesses.* This attitude was also expressed during the Senate Small Business Committee Hearings in Newark, N.J., and Harlem, New York.[1] Furthermore, Richard Nixon sensed this development when he was campaigning for the presidency and made black entrepreneurship a central point in his program for dealing with the racial problem.

The growing black interest in business represents a new environmental condition that has affected, and will continue to affect, the operations of many businesses. Those nonblack companies feeling threatened, or those already adversely affected, tend to believe that the blacks are following high-handed techniques and are turning to extortion. Yet, the blacks believe that their cause is just and that they have been patient too long.

Looking beyond the emotional aspects of these contrasting points of view, the nonblack companies involved should be searching for the most effective way to adapt to the new environmental challenge. To make appropriate adjustments, the affected companies will find it helpful to understand the black point of view, the direction of black business development, and the factors limiting the emergence of the black economic community.

TABLE 1
All Businesses in the Kenwood-Oakland Area in Chicago—1969*

Black	Category	White
	Black-Dominated Businesses	
30	Barber Shop and Beauty Parlor	...
19	Eating Establishment	2
14	Lounge and Tavern	2
14	Repair Shop	...
6	Service Station	...
4	Store Front Church	...
4	Funeral Home	...
2	Clothing	1
2	Record Shop	...
2	Pool Hall	...
13	Miscellaneous	...
110		5
	Black- and White-Shared Businesses	
15	Dry Cleaning and Laundry	11
7	Small Grocery	6
22		17
	White-Dominated Businesses	
	Laundromat	9
1	Liquor Store	8
	Currency Exchange	8
3	Drug Store	6
	Construction	6
2	Furniture	4
1	Real Estate	4
	Supermarkets	4
	Light Manufacturing	4
	New and Used Cars	3
	Supply Company	3
1	Hardware	2
1	Meat Market	2
1	Shoe Repair	2
	Optometrist	2
	Insurance Agency	2
	Storage Warehouse	2
	Medical Center	1
	Bank	1
	Wholesaler	1
	Miscellaneous	6
10		80
	Total Businesses	
142	244	102

*Survey conducted by the Kenwood-Oakland Community Organization in Chicago, Ill.

The Black Business Void

Black businessmen have had so many obstacles in their way that relatively few of them have succeeded in the more important types of businesses. For example, 1968 surveys indicated that

— Blacks held only seven of the 17,500 authorized automobile dealerships.

— The total assets of all black-owned insurance companies were 0.2 percent of the industry.

— Of the 6,000 radio stations, only eight were owned by blacks, while 108 were directly beamed at the black community.

— Blacks operated 20 of the 13,762 commercial banks with 0.2 percent of the industry's assets.

There were exceptions such as John H. Johnson, who heads three businesses—one each in publishing, insurance, and cosmetics; Henry G. Parks, a sausage manufacturer selling $7.5 million a year; and the Reverend Leon Sullivan, who has established a business conglomerate in Philadelphia. However, such examples are few in number.[2]

Blacks primarily operate those segregated businesses which would be difficult or unattractive for nonblacks to operate. Typically these businesses are either too small, or involve too frequent or personal contact with blacks to be run by nonblacks. Even in the case of the marginal type of black business, the property and building are normally owned by nonblacks.

The types of businesses operated by blacks are illustrated by a 1969 survey of businesses located in the predominantly black Kenwood-Oakland community on the south side of Chicago. Kenwood-Oakland is representative of many black communities; it is among neither the poorest nor the most well-to-do. It is a densely populated area housing 52,000 people in 1.1 square miles. Within the territorial confines of this community there are 244 businesses, of which 142, or 58 percent, are black-owned. However, the numbers do not reveal the characteristics of those businesses being operated by blacks. As shown in Table 1, the vast majority of the black-operated businesses are small, service-oriented types of establishments including barber shops and beauty parlors, repair services, service stations, lounges and eating establishments, and funeral homes.

In contrast, the nonblack businesses are generally less service-oriented with a lower labor-to-sales ratio. They are the relatively big businesses with large sales volumes, and they are the ones which tend to siphon black dollars directly out of the community. These businesses also require larger capital investment and much more sophisticated business skills. In essence, whites control the mainstream businesses, e.g., supermarkets, automobile agencies, supply companies, financial institutions, light manufacturing, contracting, and warehousing. What is left for the blacks is small and insignificant.

Associated problems

The business void has created several problems for the black community. Leadership is not broadly based and is primarily in the hands of the church. While the clergy has provided spiritual leadership, it has not been particularly skilled in providing the guidance required to reduce the acute economic and business problems of the black community. Business leaders are needed to complement the efforts of the religious spokesmen and to lead the way in the black economic community as they do in the white society.

A second problem related to the dearth of substantial black businesses is that few businesses are successful enough to serve as models of what might be accomplished through intelligent and diligent effort. Because the black businesses that do exist are typically the small service types of businesses and marginal product-retailing establishments which have little to offer the capable and ambitious black, those blacks with the capabilities to run businesses are skirting business opportunities in the black community in favor of going into government service, teaching, or working for nonblacks.[3]

A third problem linked to the restricted nature of black-business development is the lack of respect for private property in the black community. The rioting, burning, and looting of business operations in the black ghetto, which started in the summer of 1964, are evidence of this problem. Most of the businesses destroyed have been white-owned. While this problem is recognizably distasteful to the larger society, the message appears to be clear; the violent elements of the black society will strike out with the slightest excuse at the private property owned by those who to them represent their oppressors.

Finally, social and political progress will be severely constrained unless blacks develop a large number of reasonably secure and independent businesses. The resulting middle class generated by such developments would be politically active and would develop and support independent political machinery.

Black Capitalism

The approach generally being advanced for creating black businessmen and correcting the imbalance that exists is black capitalism. The concept of black capitalism was so designed that it is even endorsed by conservative whites and militant blacks. It appeals to blacks for there is growing recognition that without black capital there will be little black power. Similarly, black capitalism is acceptable to most white businessmen because they live by the capitalistic system and understand the orderly process with which change will come.

While there seems to be general support for black capitalism, there are still black and white leaders who are anxious over the prospects for this new program. Some fear it will lead to further exaggeration in the number of supposedly successful businesses in the black community. Others believe black capitalism will be directed to developing small businesses that will be swept away in the movement toward giant businesses. There is also concern it will lead to a black nationalistic spirit which will discourage outside businesses from making needed investment in the community. Finally, there are those who believe black capitalism will lead to apartheid, resulting in two separate economies in this country—the prosperous white and the desperate black economy.

Those blacks who advocate apartheid are very much in the minority and probably do not understand the consequences of what they are encouraging. Even many of the so-called militant blacks do not call for apartheid. What they are demanding is control over their own economic communities as other ethnic groups have, but not at the exclusion of all goods produced by blacks and whites in the giant enterprises of the United States. They want to become the storekeepers in their own communities as are the Jewish, Italians, and Poles, and they also want to engage in light manufacturing and distributing which does not require massive capital investment.

The growing black consciousness, pride, and self-respect made it possible for a number of organizations to assist blacks meaningfully in developing businesses. Some of these organizations, such as the National Business League, Interracial Council for Business Opportunity, and Operation Breadbasket, operate in the major black ghettos throughout the country. Others are much more local in scope, such as the economic development and investment corporations that have sprung up in major metropolitan areas with large black populations. Many new businesses have been started and existing businesses have been strengthened through the efforts of these organizations.

Business Planning Analyzed

Black capitalism has received support from blacks and nonblacks with diverse points of view because of individual interpretations of the concept. However, differences of opinion exist as to how black capitalism should be implemented. Nonblacks believe the thrust of black capitalism will be the building of new businesses by black entrepreneurs. These new businesses would probably include small retail and service businesses, distributing operations, and light manufacturers that would sell to the ghetto; also some light manufacturers selling to nonsegregated markets.

Some black leaders are skeptical about black capitalism if its programs primarily involve new businesses. They reason that, first, only a very small fraction of new businesses succeed and that the rate of failure is probably even higher for black businesses. As a result, the cost of starting a few successful black businesses will be high in relation to the gains by the black community. Second, much of the money is being poured into small businesses such as restaurants, haberdasheries, service stations, painting and decorating services, which, even if they do succeed, will not amount to more than a small portion of the ghetto business. Third, they question the viability of white capitalism or entrepreneurship today. In the early formation of our economic system white capitalism and entrepreneurship played a major role. However, conditions have changed and today big business, large chain operations, and multimillion-dollar companies control the thrust of most industries.

Transfer ownership of ghetto businesses

Those blacks who are not enthusiastic about the prospects of starting a number of viable black businesses recommend another program. They would prefer to have a large portion of the monies being appropriated for black capitalism channeled into financing buy-outs of existing businesses. These might include major U.S. corporations or ghetto businesses run by nonblacks. For example, Richard America, Jr., proposes that a cross-section of major corporations gradually be transferred from primarily white to black ownership and control.[4] There are many serious economic, technical, and political problems associated with this program which make it unworkable. However, the essence of America's proposal could be applied in the gradual and smooth transfer of ghetto businesses owned by nonblacks to blacks.

While the type of retailing in most of the businesses run by blacks, the smaller, highly service-oriented businesses (see Table 1), will continue to present limited opportunities in entrepreneurship, it will serve as an apprentice-type experience for black businessmen. However, blacks are increasingly becoming interested in the more substantial types of retail and service businesses that are traditionally run by nonblacks. Some of the more coveted businesses include automobile agencies, appliance stores, supermarkets, restaurant franchises, furniture stores, liquor stores, laundromats, and loan companies.

The aspirations of blacks to run the larger retail and service businesses are being fed by the successes of some of the first blacks who replaced nonblacks as owners of ghetto businesses. During the last three years, for example, five black automobile agencies have been established in the ghettos of Chicago. The first replacement of a nonblack by a black businessman involved a south-side Oldsmobile agency. The black business community and general public responded to this black-owned Oldsmobile agency, and sales appreciably increased. The success was then followed by the transfer of four additional automobile agencies to black ownership.

Another example is the Purity-Supreme Stores in Boston which decided to sell two of their ghetto stores to black-owned Freedom Foods, Inc. Since Purity wants to recover its investment, it is anxious to see Freedom Foods succeed. As a result, Purity makes available free management consultation and has agreed to remain a source of low-cost merchandise supply as long as Freedom Foods finds the arrangement advantageous.

Large-scale manufacturing and black businesses

It is practically impossible for blacks to engage in a large number of manufacturing businesses that require large capital investment and a high level of sales. Nevertheless, because of growing black awareness and increasing control of their community, blacks do have opportunities to run marketing-distributive types of businesses. Instead of blacks engaging directly in manufacturing, they contract to purchase merchandise under their own brand from large-scale manufacturing businesses.

For example, one newly-formed organization is making plans to penetrate the high-volume milk markets in the black ghettos throughout the country. The principals involved have experience in the dairy industry and distribution business. They have investigated the costs associated with the processing, marketing, and distribution of milk. In addition, they have studied the reasonably successful black-owned "Joe Louis" brand milk company in Chicago that purchases its products from a large dairy processing company. From their findings, the milk syndicate was able to negotiate a good contract with a large processor for products it wanted packaged under its own label.

The plans of another group of blacks is analogous to the previous example, but instead of a perishable product, it involves small household appliances. This group of black businessmen have some expertise in the small appliance business. They intend to develop a line of products under a brand name which, like the milk product, will be symbolic to the black community, but not detrimental to sales to potential white customers. Their target markets are the appliance stores, drug stores, and supermarkets in the black ghettos of Chicago, Detroit, Michigan, Cleveland, Ohio, New York City, Boston, Massachusetts, Baltimore, Maryland, and Washington, D.C.

A final example involves a black marketer of soft goods. The entrepreneur in this case resigned his job as a salesman for a hosiery company after negotiating a contract with a mill house to produce quality hosiery for him under his label. Currently he is employing four salesmen who are earning from $150 to $200 per week. He hopes to be able to branch out into new markets in the near future.

These examples illustrate how actual and planned black businesses can associate with large-scale, capital-intensive manufacturing enterprises. Without the problems of production, these companies are relatively free to concentrate on a wide range of marketing activities, such as checking variety and quality of product line, packaging and labeling, pricing, promotion, selling, and distributing.

In contrast to the private branding approach, a group of influential blacks are proposing a rather unorthodox arrangement with large-scale manufacturers. Their plans do not include the wide range of marketing activities that were involved in the cases cited. With one exception, they want manufacturers to market their products as always. The difference is that they intend to distribute the products of selected manufacturers to established retail outlets.

This planned distribution business would be tied to a black distribution center which would control the flow of certain types of products into the ghetto. Of particular interest to the blacks are the high-volume, frequently purchased products such as milk, bread, beer, cola, and newspapers. It is anticipated that many of these products would be received in trailer or boxcar loads. Similar types of products would be combined for distribution by black-owned delivery trucks to stores. The blacks believe their proposition is not unusual; in fact, they equate it to the general merchandise delivery operations existing in many cities. The primary difference is that retail operators, rather than ultimate consumers, would be the units receiving shipment.

The planned black distribution system is noteworthy because of its sponsor—the West Side Development Corporation of Chicago. This non-profit organization was formed by five groups and is located on Chicago's predominantly black west side. These five organizations have rejected old rivalries and have banded together to present a united front to Chicago's business and economic community. While such a program may be unacceptable to white manufacturers, it is indicative of the growing black determination to become involved in businesses selling to the black community.

Small-scale manufacturing businesses

The previous discussion was concerned with those businesses where actual black manufacturing of products would be particularly difficult because of capital requirements, complex technical skills, or large-scale production. However, there are light manufacturing and processing businesses where these barriers do not represent too much of an obstacle. In such industries long hours, imagination, good business practices, and hard selling are the keys to business success. Examples would include industrial product firms doing aluminum and wood fabricating, electroplating, and chemical mixing. In the consumer products field there are opportunities in food processing (sauces, bread, soft drinks, and sausage), blending of chemicals for household use (wax, bleach, and detergent), and cosmetic manufacturing (skin lotions, deodorants, and hair care products).

The plans of manufacturers in each of the three consumer products categories are illustrated by the cooperative effort of five black manufacturers having operations in Chicago. The primary products of the five manufacturers are lemon juice, floor wax, drain opener, pine oil, and a hand lotion. Initially, these products were sold only through the ghetto stores, but gradually distribution has increased to generally include most of the major chains in the greater Chicago area.

The strategy of the black manufacturers is different from most white companies with which they compete. Since the black companies cannot afford the long-run payback from advertising their products, they follow the "more for your money" approach as contrasted to the "premium product" approach. Furthermore, advertising these products does not seem to be advisable because they cannot overcome the noise level of the advertising campaigns supporting the major competitive products. What promotional dollars they have to spend are directed primarily to the trade to encourage in-store display and reduced consumer prices.

The companies producing the five products banded together during the first part of 1969 hoping to solve some of the problems they were facing. One of their objectives was a higher level of sales than could be obtained in Chicago. Individually, the companies had tried to sell their products to grocery chains outside of the Chicago market. However, for a variety of reasons their individual efforts had been unsuccessful.

Together they formed an organization called United Distributors, Inc. This organization was designed to be the vehicle by which the black companies could economically sell their products in large markets within a five-hundred-mile radius of Chicago. For a fee, United Distributors was to (1) sell the products to the major chains in the outlying markets; (2) handle the paper work associated with billing customers and receiving payment; (3) schedule pool shipments for lower shipping costs and better service of customers; and (4) arrange for a person to call upon the stores periodically to straighten and clean merchandise, to attempt to obtain more shelf space, and to encourage the store managers to reorder.

The five companies decided not to use the leverage approach in selling to chains in outlying markets—the technique which had been employed in Chicago. They did not initially want to call on the buyers, however, because of their poor experience with this level of management. As a result, an advance group was established to talk with the chief executive officers of the supermarket chains. This group explained the need for selling their products in new markets, described the characteristics and benefits of dealing with United Distributors, asked for any helpful suggestions, and encouraged questions. The meeting was concluded with a request that the executive officer encourage middle management to support and promote their products and to give them a chance to succeed. Following the liaison, contact appointments were made with buyers to sell their merchandise to the chains.

During the second quarter of 1969, the four major chains in both Detroit and Cleveland were contacted. All of the chains placed sizable orders for three to five of the products. By the end of the year an effort [was to] be made to sell to the four largest chains in the major markets within a five-hundred-mile radius of Chicago.

Determinants of Black Business Development

Blacks are generally enthusiastic about the newborn opportunities to enter the capitalistic system. As a result, there has been a great deal of planning by blacks. The extent to which plans are converted into reality, however, depends on the response of the larger society in three areas.

1. For blacks to become capitalists, large pools of funds must be made available under realistic conditions.
2. The business and technical skills of blacks must be developed and strengthened.
3. Larger numbers of white companies will have to support the efforts of black businesses if they are ever to develop markets for their products.

Capital needs

The low level of per capita income in the black community means there is very little discretionary income that can be converted into savings. As a result, blacks do not have adequate funds to invest as risk capital in black businesses. This means blacks are unable to obtain the debt financing they need because they do not have the equity cushions which act as insurance for loans. These conditions cause a "business capital trap" that has and will continue to seriously constrain black business development unless creative programs can be found to significantly increase the capital flow into the ghetto.

The Small Business Administration (SBA) is the primary government agency that is helping minority businesses obtain financing. However, for a variety of reasons, the SBA is probably only an interim agency to assist black businesses. The SBA record of making loans to black businesses has been very poor in an absolute and relative sense. In part, this is because the charter of the SBA requires reasonable assurance of loan repayment. Since most blacks do not have a credit record, their loan applications are generally looked upon unfavorably. Furthermore, loans made or guaranteed by the SBA require that the applicant raise 15 percent (the risk capital cushion) of the amount needed, which represents an insurmountable hurdle for a large number of promising black businesses. An applicant must also have adequate working capital which increases the personal investment required to start a business. An excessive amount of "red tape" and long delay in making loans has also reduced the effectiveness of the SBA assistance. Finally, SBA regulations state that loans are not ordinarily eligible for transfer of assets from one owner to another, for which there is growing need.[5]

As a result of these problems, proposals have been made that would bring badly needed capital into the black community. One bill introduced in the U.S. senate last summer was the Community Self-Determination Act which would create a series of Community Development Banks. These banks would make available funds for federally chartered Community Development Corporations that would be owned by no less than 500 residents of impoverished minority communities. The community organization would act as a conglomerate-type business that could create, acquire, and manage all businesses in its community.[6] Implicit in the bill is the assumption that the economic development of the black community can not be effectively attacked by adaptations of conventional capitalistic machinery. While the bill at one time had the support of 25 U.S. senators, it seems to be too radical a program to be enacted into law.

The Community Credit Expansion Act was introduced in the U.S. Senate in May 1970. One of the basic differences between this bill and the Community Self-Determination Act is the source of funds that would be channeled into the ghetto. Instead of public funds, private funds would be directed into the urban ghettos and depressed rural areas. A new type of financial institution, National Development Banks, would be established for this purpose. These banks would be profit-making businesses operated as independent subsidiaries of existing banks or by independent stockholders of the Development Bank. The lending powers of the new banks would include all those of national banks, plus a number of others, including second mortgages and equity investment in business enterprises. For concentrating 80 percent of their loans in the ghetto, the National Development Banks would have special authorities including liberalized entry privileges, lower reserve requirements, and longer term advances.[7] The National Development Banks closely parallel what Theodore Cross advocates in his book, *Black Capitalism Strategy for Business in the Ghetto*.[8]

A financial assistance program, analogous to that proposed by the Credit Expansion Act, would seem to have a fairly good chance of being adopted. It appears to be consistent with the political temperament of the times in that it would (1) be a program implemented by private businesses rather than government agencies; (2) involve private rather than public funds; and (3) be predicated on the belief that capitalism and not socialism can be made to work in the ghetto.

Developing business skills

Directing a capital flow into poverty areas to assist businesses is only a first step toward developing the black business potential in the ghetto. It must be supplemented by carefully thought out programs for imparting technical and managerial skills to existing and prospective black businessmen. There seems to be two types of needs:

1. Direct problem-solving assistance for the individual businessman
2. Educational programs to increase general business skills in the black community

Programs by which black businessmen can call on the advice of consultants are very much needed to help young businesses overcome some basic problems and hurdles. Throughout the country volunteers from businesses, consulting companies, and schools of business have made available free assistance. The contributions of such volunteers have been very important in areas from incorporating businesses to developing marketing programs. In addition, there has been some experience with paid consultants through programs financed by the OEO. While the cost of such programs seems high (the Chicago Economic Development Corporation budget for 1968 was $250,000 and it consulted with business projected to do $1,000,000 in sales), evidence indicates that the paid consultants have been able to work more closely with black businessmen than the volunteers. Regardless of whether the consultants are volunteers or paid, their efforts are invaluable in the building of black businesses.

While man-to-man or team consulting is important for dealing with the particular problems of individual businesses, a more formalized approach to developing basic business knowledge is also needed. One of the pioneering efforts in this area is the Free School of Business Management. The Cosmopolitan Chamber of Commerce of Chicago has primary responsibility for the program. Its cosponsor is the Small Business Administration. Their program consists of 16 two-hour class sessions taught by businessmen on a wide range of subject matters. More than 800 students have attended and completed the course. Now, specially designed courses in fundamentals of business are needed, including accounting and finance, production, marketing, and personnel. One might hope that the academic community will step forward with some creative programs.

Buy black products

The efforts put into financial assistance programs and the building of business skills will not produce maximum results unless white businesses help black businesses get started. If black businesses are restricted in their opportunities to deal with white businesses, which control the mainstream of business in both the white and black community, many will fail. To launch a large number of black businesses, white companies will have to buy black products. In essence, they will be holding an umbrella over these infant businesses until they are strong enough to stand on their own.

The efforts of the major supermarket chains in Chicago to help black companies in producing grocery products are particularly noteworthy. For a variety of reasons the supermarket chains found that black products were not being given a real chance to succeed. As a result, each chain created a position or a black liaison man to work with the producers to help them get their products moving in the chain stores. Similarly, Ford Motor Company worked with a black company to develop a new carwash product, which they are now purchasing in thousand-case quantity. There is no doubt that Ford could have purchased a comparable product for the same price, or less, from an existing supplier with much less effort. Many more companies are needed who are willing to purchase black products and give assistance to black businesses.

Conclusion

The blacks can either be shut out or brought in to the capitalistic system. Currently, the desire of blacks to participate in the free enterprise system is high. If concrete and adequate steps are taken now, the black economic community can be launched and ultimately developed to a point where it strengthens the overall economy. However, if white America turns it back on the ghetto or tries to prescribe unacceptable programs, the black community will continue to depress the total economic system.

NOTES

1. "Enterprise," *City*, July-Aug. 1968, p. 3.

2. Milton Moskowitz, *Business and Society*, Dec. 17, 1968, p. 1, and the Interracial Council for Business Opportunity (ICBO) with headquarters in New York City.

3. "Enterprise," p. 3.

4. Richard F. America, Jr., "What Do You People Want?" *Harvard Business Review*, 47 (Mar.-Apr. 1969), pp. 103–7.

5. Theodore Cross, *Black Capitalism Strategy for Business in the Ghetto* (New York: Atheneum Publishers, 1969), pp. 97–102.

6. Senate Bill 3876.

7. Senate Bill 2146, May 13, 1969.

8. Theodore Cross, *Black Capitalism Strategy for Business in the Ghetto*, pp. 97–102.

Black Entrepreneurship in the Ghetto: A Recruitment Strategy

Charles H. Levine

A partial but powerful strategy for the resolution of America's racial woes is the development of an entrepreneurial group of black business-men. While this strategy has widespread support, there has been great confusion over what is meant by "black capitalism." The ambiguity of the phrase has worked to its advantage and disadvantage simultaneously. Because everyone defines the concept differently, because the successes of black businessmen are well reported in the mass media, and because the notion conforms to the highest ideals of the American free enterprise creed, black capitalism is accepted in principle by a wide variety of people. However, the ambiguous nature of the concept has limited the development of specific programs and coordinated efforts, because its goals, purposes, and strategies remain undefined, or are defined differently by different interest groups and policy-makers.

The following analysis asserts: (1) that black capitalism can conform to widely accepted notions of business entrepreneurship and also be beneficial to the black community; (2) that blacks should be encouraged to enter forms of business activity that they have rarely been represented in before; (3) that traditional patterns of black business activity in the ghetto may not be adequate training grounds for the recruitment of the dynamic black entrepreneurs necessary for the economic development of the ghetto; (4) that to meet some of the needs of the black community through black capitalism, government, foundations, and private enterprises should encourage the recruitment of blacks from occupations other than the "mom and pop" retailers who are usually identified as black capitalists; (5) that the psychic as well as the monetary price of a successful black capitalism will confront the white community with a substantial burden.

The Ghetto Dispersal Strategy and Black Entrepreneurship

To understand the future needs and impacts of a viable black capitalism, it is important to understand the future of the American black ghetto. Among the alternative futures for the ghetto posited by Anthony Downs, the ghetto dispersal strategy is the most feasible and acceptable *long-run* alternative to the societal tensions caused by two separate and unequal societies living in the same country.[1] According to Downs, the dispersal strategy is imperative if the black man's opportunities are to be enriched by better educational facilities, health services, housing, employment, recreation facilities, etc. To make the dispersal strategy work, Downs proposes a variety of economic incentives that are designed to encourage the voluntary migration of blacks out of the ghetto and their peaceful acceptance by whites into the suburbs.

In another analysis of urban futures, Kain and Persky advocate the dispersal strategy as the more acceptable alternative to "gilding" the ghetto and urge that dispersion be supplemented by economic development in the South.[2] In the meantime, while the barriers to housing integration or new suburban housing for blacks are dissolved by a variety of sanctions and inducements, little should be done to make the ghetto more attractive to migrants. Without making the ghetto a substantially better place to live, Kain and Persky propose increasing information about jobs in the suburbs, and improving job training programs in the ghetto and linking them to job placement services. In short, nothing should be done to prevent or slow the break-up of the ghetto.

These arguments are compelling, but, again, they represent a *long-range* strategy of ghetto dispersal. In the meantime, say in the next 20 years, a mixed strategy of enrichment or "gilding" combined with dispersal will improve the living conditions of ghetto residents, offset the growth of the central city ghetto, and narrow the economic as well as the spatial gap between black and white America. This strategic mix will require innovative programs beyond the methods suggested by Kain and Persky.

Because the dispersal of the black population has not kept pace with the dispersal of jobs, industry, and whites from the central city, a gap has emerged between where jobs are located and where the jobless live.[3] While black people cannot move because of discrimination and high land and housing costs in the suburbs, strong economic, technical, and social forces are impelling industry outward from the central city.

The forces separating jobs from the jobless are also helping to accentuate the separation of society into economically unequal black and white sectors. They are also weakening the central city's economic position and tax base while welfare, education, and public service needs are increasing.

Given these trends, the economic development of the black ghetto has become critically important for American race relations. The encouragement of a viable black capitalism can contribute significantly to ghetto development. However, to make such a critically important contribution the encouragement of black entrepreneurship must be intended to serve social as well as economic objectives. Over the short and intermediate run, some of the following objectives might serve as a partial list of guidelines for the development of black capitalism if it is to add even partially to the solution of our racial problems: (1) Help to modernize the ghetto economically and make the black consumer "better off" by providing in the ghetto more efficient, economically sound, and effective businesses that will put at the consumer's disposal better quality goods and services at lower costs. (2) Provide more and better jobs for black entrepreneurs and their employees. (The increased competition may drive some marginal operators out of business, but the increased level of business activity should provide more jobs in the aggregate at higher income levels.) (3) Encourage black people committed to community development to enter business. This should serve two purposes: encourage the participation of the business community in neighborhood affairs, and provide successful role models that other blacks can identify with. Successful, community-oriented black entrepreneurs will provide the black community with some economic heroes that will serve to encourage others to accumulate capital and invest for future entrepreneurial activity. (4) In the long run, increase the amount of taxable property in the central city so that the gap between the revenue needs of the central city government and the value of taxable property will be lessened and the tax pressure on the individual property owner will decrease.

These are ambitious guidelines for black capitalism and it is therefore wise to consider how well the present pattern of black business activity serves as a resource base from which to recruit the people needed to develop the kind of multi-employee enterprises that are necessary to meet these objectives.

The present pattern of black capitalism

An inventory of the types of black-owned businesses in the typical central city would reveal mostly personal service enterprises such as barber and beauty shops, and small outlets for convenience goods such as grocery and variety stores.[4] Likewise, the types of manufacturing companies black men own tend to complement their retailing activities by providing goods such as beauty aids and caskets, that the retailer cannot (or could not) buy elsewhere. The results of this pattern of business activity are large numbers of small businesses in black neighborhoods that charge high prices for inferior goods because they cannot gain economies of scale in purchasing and operations or obtain normal business services such as insurance because they are located in the ghetto.

The present forms of black business activity are principally the result of the dual market for personal services and convenience goods caused by racial segregation in housing, discrimination in providing services by white firms, and the reluctance of large firms to locate in the ghetto. The black merchant in the ghetto has been protected from competition in the same way an industry is protected by a tariff. However, desegregation, civil rights legislation, increased social awareness and profit seeking by large corporations have increased the availability of white-owned marketing outlets for the black consumer, and most black businessmen are unable to compete in this expanded market place.

The paucity of black-owned businesses has some widely acknowledged causes. Among these are: (1) There has not been a tradition of business ownership by blacks because of their history of slavery, inability to accumulate or borrow capital, and their exclusion from occupations which would have given them experience in business and money matters. (2) The black entrepreneur is unable to give credit and use that credit to obtain chattel mortgages, because the black consumer is considered a poor credit risk by most lending institutions. (3) Landlords appear more willing to rent to white businessmen than black businessmen, because they consider white businessmen better risks. (4) The characteristics of the types of businesses blacks usually own—small, economically marginal, high-risk—and the lack of managerial ability, training, and experience of black businessmen hurts their ability to secure financing since many lending institutions place great emphasis on the experience of the management and the types of business involved when considering loan applications. As a consequence, there are approximately 70,000 black-owned businesses in the United States. If the number of black-owned businesses were in proportion to the number of blacks in the population, there would be over 400,000, and they would not aggregate so heavily in the small business categories.[5]

There have been some social as well as economic costs in the maintenance of these patterns of black entrepreneurship. In *Black Bourgeoisie,* E. Franklin Frazier charged that the black, middle-class, because of its struggle to gain acceptance from whites, failed to play the role of responsible elite in the black community and exploited the black masses as ruthlessly as did the whites.[6] According to Frazier, the masses regard the black bourgeoisie as simply those who were "lucky in getting money," which allows them to engage in conspicuous consumption. Perceived in this light, little meaningful community leadership can be expected to be generated from this group.

Toward a new black capitalism

Although the present group of black businessmen may create some noteworthy entrepreneurial achievements, pumping money and effort into much of this group and encouraging its growth may not result in stronger firms, better community leadership, or the best use of scarce resources committed to achieve these goals. To meet the goals of economic development and leadership the ghetto needs multiple employee manufacturing plants and large retail outlets. In order to have and operate large businesses, the black businessman—or for that matter any large-scale entrepreneur—must have a variety of skills and traits not necessarily possessed by the owners of small retail and service businesses.

Some important qualities often associated with successful entrepreneurship are a willingness to undertake potentially high-return, high-risk short-run investments, the managerial skill and experience to handle and pyramid complex portfolios, a source of capital, and a perception of the world as a manageable place. The outstanding business successes of the black community, for example, Truman Gibson in insurance, Henry Park in meat packing, and the Reverend Leon Sullivan with his Philadelphia conglomerate of diversified investments, share an untypical pattern for black businessmen. All three had good academic training and managerial experience before entering business, had sources of financial support, and have had the ability to master the complexities of corporate financing. Using these examples, and others, we can infer that black entrepreneurs capable of spurring ghetto economic development will need: (1) experience in formal organizations at a managerial level, (2) willingness to take calculated gambles, (3) sources of capital, (4) ability to abstract and synthesize, (5) ability to understand and calculate financial risks, and (6) training and experience in handling money and raising capital.

To be sure, these traits, abilities, and experiences are scarce in the black community, but they *do* exist, usually in the professional classes. What I am advocating is the recruitment of what W. E. B. Dubois called the "talented tenth" from the professions, military, corporations, and the public service into business enterprises. Assuming that private capital sources—banks, foundations, and insurance companies—as well as government agencies will be interested in recruiting potentially successful black capitalists, I recommend they hunt for blacks who already possess the skills, experiences, and traits needed for operating a large business in a competitive market.

The potentially successful black entrepreneurs will probably not possess only one of the six traits and none of the others, but rather a mix of all six. However, it may be feasible to assemble entrepreneurial teams of men who have skills and knowledge in specific areas and in combination possess all the traits, skills, and attitudes needed for successful entrepreneurship. An educational program should be designed to augment the talents of men currently engaged in business as well as to educate young men who demonstrate a desire to become active in the business community.

Development of Black Capitalism

If black capitalism is to have a viable future the responsibility and resources necessary for the development of a black entrepreneurial group lies in the white community. To remove the racial tension caused by a "separate and unequal" society, black men must have jobs, self-respect, and economic heroes. The white man will be doing blacks a great disservice if he encourages the recruitment of potential black entrepreneurs who have little chance of "making good" in a big way. The white man must therefore put aside his prejudicial expectations and acknowledge that the educated young leaders of the black community who will most likely be the best qualified potential entrepreneurs will be increasingly committed to the concepts of "Black Power," "Black Identity," and "Black Beauty." To shun these people as potential entrepreneurs because of their beliefs and attitudes will do great harm to efforts to bring racial peace to America, because it will reinforce black suspicions of white hypocrisy and will probably discourage the most potentially successful entrepreneurs from entering business. What heroes the black man will have will continue to remain outside the business community; and the failures of this narrow recruitment policy will reaffirm black self-doubts and white prejudices. Imagine for a moment that men with the charisma, organizational ability, imagination, drive, and racial integrity of Martin Luther King, Julian Bond, Adam Clayton Powell, and Malcolm X had entered the business world; their successes might have been monumental.

It is not enough to say that we must give the black man an opportunity to enter business or that the type of business they enter and the traits of the men recruited will affect the achievement of certain goals. In addition to moral encouragement, the foundations, private businesses, and the government must provide some combinations of services and guarantees to overcome the economic forces that make ghetto-based plants and retail outlets uneconomical. Where such services are already provided, increases in the levels of activity, service, and funding are generally necessary. Much of the logic behind these recommendations is based on the belief that the tax receipts and other income generated from an active retailing and manufacturing community in the ghetto will offset a great deal of the cost of subsidization. Such a combination of services would include: (1) *rent subsidies* for manufacturing plants and retailing outlets, (2) *wage subsidies* for training and employing the chronically unemployed, (3) *guarantees of purchases* of manufactured goods by either the government or private firms, (4) *tax incentives and write offs* by state, local, and federal governments, (5) *relaxed financing provisions and lower interest rates* for Small Business Administration loans, (6) *government guaranteed bank loans*, (7) *the encouragement of large scale cooperatives* run by teams of black professionals and businessmen, (8) *supplying modern technical machinery* for production and for training unskilled employees, (9) *supplying highly technical know-how and management training* when it is requested by the black businessman, and (10) *guaranteeing insurance* at reasonable rates for ghetto-based firms.

Conclusion

Black capitalism is a movement in the direction of equality of economic opportunity for the black man in America. It will not be a panacea for all our nation's racial and poverty problems but the benefits will be considerable if the goals set forth in the beginning of this essay are achieved.

This analysis has been intended to clarify goals, identify trends and significant variables, and to suggest strategies and their implications in order to help make policies designed to encourage the development of a strong black capitalism more intelligent and meaningful. Given the pronounced commitment of the government to "black capitalism," greater efforts at extending this type of analysis are in order lest we commit scarce resources and faith to a set of policy preferences based on a concept that is unclear and easily misunderstood when translated into specific goals and programs.

NOTES

1. Anthony Downs, "Alternative Futures for the American Ghetto," *Daedalus*, Fall 1968, pp. 1131–79. Also, *Report of the National Advisory Commission on Civil Disorders* (New York: Bantam, 1969), pp. 389–408.

2. John F. Kain and Joseph J. Persky, "Alternatives to the Gilded Ghetto," *The Public Interest*, Jan. 1969, pp. 74–86.

3. John F. Kain, "The Distribution and Movement of Jobs and Industry," in *The Metropolitan Enigma*, ed. by James Q. Wilson (Cambridge, Mass.: Harvard University Press, 1969), pp. 1–39.

4. Eugene P. Foley, "The Negro Businessman: In Search of a Tradition," in *The Negro American*, ed. by Talcott Parsons and Kenneth B. Clark (Boston: Beacon Press, 1967), pp. 555–92.

5. Richard N. Farmer, "Black Businessmen in Indiana," *Indiana Business Review*, Nov.– Dec. 1968, p. 12.

6. G. E. Franklin Frazier, *Black Bourgeoisie* (Glencoe, Ill.: The Free Press, 1957).

Community Development Corporations

Pat Patterson

Some persons have called them the last best hope to turn black and poor communities around. Others have described them in less favorable terms: social experiments doomed to failure because of governmental indifference and community impotence.

Few persons, to be sure, are neutral on the subject of Community Development Corporations (CDCs). Spawned in the 1960s in the wake of the declining civil rights movement and the aborted war on poverty, CDCs have surfaced in more than 80 urban and rural locales, nurtured by the hope that they can be vehicles for the revitalization of socially and economically blighted communities.

Although the number of CDCs is on the increase, particularly among Mexican Americans in the southwest, most observers are reluctant to predict how they will ultimately fare. To date, their performance has been spotty, due largely to the uneven level of leadership they have been able to attract. Lagging acceptance in some communities and indifferent financial support from the government and private investors have added to the uncertainty surrounding CDCs.

Moreover, the program has been troubled by a conflict of objectives, observers say. Some CDCs have emphasized social and political goals, while others have sought to maximize profits to demonstrate their viability as instruments of economic as well as social change.

"I still think we are searching for the correct form," says Bernard Gifford, former president of FIGHT in Rochester, New York, who recently stepped down as executive director of the National Congress of Community Economic Development. "So many organizations are experimenting with different forms, trying to find what will work in what area under what circumstances."

Gifford's assessment is echoed by Steward Perry, director of the Center for Community Economic Development. "The concept of community development corporations is so new and novel and different in each community that it is not immediately predictable what changes will be needed. What will take place will depend upon the community and the national environment," he says.

Indeed, community development corporations are as diverse as the communities they serve. One of the oldest and most successful is Progress Enterprises of Philadelphia, Pennsylvania, founded by the Rev. Leon Sullivan in 1962. The organization is based on a 10–36 plan. Under the plan, an individual contributes $10 a month for 36 months toward a program of community economic development. The first sixteen payments go to the Zion Non-profit Charitable Trust where the funds are used for social services, health, and education. The remaining twenty payments are used to purchase shares in Zion Investment Associates, a profit-making holding corporation.

Progress Enterprises began its operation in 1962 with 227 members and later expanded to 400 churches in the Philadelphia area. Today the organization has more than 7,000 members. Investments include an apartment building—Progress Plaza—a modern shopping center, a series of convenience stores called "Our Markets," and a garment manufacturing plant.

One of the most publicized and well-financed CDCs is Bedford-Stuyvesant Restoration Corportion in Brooklyn. Formed in 1966 by the late Senator Robert Kennedy, who toured the area and was appalled by conditions there, Restoration is actually two corporations. The Restoration Corporation is headed by Franklin Thomas, a former deputy police commissioner, and the Development and Service Corporation (D&S) is headed by John Doar, a former Assistant Attorney General.

The board of directors of D&S, which is predominantly white, is composed largely of businessmen. Restoration's board, on the other hand, is made up of a cross section of the Bedford-Stuyvesant community, headed by Thomas Jones, a New York State Supreme Court judge. Both boards, for the most part, are self-selected.

While the leadership has a decidedly elitist cast, Restoration has been most successful in attracting funding. Up to last year, it had managed to obtain $20.4 million from the federal government and $6.2 million from private sources. Thus, the Bed-Stuy CDC's average annual funding of $5 million contrasts markedly with the $600,000 that other projects average.

Its programs include a housing corporation, the highly successful $100 million mortgage pool made available for Bedford-Stuyvesant by New York banks. The corporations also created a "superblock," designed by world-famed I.M. Pei. Recently it built a six-story, 52-unit apartment house on the street.

While Restoration Corporation has been able to attract considerable federal support, most of the nation's 180 community corporations have had to manage with only modest assistance. Indeed, the Harlem Commonwealth Council, which recently was funded for a three year period, was one of the first CDCs to be funded for a period of more than one year. Until last year, most CDCs were funded for a year or less.

Not surprisingly, the uncertainty of obtaining federal funding each year affected not only the planning done by community corporations, but their ability to attract investments from private sources as well. Of the 180 community corporations, 42 are funded by the Office of Economic Opportunity. Other CDCs have been funded by the Department of Commerce, the Department of Labor, the Economic Development Administration, church organizations, foundations, and private business groups.

The Ford Foundation, for instance, whose Division of National Affairs is headed by Mitchell Sviridoff, one of the few people in the country who has been involved with CDCs from their beginning, made outright grants totalling $8 million to fifteen CDCs this year. Another $7 million from the Foundation's investment portfolio was invested in CDC businesses.

This year only $25 million has been allocated by OEO for the program, although under the "7 percent" formula—which required the agency to spend at least 7 percent of its Title I funds on Title I-D programs, which covers community development corporations—the allocation would have been $55 million. That formula no longer applies, however, the agency's general counsel asserted in a ruling earlier this year.

Washington's latest policy means that some CDCs will be funded for more than a year while others may receive no assistance at all, CDC officials contend. "What it means," says James Dowdy, executive director of the Harlem Commonwealth Council and regional vice-president of the National Association of Community Development Corporations, "is that some small CDCs will be discontinued."

Not surprisingly, the federal attitude toward CDCs has drawn fire from several quarters. Roy Innis, national director of the Congress of Racial Equality and a member of the task force that helped draw up the CDC program, says the government has reneged on its promise of support.

"The program was never properly implemented," he contends. "There was considerable reneging on the part of government and industry, especially the federal government. We tried to remedy some of the defects through the Community Development Bill which would have created community corporations that were broad based."

Innis, whose original proposal for community development also included community development banks similar to the Farm Bank, also blames black communities and big city mayors for failing to support the program. "They viewed it as a threat to them. There were the poverty pimps who didn't like it. The mayors knocked it because they thought it was a poverty program. Marxists thought it allowed for the creation of capitalism and capitalists thought it was a Marxist plot."

But the concept of community development corporations is an "old idea" says Dr. June G. Hopps, a professor of sociology at Ohio State University, Columbus, who recently completed a study of urban community corporations.

"We have witnessed the resurgence of an old idea," says Dr. Hopps, "where residents of neighborhoods shared responsibility for controlling their institutions and resources."

Dr. Hopps credits young black activists, impatient with the pace and progress of the civil rights movement, for the sudden upsurge in the number of CDCs. They began to "call for greater resident participation and control. They no longer had faith in the capacity of government bureaucracies and social work agencies to effectively assume an advocacy role when dealing with the poor or blacks," she says.

Indeed, in some rural areas of Mississippi and Georgia, community development corporations have brought about radical shifts in age-old relationships between blacks and whites. In Mississippi, the Poor Peoples Corporation (PPC), headed by Jesse Morris, started in 1965 with $5,000 and has generated a program which grossed $1 million two years ago.

Organized by a group of Student Nonviolent Coordinating Committee (SNCC) workers, PPC's record is remarkable, since it has never received any federal assistance, although it has received some small grants from foundations for its Education and Training for Cooperatives project, one of the first such programs in the country. The mainstay of the corporation, however, is the Liberty House Co-op which markets clothing and handicrafts made by its members in the delta region.

Though business slumped badly last year, PPC has managed to raise the level of income for most of its members, most of whom were domestics or farm workers, from less than $1,500 a year to close to $3,000. More important, PPC has helped to alter the view members had of themselves and, hopefully, has helped change the cycle of dependency.

In Hancock County, Georgia, the economic plight of blacks in the region is little different from that of blacks in the delta. Most blacks, who make up 75 percent of the population in the county, earn less than $3,000 a year.

But the East Central Committee for Opportunity (ECCO), which was formed in 1969, has brought hope and, hopefully, new industry to the area where little of either existed before. ECCO, headed by John McCown, a former organizer for the Southern Christian Leadership Conference, has introduced catfish farming to the region, a move he hopes marks the beginning of a bright new industry for northeast Georgia.

If McCown dares to dream that aqua-culture can help reshape the economy of rural Georgia, men like Walter McMurtry, executive director of the Inner City Business Improvement Forum (ICBIF) in Detroit, Michigan, have few illusions about the impact of their organization on the city's economy.

"I'd say our impact on the city has been nil," says McMurtry, despite the fact that ICBIF has a number of success stories to tell, notably the launching of the First Independence National Bank in downtown Detroit. "We can point to X amount of black businesses. We have a profitable stamping plant. Yet our impact on the city has been nil. There is still out migration and land blight. The unemployment rate is higher."

Organized by the clergy and businessmen in 1967 shortly after racial disorders rocked the city, ICBIF, a nonprofit corporation, has been funded largely through private sources, though it received a two-year $1 million OEO Special Impact grant in 1969.

In Cleveland, Ohio, the Hough Area Development Corporation

(HADC) is only now beginning to turn around its rubber-moulding subsidiary, which lost $300,000 in its first two years. "We made every mistake in the book," says Franklin Anderson, who recently returned to Cleveland after spending two years at Harvard where he earned his master's degree in business administration.

Anderson, who succeeded DeForrest Brown as director of HADC, believes, however, that the rubber-moulding experience was a valuable lesson. The organization has become much more hardnosed in its business practices, he says. "We are doing fairly well," says Anderson, who has seen HADC grow from the two companies it owned in its first year to seven. The properties include a supermarket that will go into the HADC-sponsored Martin Luther King Plaza Shopping Center, which is due to open this summer; Homes for Hough, a housing corporation; and two fast-food franchises.

While some community corporations like HADC and others have stumbled in getting away from the starting gate, others like Operation Bootstrap in Watts (Los Angeles, California), though not free of problems, have made steady progress.

The makers of Shindana Dolls, Operation Bootstrap, came into being in the wake of the 1965 Watts rebellion. Its introduction into doll making came via telephone from Mattel Toys, Inc., the world's largest toy maker.

"Mattel called us down to the office one day," recalled Louis Smith, Bootstrap's director, "to tell us what they were willing to do." What the toymaker was willing to do was provide $200,000 worth of equity and technical assistance for a product line of black dolls designed by a black artist.

The line became an immediate success, and the only breach in the agreement, says Smith, "was they hadn't figured we would take something and make it grow so fast." Much of the success of Bootstrap is attributed to Smith's charismatic leadership, but, according to the Hopps study, CDCs in Watts were able to draw from a larger pool of black talent.

"A large number of the Watts area CDC executives came out of established industry, primarily aerospace," says Dr. Hopps. "There were blacks who had moved up the structure into middle and upper management positions in areas of engineering, purchasing, financing, and legal work. In addition to those with experience in industry, there were men with excellent organizational skills that were developed in the civil rights movement and labor union organizations."

Dowdy, like other CDC directors, feels greater incentives must be offered if CDCs are to attract the kind of talent they need. "The ability is there," says Dowdy, "but we didn't have anything to attract top professionals. The salaries we were paying couldn't attract anybody. Today we give a guy a piece of the action and they say, 'I like longevity programs.' Now we get guys who know how to put it together. They have come back to the community."

Still, the future of CDCs is far from certain. Some basic questions have yet to be resolved. Up to now community corporations have been more corporate than community, but as their leaders rightly point out, the need to establish a track record, to gain visibility and thereby acceptance among the community and investors has not allowed for the kind of broad-based participation envisioned by those who designed the program.

Indeed, the expectations of some private groups that have invested in CDCs have raised some hard questions. Comments Dr. Hopps: "One must raise an issue regarding why foundations and church-related groups assumed that it was important for CDCs to encourage widespread control when after the experience of centuries this pattern has not occurred in our capitalistic society. Such an expectation was unrealistic, and the results of an unrealistic goal is likely to be viewed by foundations and church-related groups as a failure."

But for men like Gifford, CDCs have not failed; rather, they have not been given an opportunity to succeed. "The results are mixed," says Gifford, "simply because they have never given us the opportunity to do the job. We ought to be able to do things quickly and show people it will be followed up. The problem is that CDCs get no special treatment from HUD or other government agencies. And if there is no special treatment, why have a CDC?"

The Politics of Community Economic Development

Milton Kotler

Established Power and Poverty Reform

In 1967, three years after the passage of the Economic Opportunity Act, the White House began to have second thoughts about its original emphasis on community action and maximum feasible participation as a method for ending poverty. While the planners of the Act might have supposed originally that organized pressure by the poor could be accommodated by the system—as the system had accommodated so many interest groups—and conversely, that the organized poor would for this purpose abide by the rules of the game, the reality from the point of view of community organization was quite different. Community action based upon maximum participation was more than a tactical concept. It was the release of a potentially great force, namely, territorially organized citizen power. No other interest group has that "sovereign" base. Thus, organizations based on this principle were quite extraordinary compared to the normal varieties of interest groups which pressure the government. It soon appeared to the government, not that the poor would willfully break the rules of pressure politics, but that the government had endorsed a principle of organization that itself transcended the character of interest-group politics.

Mayors began to complain that the newly organized and funded neighborhood organizations were threatening the power of city government, and they sought to terminate these organizations and their funding, either directly from Washington or through the independent community action agencies. As a result of the complaint, Congress passed the Green Amendment,[1] permitting mayors to get control of their cities' antipoverty programs.

The new arrangement enabled the government to withdraw funding from neighborhood organizations which confronted city power and to begin to fund antipoverty programs within a pro-city framework. This rearrangement, in the sensitive world of politics, required a "felicitous" adaptation of the theory of poverty, to which the political intention of placing OEO powers in the hands of the city management would conform. The new theory was local economic enterprise, referred to as "community economic development."

But the capture of political control over OEO did not solve the mayors' poverty problems. The cities were still disproportionately populated by poor people, and their rate of increase in coming years would, by all projections, be very high. One political view was that there would have to be some absorption of members of the lower class into the established order to decrease the number of poor and to create a group from this membership which would control those who remained. Given this understanding, it seemed most feasible to shift the funds of the OEO program from those who had formerly organized the poor to confront city government to those among the poor who had the greatest ambition to enter the system. Since being in the system of our society means making money, the new patronage would go to those in the poor community who wanted to make money, rather than to those who wanted to organize the poor politically.

This signaled an important shift. While job training and manpower programs were part of the first community action programs, this training had emphasized job placement in factories and other business establishments of the city. Now the idea was to encourage the enterprising people in the communities and assist them to establish small businesses and little industries which could employ the poor people. And it was to be this group of people—those ambitious for gain—on whom established power would place the task of cooling off the cities. They thought this would demonstrate the mobility of the system and, at the same time, suppress the political movement of the underclass.

Since late 1968, and until the present, OEO funding money has gone to economic development projects. The community organizations which started earlier under the community action program had to reorient their grant proposals in the direction of economic development in order to remain funded. A variety of approaches were taken to accomplish this shift: assistance to small business in the poor community, small industrial development in the poor neighborhood, cooperative arrangements with big corporations, community ownership schemes for merchandising, and home purchasing.

This is the present state of the government's anti-poverty program, but it is already on the way out. The new program of family assistance represents the next step in the government's political program for the poor. Family assistance, which is likely to spell the demise of OEO as a program agency, returns to an old welfare notion—to wit, financial assistance on the basis of low-wage labor. The appearance of this development upon the scene raises the question of how much energy the professional should now invest in a conception of community economic development based on federal assistance. In short, while the idea of community economic development is still promoted by the government,[2] the cycle of antipoverty initiatives is turning back to a government commitment to individual labor welfare rather than to community economic development.

Family assistance is only part of the present administration's program for dealing with the political problem of the urban poor. The regional movement for metropolitan government, also part of the establishment's agenda, is hailed as the best way to cure the political ills of the city. This movement calls for the expansion of urban government on the basis of multi-county consolidation. The origins of city expansion are quite old, dating back to the first colossal enlargement of Philadelphia from an area of 1-½ square miles in 1854 to its absorption of the entire county of Philadelphia in that same year. The reasons for the annexations and consolidation in the nineteenth century were varied, but by the second decade of this century, a resistance to annexation had slowed the pace of municipal growth. Following World War II, there was a spate of annexations, particularly in the South and West, and more recently the expansion drive has reappeared in the guise of regionalization and metropolitan government. The general arguments which are advanced for this movement are based on its potential for increasing tax resources, tax equalization, and operational efficiency. But it is the political intention of this movement which must be considered as its most significant aspect.

Since the 1950s the cities have been losing their middle-class and wealthy residents to the surrounding suburbs at a fast rate. While this phenomenon has been decried from the point of view of a loss in tax base, it has also disturbed the old pattern of public services and welfare distribution which ensured the political control of downtown power. The administrative practice of giving better services to the middle-class population cannot today produce the former political results because of the decreasing population of that class in the city. In addition, the cost of applying the former service standards of the middle-classes to the poor, combined with an increase in welfare spending, is prohibitive. Aside from the cost, there is the further problem that long-established habits of public service work against any attempt to increase the services and welfare directed to the poor. Both the political structure and the administration of the city are being eroded because of the government's failure to adjust to the new class composition of the cities.

There are only two possibilities which will allow the cities to continue as viable propositions in the face of this population change. Either the city government must change its political constitution to adapt to its new class composition, or the cities must absorb the entire middle-class population that has fled to the suburbs. Apparently the politicians have chosen the latter course, opting for a program of regionalization which preserves downtown as the political and commercial center of the metropolitan area, neglects the slum city (which is fast coming to mean the entire present city limits), regains the familiar suburban middle-class as the social base for a new constituency, and proceeds with traditional patterns of public service administration.

The consequence of this movement toward metropolitan government is clear; it means the displacement of public services from within the city limits to the suburbs and the establishment of some police arrangement to control the immensely expanded slum of the present city. The economic prescription of the metropolitan strategy would nullify any necessity for community economic development in the old city neighborhoods, for the government of downtown power can find its economic foundation in the suburbs.

The Politics of Community Organizations

Turning to the question of community economic development in the neighborhood organization, we see a much different line of development of the issue. There was nothing particularly complex about the original theory of community action and its strategy of maximum feasible participation. It was thought that the best route toward eliminating poverty was to organize the poor politically in the cities or rural areas, so that they could pressure government for a greater share of public resources for services and welfare. It appeared to be an intelligent idea in three respects. First, it recognized the conventional view that to get fairer laws, better public services, and more money from the public treasury, you have to organize and put pressure upon government. The political scientists had been saying this for years, in innumerable books on pressure politics and interest groups. Thus, poverty was, like any other special interest, subject to the application of this maxim of politics.

The second element of the organization-action approach was that the neighborhood was the best base for organizing the poor. This is obvious enough because the poor, unlike doctors and lawyers, are associated in territories. The third element favoring this approach was the maximum participation stipulation. The greatest power the poor have, after all, is their numbers and their collective intention and action.

As a matter of fact, the community action method, in all its simplicity, was quite ingenious and produced results in organization and pressure. It gave a political structure back to neighborhoods which had lost their political identity because annexation and municipal reforms had destroyed the power of the neighborhoods at both the municipal and ward levels.

It was obvious to community leadership, however, that when independent, federally funded organizations based upon maximum participation began to appear, the government would withdraw support. But it was also apparent that only these principles of participation and organization could produce the political results desperately needed by the poor.

Thus, from the inception of the Community Action Program and the first funding of independent neighborhood organizations, it was clear that the crucial questions concerned the amount of funding available to those who would organize the neighborhoods as a unit of power and whether that funding could be retained in subsequent years. If the basis of antipoverty theory were community pressure, then funding would be a problem of supporting a mix of political organization and political education as well as enough programs of direct social benefit, to tie residents into the neighborhood organization.

As for the matter of getting re-funded the next year, that problem was met in terms of political strategy. It was resolved by a delicate combination of efforts at building community political power and at the same time boxing the government into a re-funding commitment. On this basis, some organizations were able to blend into the re-funding process, moving two steps forward and one step backward. Other organizations failed to take a step backwards; their militancy was too exposed, and they lost their funding.

From the outset it was apparent that eventually tactical error or a major change in government policy or law would remove most organizations from the funding train and that another source of funding—an independent source—had to be found. This problem is elaborated to draw out the reality of the economics of community organization and to show the error of the conventional notion that the economics of the anti-poverty program meant lifting individuals out of poverty—pulling people above the poverty line. It was true that many people were lifted above this line, but this was largely because of staff jobs in neighborhood organizations geared to providing either political education or the social benefits necessary to tie people to political organization.

When the federal policy changed in 1968 and favor shifted from community action based upon maximum feasible participation to community economic enterprise, it seemed to contain a possible temporary solution to the problem of funding the neighborhood political organization. The government wanted enterprise rather than political action in the neighborhood; it would move the people out of the meeting hall and put them behind cash registers. The community organization could not expect continued federal funding, and hence its survival depended upon generating enterprises whose profits could pay for the organization and its political program. An array of ventures and offers of assistance appeared, including federal grants and loans for capitalization, and training assistance from large corporations. Also, the government uncharacteristically acquiesced to such notions as community ownership. Anything, even socialism, was preferable to continued funding for neighborhood political organization.

The new line was received in the community with mixed feelings. On the one hand, political organization could not be abandoned. On the other, community ownership and enterprise assistance were also important. An infusion of wealth into the communities was consistent with the long-range need for a base of local wealth to support political organizations. And, of course, new wealth would promote the long-range objective of community prosperity. In short, at this period, it was clear that the only means to neighborhood improvement was through the establishment of independent community organizations, and it was also clear that the community had to have an internal economy capable of supporting itself.

Faced with the new economic policy of OEO, the community organizers agreed to write grant proposals promoting entrepreneurial development based on private enterprise or community ownership. But they also understood that tactically as much money as possible under these economic programs would be applied to the political objective of organization; that is, they would continue political organizing in a community-development framework. The result would be that the political organization could continue while attention was being paid to developing a local economy. Further, the priority of economic enterprise would accord with the requirements of advancing political organization. Housing projects and supermarkets were high on the economic development list, although in a number of cases workshop production of goods was undertaken. This is the state of things in poor communities at the present time. Many organizations have ceased to exist because they failed to make the economic shift, and a more radical politics have taken over in those neighborhoods. What the government failed to appreciate was that under the community action program they were indeed paying for political education and political action in the neighborhoods, but for a kind that had peaceful possibilities, albeit under a political rearrangement of the municipal constitution. By withdrawing funds, the government antagonized the communities and made their situation more desperate.

The present represents a new stage in the area of community development. Community-action organizations that lost funding had to find new sources of support. Those continuing political work with funds received under the rubric of community economic development must discover a way to free themselves from dependence on government money if they hope to achieve their political aims. Regionalization challenges the community organization in the ghetto to strive for independent political control in their own neighborhoods rather than endure the police control which would prevail under a metropolitan plan. The prospect of regional government alters the economic question as well. Since regionalization suggests a new unity between the government downtown and the middle class in the suburbs, the likelihood of a viable, independent economy in the neighborhood further diminishes. And to relate the political and economic questions, it appears that the politically organized neighborhood is obliged to be the principal developer of its own economy.

Neighborhood Self-Sufficiency

The conclusion to be reached, then, is that community-development efforts cannot rely on outside sources to improve the economy of the neighborhoods. External funding will end with the advent of the government's regionalization program. Under this condition, there is no future for the government assistance to small enterprise in the neighborhoods, or even for employment training for the poor, since the function of regionalization will be to dissociate the present cities from the economy of production in the suburbs. The problem of community economic development is rather the capacity of the neighborhood organizations to build a self-sufficient economy, first to support its own local political control and, second, to support the prosperity of its inhabitants through a local basis for internal and external trade. It is a harsh conclusion to place such great responsibility on the neighborhood organization, but this is the desperate necessity which the political maneuvers of the government have imposed upon the poorer neighborhoods. There is, however, a way by which the poor neighborhood can confront the problem of economic development and independence.

The important features of a poor neighborhood are, first, the discrepancy between the aggregate expendable income of the neighborhood and the paltry level of its commerce and, second, the discrepancy between the considerable tax revenue the neighborhood generates and the low level of benefits it receives in public services and welfare. In both cases, the neighborhood exports its income. Hence, the income and tax revenue of the neighborhood is of no service to its economic and political development. Its present internal commerce is dependent, as is its level of public services, on commerce and personnel outside the neighborhood.

With regard to expendable income, the familiar picture of the poor neighborhood is that its residents spend the largest part of their income outside their territory and another part in commercial places and for rents inside the territory to corporations or individuals who reside outside the neighborhood. In all, a very small portion of the income remains within the neighborhood. Thus there is a steady and unrelenting dependence characterized by a dollar drain which the residents replenish through outside employment.

Over the last decade, the proportion of external to internal expenditure for consumer goods has increased. There is a variety of reasons for this, including changes in residential patterns, downtown marketing, and transportation. Within the neighborhood there is, correspondingly, a sharp reduction of marketing and commerce. Small store after small store is closing up. Food marketing is confined to chain stores in a pattern which also applies to furniture and clothes.

Smaller and older shops find themselves unable to cope with either the political conditions of the neighborhood or the competition from chain stores. The business these stores might have counted on is absorbed by the stores which can offer low prices by buying in quantity and expanding to meet the needs of new shoppers. This trend has sharply reduced the commercial energy of the neighborhoods and it is likely that soon the only trade left within the poor neighborhoods will be for food and rent. Furniture, appliance, and drug stores as well as many other kinds of trading establishments are leaving poor neighborhoods. As for rent, landlords in many areas are simply abandoning their property because of the difficulty of collecting rent and the expense of repairing old buildings. As the trend develops, the proportion of income expended within the neighborhood for commodities will decrease and a greater share will go downtown.

So the picture of the neighborhood economy is one of increasing barrenness. The destruction wrought by riots in the past decade, combined with the failure of store owners to rebuild and of the city to assist commercial redevelopment, contributes to the trend. Because commercial decline is consistent with the metropolitan strategy, there is no lending and capitalization for new ventures in poor black neighborhoods. Commercial initiatives in the poor neighborhoods are viewed as adventures, not as commercial undertakings.

A similar pattern of net outflow is revealed upon comparison on the value of public services received in exchange for neighborhood tax expenditures. In his study of the Shaw-Cardozo neighborhood of Washington,

D.C.,[3] Earl Mellor reveals a tax payment of $44 million from a population of 87,000. This amount comes out of an aggregate personal income of $144 million for the area. Mellor calculates that the dollar value of visible public services and welfare received is below $34 million by the most likely measure of the distribution of public services in a city, namely wealth. Therefore, there is a net outflow of $10 million from the neighborhood tax payment.

Furthermore, taxes paid out go largely to public employees, such as policemen and teachers, who live outside the neighborhood but who come into it to perform their services, and partly to welfare recipients in the neighborhood itself. This is analogous to the expenditure of the greater proportion of income for commodities and rent in commercial establishments outside the neighborhood (or inside establishments which are externally owned). This disproportion is even more dramatic because, as Mellor suggests, out of a calculated minimum benefit of $34 million for Shaw-Cardozo, welfare payments, social security, and unemployment compensation amount to $10.9 million, or 23 percent of the payment. Thus, of the $44.6 million paid in taxes by the neighborhood, only about $10.9 million of that is received back in cash. Hence, Cardozo exports about $33.9 million a year to pay for services, just as it exports the greatest portion of its expendable income outside for shelter and commodities. If the trends in taxation continue and if the government achieves its announced intention of reducing the welfare load, the disproportion of tax revenues for public services will also increase.

The bulk of tax revenue pays for personnel who live outside the neighborhood. And, despite recent rhetoric concerning decentralization of public services and welfare administration in the city, we find that residents of the neighborhood must increasingly go outside the neighborhood for the services their taxes support. The variety of public service activity originating in, or with offices located in the neighborhood, is steadily reduced and concentrated. As an example, while the neighborhood pays taxes for education, the latest tendency is for its school children to be bused out of the neighborhood to schools in the far reaches of the city. Health care facilities are increasingly centralized, or locally unavailable. The same is true for fire prevention, welfare administration, police, and vocational rehabilitation. As with the trend in commodities, the trend in public services marks a decline in neighborhood location.

In view of these conditions, it can be said that the principal characteristic of the poor neighborhood is not its poverty but the diminution of its commerce and public administration. Its residents earn a considerable expendable income, in the aggregate, and pay considerable taxes. This payment must, however, be understood as support to the economies of neighborhoods outside the poor neighborhood. With the advent of metropolitan government, the slum city will continue to earn income, but its expenditure for commodities will constitute a primary support for a commercially renewed downtown, and its tax payments for services will be a primary support to the suburbs, whose middle class population will increasingly be involved in public employment.

The result of this tendency will be stagnation and decay for the neighborhoods of the present city. They will have few commercial or public-service activities of their own. They will be locked into a dependent relationship with the suburbs and downtown which will foster further erosion. If one accepts the statement of Rousseau that ''it is impossible to make any man a slave unless he first be reduced to a situation in which he cannot do without the help of others,'' he must conclude that the poor neighborhood has become economically enslaved, not because of an absence of income, but because of its dependence upon outside economies for commodities and public services.

The primary economic problem of the neighborhoods today is not to increase the aggregate income, for, no matter how that income increases, its flight—in payment for commodities and public services—will also speed up. The net effect will be to strengthen a downtown economy and suburban bureaucracy. This result can be prevented only if the neighborhood can create an internal economy and political control to attract and keep its expendable income for commodities and public services. The internal expenditure for these two necessities is related, in that tax payments to neighborhood employees for services performed can contribute to commercial activity in the neighborhoods. Thus, the resulting commercial prosperity can become a stronger base for neighborhood taxation.

The conventional conception of community economic development in the poor neighborhoods has been the direct organization and establishment of indigenous enterprise, whether owned privately or by some community organization. The two major difficulties with this approach have been capitalization and marketing management. If businesses were successful in original capitalization, they often collapse because of marketing difficulties, either through disorganization or because they could not meet the competition.

The problem of capitalization cannot be met simply through privately owned lending institutions because such banks cannot survive the trial-and-error of commercial development that aims to achieve a marketing and management organization suitable to the environment of poor neighborhoods. Nor can a capitalization program be based on the unreliable expedient of federal programs which may put $100 million in black banks one year and nothing in them the next. In short, the ingredients for a successful capitalization program must include substantial funding, regularly available investments, and independence from profit-making. In short, capitalization for neighborhood economic development must be conceived of as a public service and based upon an internal tax.

On the basis of the figures denoting outflow of taxes from the Cardozo neighborhood, it is apparent that funds for neighborhood capitalization programs must come from the $44.6 million paid by that area in federal and city taxes. Since Mellor's study demonstrates that there is a net outflow of tax revenue, any neighborhood which could retain this excess would have an annual capital fund of $10 million for economic development, without affecting the present level of public services and welfare. With capitalization of an internal economy as a priority, its capitalization fund might be even greater as would be the quality and efficacy of its services and welfare programs.

The question of a suitable form of neighborhood commercial organization cannot be taken up without answering first the question of whether effective commercial organization can precede political organization. If the only feasible strategy for neighborhood capitalization is neighborhood taxation, then the retention of neighborhood tax revenues and administrative control of their expenditure will of necessity be the organizational context of, and the precedent for, the appropriate organization of commercial development.

In summary, it is the thesis of this article that reliable community economic development can only evolve out of the existing fiscal resources of the neighborhood and that such resources exist in neighborhood tax expenditures. This application is consistent with the aims of community action which, although originally seeking to pressure city government for fair distribution of services and welfare, must take its course from the rebuff of government with its insistence on regionalization, and move toward self-control through neighborhood government.

NOTES

1. Economic Opportunity Act (1967 Green Amendment), 42 U.S.C., Sections 2790, 2791, 2795, 2796 (Supp. V, 1969).

2. For a brief account of the dubious nature of this support, see Boasberg, "The Washington Beat: The Urban Law Center—An Emerging Concept," *Urban Lawyer* 2 (1970): 553.

3. E. Mellor, *Public Goods and Services: Cost and Benefits* (mimeo., Institute for Policy Studies, Washington, D.C., 1969).

Ghetto Development, Community Corporations, and Public Policy

Thomas Vietorisz and Bennett Harrison

In the last several years, the twin concepts of political self-determination and economic development have caught the imagination of young blacks (and other minorities) in the urban ghetto. Community self-determination is the political program most often associated with the new spirit of racial identification—"black pride"—in America.[1] The acquisition of economic power is perhaps the only—at any rate, surely the most effective—way for the black community to acquire political influence commensurate with its numerical proportion in the population. And much socio-psychological theory (e.g., the work of Allport and Pettigrew) argues that genuine integration can only take place between groups who are cooperatively dependent on one another, such as groups of equal political status.[2]

From the spring of 1967 to the summer of 1968, the authors were associated with one of the earlier experiments in planned urban community economic development. Under a grant from the United States Office of Economic Opportunity (OEO), a group of economists who had previously worked in and studied the problems of underdeveloped countries were engaged as consultants to a new development corporation in New York: the Harlem Commonwealth Council (HCC).[3] Since 1968, the authors have published a monograph[4] and have begun to investigate the linkages between the urban ghetto and the larger, national economy, as well as the connections between urban poverty and the ways in which urban labor markets work—or do not work.[5]

The continuation of federal support to the nascent Community Development Corporation (CDC) is vital. While the Special Impact Program contained in Title I-D of the Economic Opportunity Act of 1964, as amended, is not necessarily the only or even the best way to keep these vital new institutions alive, it is at least a mechanism which has shown itself to be viable through a fairly long and rocky experimental period. Until such time as a national commitment to urban development in general and ghetto development in particular can become a reality, the

Special Impact Program represents perhaps the government's only meaningful response to the growing demand for community development in the United States.

Private Profit and Social Worth

To show why CDCs are—at least in our view—a necessary component of any development strategy and why we have implicitly discounted the social value of the so-called "black capitalism" programs of this and the preceding administrations, we must first give *our* working definition of the subject. "Ghetto development" means very different things to different people, so that any particular definition is important. For us, "ghetto development" refers to an overall social and economic transformation, with a large increase in the diversity of higher economic and institutional functions which ghetto residents are capable of sustaining, matched by a decisive improvement in the cohesion of the ghetto community (in other words, we are talking about institution-binding and not merely increasing per capita income). Specifically, we envisage the creation of a number of "inside jobs"—acquisition by the community of assets both inside and outside the ghetto; a substantial expansion of existing black businesses (particularly through cooperative forms of ownership); the large-scale transfer of ghetto property to ghetto residents and/or the community *qua* community; emphasis on the provision of pre-vocational and skill training within these ghetto enterprises; and local control of community political institutions such as schools, police, and health facilities. This kind of "local control" is, of course, already enjoyed by most suburban communities whose populations are not nearly so large as those of Harlem, Roxbury, or Watts.

Many economists and political scientists oppose investment in ghetto economic development because of its relative inefficiency in terms of the narrow criterion of jobs "created" per dollar of investment and its alleged inconsistency with the ideological goal of racial integration. Instead, these analysts propose policies designed to "disperse" the ghetto by relocating its residents to the suburbs.[6] It is not our intention to discuss this issue here; that has already been accomplished elsewhere.[7] Assuming that a development strategy is of intrest, we shall instead examine the reasons why community corporations—and the provision of federal funds for these unique institutions—are so important.

To any person seriously concerned with urban decay, enterprises that help in developing the ghetto ought to be enormously attractive given the intolerably high monetary and social costs of ghetto poverty. These islands of underdevelopment in the world's richest country lead to an appalling waste in the form of forgone productivity, quite apart from the cost of human suffering. For Harlem alone, lost production can be roughly estimated from the local per capita income of about $1,000 (as compared with the United States average of over $4,000) as $1.25 billion annually. Over and above this short-fall, there are vast cash expenditures involved in running the police stations, courts, prisons, hospitals, mental asylums, rehabilitation centers, welfare departments, and other social institutions required for keeping the lid on the ghetto.

Yet in an economy organized largely by commercial motivations, it is not the overall economic benefit that decides if an activity will be undertaken, but its commercial profitability. In the ghetto, these qualities are very nearly mutually exclusive.

Money-making ventures in the ghetto are invariably exploitative: slum-lordism, numbers, vice, drugs, and consumer credit frauds. Few and far between are the socially constructive activities that generate large enough profits—10 to 15 percent after taxes—to attract sufficient investment by the core institution of the American economy: the large, private corporation. Conditions being as they are, the ghetto is the last place to establish a privately owned and operated business having the option of alternative locations.[8] Rents are high; labor skills, morale, turnover, and absenteeism unfavorable; crime and casualty losses frightening; insurance prohibitively expensive, if available at all; public services lagging miserably behind those in more prosperous areas. The ideal business for ghetto development—one that is socially constructive and at the same time truly profitble—is rare indeed. The idea of ghetto development based on large numbers of self-contained, profit-making businesses that would generate their own capital for expansion is fantasy.

When we assert that ghetto development is technically and economically feasible, we have no illusions about the commercial prospects of isolated ghetto enterprises. A workable ghetto-development strategy must rely on tightly planned coordination and mutual support between individual activities to bring them up to the level of profitability that assures survival in an economy geared to commercial success. Yet, survival implies no more than the modest bookkeeping profits needed for paying off bank loans. This level of commercial performance by enterprises under the community-development umbrella is undoubtedly feasible, but it will not motivate the massive investments needed to develop the ghetto.

Investments for ghetto development must be motivated instead by overall social worth, not by commercial success; that is to say, in a private enterprise economy, investments must be generated by the political process. If the needed political motivation cannot or will not be provided, ghetto development and the private enterprise economy are incompatible.

We have argued that the cornerstone of a ghetto-development strategy should be the creation of a network of CDCs directed entirely by those energetic young activists inside the ghetto who are prepared to challenge existing conditions and who are responsive to and at the same time molders of the opinions and preferences of the residents of the ghetto. These CDCs, of which a growing number of forerunners already exist, should be invited into the public business of expanding job access for ghetto workers. This could be done, for example, by subcontracting

CDCs to perform outreach recruiting and prevocational training for established public and private sector employers.

But more importantly, the CDCs have the capability of establishing what we refer to as "greenhouse industries." In these industries, sympathetic nonwhite foremen can train ghetto workers on the job and in a familiar environment until their attendance level, work performance, and preferences warrant "promotion" (which may involve placement into jobs outside of the ghetto altogether).

In appending supporting bundles of consumer-oriented service activities to the core of an industrial project[9]—for example, adding credit unions, "do-it-yourself" repair stalls, and insurance claim service "centers" to a computerized automotive diagnostic center[10]—the CDC will necessarily trade off profits for the sake of community-service benefits. It is difficult to imagine how any institution other than the community development corporation would be willing and able to accept the curtailed profits and unorthodox operating procedures necessarily associated with such an experiment.

A Program for Ghetto Development

The ghetto communities, individually and considered as a potential "trading bloc," contain more than enough consumers and purchasing power to make ghetto consumer goods industries viable. In central Harlem alone (in 1966), the 250,000 residents had a combined gross income of over $200 million. Moreover, the municipal, state, and federal governments have offices and public enterprises in every city; these could certainly be made to purchase goods and services from ghetto industries as a matter of public policy, thereby opening up a market for "export" production. Roy Innis estimates that "Harlem schools purchase over $100,000,000 in goods and services each year."[11] Many of the larger ghettos (e.g., Harlem and the Chicago South Side) already have a relatively broad commercial base upon which to build.

The probability of commercial success will be measurably improved if existing establishments which are now uneconomically small can be organized along cooperative lines. There are precedents for this among white businessmen, not to speak of the eminently successful rural electrification cooperatives made up of small agricultural producers in the heartlands of America. For example, organizations of "affiliated independent" businesses are a form of producers' cooperative built around the function of joint purchasing. In American food retailing, the market share of the affiliated independents rose from 8 percent to 55 percent in the last decade, as new members were signed up. This success seems to be explained by a combination of the economies of large-scale purchasing, characteristic of the chain stores, with the high motivation and flexible adaptation to local conditions of independent entrepreneurship.

Commercial success can also be increased if the strategy of "backward integration," from control over distribution ("shelf space") to control over the production of at least some of the goods to be marketed on those shelves, is deployed imaginatively. One example is the backward integration from a chain of cooperative supermarkets to food packaging and processing plants. Supermarkets are a sensible component of ghetto-development programs for two reasons. Many areas have a definite deficiency of food outlets available within walking distance for most residents. Moreover, recent econometric research at Columbia University in New York City suggests that one of the reasons that the "poor pay more" for food is that the ghetto retail food industry is dominated by small ("mom and pop") shops. These stores legitimately must charge higher unit prices for many goods than do supermarkets because of the higher unit costs they must absorb for inventory, insurance, and most other inputs.[12] Finally, another possibility would be the wholesaling of office equipment. This could be carried out with the more than 1,200 institutional consumers in or adjacent to Harlem (churches, schools, government buildings, etc.), gradually integrating backward into metal-working and office furniture production.

Imaginative new engineering-economic studies (particularly the central city, new town, and industrial park studies financed by the Economic Development Administration and the Department of Housing and Urban Development) have shown the creative application of new technologies in building construction, industrial processing, and transportation can make central city industrial locations attractive again.[13] Moreover, new "technologies" in and attitudes toward training, to the extent that they integrate pre-vocational and on-the-job training within the context of career ladders and against the background of improved community-oriented public schools, will ensure these ghetto industries an adequate supply of capable local labor.

The limitations of physical space within the ghetto need not bottle up development. Even apart from the construction of "vest-pocket" industrial parks, high-rise industrial buildings, and pioneering multi-function structures (combining housing, school, commerce, and light industry), so long as the new activities are part of a comprehensive community development plan, their effectiveness need not be undermined by placing them in readily accessible outside locations. Examples from the Harlem development "plan" are the air space over the South Bronx, New York City, rail yards, or the recently completed Brooklyn Navy Yard industrial park. Going one step further, the plan may well include a downtown and even a suburban jobs component for ghetto residents, involving coordinated recruitment, prevocational training, placement, and follow-up support. If backed by negotiations of the CDC for block placement of trainees with large corporations and government agencies, and combined with a restructuring of publicly regulated fares for large-scale reverse commuting (from Harlem to Westchester), such a component within a ghetto development plan may well be the most effective way of securing outside employment for ghetto residents. The example certainly demonstrates the potential complementarity of "inside" and "outside" job development programs.

A social and political program of ghetto development might, apart from the coordinated planning of enterprises, contain some of the following elements:

(1) Management of local branch stores of national chains by the CDC;
(2) Administration and ownership of public housing, by a combination of tenants and community housing groups;
(3) Election of autonomous local school boards with powers comparable to those of middle-class suburban residential communities;
(4) Majority representation on the boards of directors of local hospitals and other public health facilities;
(5) Autonomous local institutions responsible to the community at large for administering manpower training and recruitment services as well as unemployment, welfare, and other transfer operations; and
(6) Community control of police, elected civilian review boards in each precinct, with powers to investigate, subpoena, and initiate proceedings for the removal of policemen convicted of brutality against the residents of the community.[14]

Several key questions remain to be explored. Contrary to the position taken by some economists, who see the problem of the ghetto primarily in terms of unemployment and are thus ready to go along with any job program no matter how poorly paid, we regard it as fundamental that *jobs paying below subsistence wages—no matter how many—have no place in any anti-poverty program.* The more we encourage the proliferation of such jobs, the more we inescapably add—since common humanity forces us to keep alive the offspring of the holders—to the already crushing welfare burden. The toleration of below-subsistence wages in combination with a family-centered welfare system merely repeats the disastrous experience of the nineteenth-century English poor laws, which encouraged textile and other manufacturers to pass on part of their payroll costs to the parishes responsible for the support of the poor. Apart from the patent inequity and social injustice inherent in this system, in the long run it grievously damaged the very industries in England which it subsidized. It robbed them of the chief incentive for the introduction of technical innovations and thereby progressively destroyed their initially phenomenal, international technological lead. If there ever were a primrose path to perdition for a country to take this surely is the one.

Our total rejection of a nonjobs strategy leads us to restrict our planning recommendations to what under the current wage structure are medium-to-high wage industries, paying from $3.50 upward.[15] Since such industries tend to be highly concentrated, entry by any new organization (let alone a black group) is at best restricted and often prohibitively expensive. Yet, without local ownership, community control of the proceeds is unlikely to materialize. We may also question the availability of a developmental infrastructure in the ghetto: water, electricity, transportation, waste disposal, etc., adequate for the support of modern industries. Since low-wage service and manufacturing facilities require relatively less social overhead capital than do high-wage "leading edge" industries, inadequate ghetto infrastructure may act as an additional obstacle to the kind of economic development we are advocating.

It must be noted, however, that both the current intrametropolitan maldistribution of social overhead capital and the feasibility of a future redistribution of these capital services are fundamentally political questions. As more and more cities attain black majorities, the economic preconditions for ghetto development will become an increasingly important object of political struggle.

And this is the central point. Ghetto development is fundamentally a political process. In a monograph on the economy of Harlem, we try to show that ghetto economic development can be

> far more than a mechanism for allocating resources efficiently, organizing production, generating profit streams, or even creating jobs . . . . Economic development, wherever it takes place, acts as a catalyst of social and political change. Jobs created inside the ghetto are the instruments as well as the objects of this change, contributing to a reduction in psychological and social pathology, an improvement in the "technology" of community organization, increased skill levels, and the re-enforcement of the community's political base and potential. Conventional economic analysis treats these social effects as external—incidental to, and not very important in light of overall economic activity. We believe, however, that economic development of the ghetto is vital because of the social externalities that it can generate, social benefits far in excess of the mere creation of even a considerable number of otherwise sterile workplaces.[16]

Policy Recommendations

The paramount national need is for the Congress to enact new national priorities and policies dealing with urbanization, manpower, subsistence wages, and poverty. We are now recommending the most desperate emergency action until the broader issues can be addressed. We suggest the following three immediate measures:

First, the existing CDCs must be kept alive for the duration. To this end, we recommend strengthening Title I-D of the Economic Opportunity Act of 1964, as amended.

Second, the mission of the CDC—development, and not simply success of showcase projects—must be safeguarded at all costs. We shall have gained little if the organizations survive but their mission is sterilized. We therefore recommend that the performance of each CDC be judged, for refunding purposes, under *self-defined success criteria,* not under conventional banking criteria or even under "development" criteria as seen by a paternalistic funding agency. In other words, let a CDC be judged on its own definition, adopted in advance, of what should be regarded as "development" under its own particular circumstances. We recommend a review process by an independent national review board not involved in funding decisions, to judge these self-defined success criteria for reasonableness, and to assist the CDCs in striking a balance between flexible adjustment of the criteria over time and the need for some continuity. We further recommend that these success criteria, once certified, be made binding on federal funding agencies involved in the support of CDCs. The funding agency would then be required to judge how well a CDC has been doing under the CDC's own definition—and not under the definition of some inscrutable bureaucratic authority. The suggested measure has the further virtue of stimulating directly community development by precipitating a debate about the very aims of development.[17] While this creates conflicts, it also contributes to public involvement, clarifies issues, and exercises the processes of democratic decision making. Most important, the measure maintains for the CDCs a lease on life in spirit as well as in fact.

Third, we recommend that the March 1971 Current Population Survey; the Labor Department's Urban Employment Surveys of 1966, 1969, and 1970; the 1966 and 1967 Office of Economic Opportunity Surveys of Economic Opportunity; the 1970 Census Employment Survey; and minor related efforts be consolidated into a standard statistical series to be assembled and published bi-annually or even (in less detail) quarterly. The series would focus on the incidence of subemployment[18] in small areas by family and by type of economic activity. In this recommendation we take our departure from the position of the unsuccessful 1970 Community Development Corporation bill, which contained just such a provision. The subemployment series would not only increase insight into labor market problems, but would also help to measure the impact of the CDCs on their environment and especially on the economic and social well-being of their constituents. While there are substantial technical and judgmental problems involved in the construction of a single composite index of "labor market failure," we have no doubt that the able and dedicated professionals at the Bureau of Labor Statistics could—if adequately funded—produce the requisite indicators.

Conclusion

Taken individually, none of the components of the development strategy we are advocating is either radical or new. Consumers' and producers' cooperatives have been established in white communities for over a hundred years. Many small towns in America have their own nonprofit development corporations which assemble land, organize local entrepreneurs, and at least occasionally give some weight to community preferences when selecting sites for industrial parks. The use of captive shelf space as a lever for backward integration to producing units is a technique prominently employed by the large food chains. The "infant industry" strategy is well known and quite commonly advocated in international economic development, for instance, by the U.S. Agency for International Development. Finally, white food merchants with small shops have, as we observed earlier, taken up the affiliated-independents approach to industrial organization to such an extent that their networks have surpassed the market share of the larger chains. We have not made any attempt to disguise or deny the fundamentally eclectic character of the elements of economic development strategy we have proposed.

New in our approach (at least in terms of domestic economic policy) is the articulation of these techniques into a system and the suggestion that blacks might use the mix of techniques to organize their communities. Used in combination—which is all that is meant by a planned, strategic approach—these not unconventional techniques constitute a formidable economic planning instrument.

Within the context of the plan—within, that is, the coordinated mix of techniques—ghetto businesses are considerably more than vehicles for generating profits for a black bourgeoisie. In this context, ghetto businesses become development instruments in their own right, devices which the community can manipulate toward many objectives, both economic and political.

The Nixon Administration [1971] has, by contrast, chosen to pursue an orthodox, atomistic business development strategy to identify and fund essentially isolated and functionally unrelated ghetto enterprises whose only common attribute is the expectation that they will yield profits to independent "black capitalists." Such a policy will (the Nixon Administration hopes) "cool" the ghetto by sustaining its middle class. In our opinion, this expectation will not and cannot be realized by such a "business as usual" approach as "black capitalism." It is the *collective* economic and political strength of the community—not the asset portfolios of a small number of its "barons"—which matters in the end.

Probably, the existing ghetto leadership will not turn to a truly planned strategic community development approach of the kind we suggest unless their more traditional approach to economic (business) development fails. We believe that it will fail; indeed, that it is already failing. Meanwhile, people within the ghetto are going to bring more and more pressure to bear on their leaders as their perceived situation becomes more intolerable. This is likely to be especially true for the young black men in the ghetto. Pressure for change, as economists and psychologists long ago observed, is a function of the relative and not the absolute position of an individual or group within society, and it feeds upon preceding changes. In these terms, there is every reason to expect an increase of tensions within the ghetto. This projection is supported by the Census Bureau's recent finding that residential segregation in American cities is actually increasing,[19] and by our own studies which show that, even for the full-time employed, married men of Harlem, additional education—up to college and possibly beyond—does not translate into perceptibly higher wages.[20]

As such pressures build, those militant ghetto leaders who are not committed to a conventional business approach—or the next generation of leaders following them—may be increasingly willing to experiment with unconventional economic and organizational strategies. We perceive their present reluctance to attempt planned ghetto development as, more than anything, a matter of mores and political style. America has been built by the decentralized efforts of individuals and small groups; there simply is no successful political tradition to draw on for organizing broad, sustained social action that follows a comprehensive economic and political design. In a word, there is no mainstream tradition for planning; on the contrary, every inbred political reflex of the average individual over thirty is "conditioned" to fend off planning, seen as conveying the threat of social coercion. Given this tradition, no American minority group that views itself as fighting for its freedom will lightly commit itself to planned community development.

Yet concerted group action in the economic and social sphere is becoming more inevitable every day, not only in relation to the problem of the urban ghetto, but also in relation to almost every aspect of modern living. Advancing population densities, the growing sophistication of technology, the rapid deterioration of the environment through all manner of pollution, the shrinkage of the globe through high-speed transport—all of these are carrying us toward a fundamentally changed world.

In this world the entire material basis of meaningful human social existence will depend on highly articulated, carefully designed technical and organizational systems, rather than on the commercially motivated maneuvering of large numbers of small social units, be they enterprises, households, or traditional political pressure groups. Political styles and structures will either ride this advancing tide or be crushed by it. We are advocating planned community development within the ghettos in the conviction that such planning is also urgently needed in regard to practically every aspect of middle-class metropolitan living right now, and will, in all certainty, become a condition of sheer physical survival within our lifetimes. The only conceivable guarantee of an open society under the material conditions facing us is the organization of the needed planning process by socially meaningful communities of limited size, as in urban neighborhoods, and the broadest possible participation of individuals in all aspects of planning, all the way down to the grassroots level. The approach we recommend is thus designed to become part of the future, not merely to serve as a palliative for the mistakes of the past.

NOTES

1. See Roy Innis, "Separatist Economics: A New Social Contract," in *Black Economic Development*, ed. by William F. Haddad and G. Douglas Pugh (Englewood Cliffs, N.J.: Spectrum, 1969); Charles Tate, "Brimmer and Black Capitalism," *The Review of Black Political Economy*, Spring/Summer 1970.

2. See Dale Hiestand, *Discrimination in Employment: An Appraisal of the Research* (Ann Arbor, Mich.: Institute of Labor and Industrial Relations, University of Michigan-Wayne State University, 1970), pp. 41–42.

3. For an early description of the goals and structure of the Harlem Development Project, see Bennett Harrison, "A Pilot Project for the Economic Development Planning of American Urban Slums," *International Development Review* (Mar. 1968).

4. Thomas Vietorisz and Bennett Harrison, *The Economic Development of Harlem* (New York City: Praeger Publishers, 1970).

5. Thomas Vietorisz and Bennett Harrison, "The Potential of Ghetto Development," *Papers and Proceedings of the 1971 Northeastern Meetings of the Regional Science Association,* and Bennett Harrison, *Education, Training, and The Urban Ghetto* (Baltimore, Md.: The Johns Hopkins Press, 1972).

6. The most widely known arguments for "ghetto dispersal" are those of John F. Kain, "The Big Cities' Big Problem," *Challenge,* Sept./Oct. 1966, and John F. Kain and Joseph J. Persky, "Alternatives to the Gilded Ghetto," *The Public Interest,* Winter 1969.

7. Matthew Edel, "Development or Dispersal—Approaches to Ghetto Poverty," in *Readings in Urban Economics,* ed. by Jerome Rothenberg and Matthew Edel (New York: Macmillan, 1972); Gerson Green and Geoffrey Faux, "The Social Utility of Black Enterprise," in *Black Economic Development,* ed. by William F. Haddad and G. Douglas Pugh (Englewood Cliffs, N.J.: Prentice Hall, 1969); Bennett Harrison, *Metropolitan Suburbanization and Minority Economic Opportunity* (Washington, D.C.: The Urban Institute, 1974); Bennett Harrison, "Suburbanization and Ghetto Dispersal: A Critique of the Conventional Wisdom," in *Controversies of State and Local Government,* ed. by Mavis Mann Reeves and Parris Glendening (Boston, Mass.: Allyn and Bacon, 1971).

8. For an excellent discussion of this issue, see William K. Tabb, *The Political Economy of the Black Ghetto* (New York: W.W. Norton, 1970), ch. 4, and the references cited therein.

9. For a geometric presentation of a procedure for assembling and scheduling such packages (or "clusters") of projects, see Thomas Vietorisz, "Quantized Preferences and Planning by Priorities," *American Economic Review/Papers and Proceedings* (May 1970).

10. Vietorisz and Harrison, *The Economic Development of Harlem,* pp. 128–36.

11. Quoted in Tate, "Brimmer and Black Capitalism," p. 89.

12. Roger Alcaly, "Food Prices in New York City: Analysis of a 1967 Survey," in *The Economy of Harlem,* Vol. 1, Office of Economic Opportunity Grant No. CG-8730. (Development Planning Workshop, Columbia University, 1968), mimeographed.

13. John H. Alschuler and Irving M. Footlik, "Industry Can Cut Costs with Multi-Story Building," *Mid-Chicago Development Study* (Washington, D.C.: U.S. Economic Development Administration, 1968); Irving Hoch, "The Three-Dimensional City," *The Quality of the Urban Environment,* ed. by Harvey S. Perloff, (Baltimore, Md.: The Johns Hopkins Press, 1969); Institute for Urban Studies, Fordham University, *The Brooklyn Naval Yard: A Plan for Redevelopment,* (U.S. Economic Development Administration, May 1968); Athelstan Spilhaus, "Technology, Living Cities, and Human Environment," *American Scientist,* 57, 1 (1969); and U.S. Department of Housing and Urban Development, *Tomorrow's Transportation: New Systems for the Urban Future* (Washington, D.C.: 1968).

14. Tom Hayden, "Colonialism and Liberation as American Problems," *Politics and the Ghettos,* ed. by Roland L. Warren (New York: Atherton Press, 1969), pp. 184–85.

15. Our threshhold for subsistence—decent poverty, no more—is measured by the "lower" (formerly "minimum adequate") family budget of the Bureau of Labor Statistics. For a family of four in the major metropolitan areas, the average "lower" budget is now about $7,000 (the figure for New York-Northeastern New Jersey region—spring, 1970—is $7,183; *New York Times,* December 21, 1970). Assuming full-time, year-round employment, with a single "breadwinner"—still the American norm—this translates into an average hourly wage of $3.58.

16. Vietorisz and Harrison, *The Economic Development of Harlem,* p. 66.

17. The self-definition of success criteria has been found to be an important characteristic of solidarity groups studied by anthropologists and sociologists. See Frank W. Young, "Reactive Subsystems" (Palo Alto, Calif.: Center for Advanced Study in the Behavioral Sciences, Stanford University, 1970), mimeographed.

18. The original Labor Department subemployment index, constructed for 10 central city ghettos in November 1966, consisted of the sum of those who were actually unemployed during the survey week, those working part-time but seeking full-time work, heads of households under 65 years of age earning less than $60 a week full-time, nonheads under 65 years of age earning less than $56 a week full-time, half the number of male nonparticipants aged 20–64 (on the grounds that they had given up looking, not because they did not want to work, but because of the "conviction—whether right or wrong—that they can't find a job"), and half of the male undercount (the "expected but unfound" adult males). The results of that initial survey are shown in Table A, below together with several benchmarks.

19. Vietorisz and Harrison, *The Economic Development of Harlem*, pp. 59–60.

20. *Ibid.*, pp. 25–30. For a study of the returns to education and training in eighteen urban ghettos, see Harrison, *Education, Training, and The Urban Ghetto;* and Harrison, "Education and Underemployment in the Urban Ghetto," *Problems in Political Economy: An Urban Perspective,* ed. by David M. Gordon (Lexington, Mass.: D. C. Heath, 1971).

TABLE A
Income, Unemployment and Subemployment in Ten Urban Ghettos

Ghetto and City	Unemployment Rate Ghetto*	SMSA	Ghetto Subemploy- ment Rate*	Median Individual Weekly Wage*	Median Annual Family Income	Bureau of Labor Statistics Minimum Adequate Family Budget†
Roxbury (Boston)	6.5	2.9*	24.2	$74	$4,224	$6,251
Central Harlem (New York City)	8.3		28.6	73	3,907	
East Harlem (New York City)	9.1	3.7*	33.1	67	3,641	6,021
Bedford-Stuyvesant (New York City)	6.3		27.6	73	4,736	
North Philadelphia	9.1	3.7*	34.2	65	3,392	5,898
North Side (St. Louis)	12.5	4.4*	38.9	66	3,544	6,002
Slums of San Antonio	7.8	4.2†	47.4	55	2,876	‡
Mission-Fillmore (San Francisco)	11.4	5.4*	24.6	74	4,200	6,571
Salt River Bed (Phoenix)	12.5	3.3†	41.7	57	2,520	‡
Slums of New Orleans	9.5	3.3†	45.3	58	3,045	‡

Source: Bennett Harrison, *Education, Training and the Urban Ghetto* (Baltimore, Md.: The Johns Hopkins Press, 1972)..

For an excellent discussion of the political history of the subemployment index, and how the regular collection of small-area subemployment statistics might facilitate the drafting of national manpower and antipoverty legislation, see William Spring, "Underemployment: The Measure We Refuse to Take," *New Generation,* Winter 1971.

*November, 1966.

†March, 1967.

‡Not available.

Problems and Techniques in Financing Ghetto Housing

Thomas F. Murray

Item: "I guess I was in the right place at the right time," Joseph Hutchinson, Jr., said last March about the approval of his home loan in Passaic, N.J. Mr. Hutchinson, a 32-year-old postal employee, had never owned his own home.

Item: In Seattle, Washington, Mr. and Mrs. Richard Parker celebrated the purchase of a new home and their son's fourth birthday on the same date. They moved from an apartment that cost them $120 a month into their own home, which costs them $90 a month for mortgage payments.

Item: In Dayton, Ohio, Mr. and Mrs. Robert W. Harris arranged a home loan which previously had been denied to them because mortgage money was not available in their part of the city.

The Billion Dollar Pledge

All these people have two things in common: They are black and their new homes were financed through the life insurance industry's billion dollar investment program in the city core areas. Their situations can be multiplied across the nation as people are given a new perspective on life in America. Hope, opportunity and dignity are being nurtured through this unique plan.

In the spring of 1967, Equitable Life Assurance board chairman James F. Oates, Jr., proposed in broad outline that American life insurance companies provide a pool of mortgage money for slum-area residential and commercial construction at the normal interest rates for low-risk investments. He called for new insurance company thinking about "venture capital in the social field."

About the same time, the executive committee of the Institute of Life Insurance recommended that the life insurance business assume a large role in seeking solutions to the serious problems facing our urban areas.

The Life Insurance Association of America and the American Life Convention unanimously approved this recommendation and formed a joint committee of top life insurance executives to formulate a program of action. The committee considered many aspects of the deterioration of our central cities, including slum conditions, air pollution, transportation, civil disorders, and the need for better employment, education and job training.

The magnitude of the problems made the committee realize that a program of substantial proportions would be needed, and resulted in a proposal that the life insurance companies commit themselves to a $1 billion investment pledge. While jobs and education were top priority needs, the committee concluded that the life insurance industry could make a significant contribution in housing and job-creating businesses. It was hoped this commitment could act as a catalyst and encourage others in the business community to participate actively in attempts to solve urban ills.

Member companies were asked to participate in the program by pledging up to 1 percent of their assets as of December 31, 1966. The response was prompt and affirmative; within a short time 149 companies subscribed well over $1 billion. Presently 163 companies are participating. With these commitments in hand, the chairman of the committee, Gilbert W. Fitzhugh, board chairman of Metropolitan Life, announced the $1 billion life insurance program to President Johnson at a White House Conference attended by industry representatives.

A route to follow

This high-level announcement triggered immediate interest in the financing of properties located in slum areas. Mortgage investment officers, who had hesitated to invest there before, found themselves plunged into the problems of the ghettos. It soon became apparent, however, that guidelines, which each company in the program could follow, would have to be established in order to attack the problem.

It was agreed that the prime objective of the program was to improve housing conditions and to finance job-creating enterprises in the city core areas. Low-income housing projects outside the core city could qualify, provided they were designed primarily for the benefit of the population of the core cities. Upon this foundation the following basic guidelines were developed:

▶ A qualified project was defined as one which, because of its location or risk, would not ordinarily be financed under normal investment practices of life insurance companies. Investments under the program would carry government guarantees or insurance of principal, unless such guarantees were not deemed necessary in the judgment of the lender.

▶ At the outset, investments were to be made under existing governmental programs, particularly FHA mortgages or loans under state or local economic development programs.

▶ Because of the availability of government insurance, such loans were to carry interest rates no higher than the regular market rates for mortgages on properties coming within the normal operations of life insurance investments. Loans to nonprofit sponsors or limited dividend corporations, under Section 221(d)(3) of the rent supplement program, would provide a statutory ceiling of 6¾ percent, with only minimal discounts possible.

▶ Each participating company reserved the right to select the loans it would make under the program and to negotiate the terms of each investment.

The framers of the guidelines believed that the great bulk of the $1 billion commitment toward solving urban problems would be invested by individual companies on their own initiative. This would occur as they searched out projects in the local areas which came within the limits of the program, as they participated with community groups and governmental units concerned with improving urban conditions.

The industry's commitment envisaged the creation of both housing and jobs. At the present time, while progress has been made in the housing field, investment in job-creating enterprises has been a problem. The insurance industry cannot ordinarily provide the capital for new or existing small firms since that is really a banking function. Efforts of insurance carriers had to be devoted to providing mortgage financing where jobs would be created—a field shown to be most difficult.

Equitable's Effort

The September 13, 1968, report of the Life Insurance Association of America stated that 19,482 jobs had been created or retained. Equitable's contribution to this total, for example, had been through the financing of convalescent homes, a hospital, a shopping center, nurses' residences, a rehabilitation center, and a medical office building.

At the outset, my company [Equitable] immediately had a problem which many other life insurance companies did not share. The Equitable does not operate under a mortgage correspondent system and, with minor exceptions, had not previously invested in FHA or VA mortgages. Inasmuch as the basic foundation of the program was its reliance on governmental guarantees of the risks involved, some rapid researching had to be undertaken to become familiar with what FHA plans would qualify under the Urban Redevelopment Program and what plans would be best suited for implementing the redevelopment program's goals.

A course of action

After a review of these various plans, the best development plan appeared to be rental housing under the 221(d)(3) rent supplement program. Further examination, however, showed that this procedure would not accomplish the most immediate objective of the Urban Redevelopment Program—visible evidence that the program was in effect.

Under rent supplement housing, it could take as long as two years to complete the units, and Federal guarantees were difficult to obtain because of limited appropriations. Some other vehicle was obviously necessary to put available funds to immediate use. This vehicle turned out to be the 203(b) (now 223E) and 221(d)(2) FHA programs which insured mortgage money for privately owned, one-to-four-family housing. In addition to the immediate advantage of employing the funds in the shortest time possible, it offered further opportunities to the inhabitants of ghetto areas by providing potential jobs in the rehabilitation of blighted properties.

Because of publicity given to the program, it was assumed that Equitable would be approached by a large number of mortgage brokers and other parties who were interested in participating. It soon became clear that this was an erroneous assumption. Very few inquiries were received at the start of the program, and the company had to actively seek out participants.

The first commitment made under FHA 203(b) was $2,000,000 in loans on one-to-four-family houses in the Bedford-Stuyvesant, East New York, and Brownsville sections of Brooklyn. On December 26, 1967, the commitment was made to Springfield Equities Limited, a small, approved FHA lender which had been active in this area for several years. All loans were made on 30-to-40-year-old, one-to-four-family, owner-occupied homes which required some rehabilitation.

This initial commitment allowed the company to become familiar with the various problems involved. As a result, an approach was formulated which has proved to be successful.

It was found that the first consideration was to apply the funds where the needs were the greatest. Because Equitable operates nationally, it was also felt that the funds should be spread out geographically. Since the company has a staff mortgage organization in most major cities, it has been able to seek out the mortgage bankers in the area who were working in this field or were capable of doing so. The primary considerations for the appointment of a mortgage correspondent were three:

▶ Top priority was given to approved FHA lenders of a minority group who had the capabilities for implementing the program.

▶ If no minority lenders were available, second consideration was given to local mortgage bankers and/or other local approved FHA lending institutions.

▶ If neither of the above were available, then the larger regional mortgage organizations were sought.

Of major consideration was whether the banker or institution selected as mortgage correspondent enjoyed good relations with the minority community and whether it had the resources to do the required job.

Project criteria

A digest of the FHA programs most applicable was sent to all of the firms' mortgage offices. This digest was also sent to all participating companies by LIAA. In addition, our mortgage departments sent a memorandum to all field offices instructing them to weigh each project on its own merits. Guidelines and questions were established to provide a flexible basis for consideration and to indicate the type of questions that should be answered in the field. Here are the criteria used:

1. The project must be one that would qualify under the requirements established by the Joint Committee on Urban Problems of LIAA.

2. Consideration must be given to the project's location and its proximity to public transportation, employment areas and shopping facilities.

3. Information is required as to the type of buildings involved, number of units, total cost, including copy of building contracts, if available, etc. Also, an opinion is required as to whether the costs are reasonably in line for the type of project being considered.

4. The particular FHA program, such as 221(d)(2), under which the project is to be submitted, must be listed.

5. The background of the sponsor and/or developer, if the two differ, should be investigated, to determine whether they have the know-how and financial capabilities to complete and manage the project.

6. While it may be difficult to obtain data as to neighborhood income range, consideration should be given to a reasonable relationship between income and the sales price or rent levels where rent supplements are not involved.

7. It is important to establish whether or not the project will have local neighborhood and community support.

How the plan works

Shortly after the industry's announcement in September 1967, the Federal Housing Administration announced a new program, in cooperation with the life insurance industry, to identify one-to-four-family housing in city core areas which would qualify for eligibility under standards established by the Joint Committee on Urban Problems. Section 203(b) and 221(d)(2) mortgages approved in these areas were identified under Categories A and B by FHA local offices. Category A included all loans in areas that have had riots or have threats of riots in the future. Category B were all loans in city core areas where there was blight in the neighborhood but the properties were acceptable. All mortgages identified under these two categories were eligible. There has since been a change from Section 203(1) to 223(e), which means that the A and B categories will not be used for new core area commitments.

FHA begain issuing commitments on such properties at the rate of 500 per week across the country, and active investment interest by participating life insurance companies has accelerated the volume of investment funds in the city core areas. This FHA program expanded the basis for greater geographical distribution and opportunities for participation by life insurance companies. As the program became known, Equitable offices were contacted by interested mortgage bankers and local banks. Upon receipt of such an inquiry or a referral from the home office, the mortgage banker or local bank was asked to submit the following information:

A. Proposal

   1. Types of loans and amounts being offered (1-4 family, Section 203(b), Section 221(d)(2), VA). How originated?
   2. General locations of loans: Category A or B?
   3. Mix—203(b), 221(d)(2) (current and future commitments).
   4. Price to Equitable (usually the purchase price is limited to one point above origination price).
   5. Delivery dates.
   6. Proposed commitment period.
   7. Servicing arrangement and fee.
   8. Average loan, size of total package, and size of blocks to be submitted periodically.
   9. Method of reporting the status of loans.

B. Background of Mortgage Company or Bank

   1. History
     a. Years in business.
     b. Types of organization.
     c. Servicing volume and background.
     d. Number of years' experience in handling FHA loans.
     e. Number of personnel and basic organization.
     f. Institutions presently serviced.
     g. Whether currently approved FHA and VA lender.

   2. Financial Statement
     a. Should include name of institution with whom mortgage banker warehouses loans.
     b. Line of credit with said institution.

In addition, the residential loan manager includes any personal knowledge he may have about the mortgage banker or local bank submitting the proposal, general comments on its reputation in the business community, and comments on the general areas in which the loans are located. These managers direct all firm proposals to the home office where the decision is made whether or not to issue a commitment.

Problems and potential

Very early in this program, the company became involved in several local situations where it was learned that handing money out on a platter to ghetto residents was not the answer to the truly urgent problems. Making money available for financing homes and other properties in these distressed areas was, by itself, not enough. It soon became evident that in each of the areas in which Equitable was intimately involved, the residents wanted a part in the plans. So it was decided to actively seek out Negro mortgage firms which were approved FHA Mortgagors, to help channel company investments in local areas.

There are not too many of these firms available on a national basis and, in fact, it was possible to work out such arrangements with only six firms in the more than thirty cities in which investments or commitments were made.

At first glance, it had been assumed that the $83 million that was to be Equitable's participation in this national program would be in major investments (largely apartment houses and possibly some commercial structures). It soon became apparent, however, that the most expeditious way to get the program rolling was to invest in mortgages on one-to-four-family residences. These mortgages usually permitted the owner or purchaser to obtain terms which were more favorable than were previously available, and often provided financing where none was obtainable before.

In many cases our mortgages refinanced a first, and second, and even a third mortgage whose combined monthly payments were practically impossible for a Negro family seeking to establish itself as an owner in a community often characterized by absentee landlords. Very often these funds permitted the owner to rehabilitate his home, or he could use the difference because of the decrease in monthly payments to modernize or improve his dwelling.

A Sense of Community

Perhaps one of the greatest mistakes that has occurred over the years in the attempt to revitalize core areas of our cities has been the relentless use of bulldozers to level entire city blocks *before* a comprehensive plan for rebuilding has been established. If the residents had been involved, they would have advised the urban planners not to tear down block after block in their city without first having a place for them to live. Time after time, this bulldozer activity has resulted in the establishment of new ghetto areas—since the inhabitants had to go somewhere before their homes were leveled. And it always takes a long time—often many years—to rebuild the bulldozed areas.

Moreover, where rebuilding did take place, the facilities often included office buildings, hotels, parking garages, luxury and semi-luxury apartments. This may be desirable to improve the economic climate of the city, but it compounds the problems of the displaced residents.

In many cities, community organizations have sprung up. These organizations are vitally interested in their neighborhoods and can be extremely helpful in guiding the redevelopment of their areas. While almost all the money has to come from outside the community, no redevelopment should be planned without full consultation with the leaders of these community groups.

Emphasis on the involvement of community leaders in the planning and redevelopment of our city core areas has been increasingly recognized by many who are seeking solutions to urban problems. John W. Gardner, [then] Chairman of the Urban Coalition, said "the nation's underprivileged, particularly the American Negro, are no longer willing to have solutions cooked up in the back rooms of the Establishment and then served on a platter." Mr. Gardner has continually emphasized the need for granting a strong voice to the Negro in helping solve the urban crisis.

Participation

It seems advantageous not only to involve Negro leaders in the planning, but to obtain, to the maximum extent possible, the involvement of the citizens of the ghettos by ownership. Ownership participation should be pursued with great vigor, even though the ownership contributions may well be a small part of the total cost of any project. Not only does the black community wish to be consulted, it wants "a piece of the action."

And a piece of the action is what many groups *are* getting. In New York City, the Hunts Point Multi-Service Corporation, a neighborhood organization, is, with the approval of the New York City Welfare Department, attempting to erect a welfare office building which will be leased by the city. Since the local group has to approve the location, it seems logical that it own the building. Their plan envisages a Negro architect and contractor who will employ some of the local residents who are on welfare. This serves a twofold purpose:

1. Pride of ownership and benefits that derive from it.
2. Reduction in the number of welfare recipients which is now approaching one million in greater New York.

Of course, a problem that must be faced is the ever-present lack of equity. Renewed efforts must be made to eliminate this hurdle.

Successful urban renewal requires the participation of *all* community leaders—the various leadership elements in the community which include: business executives, leaders, union officials, educators, political leaders, minority group leaders, religious leaders, and news media. Very often, without continued newspaper publicity, an excellent program may founder. The news media can also serve to evaluate and criticize, to record progress (or lack of progress).

It is important not to minimize the problems. They will be substantial wherever members of the business community seek to obtain community participation in any project.

In one Midwest city there are no less than 16 community organizations seeking an active voice in the urban renewal programs. It is not unusual to find that factions develop in these groups—and sometimes it is nearly impossible to resolve the militant conflicts in views regarding where and when and how the rebuilding of their city is to take place. Still, we must not get too frustrated as we find that any fine plan can be torn to shreds by opposing factions. It is in such situations that the need for communication and education, and patience, too, could never be more obvious.

Partnership

Partnership actions must encompass three main objectives: education, jobs, and housing. All of the housing that money could provide would not help if the residents had no jobs to pay the rent. And no number of available jobs would help if they could not hold the jobs after they got them.

When one of the life insurance industry committees met with leading Negro groups, these points were raised:

▶ To help overcome the spirit of helplessness and frustration of the Negro community in core areas, positive encouragement is needed to aid in the development and expansion of business firms and institutions. These include stores, plants, savings institutions, medical facilities, and the full gamut of commercial establishments.

▶ The progress of the urban investment program would be greatly advanced if participating life insurance companies would draw upon the special knowledge of Negro concerns regarding financial conditions within urban core areas. By channeling life insurance funds through qualified Negro organizations there would be much greater assurance that such funds would reach the areas where the needs are most critical.

▶ One basic cause of economic deterioration within blighted core areas has been the withdrawal of profits from business establishments operating in these areas, rather than reinvestment of earnings to expand jobs, improve housing, and provide community facilities in core city neighborhoods.

Such points as these provide an insight into the thinking of the black population regarding the insurance industry investment program.

A Sense of Purpose

As the alternatives and the economics of urban crisis are examined, it must be concluded that industry and business have a responsibility above and beyond strictly economic concerns (though this alone may often be compelling) to solve the problems of the cities. It is also quite obvious that cooperation at all levels must be sought in order to get ahead with solutions promptly.

Cooperation must be sought in each area between business and labor, between black and white, between government at all levels and business leaders, so that a maximum of resources is applied in a way, and for an objective, that meets the community needs recommended by the community leaders who, in turn, have the task of explaining these programs to the residents of the areas involved.

The Model Cities Program, which provides for studying and resolving the principal problems under four main categories—social, physical, economic, and community involvement—is a good example of the detailed planning and analysis that must be accomplished to resolve the urban crisis. The program can be successful if it achieves a maximum of citizen participation in the committees selected to study and recommend appropriate solutions in the areas listed.

One has only to scan the newspapers to learn that there is no lack of new organizations devoted to solving the ghetto problems—from the Urban Coalition, organized nationally, to innumerable local groups in most of our cities—even in the smaller communities.

There are many examples of excellent community involvements: Action Housing's Rehabilitation Program in Pittsburgh, Pennsylvania; the Bedford-Stuyvesant program in Brooklyn, New York; and such rehabilitation and education programs as the Interfaith-Interracial Council of the Clergy in Philadelphia, Pennsyulvania, Flanner House in Indianapolis, Indiana, and the Bicentennial Civic Improvement Corporation in St. Louis, Missouri.

One group with exceptional leadership and goals is the National Medical Association, made up of 5,000 Negro doctors. They have formed the National Medical Association Foundation, a non-profit foundation whose primary purpose is to erect nursing homes and group practice facilities in the core areas of our cities. The group plans to teach and employ young Negroes as medical technicians. Equitable has approved a loan, with FHA guarantees, on a prototype in Washington, D.C. This facility has all the ingredients of the proper approach. The idea is that of the association, with private industry providing the financing. The federal government has aided this project through HUD (FHA) and HEW, and the Public Health Department of Washington, D.C., has included it in its neighborhood health program.

Another interesting new group is the Tuskegee Alumni Housing Foundation. Its representatives have met with Equitable officials to explore ways in which better housing can be obtained for residents in the core areas. As with the National Medical Association, the initiative is that of the foundation.

Whenever life insurance companies—and any other kind of business organization—are involved in any project in the core areas, it is imperative that they seek out the participation and involvement of the residents of the area where the project is planned. We must not be discouraged when many of these residents and their leaders do not understand our problems; indeed, they often do not understand their own problems. Bankers, insurance executives, and other leaders of business must be patient and expect many frustrating moments as we try to involve these people, who are unskilled in financing, planning or construction, to take an active part in rebuilding our cities.

Housing the Underhoused in the Inner City

Fred E. Case

Since the inception of the federally assisted housing program in 1934, almost 10 million units have been provided with various kinds of subsidies.[1] In fiscal year 1969, 198,000 subsidized units were produced; in fiscal year 1970, 308,000; and for fiscal 1971, 503,000 units.[2] However, the Douglas Commission has estimated that at least 600,000 units are needed annually in the decade of the 70s for families who will not be able to afford decent, safe, sanitary housing without some form of assistance.[3] These include families above the poverty line who would have had to pay more than 20 to 25 percent of the family income for decent housing if they had no subsidy. Typically 70 percent of all such families would be non-white, 30 percent white; nearly one-half would be 65 years of age or older; and almost all of these underhoused families would be living in a metropolitan area, with 56 percent located in central cities.

Although the assumption in most federal programs is that the problems of the underhoused are relatively similar, or at least should yield to a reasonable number of uniformly applied housing programs, examination of major metropolises and their inner cities reveals a greater diversity than can be treated adequately under current federal housing programs. Little hard data are available about the housing needs of the bulk of the underhoused families who are concentrated in the relatively small inner cities of our metropolises.[4] Even less is known about the neighborhoods in which these families live.

The total costs of providing new "adequate housing" for the inner-city's underhoused families cannot be estimated with any degree of accuracy, but could require 50 to 100 percent increases in the amounts invested in non-farm residential structures which have averaged three to seven percent of the Gross National Product, a diversion of the major thrust of the private-housing industry from its attention to the upper one-half of the residential-housing market, and significant changes in the public-sector investment in public facilities for inner-city neighborhoods. Such efforts seem hardly likely to be undertaken given the trend in federal housing policy in recent years.

The Douglas Commission sees the problem of providing better housing for inner-city families as one of sharp expansions in total housing production, particularly in housing for moderate- ($4000–8000 annually) and low-income ($3000 and below) families. President Nixon has announced a national goal of six million new housing units during the next ten years for such families.[5] The President's Task Force on Low-Income Housing outlines in broad statements a number of suggestions for providing more housing for low-income families, but the bulk of the proposals indicate the need for providing a better housing delivery system for underhoused families.[6]

Since the estimated new home cost in 1970 in the United States was $27,500, the existing home cost was $23,000, and mortgage interest rates were 8.0 to 9.0 percent or more, even moderate-income families could purchase homes, and they found rental units which they could afford only with great difficulty.[7] In 1966 less than 12 percent of the purchasers of homes insured by the FHA under Section 203 had incomes below $6000 annually.[8] And the annual rate of 135,000 low-rent public housing units anticipated by the Housing Act of 1949 has never been reached; instead the rate has averaged only between 122,400 (1962) and 133,400 (1967) units annually.[9]

Inner-city problems are immediate and increasing and cannot wait for significant changes in federal housing policies (see Table 1). If something more is to be achieved within the framework of present and projected federal housing programs and national economic policy, then more attention must be directed to preserving and improving the existing inner-city housing stock and to finding means by which private capital might be used more effectively in inner-city housing programs.

The need for a new approach is implicit in the Douglas Commission conclusion:

> The results achieved thus far under the existing programs related to housing for low- and moderate-income families and individuals have fallen far short of objectives. No substantial progress has been made in meeting the backlog of needs. Despite the magnitude of needs and the interest in urgent action on housing and other aspects of the urban crisis, a complex of factors has inhibited the full implementation of the program: (1) Fiscal limitations, (2) Congressional limitations, (3) Administrative restrictions, (4) Inhibitions at the community level, and (5) Limitations on private participation.[10]

Significant attention was given to the needs of the underhoused families in the Housing and Urban Development Act of 1968, but even if the program were funded to its full potential, "an unprecendented expansion in the rate of production will be required to reach these goals."[11]

Rather than search for new types of programs or suggest substantial increases in federal expenditures, a series of studies was conducted in nine U.S. cities (Atlanta, Georgia, Baltimore, Maryland, Fresno, California, Indianapolis, Indiana, Los Angeles, California, Memphis, Tennessee, Newark, New Jersey, Oakland, California, and San Diego, California) in order to identify programs which had been undertaken to meet

TABLE 1

Selected Housing Data for Standard Metropolitan Statistical Areas (SMSAs) of over 250,000 Population, Poverty Areas, Other Portions. 1960
(Housing Units in Thousands)

Item	Entire SMSAs			Central Cities			Outside Central Cities		
	Total	Within Poverty Areas	Outside Poverty Areas	Total	Within Poverty Areas	Outside Poverty Areas	Total	Within Poverty Areas	Outside Poverty Areas
Land area (thousands of square miles)	203.3	52.1	151.2	7.7	1.8	5.9	195.6	50.3	145.4
All housing units	31,200	6,993	24,207	16,477	5,481	10,996	14,723	1,512	13,211
Owner occupied	16,996	2,142	14,853	7,070	1,339	5,731	9,925	803	9,122
Occupied by nonwhites	1,039	639	400	1,767	520	247	271	119	152
Renter occupied	12,217	4,281	7,936	8,487	3,728	4,758	3,730	552	3,178
Occupied by nonwhites	2,004	1,601	403	1,774	1,476	278	250	125	126
Vacant	1,987	570	1,418	920	414	507	1,067	156	911
Substandard housing units	3,018	1,755	1,263	1,784	1,352	432	1,235	404	831
Dilapidated	920	530	390	517	393	124	403	137	266
Other	2,098	1,225	873	1,267	959	308	832	267	565
Housing units occupied by nonwhites	3,044	2,240	803	2,522	1,997	525	522	244	278
Substandard housing units	765	637	128	572	520	52	193	117	75
Occupied housing units	29,212	6,423	22,789	15,557	5,067	10,489	13,655	1,356	12,300
With recent movers	9,564	2,326	7,238	5,149	1,863	3,286	4,414	463	3,951
Occupied by whites	26,168	4,183	21,986	13,035	3,070	9,964	13,133	1,112	12,022
With recent movers	8,437	1,510	6,927	4,191	1,123	3,067	4,245	387	3,859
Occupied by nonwhites	3,044	2,240	803	2,522	1,997	525	522	244	278
With recent movers	1,127	816	311	958	740	219	169	76	92
Overcrowded housing units	2,933	1,141	1,792	1,650	895	755	1,283	245	1,037
Occupied by whites	2,206	577	1,628	1,069	410	659	1,137	166	970
Occupied by nonwhites	727	564	164	581	485	96	146	79	67
Housing units in structures over 20 years old	17,478	5,492	11,986	11,449	4,674	6,775	6,029	818	5,210
Occupied by nonwhites	2,?25	1,753	472	1,953	1,623	330	272	130	142

structures	2,154	253	2,407	4,786	3,497	8,283	6,940	3,750	10,690
Occupied by nonwhites	68	41	109	233	1,152	1,385	301	1,192	1,494
Housing units per square mile	91	30	75	1,874	3,071	2,150	160	134	153
Occupied units per square mile	85	27	70	1,787	2,839	2,030	151	123	144
Percentage of all housing units vacant	6.9	10.3	7.2	4.6	7.6	5.6	5.9	8.2	6.4
Percentage of all occupied units owner occupied	74.2	59.2	72.7	54.6	26.4	45.4	65.2	33.3	58.2
Percentage of nonwhite occupied:									
Of all occupied units	2.3	18.0	3.8	5.0	39.4	16.2	3.5	34.9	10.4
Of owner-occupied units	1.7	14.8	2.7	4.3	38.8	25.0	2.7	29.8	6.1
Percentage of substandard housing units:									
Of all units	6.3	26.7	8.4	3.9	24.7	10.8	5.2	25.1	9.7
Of nonwhite-occupied units	27.0	48.0	37.0	9.9	26.0	22.7	15.9	28.4	25.1
Dilapidated units as percentage of all substandard units	32.0	33.9	32.6	28.7	29.1	29.0	30.9	30.2	30.5
Percentage with recent movers:									
Of all occupied units	32.1	34.1	32.3	31.3	36.8	33.1	31.8	36.2	32.7
Of white-occupied units	33.1	31.1	32.4	41.7	37.1	38.0	38.7	36.4	37.0
Of nonwhite-occupied units	32.1	34.8	32.3	30.7	36.6	32.2	31.5	36.1	32.2
Percentage overcrowded:									
Of all occupied units	8.4	18.1	9.4	7.2	17.7	10.6	7.9	17.8	10.0
Of white-occupied units	8.1	14.9	8.7	6.6	13.4	8.2	7.4	13.8	8.4
Of nonwhite-occupied units	24.1	32.4	28.0	18.3	24.3	23.0	20.4	25.2	23.9
Percentage of units in structures over 20 years old:									
Of all housing units	39.4	54.1	40.9	61.6	85.3	69.5	49.5	78.5	56.0
Of nonwhite-occupied units	51.1	53.3	52.1	63.5	81.3	77.4	58.8	78.3	73.1
Percentage of units in multi-unit structures:									
Of all housing units	16.3	16.7	16.3	43.5	63.8	50.3	28.7	53.6	34.3
Of nonwhite-occupied units	24.7	16.8	20.9	44.4	57.7	54.9	37.5	53.2	49.1

Source: Douglas Commission [National Commission on Urban Problems], *Reports,* Vol. 9 (Washington, D.C.: Government Printing Office, 1968), 11–12.

the needs of underhoused inner-city families and to assess their successes and weaknesses. Implicit in the analysis was the assumption that private entrepreneurship can make a substantial and unique contribution to the solutions of inner-city housing problems. Particular attention was devoted to the combinations of private and public housing activities which seemed to best serve the needs of core areas. An important question was whether private businessmen should be expected to limit or forgo their profits substantially and to act primarily as social agencies when participating in inner-city housing developments involving low-income persons and families.

The analysis rejected the notion that market forces, unaided or as administered under present federal housing policies, would produce anywhere near the needed volume of inner-city housing. For example, studies in Newark indicated clearly that the filter method of providing low-cost housing is inadequate to the needs of inner-city families. The changes which have occurred in the economic well-being of the general population appear to have inhibited rather than accelerated the providing of inner-city housing, and the announcements by federal, state, and local governments of future freeway routes, long-range land use plans, and the need for higher property tax returns have become reasons for doing little or nothing about inner-city housing markets.

The Urban Building Block

The methodology used in the research was based upon the observation that programs which treated housing problems in aggregate terms have typically served only the needs of the middle- and upper-income portions of the housing market. Apparently there are families in the market who are too poor, too old or too young, too prejudiced against, and too little understood to benefit from current housing programs. This assumption was reinforced by a conclusion of the Douglas Commission that

> the problem for analysis is that, in a period of affluence, the pockets of poverty phenomena do not emerge in the aggregate city-wide data. These gaps in prosperity can be unearthed only through the mining of small-area data: census tracts and blocks. . . . City-wide data that also reflect new development in the suburban or vacant land sectors or the city, such as New York's Queens and Richmond burroughs, tend to overshadow the declining areas of the city. . . . to the local community, however, this phenomenon spells disaster in terms of its resource ability to deal with concentrations of deterioration while newly developed areas, totally without many essential facilities, make insistent demands for service. The fact that the problem does not appear to be worsening over time, in terms of the aggregates, simply indicates that its magnitude is not as great from the standpoint of the potential charge against national resources compared with the diminishing tax base of a large proportion of the individual communities. . . . To date, however, the problem has not been accepted as national in terms of resource allocations of the Federal Government. In this sense, it can be said

that [to] the extent that the rural Negro poverty problems of America and the rural poverty problem of Puerto Rico have been transferred to concentrated central-city slums, local communities are being saddled with a problem of national concern.[12]

Equally important as the lack of disaggregated data relating to central-city housing problems is the tendency to emphasize central-city problems in terms of the slums of our largest cities. Large cities with many sources of financial support appear to attract the most attention when housing programs are being initiated, even though the evidence suggests that central-city problems of middle and small size American cities are proportionately more acute and much more poorly funded.[13] For this reason, cities studied in this report are in the middle to small range, typically averaging about one million (more-or-less) in population.

In other words, in this study we advanced the proposition that much more can be learned about urban problems and the potentials for solving them by turning from our preoccupation with the largest cities and focusing on the neighborhoods and the disaggregated data of modest-size cities. The sheer magnitude of the inner-city problems of the largest cities seem to defy any solutions. Perhaps we are saying implicitly that the biggest cities should be abandoned to their own resources, whatever they may be, confident that these cities, faced with ultimate disaster, can marshal the resources and talents sufficient to their needs but that smaller cities cannot do this.

Housing Problems of the Inner Cities

The details of the studies completed in the nine cities are presented in a series of six technical reports, but a summary of major concepts is presented here as exemplary of efforts which have provided inner-city housing in some of these cities.[14] Some of these concepts are peculiar to the cities in which they were developed, but they suggest ways in which the private sector can use imagination, innovation, and determination to achieve unexpectedly fruitful results. Some of these concepts are not new but are re-stated or given a different emphasis which has made them useful in inner-city housing programs. The values of these concepts lie in their origins in successful and unsuccessful housing programs used in the nine study cities. Few of these concepts are offered, therefore, as generalities applicable to all cities; but a major conclusion from the analyses is that the inventive imaginations of private businessmen and public officials who are determined to do something about inner-city housing can build on these concepts to meet their local city's problems.

Defining the Inner City and the Underhoused

Precision in definition usually leads to precision in solving problems, but even reasonable precision is illusive, if not misleading, when inner cities and underhoused families are defined. Data on these topics proved inconclusive, frequently contradictory and misleading, and often incomplete when used to define the nature of the housing problem to be solved.[15] More importantly, the most successful inner-city lenders and builders developed their understanding of the special needs of inner-city families through the cultivation of an understanding of the nonquantifiable aspects of inner-city housing problems.

The term "inner city" is misleading if it is assumed to be some portion of the older inner city, a predominantly minority population area, a poverty area, or a decayed, abandoned area. All of these qualities can be found in inner-city areas, but they do not give the full flavor of such an area. The inner city is characterized by a heavy concentration of the most acute physical, economic, social, and political problems of the city.[16] In some instances efforts to meet the requirements for receiving a Model Cities Program have produced the most effective delineation of the inner-city underhoused.[17]

The inner city is an area of deprivation, in which housing deprivations are the most important element.[18] In Baltimore, William Grigsby concluded that "although higher income might ultimately solve most of the shelter problems of the poor, the problems themselves are frequently a direct and indirect barrier to these incomes." In addition, if one looks at the standards of living which families experience and not at just their level of income, it is evident that being deprived with respect to housing is as much a part of what it means to be poor as is low income itself. The development of alternative programs and the establishment of priorities among housing programs require detailed client analysis with emphasis on personal, rather than institutional or research, terms.

More inner-city families than might be suspected are upwardly mobile, but their needs are obscured in those housing programs which treat inner-city problems as essentially or exclusively poverty problems; yet problems of poverty families are similar in many ways to the inner-city families who cannot improve their lot and to those families who are suffering declining fortunes. The improvement of substandard housing conditions has to start with measurements of population, income, race, tenure, age, sex of head of household and family size as a means of suggesting policy directions, but the more detailed case-by-case personal analysis is needed if programs are to be pinpointed to the real needs of underhoused families.

Inner cities are diverse in nature so that proposals for wholesale removal of existing housing and replacement with new and modern housing suggests a need for greater resources and larger programs than may be necessary. There are in inner cities many pockets of modest, even occasionally luxurious residential units usually populated by families who choose to stay in the inner city even though they might move elsewhere.

Success and Failures in Inner-City Housing Programs

If only one conclusion were to be drawn from the studies of the nine cities it would be that there are viable residential real estate and mortgage-

lending markets in inner cities, but these markets have special characteristics and problems which must be recognized and dealt with imaginatively if the market potentials are to be exploited successfully. Finding
solutions to inner-city housing programs requires attention to the major
considerations relating to inner-city characteristics as a housing market; a
change in lenders' procedures and lending policies; unique treatment of
inner-city borrowers; renewed efforts by the public sector with special
attention to the inner-city "community," and a restatement of market
principles for inner-city housing markets. However, since private industry must make a profit in servicing these markets, approximately one-
third to 40 percent of the market will require maximum kinds of subsidies.
In other words, inner-city markets represent a substantial minority of
metropolitan markets, but only a minor portion of these markets requires
the kinds of subsidies associated with full or major supplementation of
family income.

The development of an effective housing-supply system for inner-city.
markets requires the creation of programs and policies in five areas:

1. Attention to the inner city, its characteristics, its variety and its stability,
2. Inner-city lending and lender programs,
3. Inner-city borrowers,
4. The public sector and the inner-city community,
5. The inner city as a market area.

Inner-City Characteristics

Although much has been written about the inner city, there are really
very few accurate or complete data on the characteristics of the inner city
and the persons who live there. Any program of mortgage lending or
housing supply in the inner city, therefore, has to start with a careful
inventory of the special characteristics of the inner city in which the
programs are to be developed. The inner city of Baltimore, for example,
consists of rows of housing built closely together around special kinds of
courts. It's a very old area, where some of the earliest housing in the
United States was built. The substantial quality of the brick construction,
the strong sense of culture that has been built in these areas suggest that
this is where rehabilitation might be effective. On the other hand, in
Atlanta the inner city consists of street after street of flimsy wooden
structures in poor stages of repair so that this inner city would have to be
totally rebuilt. The problem in Atlanta is compounded by the fact that
most of the inner city is populated by Negro families. On the other hand,
in the Fresno inner city there are all kinds of structures and all kinds of
racial mixtures.

Variety in the inner city

Inner-city housing is not homogeneous in character. There are frequently islands of excellent housing mixed in with the decayed slum

housing which most of us associate with inner cities. An examination of the inner city in Los Angeles revealed pockets of good housing owned by people with good credit ratings, with the result that one lender who attempted inner-city lending found the potential for more than 400 loans in areas where he had never really attempted to make such loans. A major problem facing the lender, therefore, is to examine the inner city and to classify it according to risks which are found there and the kinds of loan treatments which are needed by the people who own the properties in those areas. The varieties of neighborhoods, properties, and life styles in the inner city and their profit potentials are not appreciated by the lenders and the builders who could provide housing and financial assistance in these areas.

Stability of inner-city property values and lenders' expectations

Mortgage lenders are willing to make high percentage loans on suburban properties, because they expect prices to increase sufficiently to provide a continuously comfortable margin between the amount of the loan and the value of the property. On the other hand, these same lenders feel that in the inner city these kinds of price increase do not occur and that probably property values and loan margins will shrink to almost nothing or perhaps even disappear. Evidence about what happens to property values in the inner city is very mixed, but in our surveys we found inner-city areas in which property values were not only stable but did increase as inflationary influences increased. These properties do not represent the high quality of security of the suburban properties, but nevertheless they do provide a consistent, if narrow margin between loan value and property value. There are costs, of course, to finding these areas and identifying particular loan policies which should be associated with them, so that the profit margin on such loans may not be as great as lenders would require.

Durability of the inner-city housing inventory

In none of the inner cities included in this study was there any substantial amount of new construction under way. In fact, in some instances not even rehabilitation or modernization was being undertaken. On the other hand, the inner-city housing is remarkable stable. Since there is small chance that a substantial amount of new construction will be provided in the inner city, some cities have started programs to preserve the existing inner-city housing. This is not an effort to "gild the ghetto" but rather a recognition of the hard fact that if inner-city families are to be provided housing, they will have to find it in the current inventory. Improving the current inventory, therefore, takes care of some of the more immediate problems of inner-city families and provides some breathing space until federal and private groups can find more appropriate and effective ways of housing inner-city families. In Baltimore, for example, an investment of as little as $1000 per unit could make many of the deteriorated units reasonable living places for inner-city families. But the rate of deterioration of these units in Baltimore is accelerating, and unless something is done immediately, the entire inventory could very well be lost.

Inner-City Lending and the Lenders

In this study we made no effort to measure the profitableness or lack of profitableness of inner-city lending efforts. We assumed that the lenders were interested in making inner-city housing loans and that the decisions about profit would have to be made after they had studied the area and experimented with making loans in it. Again, we refer to the diversity that is found in inner cities and believe that a study of profitableness of lending in one inner city would provide very little information useful in another inner city. The general opinion among many institutional lenders is that unless the private segment makes a serious effort to move in voluntarily, federal regulatory authorities are likely to require those who specialize in home lending to place a portion of their lending portfolios in the inner cities even when profits are minimal. The conclusions and recommendations in this section suggest ways in which lenders can maximize their profit potential if they decide to enter inner-city lending markets.

Risk analysis

Home lenders have concentrated on providing credit for the suburbs and have not have the experience in lending in inner-city markets which would help them evaluate the risks and the associated problems. When normal lending policies and risk analysis are used as a basis for providing credit in the inner city, they prove to be inadequate for three reasons:

1. They do not match the kind of lending risks which exist there. Essentially these risks are related to the difficulties that borrowers will have in meeting regular loan payment requirements, and the potential that the property on which the loan has been made might be examined for code violations and might have to be demolished.

2. They do not provide for sufficient and complete credit evaluation which would uncover the real nature of the credit problems to be anticipated if the loan is made. Typically, an inner-city resident has intermittent employment, which means that he can probably make home payments only ten or eleven months in a year. Loan penalties may create a situation in which he is unable to make any payments. Inner-city families usually have to spend up to 30 or 35 percent of their family incomes in order to acquire even modest shelter, so that any increases in the amounts they have to pay because of penalties puts an almost impossible strain on their budgets.

3. They do not anticipate the kind of credit-collection problems which are found in inner cities. Because the family income is so low, a

crisis of any kind may cause the family to decide not to make a loan payment. On the other hand, lenders who have worked in the inner city understand that these families would be willing to make at least a partial payment if they were given the opportunity. Therefore, credit collection becomes a fine art in which an experienced collector understands how to balance the needs of his organization against the needs of the family which owes the money.

Viable lending policies

In order to have a satisfactory lending experience in inner cities, lenders must consider three things in setting up their lending policies:

1. Land uses are in a constant state of change in the inner city. This change results from the introduction of freeways, urban-renewal programs, model city programs, and the fact that the zoning in many inner cities is so outdated that almost any kind of a use can be undertaken because a variance is easily obtained. Most mortgage lenders do not understand how to deal with this kind of change.

2. Even the inner-city families who have overall good credit records typically could not qualify under the standards which lenders now enforce. This is true because of their low income, their minority status, and their special cultural problems which make the evaluation of them for home-lending credit a difficult process.

3. Contracts for home lending in the inner city have to be drawn in such a way that the lending officer has some flexibility in enforcement. In the inner city, each loan considered has to be treated as a unique process in which the lending officer balances the borrower's needs and the earning potential which was represented in the contract, the quality of the security, and alternative procedures to prevent the loan from going into foreclosure.

Know the territory

The most successful inner-city loans are made by loan officers who have been operating in those areas for some time and who understand the inner-city life styles and values. Loan officers who are transferred to inner-city branches from the suburbs should be given at least a 6- to 12-month education and retraining program if they are to make successful inner-city mortgage loans.

Flexibility in negotiating delinquencies

Income interruption and unemployment are constant problems for inner-city families. Any lender who provides funds must anticipate that loan payments will be interrupted. When this occurs, the lending officer must understand how to work with the family in order to help it solve its financial problems. He may have to be willing to take a smaller payment,

payment only on interest, or even to postpone the entire payment if this will solve the immediate pressing income problem of the family. Mortgage lenders should understand that housing is so diffuclt to obtain in the inner city that most families, whether renters or owners, will go to great lengths to protect the housing which they now occupy for fear they will not be able to get the same quality if they are forced to leave.

Large lenders and problems of internal communications

Some of the major institutional lenders have engaged in limited programs of inner-city home mortgage lending. A survey of what is actually happening in these programs suggests that local lending officers have been trained in the traditional methods of mortgage lending and simply cannot or will not adapt themselves to the requirements of inner-city lending programs. When some of these lending officers were queried about their problems, they said they felt it was incumbent upon them to protect the stockholders of the institutions for which they worked, or they said they couldn't understand why they should provide loans to poor people who were relatively undeserving while the people who were working hard and earned consistently but had low incomes couldn't get the same types of loans and terms. Such officers were extremely selective in the kind of inner-city lending which they were doing, and not really carrying out the lending policies which had been announced by the institutions for which they were working.

Inner-City Borrowers

Several allusions have been made in the previous paragraphs to the special problems associated with inner-city borrowers. Some of these problems and ways in which they can be dealt with are discussed in these paragraphs.

Lack of access to any kind of credit

Many inner-city families have such low incomes that they have not had access to normal kinds of credit and do not understand the credit processes. Some of them have had the experience of having their wages garnisheed or had other difficulties connected with the purchase of goods and services which have led them to shy away from the use of any kind of credit. They prefer to avoid institutional lenders who might provide more reasonable terms and credit, on the assumption that these lenders would be even more reluctant to approve credit for a loan. This is unfortunate, because many of these families would represent good credit risks for the typical lending institution, but these families have to be discovered.

In other words, even though a lender may announce that he is providing loans for inner-city families, some of the most deserving and qualified families will avoid taking advantage of these opportunities simply because they are afraid of all institutional lenders. One implication of this is that not only do lenders have to announce the programs, but they must engage in a vigorous search effort to find families who will qualify for the programs.

Alien debtor values

Borrowers of the inner city are constantly being bombarded by all kinds of "shady" propositions. There are many sellers who go into the inner city with the full intention of taking advantage of the ignorance of inner-city families. Some sellers do this unintentionally, assuming that if families agree to buy cars, even though the cars may be an extravagance, the families understand what they are doing. When inner-city families realize that what they have agreed to purchase is not equal to the price which they are paying for it or that it represents an unwarranted extravagance, they frequently refuse to pay additional amounts. This entails foreclosure or seizure of the property and more importantly, creates a permanent record of a bad credit reputation for that family.

A sense of obligation to repay

Lenders frequently refuse to provide loans to inner-city families on the assumption that these families have not developed a sufficient sense of the need to repay credit according to contract terms. The lenders point to the records of credit collection difficulties which are found for many inner-city families. Apparently, modern credit practices are such that a bad credit record follows a family wherever it may go, even though in many cases the family has overcome the difficulties which led to the original bad record. Unfortunately, even though the family may now have good credit records, it is unable to get credit because of its poor early credit history.

Home mortgage lenders can anticipate that most of the credit problems of inner-city families will be related to one or more of the following:

1. Medical problems—the typical low-income large inner-city family cannot afford medical insurance so that an accident or an illness which might be no problem to the typical middle-income family represents a financial catastrophe for such a family. The large numbers of children in these families usually lead to a series of medical hardships or accidents which prevent the families from meeting their other credit obligations on a regular basis.

2. Marital problems—there is a high incidence of marital breakups among inner-city families; there are many one-parent families, and usually this one parent has a great difficulty in adjusting family income to family needs. On the other hand, these families consistently exhibit a willingness to pay their debts if they can only be given an opportunity to do so and if they are provided with a program which will match their capacities.

3. Large low-income families—the most typical reason for credit difficulties in the inner cities is that families are too large and incomes too

low and too intermittent. Frequently the family has to make a choice between paying for food or shelter, or paying for utilities, transportation, clothes, and other items. When faced with this choice, families usually prefer to pay for the house or to pay for food, and then to meet their other obligations. However, when they are forced by the credit collection policies of the non-mortgage lenders to make payments which are beyond their expectations or capacities, then the mortgage lending payments suffer.

The major problem with inner-city families is that they are constantly being enticed to use more credit than they should, and for the wrong kinds of items. For example, in one of our cities, free credit cards were distributed among the inner-city families. Because some of the families did not understand the full implications of such cards, they incurred debts which they could never hope to repay. Such families, however, should be balanced among the large number of them who have reformed their credit habits after having had a bad incident, because they now understand that they must not use credit in a way that injures their ability to borrow.

It is the historical credit records of inner-city families which give an impression that almost every inner-city family is a bad borrowing risk and will not want to repay its obligations. Perhaps one indication that even those who get into credit difficulty are really interested in repaying can be found in the experiences in Fresno in which a number of inner-city families chose to accept bankruptcy but still attempted to work out with their creditors ways in which they could settle the full amounts of the claims which existed.

Multiple loans and family emergencies

Many inner-city families have had to face financial emergencies by obtaining second and third mortgages on their homes. Whenever a new home lending program is announced, these families find that removing the mortgages on their properties is too difficult and too expensive. For this reason they do not attempt to take advantage of opportunities to remodel, to repair, or even to buy new homes. Some lenders have found that they could solve this problem by finding ways in which the families could pay off those extra high-cost loans and consolidate them into a single loan which provided for payments which were manageable within the family resources.

The Public Sector and the Inner-City "Community"

In many ways, the inner cities represent some of the most neglected areas in terms of public services and facilities. The insistent demands of the suburbs, the ability of the suburbs to provide political power and revenue usually force most public officials to give the bulk of their attention to the needs of suburban homeowners. The inner city is looked at only in terms of its requirements for police protection, welfare, and other services which are considered to be a drain on city resources. As a result of the attitudes of public officials and the general public with respect to the inner city, inner cities continue to become almost abandoned areas in terms of the public services and facilities provided to them.

Irrational public actions

Because public officials frequently fail to see the inner city as a family-living area for those who must or who choose to live there, these officials frequently engage in what are irrational attitudes and practices with respect to the properties in these areas. These irrational practices find outlets in the assessments for tax purposes, code enforcement, and the provision of facilities and services to the inner city. This, perhaps as much as anything else, contributes to the decay of property in the inner city. It is these practices which have been given so much prominence and so many other kinds of reports, and they are mentioned here only as a reinforcement of the recommendation that attention be given to remedying these problems. It is interesting to note that in Los Angeles, in the period between 1960 and 1965, even though the inner-city area had been neglected and was decaying, there were many properties which continued to have stable property values or even some increases. Property values in some portions of the South Central Los Angeles riot area had increased by as much as 15 to 20 percent even in the five years following the 1965 riots.

Security for residential loans

The typical property offered for security in the inner city is usually far below the quality and maintenance levels of properties in the suburbs. Inner-city properties are older and sometimes in poor repair, located in neighborhoods which are deteriorating. One of the major reasons why these properties are such poor loan security risks is action by the city. For example, such areas are frequently zoned for industrial uses or commercial uses, and these uses may be there even though the area is a predominantly residential area and has been for some time. When the city fails to maintain these areas for residential purposes, more and more families find maintenance of their properties impossible, and more and more landlords see little reason to keep their properties maintained.

A rather unique experience was found in Oakland where wooden curbs were provided in lieu of cement curbs in some of the older inner-city areas. Lenders in such areas will not provide mortgage loans unless the wooden curbs are replaced by cement curbs, but the city will not replace the curbs without charging the homeowner. The homeowner cannot pay for these new curbs without a loan, and he cannot get a loan until the new curbs are installed. It is this "wooden curb syndrome" or variations of it, which are found in many inner-city areas and which provide the gordian knot for those trying to encourage a flow of funds into inner-city areas for property modernization and rehabilitation.

Community participation

Many home lending programs include provision for some kind of community participation, usually through some form of organized community group. The experiences which occurred in our nine study cities were quite mixed, and a great deal more needs to be known about community participation processes before the requirement for participation by organized community groups is included in housing programs. Frequently there are several groups vying for control of a given inner-city area so that they can get the prestige, money, or other advantages that would come with being associated with such programs. Frequently, these community groups are headed by persons who seek to maintain their popularity and their power by trying to obtain for their communities a great deal more than what the communities really want or need. It is these kinds of leaders who mislead the communities and who destroy many of the programs which have been undertaken to help the inner cities.

Sometimes, when those who are trying to introduce home lending programs to the inner city, are faced with "difficult community groups," they pick out the trouble makers and make them the leaders, then attempt to deal with these leaders. This procedure simply complicates the problem of solving inner-city housing market problems. Too many institutional lenders do not understand the nature of inner-city life and, when faced with an inner-city group which is headed by militants or which is composed of what seems to be radical or left-wing groups, write the whole inner-city community program off as being dangerous and too much of an effort.

There is an art to working with community groups in the inner city which can be learned only through hard experience, and it is this art which most lenders must acquire if they are going to have viable inner-city programs.

The nonprofit corporation

Increasing consideration is being given to the creation of nonprofit organizations which can undertake inner-city housing programs. In fact, there are some federal housing programs which require that such corporations be created before the funds can be secured. Again, the experience with nonprofit corporations is mixed, but on the whole it is disastrous. In Indianapolis, for example, a major corporation made substantial donations to a nonprofit corporation in an effort to help it provide inner-city housing, but the effort finally failed. After more than a year's efforts in Indianapolis, the corporation finally wrote off several hundreds of thousands of dollars which it had donated to nonprofit corporations who were going to provide inner-city housing in Indianapolis.

Unfortunately, many such nonprofit corporations are organized as a collection of equals who will use democratic processes to decide what should be done, when it should be done, and how it should be done. These amateur efforts typically lead to disaster since the providing of inner-city housing is a highly complex matter that requires professional technicians to work on it. Calling the organization nonprofit is misleading since no business organization can stay in operation unless one of its objectives is the making of some profit with the expectation that a small profit margin goal may actually lead to a nonprofit operation; but at least a goal should lead to covering all the costs of operations.

Federal programs

The experiences with federal programs were quite mixed in the nine cities which were studied. In some cities, such as Fresno, the regional FHA officers worked closely with local builders and lenders to inaugurate 235 and 236 programs, and these programs are proving most effective. On the other hand, in other cities the requirements imposed by regional federal housing officials were such that the programs were never undertaken. In some cases, the regional officers appear to be unwilling or unable to understand the risks associated with providing housing in the inner city. As a result, they often imposed requirements which would certainly protect the federal agency but which frequently lead to bankruptcy for the builder attempting to use FHA programs. For example, in Indianapolis, one case took eighteen months and a re-submission of the same forms several times in order to get clearance to start a program which was to be supported through federal funds.

The regional offices which were most successful in aiding inner-city programs usually have in them FHA experts who understand inner-city problems and who will, when necessary, communicate directly with the Washington central office or with the appropriate officials in order to clear away regulations which are inappropriate for the project at hand. In fact, one large builder in Fresno maintains on his staff a man who has no other task except to communicate with the FHA, at the local office, the regional office, and in Washington, in order to facilitate the interpretation of regulations or the submission of forms affecting inner-city lending programs.

The long tradition which the FHA has had in dealing with suburban properties frequently means that its local officers are not at all comfortable working in inner-cities where properties, borrowers and neighborhoods are quite different from those with which they have worked in the past.

The Inner City as a Market Area

Builders have as great difficulty as lenders in understanding how to operate successfully in the inner-city market areas. Methods of construction, property types, and other practices which are successful in the suburbs cannot really be adapted to inner-city housing needs. Instead, new and imaginative efforts must be undertaken after a careful analysis of the needs of each of the particular inner cities in which new housing is to be supplied.

Technology, land assembly, and scale

As an inner city ages, the removal of residential properties sometimes accelerates, and the rate of removal is never again matched by an equal volume of new additions. Code enforcement, rehabilitation, modernization can relieve the pressures created by removals to a limited extent, but clearly some means has to be found to provide a substantial volume of new housing in the inner city. In cities such as Memphis, a reasonable amount of new housing was provided by building it in some of the close-in outlying suburban areas. In Chicago, prefabricated units were moved in very successfully by two different housing corporations. But the one lesson which can be learned from these successful efforts is that unless those who have some power in the local community exhibit a "political" will which will overcome the various kinds of local restrictions which always exist, new housing is not likely to be provided for inner-city families.

Although the technologies which can provide new housing were not investigated in this study, the possibilities of using these technologies were analyzed. The major conclusion which came out of these investigations was that unless large parcels of land could be assembled on a sufficient scale to warrant the development of special kinds of prefabrication programs for inner cities, this solution was not viable at this time. In other words, there are varieties of technologies which can produce the kind of housing needed in the inner cities' but the character of the land and land ownership in the inner city is such that sufficient volumes of vacant land cannot be provided to warrant the creation of special corporations which could use the technologies which now exist to build new inner-city housing.

Markets and marketing

Most inner-city families appear to have resigned themselves to accepting whatever housing happens to be available or provided for them. They do not see themselves as taking the initiative in finding or asking for the kind of housing they want. They have not had the opportunity of going into markets where they can make a selection among various kinds of housing or make their demands known. As a result, both builders and lenders must expect to go out into the inner-city community and use interviews or other devices to find those families who may have given up hope but who could be convinced that they should be interested in securing some of the new housing or some of the new loans which could be provided under the inner-city lending programs.

Long-term problems and solutions and short-term needs

The numerous studies which have been made about the housing needs of inner-city families tend to summarize their findings by stating the problem in large terms requiring large solutions. Unfortunately, most of these solutions require resources and programs which do not seem to be contemplated in national economic policy. Moreover, all of these reports appear to have stated the problems and have suggested solutions in general terms but not the necessary details which would permit implementation of their recommendations.

An examination of the literature related to housing problems of inner-city families suggests that consistently this nation has attempted to ease its national conscience through a series of studies which manage to define the problems in such ways that they will yield only to long-term solutions. At some point it will be necessary to face up to the problem that the inner-city families have housing needs which are current, immediate, and requiring attention now. Some agency, some program must go first in aiding inner cities. Federal housing officials frequently explain their actions as doing what they can with the resources provided to them and in accordance with instructions received from Washington. At the national level, economic policy apparently assigns housing a somewhat minor role and the provision of housing for inner-city families is only a portion of the total federal housing effort. Under these circumstances, it would appear that if anything substantial is to be done for inner-city housing programs, then the private sector must find ways of multiplying available federal housing programs and resources in ways which will produce more inner-city housing per dollar than has been possible in the past.

A delivery system

In every inner city that was studied, a variety of efforts were being made to provide housing. None of them were especially large, but unfortunately few of them appear to be cooperating with each other in an effort to increase their efficiency and to multiply the results which they could achieve. More importantly, the problem of providing housing had been viewed as essentially temporary in nature with the principal reliance on some kind of subsidies to those who are demanding housing.

One of our tentative conclusions, which is supported to some extent by other studies but which really needs additional verification, is that housing is a part of a cycle which is involved with the kind of education and training that inner-city residents receive, the kind of business or employment opportunities they have, the amount of family income which can be earned, the ability of the family to obtain housing, and the kind of neighborhood and housing which the families can afford or which they get. A careful cost-benefit analysis of inner cities and their housing might show that the extent to which any element of the cycle is neglected is the extent to which the public sector pays an increasingly greater cost for ignoring the total problems of inner-city families. If poor housing leads to poor family life, which makes education difficult to obtain, which therefore leads to poor employment opportunities, then we must ask whether there is not a social cost associated with this process, which finds outlets in higher police costs, higher fire protection costs, higher welfare costs, and generally higher public service costs to inner-city families.

NOTES

1. U.S., Department of Housing and Urban Development, *1968 HUD Statistical Yearbook* (Washington, D.C.: U.S. Government Printing Office, 1969).

2. *Second Annual Report on Housing Goals*, Message from the President of the United States, 91st Cong., 2nd Sess., House Document No. 91–292.

3. *A Decent Home*, The Report of the President's Committee on Urban Housing (Kaiser Committee), (Washington, D.C.: U.S. Government Printing Office, 1968), p. 3.

4. *Urban Housing Needs through the 1980's: An Analysis and Projection*, Research Report No. 10, National Commission on Urban Problems (Douglas Commission), (Washington, D.C.: U.S. Government Printing Office, 1968), p. xi.

5. *Housing America's Low- and Moderate-Income Families*, Research Report No. 7, National Commission on Urban Problems (Douglas Commission), (Washington, D.C.: U.S. Government Printing Office, 1968), p. 1.

6. *Toward Better Housing for Low-Income Families*, The Report of the President's Task Force on Low-Income Housing (Washington, D.C.: U.S. Government Printing Office, May 1970).

7. U.S., Department of Housing and Urban Development, *Housing Statistics* (Washington, D.C.: U.S. Government Printing Office, May 1970).

8. Douglas Commission Research Report No. 7, p. 1.

9. *Ibid.*, p. 5.

10. *Ibid.*, pp. 13–20.

11. *Ibid.*, p. 21.

12. Douglas Commission Research Report No. 10, p. 49.

13. *Housing Conditions in Urban Poverty Areas*, National Commission on Urban Problems (Douglas Commission), (Washington, D.C.: U.S. Government Printing Office, 1968), Table 8, pp. 14–19.

14. Technical Statements of the Housing the Underhoused Project: Carl J. Tschappat, "Housing the Underhoused in Atlanta, Georgia" (Georgia State University), Wm. Grigsby, *et al.*, "Housing and Poverty in Baltimore, Maryland" (University of Pennsylvania), Fred E. Case, *et al.*, "Housing the Underhoused in California" (UCLA), Dr. George Bloom and Thomas L. Lemon, "Housing the Underhoused in Inner City Indianapolis, Indiana" (Indiana University), P. R. Lowry, *et al.*, "The Underhoused of Memphis" (Memphis State University), and George Sternlieb, *et al.*, "Housing Costs and Housing Restraints in Newark, New Jersey" (Rutgers University).

15. Douglas Commission Research Report No. 7, and *More than Shelter: Social Needs in Low- and Moderate-Income Housing*, National Commission on Urban Problems (Douglas Commission), (Washington, D.C.: U.S. Government Printing Office, 1968), Research Report No. 8.

16. Newark Technical Statement, p. 24.

17. Indianapolis and Atlanta Technical Statements.

18. Baltimore Technical Statement.

Black Central Cities:
Dispersal or Rebuilding

Peter Labrie

It is a widespread practice to hold the ghetto responsible for much of the burgeoning financial burden which metropolitan areas are currently experiencing. The increasing fiscal and administrative pressures placed upon central city governments to enable them to provide adequate municipal facilities and services for their large black and lower-income resident population, and the demand for more expensive transportation systems to handle the expanding traffic flows between the central city and the fringe are examples of these burdens. Indeed, John F. Kain states that the ghetto has "produced" these imbalances. But this is not historically accurate. Imbalances among population, housing, and employment growth have always been a part of American urban development. Housing production has always lagged behind population growth, both nationally and locally. The physical and social manifestations of housing shortages predominate, of course, in the overcrowded and deteriorated residential areas of the central cities. The point is that the black population has been a prime recipient of imbalances inherent in American urban growth. Problems resulting from these imbalances have been compounded by the black population's greater degree of poverty inherited from slavery and the plantation system of the South and the huge volumes and rapid rates of their urban migrations. These complications have undoubtedly accelerated the white suburban flow, aggravated metropolitan transportation problems, and increased the fiscal and administrative burdens of central city governments. However, it will help to take a closer look at the underlying ramifications of some of these problems.

It has been pointed out, for example, that the increase of blue-collar jobs in the suburbs and of white-collar jobs in the central cities is ironically creating numerous travel difficulties for both lower-income, central-city residents traveling to work in the suburbs and upper-income, suburban residents traveling to work in central cities. It would, of course, be more efficient to have the population living near its place of employment. But to what extent have urban areas ever developed efficiently? Don't urban residents continually absorb public inefficiencies to realize private choices? They have continually shown this by their widespread preference for the automobile over public transportation, which produces increased congestion and numerous other traffic problems. After all, as is so often stated, transportation is a function of land use. Transportation problems are a function of a host of land-use choices made by urban residents, private enterprises, and public agencies. In the case of the metropolitan racial situation, the trend toward predominantly white upper-income suburbs and predominantly black lower-income central cities evidently means that residents are willing to absorb the transportation costs and difficulties mentioned by the Douglas Commission[1] in order to maintain their respective residential environments. Planners may entertain the possibility of rearranging residential land uses to meet this particular transportation problem, but it would mean putting the cart before the horse. It would be absurd to hold that land uses can or should be considerably rearranged to satisfy transportation efficiencies, even if these efficiencies could be adequately defined.

The Ghetto and the Decline of the Central City

Another point needs to be considered in regard to claims that the huge influx of black and other lower-income groups to the central city, coupled with the exodus of the upper-income white groups to the suburbs, has led to the decline and decay of the central city. Many analysts go so far as to state that the spread of metropolitan economic growth outward to the suburbs means that the central cities have no more potential for further growth. For example, Linda and Paul Davidoff write that

> the decentralizing forces of American life are not reversible. The absence of vacant land within central cities, coupled with the existence of an enormous supply of vacant land on the urban periphery, will not permit a major expansion of the employment capacity of central cities. Public programs that seek only to rebuild the central city housing stock and to encourage industry to locate within central cities and within ghettos run counter to the movement of the private economy.

Yet more intensive analyses of metropolitan economic decentralization have revealed that there is potential for growth in the central cities but that meaningful policies for realizing this potential are lacking. To be sure, as the Davidoffs and Gold point out, the land situation in the central cities is tight and the suburbs offer more room for development. The economic function of the central city is declining both relatively and absolutely in relation to the suburbs, but this does not mean it is on the verge of collapse. For example, redistribution of more central business-district businesses to the suburbs does not mean that the central business district will not retain a central economic focal point in metropolitan structure. Undoubtedly many businesses will remain and continue to expand in the urban core. As Raymond Vernon puts it: "The central cities may not capture quite as high a proportion of such [office] activity as they have in the past, but there is not much doubt that absolute increases in such employment will occur. Nor is there much doubt that, to the extent that they occur, they will offer a continued stimulus to some central business districts."[2]

The problem areas in the central city are those older residential communities and business districts surrounding the central business district. It is here where blight and decay are setting in and where most black ghettos are located. As the structures in these areas become so old and dilapidated that they are no longer useful, a potential for reuse appears. But so far very few local governments have developed meaningful renewal policies for developing this reuse potential. It is widely acknowledged by housing experts and specialists that thus far the federal renewal program has been manipulated in such a manner as to hamper, if not set back, the redevelopment of declining central-city areas. The many destructive consequences of the program in reducing the amount of housing accessible to minority and lower income groups—thereby increasing the amount of overcrowding and blight—have been widely publicized.

But it should be remembered that what is lacking is not the need for central-city renewal itself, but the adoption of realistic and effective policies for achieving renewal. Indeed, the need for realizing the potential of central-city renewal is especially pressing. As Alonso has stated: "Without positive action the urban center may wither and the metropolis may become a vast, amorphous, headless amoeba. A strong center is needed socially, economically, and psychologically, for it is here that urban life is lived in full, and virtually all activities in the metropolitan area focus toward it."[3] This paper proposes that ghetto rebuilding become a major component of a general metropolitan effort to build a strong urban center.

The position of the ghetto in metropolitan structure: monopolistic control

In order to get at the more vital linkages between the ghetto and metropolitan structure, it is necessary to move away from the views, fostered by the case for ghetto dispersal, concerning metropolitan imbalances "produced" by the ghetto. Instead we must delve more closely into the economic imbalances which surround the emergence of the ghetto. We know that a vast majority of the black population entered the cities at the bottom of the economic structure and has remained there throughout its urban history. Also, it is widely acknowledged that whites who departed from the areas occupied by black migrants nonetheless retained control over the areas' business and real estate. This can be readily seen in many examples: slum landlords who capitalize on the general metropolitan housing shortage to squeeze excess rent from black tenants for substandard dwellings; marginal central-city businesses which rely upon the cheap labor supply in the ghetto for employment; and the mortgage-lending policies of FHA which enabled millions of white families to move from the central cities and maintain segregated suburban communities. In effect, the severe competitive disadvantage of the black community in the political economy of the cities has provided a base for the acquisition of varied economic and political interests by the white community. Over the years the accumulation of these interests becomes institutional and structural; the interests become monopolistic.

Quantitative evidence on monopolistic advantages achieved by the white community is supported by the investigations of Lester Thurow reported in his recent book, *Poverty and Discrimination*.[4] Using econometric techniques to investigate the relationship between poverty and discrimination in the United States, he shows that black poverty is considerably more extensive and enduring than white poverty and, more importantly, that various economic gains acquired by the white community result in economic losses for the black community. In light of such facts it is misleading to view economic discrimination through the lens of formal bourgeois economic theory, which traditionally conceived of economic discrimination in terms of physical distance, in terms of the white population's willingness to pay for not associating with blacks. As Thurow and others have pointed out, it is more realistic to view economic discrimination in terms of social distance—in terms of whites defining black people's points of entry into the marketplace in order to reap substantial economic advantages. For example, employment discrimination exists not only in white employers' refusal to hire blacks but also in their relegation of blacks to inferior occupational and income positions, such as domestic servants, chauffeurs, messengers, file clerks, etc. The power to carry out such relegations is a function of the monopolistic institutional advantages acquired by whites relative to blacks.

Thurow's conclusions reveal: "Quantitatively the monopoly powers of the white community vis-à-vis the black community are a major force leading to lower Negro incomes and higher individual white incomes. Negro losses and white gains amount to approximately $15 billion per year." In discussing the policy implications of this conclusion he makes the significant point that the "policy instruments must be color conscious. The package of progams that will cure white poverty will not cure Negro poverty. Something extra is needed."

Although he does not fully articulate it, the theoretical thrust of Thurow's findings points toward what many black community groups have been maintaining for several years, namely, that the ghetto functions as a colonial appendage of the dominant white metropolitan community, which drains the ghetto of its ability to develop its own capital and resource base. This view carries much more theoretical and empirical weight than the references to ghetto-produced imbalances made in the case for ghetto dispersal. American metropolitan growth has never been balanced in either the economical sense of an efficient utilization of resources or the normative sense of an equitable distribution of resources. The locus of metropolitan imbalances associated with the ghetto structure can usually be traced to the monopolistic control over the ghetto structure by the white community.

The ghetto and social pathologies

In examining the pathologies of the ghetto it is necessary first to distinguish between the ghetto and pathologies. After all, a ghetto is not synonymous with the pathologies of social and economic deprivation, as Martin Grodzins, Kain, and others seem to imply. A ghetto is only a residential area inhabited by a common ethnic group. Economic poverty, for instance, is not a necessary characteristic of ghettos. Many Jewish ghettos in Europe have maintained a higher standard of living than most of the surrounding European population.[5]

Moreover, while black ghettos in America manifest many social pathologies, these represent only one aspect of black urban life and do not characterize all of their residential areas within the central cities. Instead of referring to the works of Kenneth Clark and Claude Brown to characterize the ghetto as "institutionalized pathology," Kain would have done better to refer to the works of E. Franklin Frazier, who has done more comprehensive and thorough studies of black urban communities over a longer period of time than either Clark or Brown. His studies on the ecological settlement of the black population in Harlem, New York, and Chicago, Illinois, have revealed that neighborhood differentiation by family organization and socio-economic status tends to follow in broad outline the same general pattern within black residential areas as it does within white residential areas.[6] The ghetto slum areas which Clark and Brown refer to would constitute only one type of black residential neighborhood. Moreover, the increased suburbanization of the white population since 1950 has opened up more and better residential areas within the central cities for black families and households. Thus, one finds greater neighborhood differentiation among the black central-city population today than existed at the time Frazier conducted his studies. The hard-core slum ghetto is no more characteristic of black urban communities than skid row is of the white central-city communities.

In looking at the pathologies associated with the polarization of the races, it is important to recognize the difference between polarization in terms of racial attitudes and the actual forces of ecological segregation between blacks and whites. Polarization of the races did not occur with the black concentration in the central cities and the white flight to the suburbs. The races have always been polarized in a moral and social sense that has little to do with spatial segregation. In fact, blacks were probably most integrated in a spatial sense during the slavery and early post-slavery periods when their servant dwellings were freely intermixed with the mansions of their white masters and employers. The current crisis of racial polarization simply reflects the extent to which the white population has recently become aware of the plight of the black community. In regard to the ghetto, it is crucially important to recognize that it represents a form of moral and social isolation more than a physical or spatial isolation. Moreover, rather than producing this social isolation, the ghetto structure is an important shield from its damaging effects. Consider very carefully the words of Frazier in referring to the plight of the Negro middle class:

The middle class owes its growth and form of existence to the fact that the Negro has been isolated mentally, socially, and morally in American society. Therefore, in some respects, the Negro community may be regarded as a pathological phenomenon. It is not surprising, then, that the Negro middle class shows the mark of oppression...in its mental and psychic make-up. The middle class Negro shows the mark of oppression more than the lower class Negro who finds a shelter from the contempt of the white world in his traditional religion, in his songs, and in his freedom from a gnawing desire to be recognized and accepted. Although the middle class Negro has tried to reject his traditional background and racial identification he cannot escape from it. Therefore, many middle class Negroes have developed self-hatred.[7]

The ghetto, of course, is the primary locational base for the ''shelter'' institutions of the black lower class referred to by Frazier. These institutions are vital to the social sustenance of a vast majority of the black population. In light of the profound historical roots of the American racial problem, it is doubtful that the ghetto will lose its shelter function in the forseeable future.

To recognize positive functions of the ghetto is not to deny its many problems. The point is that the problems should be put in their proper perspective. Thus, such problems as those of the central-city ghetto schools cannot be seen simply as a product of the expanding boundaries of segregation. It is not the expansion itself which leads to high dropout rates, insufficient college preparation, poor classroom environments, etc. Solutions to such problems are too complex to be found in policy structures of school integration. Indeed, in the South and various parts of the North and West, white politicians and educators have used the federal guidelines on school desegregation to make integration a one-way street, in which black students, teachers, and principals are transferred to white schools and the black school system is eliminated, bringing about loss of occupational mobility for black teachers and educators. And in large black ghettos, such as those in Washington, D.C., Los Angeles, California, and Chicago, it is doubtful that school integration is attainable in the near future. Thus, it is not surprising that, in the past couple of years, interest of many black community groups in the school issue has shifted from integration to community control. As manifested in the widely publicized Ocean Hill–Brownsville school crisis in Brooklyn, New York, in 1968, ghetto parents are increasingly recognizing that many of the formal educational problems of their children are closely related to the lack of control which they can exert on the school board and other local institutions that determine the development of public-school facilities and educational programs.

The false search for market balance

In sum, the case for ghetto dispersal rests upon a false search for metropolitan market balance. The studies tend to connect the growth of metropolitan structure to the movement of the market mechanism. They view the private economy of the metropolis as shifting toward the suburbs and, therefore, postulate that ghetto inhabitants should also shift in order to have access to growing metropolitan resources. Not only do such analyses reflect an incomplete and inaccurate assessment of the metropolitan economy and the problem of accessibility to its resources, they also underrate the scale and nature of the ghetto's economic and employment situation and completely ignore its vital geo-social functions. More importantly, by continually drawing simplistic and naïve connections between economic needs and resources, they are deterred from the most fruitful course to their ultimate objective of recommending policies for change. As Myrdal has stated,

> in most questions of economic policy there are conflicts of interests. This in fact cannot be concealed by obscure talk of *a priori* principles. In those cases neither an economist nor anybody else can offer a "socially" or "economically correct" solution.... It should be one of the main tasks of applied economics to examine and to unravel the complex interplay of interests, as they sometimes converge, sometimes conflict.[8]

The object of this critique has been to indicate that the relationship of the ghetto to metropolitan structure can be understood only in all of its dimensions: economic, political, social, and cultural. The problems inherent in ghetto-metropolitan linkages involve institutional and interest conflicts that permeate all these dimensions. The black ghetto is a pathological community; the political, economic, and social deprivations experienced by its inhabitants are a function of monopolistic interests built upon its structure by various groups of the white metropolitan community. Such a relationship has severely dissipated and constructed the ghetto's political and economic institutions.

To remove these constrictions does not imply a large-scale displacement and removal of ghetto blacks to the suburbs. The high rates of natural increase among the central-city black population will undoubtedly lead to increase in the rate of black suburbanization. But this does not mean that the central-city ghetto will suddenly wither away. Quite to the contrary, the ghetto is seen as a highly durable community which will be around for some time to come. The problem, then, is one of creating conditions which remove the political and economic constrictions on existing ghettos and encourage their inhabitants to assert themselves in the control and management of their community environment. Such control and management are at the very heart of the black struggle to achieve a wholesome and decent community life.

Policy Case for Ghetto Rebuilding

Our program proposals for reconstituting the black central-city communities do not in any sense reflect a belief that their successful implementation would secure full collective freedom for black people. It is our firm conviction that the substantial majority of black people cannot gain relief from their oppression, from their material and spiritual degradations and frustrations, until they completely sever their subjection to the tentacles of the dominant white society. To us, this necessarily means the achievement of black nationhood—the formation of a black nation-state with its own land base. To deny the possibility of this achievement is to deny history. Yet at the same time one must also recognize certain minimal preconditions to the formation of black nationhood: the existence of a mass consensus for black nationhood with strong unified leadership to implement it; sophisticated black political and economic institutions that command respect and exert influence among other nations of the world; and favorable domestic and international circumstances which make it opportune for blacks to acquire a land base. To us, all evidence suggests that the maturation of the these preconditions is at least another generation away; hence our current energies are directed to their fulfillment. It is in this light that our ghetto-rebuilding programs are proposed. They represent interim, middle-range objectives toward which black people can strive toward until they are able to bend national and international circumstances to the interest and fulfillment of black nationhood.

Also, although our proposed programs deal primarily with urban areas, this does not mean we view the cities as the most suitable environments even for black interim objectives. Nor does it mean that we deny the need for a substantial black rural development program. But the central cities are where most black people now reside. Furthermore, their large-scale urban concentrations are the product of tremendous migrations which began during World War I and gave no indication of leveling off until the past decade. The rates and volumes of these migrations are the most rapid and largest in modern world history and have caused considerable disruption and uprooting of black social and cultural ties. Thus in many regions, particularly in the relatively new black communities of the West, many blacks are still involved in the process of establishing themselves in the cities. To advocate programs involving further substantial migrations within the confines of white America would appear to be out of touch with the tempo and process of black community settlement unless the programs can guarantee definite improvements in black living situations.

In assessing the economic resources available for black development one should not get hung up on facts and figures used to show the paucity of resources available to black people in the central city. It is true that they are meager. According to most established economic indices and criteria, central cities are relatively insignificant units in the total economic system and offer no genuine access to the chains of command in white America's dominant institutions. But these facts have nothing to say about the potential of black central-city development. The "hard" facts of economics should not make one lose sight of the more basic fact that economic activities, like all other societal activities, are no more than a function of human behavior, a product of the human will. People do not simply live according to general economic stages and systems. People possess economies. The flexibility of people in providing for their material welfare can never be absolutely circumscribed. The ability of black people to provide for themselves in the central city will ultimately depend on the caliber of their own community organization and leadership. This necessarily means that the black leadership must demonstrate considerable shrewdness and tenacity in extracting resource subsidies from white public and private institutions to help support direly needed community development projects, such as housing renewal and construction, daycare centers, community colleges, and business and commercial endeavors. The central city is no more undesirable for meeting these challenges than any other locational base within the confines of white America. The white suburban residents and businesses who have left the central city in an impoverished state may neglect it, but they cannot write it off. The central city is still an indispensable unit in the over-all distribution of metropolitan activities. Important financial and commercial offices, strategic government and military functions, public-utility and transportation facilities, and many other integral metropolitan facilities and services are concentrated in central cities and offer potential leverage to their black inhabitants in extracting overdue economic support from the white metropolitan community. Moreover, whether blacks ultimately remain in the United States or separate to another land, they can never escape the delicate and difficult problems of contending amid rival forces to provide for and protect their material and social interests. The central cities are just as good a place as any to realize the far-reaching implications of a statement made by Frederick Douglass over a century ago: "Society is a hard-hearted affair. With it the helpless may expect no higher dignity than that of the paupers. The individual must lay society under obligation to him or society will honor him only as a stranger and sojourner."

Policy framework

The policy proposals that follow consist of four program elements considered to be essential to any national effort to bring about effective renewal of ghetto communities. They apply primarily to those major central cities and smaller town and villages in various parts of the country which contain a significant proportion of black people and whose communities are marked by a predominance of low incomes, substandard housing, low indigenous capital base, and deteriorated physical environments.

The proposals do not go into specific program designs in terms of indicating detailed fiscal and organizational alternatives for implementation. This would be a considerable task that goes far beyond the scope of this paper. Within each proposal element, much applied research and planning needs to be done. The proposals themselves simply represent the general ends and organizational forms toward which many existing black community-development efforts can be directed. Because of tremendous, deeply rooted problems within the ghetto and the powerful, complex political and economic forces impinging upon its structure, ghetto rebuilding must necessarily be conceived of as a fairly long-run process consisting of a host of sustained organizational efforts and involving major political struggles and conflicts within the metropolitan and national structures.

A primary feature of the proposals is their reliance upon existing and incipient ideas and organizational resources within the black community. The programs are conceived of as being built from the bottom up rather than from the top down. Hopefully this approach would avoid many of the "community-participation" difficulties that permeate existing efforts, such as the Model Cities program, which attempts to solicit community support for a program conceived in Washington which offers no real promise of physical and social improvement. Only one of the proposals is the writer's original. The others reflect a synthesis of various ideas and organizational thrusts that have emerged from the black community over the past decade. In effect, ghetto rebuilding is simply an encouragement of black initiatives toward community control.

1. *Develop black municipal corporations.* The creation of a proto-municipal structure within specified ghetto boundaries of each urban area would involve the development of a black municipal authority elected by and responsible to ghetto inhabitants. This black municipal authority would be the primary body responsible for the general physical, social, and economic reconstruction of the ghetto. Its board of councilmen, and perhaps its mayor, would be responsible for the provision of all basic community services, from housing and urban renewal to public education to law enforcement.

In large urban areas, such as Detroit, Michigan, and Chicago, Illinois, the corporation could exist along with regular city government, but it would assume responsibility for most of the services usually provided by that government. Also, it would be the primary body representing the black community in any discussions and negotiations between city hall and the ghetto. Of course, in small, unincorporated, all-black towns of the rural South it would simply be a matter of acquiring legal corporation and setting up the administrative machinery for municipal government, a trend which has already begun in Mississippi, Alabama, and other Southern states.

The black municipal structure would also serve as the prime recipient of funds from the Departments of Housing and Urban Development and of Health, Education, and Welfare, and from other federal agencies, to provide basic community improvements in the ghetto. This arrangement would eliminate many of the conflicts that now occur between the black community and city hall when funds "disappear" as they filter indirectly to the community through city hall. In a sense, the black municipal corporation might sponsor the same broad set of community services that the Model Cities program is trying to provide. Only its organizational structure would maintain closer links to the residents and a more reliable system for the accounting and provision of community services.

Movements in this direction are evident in many places. Most notable are the achievements of the Nation of Islam, which has an internal system of black self-development. Relying primarily upon the self-sacrifice and devotion of its members, it is building through a central organizational mechanism a number of schools, farms, businesses, and educational and health centers in various parts of the country. As an actual model of black community development it is similar in broad outline to the development approaches taken by certain developing countries. China and Tanzania, for example, stress reliance upon the indigenous resources of their predominantly rural populations to embark on the arduous road to industrialization and modernization. One can also see the trend toward black municipal organization in the black neighborhood organizations that have been developed in Oakland, California; Brooklyn; Harlem; Chicago and other urban areas. One can further see it in the Afro-American police societies organized across the Northeast and Midwest, one of their main objectives being to work for the patrol of black communities by black policemen. The black municipal authority then would strengthen and legitimize these incipient black efforts in law enforcement, public education, and the whole range of community services. It would support, coordinate, and channel the increasing indigenous efforts toward community control into the tremendous task of rebuilding the social and physical fabric of the ghetto.

2. *Build black economic development institutions.* One of the primary challenges and responsibilities facing the black municipal corporations would be to eliminate the poverty and restructure the economic base of the ghetto; that is, to increase the ghetto's capital and employment base, diversify and enlarge the productive capacity of its businesses, and provide for black control and determination over the ghetto economy. This responsibility could be met by the establishment of community-based development corporations operating under carefully prepared and organized economic programs to increase the standard of living among ghetto inhabitants. Two of the most widely discussed proposals for bringing about such innovations are the CORE Community Self Determination Bill, sponsored before the 1968 session of Congress, and the Ghediplan, devised by black economist Dunbar S. McLaurin. These proposals call for the creation of an elaborate system of community corporations, banks, and other entrepreneurial mechanisms to establish a capital base in the ghetto and carry out far-reaching programs of black economic development. While they differ in many respects and would have to be modified to fit the particular local conditions and circumstances of a given black community, they do offer a fertile basis for examining ways in which black groups can use their organizational and political strength to help achieve ghetto economic control and growth.

For example, one of the main features of the Ghediplan is the design of a framework by which ghetto development corporations can productively utilize fiscal and economic resources from government, business, and labor institutions to acquire the necessary capacity and experience for large-scale productive activity. It rests not so much upon direct grants from the government as on creative utilization of existing governmental fiscal resources to provide "guaranteed" markets and financing for ghetto businesses and industries. A significant proportion of the city, state, or national government's purchase contracts, for instance, would be allotted to ghetto corporations to provide their businesses with a built-in market for the sale of their products and services. Such an act by the government, it is felt, would probably induce similar acts from large private businesses and labor unions. Likewise, "guaranteed financing" could be provided by governmental bodies using their security bonds and other deposits to encourage banks and financial institutions to furnish the necessary credit and loan capital for ghetto development business ventures. The commitment of these marketing and financial resources from the government and other dominant institutions would provide some of the vital economic ingredients required by the black businesses and industries at their early stage of growth.

Well-organized black municipal corporations and political organizations would be in a strategic position to help extract and mobilize the types of fiscal and economic supports mentioned in the Ghediplan. In cases where such organizations achieve control over the management and operation of various city services, they could act as primary agents in providing the "guaranteed" markets and financing to the development corporations. In addition, black organizational pressure, in the form of economic boycotts, strikes, and other confrontation tactics, might be used against large white businesses and labor unions to garner their support. Black community organizations could also be instrumental in bringing pressure to bear on elected political officials of predominantly black constituencies to endorse and help mobilize resources for their economic development programs. Too often these elected officials use the fragmented organizational state of their consituencies and the prestige and power of their positions to set themselves above the people, advocating all sorts of ill-conceived and worthless programs for "curing" poverty. Unified black community groups with well-defined economic programs and strong political organization would narrowly limit the range of irresponsible actions and maneuvers their politicans are accustomed to performing.

Regardless of the various tactics used from locality to locality, the ultimate objective is one of establishing a black institutional and organizational base for carrying out thorough and diversified economic development of the ghetto. Moreover, it is important that black municipal and political organizations play a strategic role in this process, stimulating and catalyzing it by using political leverage to extract support from the dominant white institutions and acting in a regulatory capacity over the development corporations so as to ensure their commitment and responsibility to the economic improvement of ghetto inhabitants.

3. *Combine ghetto rebuilding with central-city renewal.* This program could serve as one of the primary development activities of the black municipal and private corporate structures. It would involve the black municipal and development corporations acting as primary partners in a general metropolitan effort to revitalize declining areas of the central

city, particularly the central business district, with the black corporations assuming complete responsibility for the physical, economic, and social renewal of specified portions of the district.

It was mentioned earlier that, in most metropolitan areas with large black populations, various commercial and industrial areas within the central city are declining both economically and physically, marked by empty office space and marginal businesses with high turnover rates, as a result of the business exodus to the suburbs. Since the expansion of commercial and financial offices remaining in the urban core will occupy a relatively small amount of space, a potential demand is developing, but so far there has been little actual demand for reuse. The need for land-development outlets by black municipal and development corporations could readily fill much of this demand. Access to these declining areas would provide much-needed space for their residential renewal and business-development activities. In residential renewal it would enable the construction of significant numbers of new dwellings to house both new black family formations and those households displaced by clearance of the worst ghetto areas. Also, it would furnish space for the community development corporations to launch major industrial and commercial enterprises. By establishing these business enterprises within or near the central business district, the corporations would be in a strategic location to capture significant proportions of the metropolitan economic market, for, despite its decline, the central business district still attracts for a variety of reasons a major part of the metropolitan population.

In addition to these economic benefits there would be important social and cultural benefits. It is widely recognized by urban analysts that the urban core must renew its role as a political, economic, and cultural center if the metropolis is to be prevented from becoming "headless" and monotonous, a city without diversity and excitement. Also, it is apparent that one must begin to think in terms of new images regarding the city center. A center within a decentralized metropolitan structure will necessarily have to be different from one in a centralized structure. A new city center cannot restrict itself to large-scale commercial development, but must cater to a wider variety of smaller attractions. As Charles Abrams has suggested, the center might increasingly provide a variety of cultural, recreational, and tourist retail enterprises.[9] While these enterprises would be small relative to the huge corporations of the white community, they would be of an attractive size for the developing black corporations. What better way to revitalize the city center than by providing for the development of black cultural centers, theaters, restaurants, Afro-Asian import and export exchanges, and various other enterprises? It is widely recognized that the black population—the largest, and, except for the Indian, the oldest nonwhite ethnic group in the country—has made unique and permanent social and cultural contributions to the development of the society. What better way to acknowledge these contributions than by the development of major black political, cultural, and commercial establishments at the heart of the metropolitan area?

Too often when people think of interracial communication, they think in small group terms, in terms of black and white residents living together in interracial housing projects or students going to integrated schools. But perhaps more important is the communication one receives through public images, the urban sights one sees while walking along city streets, attending musical and theatrical performances, and eating at restaurants. City centers with black people managing and operating their own establishments would stand in sharp contrast to those of today with black people serving primarily as waiters, cooks, and stock and file clerks for predominantly white establishments.

4. *Develop black institutions of higher education.* A crucially important need generated by the above programs would be increased demands for black skills in all phases of urban and rural development: engineers, accountants, community planners, statisticians, public and business administrators, agricultural economists, research analysts, etc. While increased black access to the educational resources of predominantly white colleges would be needed to meet some of these demands, it would also be essential that predominantly black colleges and universities be overhauled and developed to meet the skill demands and needs for ghetto rebuilding. All black college development programs would, of course, have to be coordinated by a national group of black educators and administrators who have an experienced and sincere interest in the higher education of the black population.

The first focus of any general black college development program should be the existing predominantly black colleges and universities in the Southern and border states. It is acknowledged by black and white educators that these colleges have been beset by a host of major problems in the postwar period due primarily to large migrations of blacks from the South to the North and West and to the rapid pace of social and technological changes in the society. Handicapped by low budgetary funds, increased educational costs, and excessive control by paternalistic white boards of trustees and state officials, many have become increasingly unable to make necessary improvements in their facilities and instructional programs. As a result, they have been severely hampered in preparing students for worthwile tasks in the modern world. Despite this decline, most of the colleges will survive, one way or another, because of the sheer growth pressures of the rapidly increasing black student population. Yet there is no reason why they should not be upgraded to meet the modern skill demands and requirements of the black population. Many have unique and valuable assets to rebuild upon. Tuskegee has important schools in agriculture and veterinary science built upon the scientific accomplishments of the late George Washington Carver. Atlanta University, Georgia, Fisk University, Nashville, Tennessee, and many others have valuable library and research materials on the black community. With the abundant resources in this country there is no reason why these colleges should be allowed to decline. What more reliable avenue for the flow of public and private subsidies than to institutions whose administrative machinery is already intact? Programs and struggles to break the tight control paternalistic whites have over these colleges and to increase the flow of funds for overhauling their administrative and educational structures would greatly accelerate the number of black college graduates with the skills and motivation necessary to accomplish the task of rebuilding their communities.

A second focus should be on the creation of black community colleges in every urban area with a large black population. In the North and West some have already started, such as Malcolm X University in Chicago and Nairobi College in East Palo Alto, California. Colleges such as these could supply training in a range of essential practical skills that are not provided by prestigious white universities. It is no secret that college-educated blacks have been traditionally shunted into nonpractical subjects, such as sociology, political science, and English literature, most of which reflect white ethnocentric intellectual biases and are not relevant to black world views and skill needs. What would be needed in abundance are more useful skills, such as how to manage and operate a business cooperative, building-construction contracting, and management, book-keeping, etc. The training in many such skills could be provided within a year or two and would be highly relevant opportunities for many black youths seeking a "second chance" in life. Black community colleges situated in the ghetto would be in a strategic position to provide such opportunities.

Summary

In general the case for ghetto rebuilding rests upon a different conception of the relationship between the ghetto and metropolitan decentralization than does the case for ghetto dispersal. The case for ghetto dispersal holds that the dominant movements of the white population and economic resources to the suburban fringe have isolated the black ghettos in the central city and limited their residents' geographic accessibility to direly needed socio-economic resources. The isolation is seen as accentuating the economic poverty and social pathologies of the ghetto in addition to creating imbalances in metropolitan growth. If these problems are to be resolved, then it is considered imperative that barriers which limit the ghetto residents' access to the suburbs be eliminated so that they can move to the dominant resources on the fringe. Therefore the focus is on the creation of conditions which make for the dispersion of the black population from the central-city ghettos to the suburbs.

The case for ghetto rebuilding does not see the social and economic deprivations of the ghetto as a product of its geographic isolation from the suburbs but as a product of much more complex forces at work within the metropolis and the nation as a whole. First, as a different ethnic group from the majority white population with a different set of historical experiences resulting from conditions of slavery and servitude in the rural South, the black population has never been fully assimilated into the cultural fabric of the country. This cultural difference has been reinforced by the socio-economic position which blacks inherited when they moved in large number to the cities. Their general economic position has always been at the bottom of the urban structure, which means that they have continually suffered from housing and employment shortages and imbalances that have continually existed in the national urban economy and that the structure of their ghetto community has provided a basis upon which white community groups have built monopolistic economic and political interests. Thus, the economic poverty and consequent social pathologies of the ghetto are a function of profound imbalances in the national urban economy and of monopolistic interests accumulated by the white community

Relieving the problems of the ghetto is not so much a question of eliminating barriers to black movement to the suburbs as it is that of eliminating the monopolistic control which white groups hold over the ghetto structure and mobilizing unprecedented resource subsidies at national and local levels for resolving the economic imbalances affecting the depressed situation of the black community. While these problems are not spatially determined, they do tend to have a fixed spatial character. The national economic imbalances find their primary locational bases in the declining commercial, industrial, and residential areas of the city center, in which most urban blacks reside. Thus problems of improving the ghetto are closely related to those of revitalizing the city center. To try to resolve these problems by returning white middle and upper income families to the city center and dispersing black families to the suburbs not only runs counter to historical forces of ecological segregation in American cities, but in all probability would neither relieve the social and economic deprivations of the black population nor renew the city center. Hence the problems have to be faced where they are. Such a situation naturally points to ghetto rebuilding as the more effective and desirable alternative.

Ghetto rebuilding is seen as a process already at work in existing efforts by black community groups to attain control over various governmental, business, and educational activities within ghetto areas. The proposals for ghetto rebuilding consist simply of recommending the long-run organizational forms toward which these efforts should be directed if blacks are to attain firm control over their community environment and effectively utilize resource subsidies for its physical and social reconstruction. The proposals recommend the development of black municipal and business corporate structures as the primary instruments for carrying out the ghetto-reconstruction process. To enhance the social and economic viability of this process it is recommended that ghetto rebuilding be part of a general metropolitan effort to revitalize the city center. The final proposal recommends the overhauling of existing predominantly black colleges and universities and the creation of new community colleges in black urban areas to help supply the skills required by the ghetto-rebuilding effort.

NOTES

1. U.S., National Commission on Urban Problems, *Building the American City* (New York: Praeger, 1969).

2. Raymond Vernon, "The Changing Economic Function of the Central City," *Urban Renewal: The Record and the Controversy*, ed. by James Q. Wilson (Cambridge, Mass.: The M.I.T. Press, 1966), pp. 22–23.

3. William Alonso, "Cities, Planners, and Urban Renewal," *ibid.*, p. 449.

4. Lester C. Thurow, *Poverty and Discrimination* (Washington, D.C.: The Brookings Institution, 1969). See pp. 111–38 and 158–59.

5. Peter Labrie, "Ghettos: A Comparison of Jewish Ghettos in Europe and the European Ghetto in Shanghai" (unpublished manuscript, 1964).

6. See "The Negro Family in Chicago" and "Negro Harlem: An Ecological Study," included in *E. Franklin Frazier on Race Relations*, ed. by G. Franklin Edwards (Chicago, Ill.: University of Chicago Press, 1968).

7. "The New Negro Middle Class," *ibid.*, p. 265.

8. Gunnar Myrdal, *The Political Element in the Development of Economic Theory*, trans. by Paul Streeten (New York: Simon & Schuster, 1969), p. 198.

9. See Charles Abrams, *The City Is the Frontier* (New York: Harper & Row, 1965), pp. 308–14.

Topics for Discussion

1. Discuss the financial problems of the community development corporation, the problems inherent in its dependence on outside sources for financial aid, and particularly the political implications and uncertainties of depending on government funding and refunding in changing economic and political environments. How does this affect the degree to which CDC's can carry out various social and political aims?

2. What is the role of the community development corporation? Relate your answer to the need for development, diversification, and coordination of commercial activities in low-income areas.

3. How does the community development corporation respond to the needs of low-income individuals? How does the CDC meet the needs of the middle-income black individual? Compare and contrast.

4. How do traditional consumer credit evaluation practices fail to identify and analyze properly the potential for mortgage loans to low-income persons? What factors must be considered to minimize the perceived risks of granting loans to low-income persons?

5. Whether or not black dispersal and integration into the suburbs is desirable is the subject of considerable debate. Irrespective of the desirability of dispersal, it appears that a substantial proportion of the black population will be located in city areas in varying degrees of decay for some time to come. Given this situation, what steps can be taken towards rebuilding inner-city residential and commercial areas? How can the blight be minimized?

6. A. Efforts towards black economic development have been identified basically as two approaches: (1) the moderate or integrationist approach, and (2) the militant or separatist approach. Both claim that the programs offered, while aimed at improving the economic well-being of the black community, are not aimed at economic development as an end in itself but as a vehicle for achieving other complex and related social and political goals. Both approaches assume a direct relationship between the acquisition of economic controls and the acquisition of social and political leverage. What common elements will be found in these two approaches with respect to how the task of economic development is pursued and to what problems may be encountered (skills, market limitations, mobility, entry barriers, capital problems, management development, etc.)?

B. The so-called separatist approach is based on the belief that the present socio-economic system, while possessing the technological capability to provide an adequate standard of living for all, is structured in terms of goals and priorities implied by the way the system functions to prohibit full participation by the black community and to inhibit the utilization of the full potential of members of the black community. How is this belief reflected in programs and proposals classified as "separatist"? What limitations of "traditional" or "integrationist" methods support the separatists' belief?

7.   A.   Banking regulations typically provide for a justification before a charter is issued to a new bank. Black bankers purport to meet far more tangible needs than the obvious psychological satisfaction felt by having blacks more highly visible in the area of finance. Discuss the merits of the justifications for chartering black banks.

B.   What operational differences (asset distribution, income generation, profitability, etc.) exist between black banks and other banks of comparable size? Explain these differences in terms of managerial resources available and in terms of the characteristics of the markets typically served by black banks. What does this imply about the future of black banks' assimilation into the total banking system?

C.   The re-emergence of black banks is generally considered consistent with the overall quest for black economic development. To be successful the black bank must compete effectively within a mature commercial banking environment. What problems does the black bank face in operating as a successful commercial banking enterprise while at the same time pursuing the developmental commitments which in many ways justify its existence? How does the resolution of such problems depend on an overall solution to the capital problems of the black community?

8.   A.   The successful entreprenuer or manager has been identified as one who is willing to undertake high-risk investments for potentially high returns and one who possesses managerial skills and perspectives. To contribute to black economic development in terms of its congruent social and political goals, a black entrepreneur should provide involved and responsible community leadership. In this context what characteristics will be necessary for successful black business persons? How can persons with such potential be identified and recruited for business careers in the black community?

B.   Financial and technical assistance are widely recognized as necessary aids to the development of black business enterprise. These are not sufficient, however, to insure the success of the business undertaking. What other management related factors determine success? How can these factors be incorporated into an assistance or development program?

Suggested Readings

Blaustein, A.I., and Faux, G. *The Star-Spangled Hustle: Black Capitalism and White Power.* New York: Doubleday & Company, Inc., 1972.

"Where It's at: Black Capitalism." *Business and Society,* December 17, 1968, p. 108.

"A Model of Black Success in Business." *Business Week,* April 13, 1974.

"Where Negro Business Gets Credit." *Business Week,* June 8, 1968.

Profiles in Community Based Economic Development. Cambridge, Mass.: Center for Community Economic Development, 1969.

Coles, Flournoy A., Jr. *An Analysis of Black Entrepreneurship in Seven Urban Areas.* Washington, D.C.: National Business League, 1969.

Goldsmith, W. "Black Economic Development—What Should City Planners Do?" Ithaca, N.Y.: Dept. of City and Regional Planning, Cornell University, April 1972 (mimeo).

Irons, Edward D. "Black Banking: Problems & Prospects." *The MBA,* February 1971, pp. 20–26.

Ofari, Earl. *The Myth of Black Capitalism.* New York: Monthly Review Press, 1970.

Olken, C.E. "Economic Development in the Model Cities Program." *Law and Contemporary Problems* 36 (Spring 1972), pp. 205–26.

Perry, S. "Federal Support for CDC's: Some of the History and Issues of Community Control." *Review of Black Political Economy* 3 (Spring 1973), pp. 17–42.

Phemister, J.M., and Hildelbrand, J.L. "The Use of Non-Profit Corporations and Cooperatives for Ghetto Economic Development." *Journal of Urban Law* 48 (1970–71), pp. 181–232.

Schiller, B.R. "The Little Training Robbery" (Parts I and II). Dept. of Economics, University of Maryland, College Park, 1972.

CDC's: New Hope for the Inner City. Twentieth Century Fund Task Force on Community Development Corporations. New York: The Twentieth Century Fund, 1971.

U.S., Dept. of Commerce, Office of Minority Business Enterprise. *Progress of the Minority Business Enterprise Program.* Washington, D.C.: U.S. Government Printing Office, 1972.

IV

Proposals
and Implications

New Directions for Minority Enterprise

Samuel I. Doctors and
Sharon Lockwood

The Need for New Directions

Minority enterprise has historically been limited to primarily small retail establishments, personal service businesses, and small construction contractors. Despite the fact that minority groups constitute about 17 percent of our population,[1] they own less than 3 percent of the nation's businesses.[2] Perhaps even more significant is the fact that these businesses control less than .5 percent of the nation's business assets.[3]

Present programs for minority business development have emphasized loans, grants, and subsidies to small businesses in retail services and construction areas. These businesses are often in crowded business sectors—small margin, low-growth potential areas such as gasoline service stations, barber shops, or small retail food markets—and often serve an impoverished clientele. The historic failure rate for these types of business is quite high.[4] Although data is scarce in this area, it appears that less than 20 percent of all new small businesses survive their first five years.[5] New minority businesses are even more vulnerable because they lack access to financial and technical resources.[6] However, even those which do achieve some modest degree of success are unlikely to achieve growth rates that would create high leverage business opportunities for very many members of the minority community. Moreover, these businesses often lock their owners into a life of long hours, and hard, unstimulating work with little or no opportunity to branch out of the pattern of marginal growth opportunity.

Surveys of existing minority businesses indicate that there are very few with gross sales as large as $1 million a year and none which approaches the size of the 500 largest white owned and controlled corporations.[7] Nor do we find minority group members in positions of control or decision making in the large American corporations where they could gain the managerial experience to start companies which might grow to a place among the largest American businesses.

Other data indicate that minority business development, although receiving some stimulus from present public and private efforts, still shows no signs of the exponential growth rate needed to catch up with white business development and may in fact be falling farther behind. We have raised the expectations of our minority groups for examples of such exponential growth but have neither formed nor created models capable of achieving these catchup growth rates.

As may be seen from the sample of minority businesses presented in Tables 1 and 2, the minority entrepreneur tends to enter the more marginal types of business. Table 1 indicates that a disproportionate number of minority entrepreneurs are in the personal service area. While some facets of the service industries are higher growth areas, the more disaggregated data in Table 2 reveals that the minority entrepreneurs are not in these higher growth areas.

TABLE 1
Distribution of Minority and Nonminority Business Enterprises

Type of Business	Minority-Owned	Nonminority-Owned
Personal service	26.9	7.3
Other service	15.1	20.3
Construction	10.8	9.0
Manufacturing	2.2	7.9
Retail trade	34.0	34.9
Other industries	11.0	21.6
All other industries	100.0	100.0

Source: Office of Planning, Research, and Analysis of the Small Business Administration, "Distribution of Minority-Owned Business," June, 1969, p. 7 (unpublished report).

TABLE 2
Categories and Types of Black Business Enterprises

Category	Number	Percentage
Food and beverages	173	30.7
Public services	101	17.9
Merchandise sales	37	6.5
Professional services	35	6.2
Contracting services	31	5.5
General sales and service	169	30.0
Other	18	3.2
TOTAL	564	100.0

Source: F. Coles, Jr., *An Analysis of Black Entrepreneurship in Seven Urban Areas,* app. I (1969), pp. i–ii.

Little effort has been made to guide the minority entrepreneur to more lucrative business opportunities. Most government and nongovernment programs are grounded in the concept that simply establishing a minority member in a business is sufficient. This reasoning requires serious reconsideration. If minority businessmen are not guided to the higher growth areas, their businesses will not help the minority economy approach the national economy.

To lift minority enterprise from the ghetto and the barrio to which it has been consigned, a strategic thrust must now aim at providing opportunities for higher growth potential in models of minority enterprise. These model businesses should be capable of growing at the rate of 10 to 20 percent or more per year over the next five- to ten-year period.[8] Such new enterprises will help meet rapidly rising expectations, provide for true upward mobility, stimulate capital formation, and provide attractive alternative routes for minority employment and provide success models for future programs.[9]

Many new opportunities for minority entrepreneurs to obtain financial assistance have become available, not only in the Small Business Administration (SBA), but also in the Department of Commerce, the Office of Economic Opportunity, and in the private sector. New and expanded business opportunities capable of leveraging these expanding sources of capital funds must be provided to stimulate the creation of enterprises which can multiply their initial investments many times over.

Much of this development should occur in higher-growth industries, although medium- and low-profit, low-growth potential industries should not be completely excluded. They may provide needed goods and services for the community and serve to keep a larger amount of capital within the ghettos and barrios. Medium or lower growth potential businesses may also provide some training opportunities for a number of potential minority entrepreneurs and managers. Thus, this latter type of business may also play some role in long-term economic development of minority communities.

Today's minority entrepreneur is finally ready to gain a more advantageous position in the economy. Higher minority educational levels, increased minority incomes, a wider range of business opportunities, the changing attitude of public and private institutions toward minority entrepreneurs, and an attitudinal change in the minority community towards business as a career have combined to bring about an environment which can fit the minority entrepreneur for entering higher-growth industries. The educational level of minorities appears to be improving more rapidly than that of the population as a whole. As entrepreneurs are usually drawn not from the most disadvantaged groups, but from the middle classes,[10] this increase in educational level will undoubtedly be reflected in a growing pool of potential and actual entrepreneurs (Table 3). The rapidly increasing family income of minority groups (Table 4) is reflected in the growing purchasing power in the minority community. This increased purchasing power can support a larger number of minority businesses and a wider range of products and services. Thus, an increased range of business opportunities should be available within the minority community. The increased educational level and the extensive needs of the general public in the areas of goods and services should increase the range of business opportunities for the minority entrepreneur.

TABLE 3
Percentage of Distribution by Years of School Completed for Persons
20 Years Old and Over, by Age, 1969

Age	Less than 4 Years of High School	4 Years of High School	1 Year or More of College	Median Years of School Completed
NEGRO				
20 and 21	42.1	36.6	21.2	12.2
22 to 24	43.9	37.1	19.1	12.2
25 to 29	44.3	40.1	15.7	12.1
30 to 34	49.8	36.7	13.5	12.0
35 to 44	62.8	26.8	10.5	10.6
45 to 54	70.8	18.9	10.3	9.1
55 to 64	85.2	8.7	6.2	7.6
65 to 74	89.7	5.5	4.9	6.1
75 years and over	92.4	4.1	3.5	5.2
WHITE				
20 and 21	18.1	41.6	40.1	12.8
22 to 24	19.6	44.8	35.7	12.7
25 to 29	23.0	44.8	32.1	12.6
30 to 34	27.3	44.9	27.6	12.5
35 to 44	33.9	41.0	25.1	12.4
45 to 54	40.7	39.3	20.0	12.2
55 to 64	55.2	27.5	17.3	10.9
65 to 74	67.6	18.9	13.4	8.9
75 years and over	75.1	13.8	11.1	8.5

Source: Bureau of the Census, in U.S., Dept. of Labor, Bureau of Labor Statistics, *The Social and Economic Status of Negroes in the United States* (1970), p. 50.

TABLE 4
Median Family Income in 1968 and Negro Family Income, 1965–68
as a Percentage of White Income by Region

	Median Family Income, 1968		Negro Income as a Percentage of White Income			
	Negro	White	1965	1966	1967	1968
United States	$5,359	$8,936	54	58	59	60
Northeast	6,460	9,318	64	68	66	69
North Central	6,910	9,259	74	74	78	75
South	4,278	7,963	49	50	54	54
West	7,506	9,462	69	72	74	80

Source: Bureau of the Census, in U.S., Dept. of Labor, Bureau of Labor Statistics, *The Social and Economic Status of Negroes in the United States* (1970), p. 15.

There has been an increasing concentration of the minority community in the urban area during the decade of the fifties and the sixties (Table 5). This increasing concentration in the urban areas may, on the one hand, help consolidate purchasing power to the advantage of the minority entrepreneur. On the other hand, with the move to the suburbs by the nonminority middle class, much of the capital and many markets needed for economic development are no longer available in the central city.

TABLE 5

Negroes as a Percentage of Total Population by Location, inside and outside Metropolitan Areas, and by Size of Metropolitan Area, 1950, 1960, and 1969

	Percentage of Negroes		
	1950	1960	1969
United States	10	11	11
Metropolitan areas*	9	11	12
Central cities	12	17	21
Central cities in metropolitan			
areas of:			
1,000,000 or more	13	19	26
250,000 to 1,000,000	12	15	18
Under 250,000	12	12	12
Suburbs	5	5	5
Outside metropolitan areas	11	10	9

*Population of the 212 SMSAs as defined in 1960.
Source: Bureau of the Census, in U.S., Dept. of Labor, Bureau of Labor Statistics, *The Social and Economic Status of Negroes in the United States* (1970), p. 15.

One of the most interesting elements in today's minority enterprise climate is the changing attitude in the minority community toward the status of the entrepreneur. Heretofore, the ambitious black perceived the obstacles to a business career and often chose a career in the professions. He had access to professional education in black educational institutions and he had a captive clientele, since white doctors, dentists, or lawyers frequently did not or would not provide these services to the black population.[11] Highly motivated blacks, unlike the highly motivated in other racial groups, were discouraged from entering business. The black population valued the contribution of the black professional man but tended to diminish the contribution of the black businessman. In fact, until recently it was considered prestigious in the black community to purchase name brands from non-minority enterprises. The goods of the black merchant were thought to be inferior, apparently for no reason other than that the proprietor was black.[12]

Growth Potential Industries

Minority enterprise opportunities should be developed which:

1. Contribute to the capacity of the various minorities to take advantage of business opportunities beyond particular ethnic or racial markets;

2. Have a capacity for growth and capital creation;

3. Capitalize upon the skills and knowledge of all elements of the population;

4. Promote areas of comparative advantage such as health care, job training, day care and communications in the minority community;

5. Promote short- and long-run community development objectives;

6. Make effective use of government-created and government-protected markets, particularly in new, higher growth areas.[13]

Economic indicators show where the potential for minority business lies. Real economic growth of the United States is expected to average 4.4 percent per year, so that the Gross National Product (GNP) will increase from the third quarter 1970 level of $985.2 billion to almost $1.4 trillion by 1980.[14] With this increase, the consumption rate of nondurable goods is expected to decline from 62 percent to 60 percent during the period from 1967 to 1980.[15] At the same time, increases in family formation, rising incomes, and replacement of old and substandard housing will push demand for new housing to 2.4 million units per year in the late 1970s. This factor will account for the rise in private domestic investment growth from the 1967 level of 15 percent to over 16 percent of the 1980 GNP.[16]

Expenditures on consumer durable goods will show the highest rate of growth, largely because of rising affluence. Between 1967 and 1980 real disposable income per capita is projected to increase at an annual average of 3.1 percent, doubling the proportion of families with real incomes of $10,000 or more from around 25 percent of all consumer units to around 50 percent. Higher incomes, along with increased leisure time, will influence demands for recreation equipment, such as boats, motors, automobiles, televisions, pleasure aircraft, and sporting goods. There will also be large demands for household furnishings because of the large increase in the 25–34 age group.[17]

Consumer spending for nondurable goods will continue to grow at a slower rate than total spending. By 1980 Americans are expected to spend only 38 percent of total expenditures on consumer nondurables, compared to 44 percent in 1967 and 55 percent in 1968. A large share of the consumer nondurables will be for clothes, household supplies, gasoline and oil, drugs, personal grooming aids, and reading materials. Spending for food and beverages will decrease as a proportion of total nondurable expenditures.[18]

Statistical data from the Department of Commerce indicates that consumers will, for the first time in American history, spend more money on services—air travel, car rentals, beauty parlors, advertising and management consulting, life insurance, and so on—than for nondurable goods. Even though the prices for services have risen at a faster than average rate, services have proliferated, and their coming preeminence will present a whole new set of opportunities and challenges. Major components within the services field will be housing, business expenditures, medical services, and education and research.[19] These then are prime areas for minority enterprise to enter.

An examination of output demand by using projections from the Bureau of Labor Statistics, can show a national trend in higher growth businesses. The data reveal obvious business opportunities in those industries with projected substantial increases in growth rate. These include the following industries: optical, ophthalmic, and photographic equipment; electric, gas, and sanitary services; business services; and office supplies.[20]

Industries for which the projected demand for output is expected to grow at medium high and increasing rates include the following:

nonferrous metal ores
new construction
household furniture manufacture
manufacture of other furniture and fixtures
manufacture of paper and allied products, except containers
printing and publishing
manufacture of stone and clay products
the wholesale and retail trade industry
medical, educational services, and non-profit organizations
primary nonferrous metals manufacture
manufacture of electrical industrial equipment and apparatus
manufacture of miscellaneous electrical machinery, equipment, and
    supplies
scientific and controlling instruments
miscellaneous manufacturing
hotels, personal and repair services, except automobile repair ser-
    vices

Some discretion must be used in evaluating those industries which will show high rates of growth during the 1965–80 period but for which the growth rate has decreased since the 1957–65 period. Whether or not opportunities exist for minority entrepreneurs depends on such factors as: (1) the production capacity of existing firms, (2) the number of new firms to be developed during the coming decade, (3) new-product development, (4) the ability of minority firms to reduce costs, (5) the relative sales promotion success of minority versus rival firms, (6) the availability of capital, and (7) the availability of trained minority managers and technicians.

Technology-intensive industries

A large number of higher-growth opportunities exist in technology-intensive industries.[21] In the past, entry into these industries has been eased in many cases by government-contract support, both in terms of direct support for research and development expenses and through creation of a market for at least a limited number of the new products. The importance of government market creation has been dramatically demonstrated by the hundreds of new firms initiated in the Boston, Palo Alto, and Los Angeles areas since World War II. Research and development is a potentially profitable area, but it presents many problems, such as the need for substantial investments. In addition, these areas require technological expertise, managerial and entrepreneurial expertise, and sales promotion expertise.

Given these requirements, how can a minority enterprise launch itself into a high-growth potential industry? The answer may lie in nonminority corporate support of minority spin-off firms, perhaps in conjunction with direct government grants or tax incentives. For example, a large manufacturing firm could set up a minority-run supplier to manufacture components for the manufacturer or to provide a specialized service. One example of such a high technology spin-off is that established by the Bendix Corporation's Communications Division—Baltimore Electronic Associates, Inc.[22]

In a study of more than 200 new technology-based firms founded by former employees of the Massachusetts Institute of Technology research and development laboratories, the total proportion of failures found during the first five years of these spin-off firms was only 20 percent, as compared with 80 percent failure during the same period for all firms.[23] In addition, the spin-off firms showed an exponential growth in sales during this same five-year period. During their preliminary stages, these firms were mainly preoccupied with government research and development, but tended to diversify rapidly into consumer markets.[24]

Potential minority businessmen seeking out areas of high growth might also look to those industries in which significant technological advances are expected, as there appears to be a correlation between research and development or technological research expenditures and long-run profits.[25] Not only must minority businessmen enter fields in which subsidized research and development will occur, they must also enter fields which are already technology intensive and in which expenditures on innovation will translate themselves into substantial profits during the coming decade.[26]

One cannot predict with certainty which industries will experience significant technological changes, nor can one readily predict with absolute certainty where an innovative thought will occur. But the growth of investments in, and profits from, research and development expenditures appear to be closely correlated with government expenditures in any given area.[27] While government expenditures for the 1960s were concentrated in the areas of aerospace, electronics, and atomic energy, increased emphasis will be placed on research and development in such areas as medical research, education, sanitation, housing, and safety.[28] If minorities are seeking high-return investments, they must look toward these new areas of large government investment.

America has typically accepted technological advances with insufficient consideration for problems of physical health, sanity, and aesthetics, such as the noisiness of airplanes and air pollution from automobiles. Thus, one higher growth business opportunity (in terms of government expenditures) will be the technology-intensive research and development industry which will deal with the problems created as by-products of advanced technology.

Discretionary purchase industries

Another source of high-growth opportunities is the discretionary purchase industry. Business opportunities may be said to lie in the areas of fad industries and intermediaries for labor-intensive production. The fad industry is one area of business opportunity which can show high growth but which does not necessarily involve a high level of technology. Increasing income and increasing leisure time will stimulate a tremendous increase in goods and services which will soon outgrow their stylishness. Despite the fact that employment for minorities may be cyclical or unpredictable and sporadic in these industries, the fad industries give unusual returns on capital. The toy industry is one example of business opportunity requiring relatively little capital outlay but much innovation, extremely good sales promotion, and market appraisal.

An additional source of business opportunity is the area of businesses which provide special services as well as social services. The following areas of comparative strength may contribute to rewarding business opportunities by drawing on the strengths and knowledge of an ethnic or racial group: developing minority resources; capitalizing on ethnic or racial identities, experiences, and attitudes; providing (and researching) social services to minorities.

In the first area—resource development—minorities could act as developers and agents for talented minorities. For example, black recording stars, actresses, athletes, artists, and writers might also have black agents—provided adequate training, financing, and necessary contacts were available. The entrepreneurial aspect requires an aggressive sales promoter. Not only might this minority-talent, public intermediary operate a highly successful business, but also this business venture would be one means of stopping the flow of minority talent to nonminority capitalists. For Indians and Mexican-Americans (many of whom are engaged in the making of handicraft, pottery, dolls, and carved items), an intermediary might exploit the rising market for custom goods by acting as a go-between for labor-intensive producers and retailers. Where possible, both types of intermediaries might also function in the final stages of trade or production.

Minorities operating in minority-identity fields might have a better understanding of minority needs than would other business firms. A chain of soul kitchens might be highly successful, especially if it combined good food with pleasant surroundings and served both minorities and nonminorities. Cosmetics, clothes, and hair products catering to minorities have, on the whole, met with widespread acceptance, although they are often so expensive that they are beyond the means of many potential customers. In an allied area, Latin minorities could investigate the development of import-export linkages with the increasingly important Latin

American market; blacks could likewise involve themselves in African trade exchange.

An important minority comparative advantage includes the administration of social services in minority communities, since a minority individual, capitalizing on shared experiences, can better communicate with others of the same minority group.[29] In the areas of mental health programs, drug and crime rehabilitation, and social welfare, a minority enterprise to administer social services, staffed by professionals in their respective social fields and with paraprofessional minority community residents, might have considerably more success and prove to be much less expensive than a similar governmental agency.[30] Formal education and professional experience cannot overcome lack of communication, distrust, and lack of common experience. Among groups with language problems, language training by bilingual minority members may capitalize upon a strategic weakness. In addition, a minority firm could do urban research into the quality of public services, and might well have an advantage over a similar nonminority firm.

Government Creation and Encouragement of Market Development

Since World War II, the federal government has become an important force in the creation of new markets in both the public and private sectors of the economy.[31] A familiar example is the visible market created by the federal government in the aerospace area, which has amounted to several hundred billion dollars over the last ten years.[32] But the government also creates market demand in many other ways, such as licensing, grants of insurance, and protection of monopoly status. Perhaps most important for minority enterprise development, the government can use its market creation power to provide numerous protected market areas so necessary for the development of most new enterprises, and the government can assume the role of the primary risk taker.

Of course, there are numerous other ways in which the government may create a protected market, as by the granting of a radio, television, or interstate commission carrier license. As previously noted, the government may also create substantial incentives for nonminority business to assist minority business with financial guarantees, subsidies, and grants. There is a variety of ways in which the federal government may use its powers to promote the development of minority enterprise. The following list is a brief survey of federal government market creation and development powers:

1. *Risk taking.* The government has become the primary risk taker in many new technical areas such as radar, computer development, microelectronics, and, more recently, supersonic air transportation, and artificial organs.

2. *Direct purchase of goods and services.* Many hundreds of new companies have been initiated and sustained through government contracts, including almost the entire aerospace industry.

3. *Tax incentives.*[33] The use of tax incentives has stimulated many different types of industrial development. The most widely publicized have been the various mineral depletion allowances and the investment tax credit. However, a large variety of taxes is commonly used by government at all levels for selective stimulation of business development.

4. *Allocation of scarce resources.* The insuance of licenses in regulated industries, such as air transport, communications, and interstate transport, has provided substantial opportunities for business development. The grant of grazing, mineral, or timber rights on federal lands has also been quite important.

5. *Insurance.* The guarantee of investments by agencies, such as the Agency for International Development (AID), or the guarantee of loans by SBA or EDA, have been important in business development. New areas of proposed government insurance include surety bonding for minority contractors and guarantee of equity investments in minority enterprise.[34]

6. *Direct loans.* The government makes a significant amount of direct loan money available, particularly through SBA and EDA programs.

7. *Tariffs and quotas.* The selective use of trade barriers has provided substantial opportunity for industrial development in a number of industries.

8. *Supply of capital equipment.* The government has often stimulated industrial development by allowing private firms to use or buy government-purchased equipment at reduced rates.

9. *Subsidized markets.* The use of agricultural subsidies has provided a substantial impetus toward the creation of a highly efficient agricultural industry in this country.

This list indicates ways in which the federal government can use its powers to stimulate business development. However, minority businessmen have been almost totally excluded from such government programs. They have participated, if at all, only recently, and then primarily through the direct business loan.[35]

At present, spending by federal, state, and local government is approximately one-fifth of GNP and is projected to increase during the period from 1967 to 1980 by an average annual rate of 7.08 percent (Table 6). The greatest increase in government spending will be for housing and community development, both of which are concerned with fulfilling social needs. In general, government expenditures will exhibit increased focus upon housing, urban renewal, and other social benefits. Large increases in government expenditures for health and hospitals, conservation, and recreation will occur, while spending on national defense is expected to show the slowest growth rate of government spending. Thus, much government spending for the coming decade will complement high-growth industry in such areas as housing, education, and health care. All are areas which will also assist in community development and over which the community should be able to exercise some control in the letting of contracts and grants. Thus, minority enterprise could be given a substantial portion of this new, higher growth business.

TABLE 6
Government Spending by Function, 1967 Actual and 1980 Projected

Program	Total Government Millions of Current $		Average Annual Growth in Percentage
	1967	1980	
Total expenditures.........	241,253	587,164	7.08
Defense..............	74,555	116,179	3.47
Nondefense...........	166,698	470,985	8.32
Education...........	39,677	123,324	9.12
Health and hospitals......	8,547	35,087	11.48
Sanitation...........	22,006	7,672	10.87
Social security and welfare	40,994	103,683	7.40
Civilian safety.........	6,248	21,073	9.80
Labor..............	1,087	5,176	12.75
Transportation........	15,118	38,643	7.48
Development.........	713	11,052	23.47
Conservation and recreation	4,492	16,620	10.60

Source: National Planning Association, in Looking Ahead, May, 1969, p. 11.

Demographic-Economic Trends and Business Opportunity

Population growth or decline by geographic area, together with growth or decline in the work force and the number employed by occupation, suggests increases in manpower resources to take advantages of emerging business opportunities, and in manpower to provide purchasing power. Such population changes constitute significant changes in business opportunities. Four sets of interacting population movements affecting business opportunities and markets can be identified: (1) regional population trends; (2) the movement from rural to urban areas; (3) the movement of city population to the suburbs; and (4) an exchange of population according to race.

In general, the greatest rate of job and population growth has occurred along the rim of the country—moving along the West Coast, through the Southwest, and over to Florida. Higher-than-average growth increases also took place in the South and the West. The West will show the fastest gains in population and income, and the Southwest will show the fastest gains in employment. Florida (Southeast), Arizona (Southwest), Colorado (Mountains), California and Nevada (West) will be the states spearheading the growth of their respective regions.

There has been a substantial decline of rural populations, and an increase in metropolitan areas. Rural population increased from 61.4 million to 70.7 million in the 19 years from 1950 to 1969. At the same time, metropolitan population increased from 89.2 million to 127.5 million people.[36] Thus, while the rural (nonmetropolitan) population was increasing by an annual average of .85 percent, the metropolitan population was increasing by 3.4 percent.[37]

There is also a geographical concentration present among the states experiencing the fastest growth in services. Of the six states experiencing the greatest increase in service dollars spent (Maryland, South Carolina, Georgia, Florida, Alabama, and Hawaii, in that order), the fastest growing five are in the Southeast. Moreover, the service field, compared to retail trade, is a highly concentrated market geographically. The two leading states in spending for services are New York and California. These two states do more than one-third of the nation's service business, although they contain only one-fifth of its population. Illinois, Pennsylvania, Texas, and Ohio are the other national leaders in service dollars spent. All of these states contain substantial minority populations which could benefit from the growth of these service industries if an appropriate national strategy were developed now to channel substantial amounts of this new business to minority enterprise.

Given the above facts, it is obvious that business and job opportunities do not necessarily lie either in the northern United States or in the large cities. Business opportunity is growing more rapidly in the South (where the minority population is concentrated) than the national average. Medium-size cities may have better business growth opportunities than the inner-city areas of the large cities.

Finally, there have been surprising increases in the population of small nonmetropolitan cities. In other words, the movement from the farms is not necessarily to the big city. This suggests that there are important nodules of business opportunity in cities of this smaller size, even in predominantly rural states.

It is important to realize that these population trends are not merely population movements, but are *opportunity* movements—opportunities for jobs and business—because they reflect an underlying growth of business and government in the fast-growing areas. This data gains importance when it is realized that the movement of the minority population is not in the direction of greatest opportunity. The movement of the minority population appears to be going in almost the opposite direction, although it must be cautioned that conclusions in this area are often impressionistic, since data on the movement of race is scarce. But an example which supports the hypothesis is New England. Its average annual employment growth rate during 1961–68 was next to the lowest of the regions, 2.3 percent,[38] but its increase in nonwhite male workers was the fastest in the nation; and this increase is expected to continue to grow at a rapid rate in the 1970s.

During the past 25 years, the proportion of nonwhites in the central city population has doubled, but it has declined in suburbia. In fact, between 1960 and 1966, the Negro population in American central cities increased 22.9 percent. It declined by 1.8 percent for whites.[39] Meanwhile, industry and manufacture have abandoned their old quarters, and have followed or even preceded the general movement of the more affluent population and business to the suburbs. The contrast is apparent: blacks go into the city while the jobs and businesses are moving away.[40]

The South has increased in population, but the net growth is accounted for by the white population; the blacks have moved to the North and to the big cities. In the 1950s, the South experienced a net loss of over 1.4 million nonwhites. Estimates place the net outmigration from the rural areas during the 1960s at an average of more than three-quarters of a million persons a year.[41] When total population movements are related to the population trends of minorities, it appears that there is increasing emigration of nonwhites from higher-growth areas. This result suggests the need for a network to inform minorities of business opportunities based on demographic changes. At the very least, such information is needed to enable the minority entrepreneur to make realistic calculations about risks and opportunities. Rather than proposing a mass migration of minorities to higher-growth areas, it is proposed that some business opportunities for minorities be matched to specific areas of comparative advantage. Fortunately, there will exist in the 1970s not only expanding horizons for business growth in geographic districts which are rapidly developing, but also opportunities in the inner city and the large metropolitan areas. These are often considered *passé* by nonminority entrepreneurs who think in terms of economic and business growth opportunities.

Conclusion

It is clear that greater opportunities for business development must be made available to minority entrepreneurs in order to provide one important component of total community development. It has not been suggested that minority business development without other facets of development—such as greater education and health care opportunities, as well as greatly expanded job opportunities in non-minority business—is a panacea. But minority business development must provide a significant element in building the capital base in the minority community, in providing success models, and in providing opportunities for self-development.

Present programs for minority enterprise development are largely focused on short-term goals, such as providing quantities of equity and debt capital to numbers of minority enterprises, almost without regard to the growth potential of these enterprises. If the vast bulk of minority business is investment in low-growth, low-profit potential businesses, then present programs may have the long-term impact of widening the gap between minority and nonminority businesses. It is, therefore, important that we attempt to make available to minority entrepreneurs the full range of business opportunities, with particular emphasis on higher growth potential opportunities.

It is possible to identify a number of areas of higher growth potential through a variety of indicators, such as projections of government spending, consumer demand, socio-economic patterns, and demographic projections. All of these changes represent new and often important opportunities with higher growth potential. It is important to identify these areas, make this information available to minority entrepreneurs, and provide necessary financing, management and technical assistance. Such a program of business development must include a broadly based strategy designed to meet the many development deficiencies in the minority community. Such a comprehensive program has recently been proposed by the National Advisory Council on Minority Business Enterprise (NACMBE), which includes more than seventy-five recommendations for new and expanded programs in business opportunities, education, community development, and finance.[42] Only a comprehensive program of this type will provide the human and technical resources needed to implement the business development strategy discussed in this paper.

The role of the federal government is crucial in the implementation of the proposed strategy. It may be desirable to delegate much of the actual implementation of the proposed strategy to the private sector, but only the government can provide the financial incentives and create the markets needed to provide numbers of higher growth potential minority enterprises. The government can fill this latter role by: (1) the direct purchase of goods and services; (2) acting as a guarantor and subsidizer; (3) providing licenses; (4) acting as a risk taker; and (5) providing tax incentives or direct grants to motivate involvement by nonminority business.

To summarize the proposed business opportunities analyzed, a comprehensive business opportunity strategy should concern itself with moving on all possible fronts. It must match community and individual resources with business opportunities. It must focus on higher-growth areas while performing a variety of community development functions, including employment, capital creation, and the production of needed goods and services. This mix of functions will provide a "staging area" for entrepreneurial development which can make a meaningful contribution to overall minority economic development.

NOTES

1. "Minority group" is defined for this paper to include only blacks, persons of Spanish-speaking ancestry, and American Indians.

2. Office of Planning, Research, and Analysis of the Small Business Administration, "Distribution of Minority-Owned Businesses," June 1969, p. 1 (unpublished report). Theodore Cross has estimated that there are only a dozen black businesses in Manhattan which employ ten or more people. T. Cross, *Black Capitalism* (1969), p. 60.

3. S.B.A., "Distribution of Minority-Owned Businesses."

4. See generally *The President's Task Force Report on Improving the Prospects of Small Business* (1970), pp. 21–27.

5. See also MIT Conference on the Human Factor in the Transmission of Technology, 1966, Roberts, "Entrepreneurship and Technology," in *Factors in the Transfer of Technology*, ed. by William H. Gruber and Donald G. Marquis, (Cambridge, Mass.: MIT Press, 1969), pp. 219, 224–25, and Addison W. Parris, *The Small Business Administration* (New York: Praeger Publishers, 1968), pp. 51–55. Of course most business discontinuances are not outright bankruptcies; still, for every five new businesses started, another three to five go out of business each year.

6. One estimate of minority business failure or discontinuances may be obtained by examining the relative default rates of SBA loans between nonminority and minority borrowers. Parris estimates that minority defaults were running ten to twenty times the rate of nonminority defaults (3 percent). A. Parris, *The Small Business Administration*, p. 116. However, this estimate is based solely on the Economic Opportunity Loan (EOL) program through 1968, and a more recent analysis of the SBA minority loan program indicates that overall default rates are likely to be lower than was previously true for the EOL program. See Small Business Administration, "Evaluation of the Minority Enterprise Program," Jan. 1971 (unpublished report). For a discussion of the difficulties in running a ghetto-based small business, see T. Cross, *Black Capitalism*, pp. 21–30.

7. See "Distribution of Minority-Enterprise." A recent Office of Economic Opportunity (OEO) survey of larger minority businesses attempted to identify minority busineses with annual sales in excess of $500,000 and which showed a profit for the last two years. The largest business so identified was Johnson Publications, Inc., with annual sales in 1969 of about $33 million, and this was three times the size of the next largest minority business, Johnson Products, Inc. About 100 companies were included in this study; of these, 24 met the sales and profitability criteria. (OEO memo from Paul London and Susan Davis to Theodore Cross, Minority Business Successes, May 19, 1970.) The smallest company listed among the *Fortune* 500 had sales of $162 million in 1969. *The Fortune Directory*, May 1970, p. 23.

8. The 216 Boston "route 128" spinoff companies studied by Edward Roberts and his colleagues had an annual five-year growth rate of over 20 percent per year. Roberts, "Entrepreneurship and Technology," pp. 225–27. The same type of growth rate was exhibited by a sample of 13 companies used in a technology transfer study by the author. S. Doctors, *The NASA Transfer Program: An Analysis* (New York City: Praeger Publishers, 1971). Much of the growth achieved by these companies has been made possible through the creation of a protected market by a federal government. Clearly this same federal government power could be used in the development of minority enterprise as it has been used to develop an aerospace industry.

9. It is assumed, contrary to Andrew Brimmer, that the promotion of minority enterprise does not have the sole objective of providing employment for larger numbers of blacks. It is assumed that the creation of numbers of viable minority-owned enterprises may serve a number of other socioeconomic objectives. It is also assumed that minority economic development requires a holistic approach to such development, including the parallel provision of improved employment, business, educational, and health-care opportunities. Just as in the nonminority community, it is the synergistic interaction of a variety of factors which will result in significant development. See A. Brimmer and H. Terrell, "The Economic Potential of Black Capitalism," Dec. 29, 1969 (paper presented before the 82nd Annual Meeting of the American Economic Association).

10. This idea is suggested by the work of Frazier, McClelland, and Roberts: E. Frazier, *Black Bourgeoisie* (1968); D. McClelland and D. Winter, *Motivating Economic Achievement* (1969); Roberts, "Entrepreneurship and Technology" in *Factors in the Transfer of Technology*.

11. A recent survey of the graduates (346 from 1946 to 1969) of Atlanta University's (AU) School of Business Administration indicated that prior to 1968 most of the graduates had entered nonbusiness occupations. AU has produced over half of all the black M.B.A.'s in the period 1908 to 1969.

12. This is especially true for the black middle class. See E. Frazier, *Black Bourgeoisie*.

13. The core recommendations of the National Advisory Council on Minority Business Enterprise (NACMBE) placed stress on the need for greatly expanded training and educational opportunities and recommended the allocation of $160 million over the next three years to assist materially in this area.

14. Department of Labor *Forecast*, Nov. 1970.

15. *Predicasts*, April 20, 1970, p. 3.

16. *Ibid.*

17. *Ibid.*

18. *Finance Facts Yearbook,* National Consumer Finance Association (1970).

19. *Sales Management–1970 Survey of Buying Power,* June 10, 1970, p. A–21.

20. It should be noted that the SIC code groupings may, in general, bring together different kinds of growth areas within one industrial code. Thus, further breakdowns of a given area may be necessary to find particularly desirable opportunities.

21. Technology-intensive industries may be defined as those industries which have such characteristics as a much larger than average amount of their funds being spent on research and development, a significantly higher than average percentage of technologists in their employ, and a reliance on the production of new technology-based products for their retention and expansion markets. Such industries would include aircraft, scientific instruments, chemicals, and electronics. National Science Foundation, *Research and Development in Industry,* 1968 (1970).

22. Bendix helped several of its minority employees establish a business to manufacture electrical components needed by Bendix. Originally the components were manufactured by the company, but it was thought that they could be produced less expensively by an outside source. Bendix has supplied management and technical assistance as well as help in purchasing for the new corporation, Baltimore Electronics Associates.

23. Roberts, "Entrepreneurship and Technology," pp. 224–29.

24. *Ibid.,* p. 228.

25. See also U.S. Panel on Invention/Innovation, *Technological Innovation: Its Environment and Management* (Washington, D.C.: Dept. of Commerce, 1967); E. Mansfield, *The Economics of Technological Change* (New York: W.W. Norton, 1968), pp. 43–98; and C. Freeman, *et al.,* "Research and Development in Electronic Capital Goods," *National Institute Economic Review* (Nov. 1965), pp. 40–91.

26. S. Doctors, "Federal R&D Funding and Its Effects on Industrial Productivity," Jan. 1968 (unpublished paper prepared for the New England Research Application Center, University of Connecticut).

27. *Looking Ahead,* National Planning Association, May 1969, p. 11.

28. See the discussion of new career opportunities in A. Pearl and F. Riessman, *New Careers for the Poor* (New York: The Free Press, 1965), Chs. 3, 4, 5, 7.

29. *Ibid.*

30. U.S. Dept. of Commerce, Business and Defense Services Administration, *Selected Industry Profiles: Detailed Analysis of Minority Business Opportunities* (1969), Parts I–V.

31. State and local governments also purchase large quantities of goods and services and create markets in many other ways, but this article will concentrate on the role of the federal government, leaving for future works the exposition of the importance of the nonfederal public sector for minority-enterprise development. The ratio is about two to one in terms of present tax collection expenditures in favor of the federal government. Dept. of Commerce, *Survey of Current Business* (1970).

32. Aerospace research and development expenditures alone have totaled over $100 billion during the last decade. National Science Foundation, *Federal Funds for Research, Development, and Other Scientific Activities: Fiscal Years 1968, 1969, and 1970* (1969).

33. NACMBE has recommended the use of tax incentives for both direct nonminority business assistance to minority businesses and for training minority managers.

34. OEO's newly initiated Opportunity Funding Corporation (OFC) will attempt to determine the efficacy of using federal government guarantees in a wide variety of applications to stimulate minority business and capital base development. See Office of Economic Opportunity, *Opportunity Funding: An Economic Development Demonstration Program* (1970).

35. A recent survey (by NACMBE) of SBA lending practices revealed that most loans to minority entrepreneurs were direct Equal Opportunity Loans (EOL) of $25,000 each, while those to nonminority entrepreneurs were considerably larger, averaging $56,000, and were guaranteed. The findings of the NACMBE indicated that minority businessmen have been almost totally excluded from most government business development programs.

36. U.S., Bureau of the Census, *Current Population Reports,* 1969.

37. *Ibid.*

38. 1969 *Manpower Report of the President,* p. 35.

39. U.S., Dept. of Commerce, Bureau of the Census, *Current Population Reports,* Series P. 20, No. 181, Apr. 21, 1969, p. 1.

40. 1968 *Manpower Report of the President,* p. 132.

41. Sheridan T. Maitland & Stanley M. Nebel, "Rural to Urban Transition," *Monthly Labor Review,* June 1968, pp. 28–32.

42. 1971 *NACMBE Final Report* (1971).

Implications of Revenue Sharing for Black Political and Economic Goals

James A. Hefner and
Marguerite Ross Barnett

The natural consequences of haphazardly planned, rapid urban growth compounded by racism, ethnic and class conflict, public malaise, and official neglect have created the elements of the "urban crisis." There are many manifestations of the urban crisis. Among the most serious is the growing inadequacy of urban public services. Emergence of sprawling, metropolitan areas has created the need and demand for new, unanticipated forms of publicly financed services. However, cities, in a nation which has spent approximately $100 billion between 1966 and 1971 on the Indochina War,[1] find it difficult to halt the decline in quality and quantity of traditional public services.

For blacks, the increasing fiscal impoverishment of cities is a threefold problem. Financial constraints have forced local governments to curtail vital public services; suburbanization of an increasing number of industries limits job opportunities and contributes to black unemployment, impoverishment, and geographic immobility, while at the same time these exiting industries weaken an already faltering tax base; and, finally, contemporaneous and historic economic deprivation means blacks require many special public services which cannot be financed in a time of fiscal crisis.

Furthermore, blacks are becoming increasingly urbanized. Between 1960 and 1968 the proportion of blacks in the total population of the Northcentral cities rose from 17 to 23 percent and of Northeastern cities from 13 to 18 percent.[2] For Northcentral cities this is an increase of 28 percent and for Northeastern cities an increase of 37 percent. In the South there was a slight increase from 25 to 27 percent and in the West central cities from 8 to 10 percent. The proportion of blacks in the suburbs remained stable at 3 percent in the Northeast and Northcentral regions, declined from 12 to 10 percent in the South, and doubled to 4 percent in the West. While 54 percent of blacks live in central cities, only 26 percent of whites do. Of those whites residing in cities, half are living in small

TABLE 1
Percentage of Blacks in the Total Population of Each of the Thirty
Largest U.S. Cities, 1950–67, and 1972 Black Voting Age Population by City

Size Ranking*	City†	Percentage of Blacks			Change in Percentage 1960–67	Imputed Annual Rate of Change in Percentage 1960–67‡	Blacks as Percentage of Voting Age Population
		1950	1960	1967			
9	Washington, D.C.	35	54	69	+15	+3.5	66.8
30	Newark	17	34	49	+15	+5.3	48.6
24	Atlanta	37	38	44	+6	+2.1	47.3
6	Baltimore	24	35	41	+4	−1.5	39.7
15	New Orleans	32	37	41	+4	+1.5	39.7
22	Memphis	37	37	40	+3	+1.1	36.2
5	Detroit	16	29	39	+10	+4.3	39.4
10	St. Louis	18	29	37	+8	+3.6	35.9
8	Cleveland	16	29	34	+5	+2.3	35.1
4	Philadelphia	18	26	33	+7	+3.5	31.1
2	Chicago	14	34	30	+7	+3.8	28.2
21	Cincinnati	16	22	24	+2	+1.3	24.4
26	Indianapolis	15	21	24	+3	+1.9	14.5
27	Kansas City	12	18	22	+4	+2.9	18.8
7	Houston	21	23	22	−1	−0.6	24.1

14	Dallas	13	19	22	+ 3	+2.4	22.3
16	Pittsburgh	12	17	21	+ 4	+3.1	18.4
1	New York	10	14	19	+ 5	+4.5	19.0
28	Columbus	12	16	19	+ 3	+2.5	16.5
3	Los Angeles	9	14	18	+ 4	+3.6	15.9
20	Buffalo	6	13	17	+ 4	+3.9	17.8
13	Boston	5	9	15	+ 6	+7.5	13.2
11	Milwaukee	3	8	14	+ 6	+8.3	11.5
12	San Francisco	6	10	14	+ 4	+4.9	11.1
23	Denver	4	6	9	+ 3	+6.0	NA§
17	San Antonio	7	7	8	+ 1	+1.9	NA
18	San Diego	5	6	7	+ 1	+2.2	NA
19	Seattle	3	5	7	+ 2	+4.9	NA
29	Phoenix	5	5	5	0	0.0	NA
25	Minneapolis	1	2	4	+ 2	+10.4	NA

* Largest size is ranked #1. These are 1960 size rankings before 1970 census data were available.
† Arranged in order of estimated percentage of blacks in 1967. The 1970 Census figures will undoubtedly show that a number of additional cities are more than 50 percent black.
‡ This is the annual compound interest rate required to account for the recorded change in the proportion of blacks in the total population between 1960 and 1968.
§ Not available.

Source: "Trends in Social and Economic Conditions in Metropolitan Areas," Current Population Reports, 1969, p. 9. The percentage figures for 1950 have been included to give additional perspective to the changes in the last decade. Reported in Michael T. Flax, Blacks and Whites: An Experiment in Racial Indicators (Washington, D.C.: The Urban Institute), pp. 54–5. Black Voting Age Population by City from Joint Center for Political Studies, Washington, D.C.

rather than large cities. As Table 1 indicates, the magnitude of the demographic shift in black population has had important political implications. *Reynolds* v. *Sims* and the so-called "Reapportionment Revolution" underscore the increased potential of black political power. Table 1, showing black concentration in the thirty largest American cities and the high levels of black voting-age population, indicates the particular importance of urban development to the black community.

Recent revenue sharing proposals for urban areas direct our attention to the fiscal aspects of the urban crisis. Yet that crisis, and even the broader issue of establishing a sound financial base for the cities, is intrinsically both political and economic. It is a crisis created by social values, political philosophy, and inadequate institutional organization as well as by diminishing financial resources. Ponder this fact: "The metropolitan areas of the United States account for 80 percent of the nation's bank accounts, three quarters of federal personal income tax collections, and 77 percent of the value added by manufacture."[3] Why is there a crisis? One answer is that the resources exist within the domain of one set of jurisdictions and the problems within another; one segment of the population controls the distribution of the resources, and another segment experiences the problems and clamors for resource redistribution.

Within the metropolitan areas, political fragmentation[4] has resulted in the creation of governmental barriers which often isolate poor communities with massive public service needs from wealthy communities with surplus resources. Racism, the concept of grassroots government, and the supposed intrinsic value of suburban bliss provide the underlying ideological rationale for political fragmentation and segregation. Metropolitan political fragmentation, created largely by suburban demands for autonomy, creates, protects, and exascerbates fiscal disparities. It also creates social costs, borne by all, but more dramatically by the poor. Often the units of government designated to perform certain public service functions do not have the population base to perform those services adequately. To a certain extent cross-cutting, over-lapping jurisdictions fragment the performance of services and thus increase their cost. More important these jurisdictions create anomalous situations in which neighboring communities might have vastly different levels of public service. The characteristics and dilemmas of American urban growth, as they set constraints for and provide opportunities to urban blacks, structure the framework in which we shall analyze the Nixon and Mills Revenue Sharing proposals.[5]

We shall first outline the components of the two tax-sharing plans, compare revenue sharing to the present system of federal aid to state and local governments, analyze revenue sharing as it relates to black political and economic goals, and suggest some tentative conclusions concerning the most profitable way for blacks to utilize revenue sharing.

The Mills and Nixon Revenue Sharing Proposals

Revenue sharing got its initial impetus from the tremendous expansion of federal tax revenues in the early 1960s and the resulting prospects for a continuing federal fiscal surplus. However, the costs of U.S. involvement in the Vietnam conflict (which became important around 1965) precluded any action on revenue sharing during that decade. All discussions of revenue sharing included a statement somewhat like Walter W. Heller's:

> The important thing is to be ready to move from talk to action once Vietnam relents. . . .[6]

Now, in 1972, the situation has changed once again. Property taxes have been criticized as a basis for support for public education.[7] The problems of the cities have grown steadily and visibly worse; the Nixon Administration has predicted an end to the conflict in Vietnam,[8] and it is widely believed that there is a "taxpayer revolt" in middle America. All of these factors provide a climate in which Congress is expected to enact some revenue-sharing proposal this year.

Two specific proposals for revenue sharing have currently gathered substantial support in Congress. The first is one which President Nixon has backed for several years. Under its terms as originally proposed in 1969, the states would share in a progressively increasing percentage of the federal tax base. In 1970, they were to receive one-sixth of 1 percent (or about $500 million), with regular increases until the total appropriation reached 1 percent (or about $5 billion) at the end of 1975. The funds are to be divided among the states on the basis of population, weighted to consider incremental tax effort.[9] Under the present plan each state would be required to set aside at least 50 percent of its allocation for local use,[10] with allocation among localities determined by the amount of total local revenue in the state raised by each community. Alternative allocation plans can be drawn up through the cooperative efforts of the state and its local governments.[11]

Wilbur Mills, House Ways and Means Committee Chairman, calls for the allotment of about $5.3 billion on the basis of a state's population and the extent to which the state utilizes a personal income tax. The thirteen states which still have no income tax would get a two-year grace period during which they would receive an arbitrary amount. States with a high degree of urbanization or with a large number of families having yearly household earnings under $4000 would receive additional allotments. A state would be required to plow two-thirds of its allotment into city and county governments. The amount of the total national appropriation would not vary directly with the federal tax base, but instead would be set in a five-year pattern of increases, with congressional review of the entire system every five years. The money would be required to go for so-called high priority items—public safety, environmental protection, public transportation, youth recreation, health, financial administration, and related public works (presumably including possible public housing).[12]

Revenue Sharing Compared to Present Federal Aid to State and Local Governments

Resources of major metropolitan areas are, in general, far from equal to the demands which their citizens make. There is overwhelming need, especially in poor and black sectors, for more and better housing, schools, transportation, employment, utilities, and a whole range of social services unanticipated until recent years.

Intrinsic to the declining quality and quantity of urban public services is a growing inadequacy in state and local sources of revenue. Federal government use of income taxes as a source of revenue has limited the level of income tax state and local governments can levy on their citizens without creating an intolerable tax burden. As a result these governments have turned to property taxes and sales taxes. Local tax revenue in the United States consists mainly of property taxes. In 1966 the total amount collected in property taxes was $23.8 billion, 87.1 percent of the total local tax revenue.[13] Yet even with property and sales taxes, state and local governments are limited by competition in the size of levies they can make. They must adjust their rates to what industrial firms are willing to pay or risk losing the substantial increment to the area's economy which those firms represent. This creates pressure for a more regressive structure in a case where from the standpoint of distribution the taxes involved are already distributionally inferior to a progressive income tax.[14] To meet the rising expenditures, cities have sought higher tax rates only to discover new political and economic constraints. The recession of the late 1960s initiated a wave of political defeats for tax levies by people experiencing a growing economic squeeze. When higher taxes were passed, they contributed to the middle-class taxpayer exodus to more affluent suburbs.

The changing demographic pattern of the cities and the nature of tax-revenue growth combine to paint a bleak picture of the future of the cities under existing fiscal structures. Between 1957 and 1965 population grew 17 percent overall, but that growth included a 37 percent rise in the number of school-age children and a 25 percent rise in the over-65 group. Thus, not only did rising population and expectations increase the demand for services, but there was a tremendous, disproportionate increase in the demand for schools (already the largest component of the local budget) and special services to the elderly.[15] Revenues from property and sales taxes barely kept pace with growth in Gross National Product (GNP),[16] whereas revenues from the progressive income taxes relied upon by the federal government have been estimated to rise about 1.5 percent for every 1 percent rise in GNP.[17]

The state and local fiscal gap is dramatically represented by changes in expenditure patterns at that level. These expenditures for goods and services have taken up an increasing proportion of the GNP over the last two decades as shown in Table 2.

Estimates show that for every 1 percent rise in GNP in the period since 1954 state and local expenditure has risen on an average of about 1.7 percent, while general revenue has averaged about 0.9 percent (somewhere between 0.8 percent and 1.01 percent).[18] Given this trend, the fiscal gap as reflected in the GNP elasticity of state and local expenditure and revenue will probably grow larger in the future.

TABLE 2
State-Local Expenditures as Percentage of GNP 1950–1970

Year	State-Local Expenditures as a Percentage of GNP
1950	6.8
1955	7.5
1960	9.1
1962	9.6
1964	10.0
1966	10.4
1967	10.9
1970	11.3

Source: U.S. Congress, Joint Economic Committee, *Revenue Sharing and Its Alternatives*, 3, p. 1231.

Initiatives by the federal government, and to a lesser degree by some state governments, helped mitigate the extent and magnitude of the fiscal crisis. As Table 3 indicates, from 1952 to 1964 federal aid to local governmental units quadrupled. State aid to local units has continued to exceed state receipts from the federal government, but the net difference has leveled out in recent years.

TABLE 3
Federal and State Share to Local Government
(in Millions of Dollars)

Year	Total Local Direct Expenditures	Federal Grants-in-Aid To Local Units	To States	State Aid to Local Units	Excess of State Aid to Local Units over Federal Aid to States
1902	959	4	3	52	49
1927	6,359	9	107	596	489
1952	20,073	237	2,329	5,044	2,715
Fiscal Year 1963–64	50,964	956	9,046	12,873	3,827
Budgeted-Fiscal 1966–67		14,700			

Source: Research and Policy Committee, *Modernizing Local Government to Secure a Balanced Federalism* (New York: Committee for Economic Development, July 1966).

In the face of snowballing federal revenues and inadequate state and local revenues, it appears that continued and expanded federal aid to state and local governments is a logical and defensible solution to the services gap. Without an increase in this aid, there seems to be little hope for reversing the trend toward increasingly regressive taxes and widening disparities between the services offered by rich and poor states and cities. The demand for services in poor communities will continue to necessitate more taxation, which will in turn tend to drive away prosperous citizens and industrial firms. This will shrink local tax bases, necessitating an even greater tax effort, until those cities are drained of taxable resources.

Under the present structure of intergovernmental fiscal relations, the standard (and for most purposes, the only) form of federal aid is the conditional or categorical grant-in-aid. Most of these grants are made for strictly limited, explicit purposes (the funding of some governmental service). Often they require that the recipient provide matching funds and/or administrative staffs and set minimum standards for continued eligibility.[19] The federal government employs these grants where substantial benefit-spillovers exist outside the jurisdiction of the recipient, and traditionally it has justified them on the basis of those spillovers rather than the financial needs of the recipient. The rationale is that the local government will not provide a service when costs exceed direct local benefits, even though the existence of spillovers may mean that benefits to the nation as a whole exceed costs. The federal government pays a portion of the costs through its grant, the amount of which is determined by the ratio of local benefits to total benefits, the fiscal resources of the recipient, and the unmet needs of that community.

An alternative to conditional grants-in-aid is a national tax-credit system. Under such a system, the individual taxpayer can credit a given percentage of his state and local income taxes to his total federal income tax payment. This would make it easier for states to levy substantial personal income taxes, thus tapping an expanding source of revenue hitherto reserved for the federal government. The plan would also allow state and local governments to rely less on regressive property and sales taxes. However, its effects would be dampened by two factors: first, there is still an incentive (in interstate competition for industry) for a regressive tax structure; second, seventeen states still levy no personal income tax, and many have constitutional provisions against such a tax.[20]

Unconditional grants-in-aid, or revenue sharing, constitutes another alternative to the present fiscal structure. As mentioned above, in its most general form, revenue sharing sets aside a fixed portion of the federal income tax base for allocation to the states purely on the basis of population.[21] Specific proposals in Congress have included various allocation factors in addition to population for determining relative state shares in the tax pool, among them are: general tax effort (intensiveness of taxation) by the state; income tax effort, degree of urbanization; amount of tax originating in a given state; general incidence of low-income residents, and special subsidy provisions for the seventeen states with the lowest per-capita income.[22]

Revenue sharing could perform several important functions not performed by present methods of federal aid to localities. In providing revenue for state and local governments it could supplement conditional grants-in-aid; it could equalize the availability of services among states and cities and halt the regressive trend in state and local fiscal structures. At the aggregate level, such a system might provide a new tool of fiscal stabilization.[23]

As a supplement to conditional or categorical grants-in-aid, revenue-sharing could meet their inadequacies and correct the distortions which they cause.[24] Because they are limited in the purposes for which they may be used, categorical grants-in-aid tend to revitalize some needed public services while leaving others neglected. Because the grants also require matching funds, they tend to reinforce the neglect of other services by siphoning off funds to match the federal requirements for the services covered in grants. State and local politicians aggravate the problem by over-allocating funds to services covered by grants in order to stimulate still more federal interest and funds.[25] The general funding supplied under revenue sharing would, through ensuring local governments of a given minimum level of revenue, allow them to fill in the gaps between grants-in-aid (i.e., to supply services not covered by grants-in-aid). At the same time, by assuring localities of a guaranteed minimum level of revenue it could allow them to allocate funds to services in the order of their utility rather than according to the incidence of federal matching-fund grants.[26]

Because revenue sharing is based on population, it provides more equal access to its funds for all states. As a result it inherently tends to equalize the availability of public services from state to state. There are three factors which tend to make revenue sharing fiscally progressive. First, it lessens the dependence of state and local governments on regressive property and sales taxes. Second, the revenue which is shared is derived from the federal income tax, which is progressive. Third, the pattern of state and local expenditures is *very* progressive (amounting to 43 percent of income for the poorest families but only 6 percent of income for the middle class), while federal expenditures are slightly less so (varying from 42 percent of poor incomes to 16 percent of incomes over $10,000).[27]

But there are also substantial problems and unanswered questions associated with revenue sharing. First, although revenue sharing will channel more funds to the cities, these additional funds will not be sufficient for the expansion of the public services central cities require. Even if these grants were large enough for expansion of vital public services, if federal income, on which these grants depend, were to decrease (for example, as the result of a recession), these services would have to be cut back or eliminated. Elasticity in revenue sources has both advantages and disadvantages. Although the advantages of elastic revenue sources may outweigh the disadvantages, the question of what to do about services based on a revenue source that may decrease or disappear is particularly acute given the specific five-year limitation of the Mills proposal and the possibility of fund cut-backs, in any proposal. While heightened fiscal stability is possible under revenue sharing, increased fiscal instability is also possible, depending on the specific terms of the legislation.

Furthermore, the most important aspects of the urban crisis will not be resolved by the simple addition of a little more money. Certainly political fragmentation and economic differentiation will not be changed by revenue sharing. While the Mills proposal does contain a germ of potential redistribution impact, without federal conditions specifying metropolitan fiscal reorganization, political fragmentation will probably be reinforced by either the Nixon or Mills revenue sharing proposals. Although there may be some increased participation and innovation on the local level stimulated by revenue sharing, neglect of unpopular public services or of public services utilized disproportionately by unpopular groups will not be affected by revenue-sharing. States might even use the funds to lower taxes rather than to improve public services.

Many discussions of revenue sharing have questioned the capacity of state or local governments to handle additional funds. Usually this point is made in the context of calling for governmental reorganization. Critics of the web of overlapping local governmental jurisdictions as well as of local government inefficiency, incompetence, and corruption have demanded that funds be allocated only if there is a requirement of governmental reorganization. However, there are more important aspects of this issue. The basic assumption of revenue sharing is that states and localities can solve their problems if they have the funds to do so.

One could argue with a good deal of cogency that very few states and local governments have provided clear evidence that they possess the creativity, capability, or understanding to handle the problems of urban development.[28] This point is most poignantly demonstrated by the conservative, insensitive, often hostile and unhelpful attitudes of many state houses to their major cities. Reapportionment has enhanced both central city and suburban political power. When many middle-class whites left the central cities, they did so to escape problems. State legislatures invariably reflect suburban and rural apathy, hostility to the central cities, and racism.

When we consider local governments as recipients of these funds, we must keep in mind the fragmented and differentiated character of the metropolis.[29] We have already pointed out that the serious financial problems which confront local governments are not uniform within the greater metropolitan area. The intrametropolitan fiscal pattern is sufficiently diverse to mean a differentiated impact of revenue sharing. Some localities will be able to expand their already ample supply of public services, thanks to revenue sharing, while others will find the extra resources too little and too late. Some local governments will have the initiative and capacity to make innovative use of additional funds, while others will fritter them away or, even worse, use them to expand unnecessary services or to pander to influential local constituencies.

Finally, in contrasting earlier federal subsidies with revenue sharing it should be remembered that categorical grants sometimes had the effect of forcing local communities to follow federal guidelines, which meant the imposition of national standards which are often more progressive than those of local communities.

Revenue Sharing and Black Power

What are the implications of each of these proposals for metropolitan areas with significant black political power or potential? How will blacks located in areas of low black concentration or weak political organization fare? What initiatives might black politicans take with respect to revenue sharing?

A first step in this analysis is simply to review the financial position of a selection of metropolitan areas with significant black voting age populations under the Nixon and Mills proposals (see Table 4).

The Mills plan comes out far ahead of the Nixon plan on immediate aggregate benefits to the cities. First, the Nixon plan would provide an initial aggregate revenue fund of far less than the $5.3 billion called for by Mills. By late 1975 Nixon's fund would build up to about $5 billion, but by then the Mills fund would have been increased twice. Next, the Mills plan insures minimum pass-through from state to local government of over 66 percent, while the Nixon plan only stipulates a 50 percent pass-through. Thus, under the Mills plan the cities get a larger slice of a larger pie.

Nixon's plan parcels out more money to those areas that are trying harder to generate revenue, thus creating an incentive of sorts. Mills' plan, however, specifically ensures that those areas which are *least capable* of meeting their own fiscal need (heavily urbanized communities with large numbers of poor families) get the most. Furthermore, the Nixon plan rewards areas which have high taxes, regardless of how progressive those taxes are. Under the Mills system, all state revenue sharing would eventually be based upon the degree to which a state utilizes a progressive income tax.

Even the specific impact on the sixteen cities we have selected as examples favors the Mills plan. Each of these cities is one of the dominant cities of its particular state. Because they are large and urbanized, even though most contain a high concentration of poor families, all will tend to be among the most intensive per-capita revenue sources in their respective states and as such will rank high on the Nixon funding list. However, these same characteristics also rate them a high place in Mills' priorities. If we examine the results of applying Mills' plan to allocate $5.3 billion in comparison to Nixon's plan at the $5 billion level, we find that the change in state revenues ranges from a 50 percent increase in Maryland to a 12 percent cut in California and Michigan. But if we consider that Mills guarantees local governments 66 percent pass-through while Nixon guarantees only 50 percent, this means an overall increase for the cities in each state, ranging from 50 percent in Maryland (Baltimore) to about 9 percent in California (Los Angeles) and Michigan (Detroit). Furthermore, of the six cities whose states face a cut in federal aid (Philadelphia, Los Angeles, Detroit, New Orleans, Newark, and Indianapolis), all but one (Los Angeles) have very great concentrations of relative poverty in the center city and would thus qualify for additional consideration under the Mills plan.

Insofar as the choice is between the Nixon and Mills revenue sharing proposals, the Mills plan seems to offer some slight economic advantages. Since it has the political support of a large body of national and congressional opinion, it is likely to pass in some form. However, both proposals raise serious questions for black communities. Mills' proposal requires that substantial funds be allotted for public safety, environmental

TABLE 4

Financial Position of Representative Metropolitan Areas with Significant
Black Voting Age Populations (VAP) under the Nixon and Mills
Revenue Sharing Proposals

City	Lower Income in Black Sectors*	Lower Expenditures on Central City	State Income Tax	Lower or Higher State Aid Under Mills (vs. Nixon)?		Blacks as Percentage of VAP
New York, N.Y.	Yes	No	Yes	+ .25	Higher	19.0
Washington, D.C.	Yes	—	Yes	+3.00	Higher	66.8
Philadelphia, Pa.	Yes	No	Yes	– .04	Lower	31.1
Chicago, Ill.	Yes	No	Yes	+3.30	Higher	28.2
Los Angeles, Calif.	No	Yes	Yes	– .12	Lower	15.9
Detroit, Mich.	Yes	Yes	Yes	– .12	Lower	39.4
Baltimore, Md.	Yes	No	Yes	+ .50	Higher	43.7
Houston, Tex.	No	Yes	No	+ .09	Higher	24.1
Memphis, Tenn.	No	No	No	+ .12	Higher	36.2
New Orleans, La.	No	No	Yes	– .09	Lower	39.7
Newark, N.J.	Yes	No	No	– .05	Lower	48.6
Louisville, Ky.	Yes	Yes	Yes	+1.77	Higher	21.2
Atlanta, Ga.	No	Yes	No	+ .09	Higher	47.3
Columbus, Ohio	Yes	Yes	Yes	+ .004	Higher	16.5
Indianapolis, Ind.	Yes	Yes	Yes	– .05	Lower	14.5

*It is pertinent to note that not only does income tend to be lower in the black sectors, but there is also dramatic differentiated growth in job opportunities between city and suburbs. For example, between 1951 and 1968, Baltimore central city experienced a 6 percent growth in number of jobs while the suburbs had a 161 percent increase; St. Louis central city declined 9 percent in jobs while the suburbs increased 144 percent; Philadelphia central city remained approximately the same while the suburbs had an 86 percent job increase; Washington, D.C., had a 38 percent increase and its suburbs 352 percent; New York a 10 percent increase, its suburbs 51 percent. U.S., Department of Commerce, Bureau of the Census. Quoted in Michael N. Danielson, ''Differentiation, Segregation, and Political Fragmentation in the American Metropolis,'' *Governance and Population: The Governmental Implications of Population Change 4,* (Washington, D.C.: Commission on Population Growth and the American Future, 1972), p. 27. Danielson also reports: ''Twice as many families with incomes below the poverty line lived in cities [as lived] in suburbs in 1969. On the other side of the ledger, 58 percent of all families in the suburbs (10.7 million) had incomes over $10,000 compared with only 44 percent in the city (6.5 million families),'' p. 24.

Sources: U.S., Advisory Commission on Inter-Governmental Relations (ACIR); *U.S. News and World Report,* Aug. 1970; and The Joint Center for Political Studies.

protection, public transportation, youth recreation, financial administration, and other public works. While this requirement obviates the possibility mentioned earlier of localites' using funds to lower taxes rather than to improve and expand public services, the Mills order of priorities hardly coincides with the desires or needs of blacks.

Blacks can only view with dismay channeling of further funds into already massive, repressive police establishments. While it is true blacks suffer more than other groups from urban crime, it is also frivolous (at best) to seek to stem rising crime rates through repressive laws with more guns and so-called tough cops to enforce them. "Law and order," if it is to be more than a code phrase for racism, must be linked to policies which emphasize jobs, justice, and efforts to vitiate alienation.

Since Mills' proposal already embodies the idea of federal stipulation of the use of funds, it might be easier, now or at some future date, to earmark certain funds for projects of high black priority and/or to specify that certain kinds of public-service equalization and quota conditions must be fulfilled. For the majority of blacks who do live in white-controlled local communities, Mills' conditional revenue sharing (given appropriate modifications) is preferable to the Nixon plan. However, for cities with actual or potential black political control, the Nixon plan appears preferable since funds unconditionally allocated could be earmarked by local black officials for innovative projects of black interest. In their March 25, 1971, statement to the President, the Congressional Black Caucus resolved this apparent contradiction by expressing support for the general principle of giving states and localities greater flexibility in administering federal grants but insisting that "national priorities requiring accountability for delivering services to those most in need of them must be maintained."[30]

Fundamental reform

While tying revenue sharing to minimal federally imposed standards is a laudable attempt to avoid some of the worse pitfalls, at bottom revenue sharing (as presently proposed by Mills and Nixon) is a stop-gap measure. It does not address itself to the structural aspects of urban fiscal problems. The form and character of the urban crisis cannot be separated from the nature of American society. National policy priorities (and particularly the cruel illusion of the possibility of the economy supporting "guns and butter") constitutes the central constraint on development of a national urban economic policy. A truncated opportunity structure which specifically excludes the overwhelming majority of blacks from positions of economic and political power and the limited scope for black wealth accumulation and upward mobility contribute to the form which the urban crisis takes for blacks. More important, it is the structural features of the urban crisis which have created an environment in which gargantuan effort is needed to achieve even modestly progressive change.

Furthermore, political fragmentation breaks up metropolitan areas into overlapping, inefficient small units with vastly different economic resources. Flight to the suburbs has created the incorrect impression of dying cities. Actually central cities still perform crucial economic, cultural, and social services for the metropolitan areas they serve. Fundamental fiscal reform must be based on recognition of the organic character of metropolitan areas as well as on an appreciation of the right of urban centers to community control. A two-tier political and economic reform is called for which allows urban and suburban centers to determine policy priorities but share economic resources in ways which guarantee equalization of public services. Of course the separation of fiscal organization from control over policy is no easy task. But thinking along these lines avoids the perils of metropolitan government with diluted black political power, on the one hand, and of fragmentation and continued urban fiscal inequities, on the other.

As many politicians and political analysts have pointed out, revenue sharing cannot become a substitute for other economic measures such as welfare nationalization, manpower programs, etc. The principle must be maintained that there are additional areas which demand special federal support outside any other system of appropriations. Welfare is one area, another is education.

Increased federal support of urban education is justifiable on several grounds. Because of the high degree of mobility in American society, education in one area affects other areas, and the external diseconomies to the entire society resulting from inadequate eduation are great. There is substantial and immediate need for federal support of minimum educational standards because of the increasing "dollar gap" between per-pupil expenditures in the central city and expenditures outside the central city. This fact has resulted in the situation summarized below in our sixteen selected metropolises (see Table 5).

Furthermore, the plight of the center city is accentuated by the fact that in the fifteen largest metropolitan areas, about 37 percent of all center-city school buildings are over forty-five years old. Table 5 becomes even more significant when we realize that the central city generally spends more *per capita* on services than the suburbs, except for education. Table 5 shows dramatically that the children who need the most get the least.

Assumption by the federal (or state) government of local costs of education would equalize educational opportunity and release financial resources from the property tax and revenue sharing for provision of other services. It could even decrease the incentive for exclusionary zoning practices aimed at exclusion of large, low-income families. Of course, insofar as exclusionary zoning has a racist as well as economic intent, it will remain. We have emphasized the special character of education in fiscal reform because it is of central importance to long-range black political and economic goals.

Conclusions

Thus far urban development has been subject to the regulation of forces generated by the market economy. Such planning as has existed

TABLE 5
Urban and Suburban Per-Pupil Educational Expenditure

City	Center City	Outside Center City	Gap (In Percentage)
Los Angeles	$424	$654	31
Washington, D.C.	508	562	11
Atlanta	342	403	18
Chicago	433	578	33
Indianapolis	407	579	42
Louisville	350	455	30
New Orleans	310	369	19
Baltimore	407	452	11
Detroit	454	539	19
Newark	515	619	20
New York	728	889	22
Columbus	368	500	36
Philadelphia	477	656	38
Pittsburgh	419	544	30
Dallas	334	597	80
Houston	311	794	155

Source: U.S., Advisory Committee on Intergovernmental Relations, *Fiscal Balance in the American Federal System*, 2 (Washington, D.C.: U.S. Government Printing Office, 1967), p. 66.

has been overwhelmed by the dynamics of market forces, perverted priorities,[31] political fragmentation, and economic differentiation. The joint goals of removing the crisis elements of urban growth and of expanding black political potential have provided the framework in which we have analyzed both the general ideal of revenue sharing and the specific Nixon and Mills proposals, comparing these as proposals to present federal aid to state and local governments.

While we believe the Mills proposal to have some slight advantages over the Nixon revenue-sharing plan, we have emphasized the importance of further fiscal and political reforms. Even with revenue sharing, it should be a priority item on the agenda of urban politicians to press for both restructured intrametropolitan fiscal structures and a modernized version of the property tax. Even in equal application, property taxes may be regressive. Incompetent or dishonest assessors, local favors to special interest groups, and often the rate structure itself render American property taxes in general a spectacularly regressive system. Wherever feasible, a highly progressive state income tax system is also preferable. Certainly, the regressive systems, such as those in Illinois, Indiana, Massachusetts, Michigan, and Mississippi, and even the slightly less regressive rate schedule in West Virginia are severely in need of change.

It goes without saying that whichever revenue-sharing proposal is passed, the most minute monitoring will be necessary to insure that funds are used to equalize public-service delivery. For example, an appropriation as seemingly laudable as the federal highway systems matching-fund pool becomes suspect once we realize that the massive expenditures made in the past few years on the national highway system have contributed almost nothing to central cities. Instead, road building has caused the uprooting of urban areas, the destruction of parks, congestion, and pollution while at the same time draining resources away from other, more beneficial programs.

While the short-range results of revenue sharing might be of some slight benefit to central cities and specifically to the black community, the long-range implications of revenue sharing may be less salient. One writer has predicted:

> Implementation of revenue-sharing could lead to a situation in the United States where, insofar as development and implementation of programs are concerned, this nation will become fifty separate states, not one country. Instead of developing domestic programs consistent with national interests, priority for establishing domestic programs would be left to governmental units which to the present have demonstrated neither will nor capacity to act.[32]

Of particular concern to blacks is the fact that as unsatisfactory, ineffective, and hypocritical as federal domestic programs have been, they have been better than state and local apathetic neglect. What little political redress blacks have experienced has been federally initiated. Until recently it has been much easier for the most reactionary forces to gain and maintain control of local communities and influence state legislatures than it has been for them to be effective on the national level. On the other hand, more local autonomy, buttressed by federal funds, could be important for black-dominated or -controlled cities. Where progressive politicians are seeking to mitigate racial and class exploitation and oppression of large segments of the urban poor, unconditionally granted funds could provide the basis for an innovative attack on these problems.

Every caveat we have entered and every scenario we have traced underscores the importance of a national black political organization that can monitor legislation and lobby on the national level as well as organize on the local level to insure that fiscal issues get a more rational public discussion, to press for changes in intrametropolitan fiscal administration, and to press for the equalization of public services under revenue sharing. Whatever the long-range implications of revenue sharing, a national, black, multi-functional, organizational infrastructure is of central importance.[33]

NOTES

1. *Air War: The Third Indochina War*, Project Air War and the Indochina Resource Center, Mar. 1972. It was estimated by Senator W. Proxmire that the future costs of the war could be as high as $20 billion per year (CR, 7/13/70). The cost of the 1971 air war alone was $7.64 million per day.

2. Michael T. Flax, *Blacks and Whites: An Experiment in Racial Indicators* (Washington, D.C.: The Urban Institute, undated), pp. 47–8. All population figures in this paragraph are from this source. Also see "Demographic Aspects of the Black Community," *The Milbank Memorial Fund Quarterly* 48 (Apr. 1970), Part 2.

3. Advisory Commission on Intergovernmental Relations (ACIR), *Urban America and the Federal System*, 2, Washington, D.C. 20575, Oct. 1969.

4. Political fragmentation refers to the pattern of urban-suburban development in which typically a central city is surrounded by many smaller suburban units, each with the power to tax and the responsibility to provide public services.

5. We are analyzing the Nixon and Mills proposals as introduced in the 91st Congress. It is likely that the more popular Mills proposal will have a better chance of passage and will be amended in the process. Since our analysis is primarily concerned with the implications of the principle of revenue sharing and the major differences between the Mills and Nixon plans, our general arguments will hold assuming no fundamental revisions in either plan. [The Mills Bill (HR 14370) "The State and Local Assistance Act of 1972," was passed by Congress on Oct. 20, 1972, and became PL 92–512—eds.]

6. Walter W. Heller, Richard Ruggles, *et al.*, *Revenue Sharing and the City* (Baltimore, Md.: Johns Hopkins Press, 1968), pp. 32–35.

7. John E. Coons, William H. Clune, and Stephen D. Sugarman, *Private Wealth and Public Education* (Cambridge, Mass.: Harvard University Press, 1970), p. 2; also see *Serrano* v. *Priest*, Los Angeles 29820 (Superior Court #938254), Calif.

8. "Actually costs have shifted from maintenance of a ground army to military aid and development of electronic counterinsurgency weaponry." *Air War*, p. 18.

9. U.S., Congress, Congressional Record,91st Cong., 1st sess., pp. 237–64.

10. "Who'll Get What from Tax-Sharing," *U.S. News and World Report*, Aug. 17, 1970, p. 56.

11. *Congressional Record*, 91st Cong., 1st sess., pp. 237–47.

12. "Tax-Sharing: Mills' Plan vs. Nixon's," *U.S. News and World Report*, Feb. 21, 1972, pp. 51–2.

13. John Riew, "Metropolitan Fiscal Disparities and Fiscal Federalism," in *Financing the Metropolis*, ed. by John P. Crecine (Beverley Hills, Calif.: Sage Publications, 1970), p. 139.

14. Walter W. Heller, *New Dimensions in Political Economy* (Cambridge, Mass.: Harvard University Press, 1966), pp. 126–27.

15. *Ibid.*, p. 128.

16. *Ibid.*, p. 127.

17. Selma T. Mushkin and John F. Cotton, *Sharing Federal Funds for State and Local Needs* (New York: Praeger, 1969), p. 137.

18. U.S., Congress, Joint Economic Committee, *Revenue Sharing and Its Alternatives*, 3, p. 1234.

19. For further analysis of the complexities of federal aid to local communities see Tax Institute of America, *Federal-State-Local Fiscal Relationships* (Princeton, N.J.: Tax Institute of America, 1968), pp. 34–41; also, Mushkin and Cotton, *Sharing Federal Funds*, pp. 43–66.

20. Heller, *New Dimensions*, pp. 156–58; also see Appendix on "State Individual Income Taxes: Rates," Dec. 31, 1970.

21. *Ibid.*, p. 145.

22. Mushkin and Cotton, *Sharing Federal Funds*, pp. 140–41.

23. *Ibid.*, p. 134.

24. Heller's original proposal was based on the assumption that there would be budget surpluses and revenue sharing would *supplement* categorical grant programs. For an analysis of recent departures from the original Heller proposal, see Leonard Opperman, "Aid for the States: Is Revenue Sharing the Answer?" *Review of Politics*, 30 (Jan. 1968): 43–50.

25. Heller, *New Dimensions*, p. 142.

26. Mushkin and Cotton, *Sharing Federal Funds*, p. 134.

27. Heller, *New Dimensions*, p. 153.

28. Leonard Opperman does a compelling analysis of Indiana State politics and finds a ". . . lack of commitment to positive government." He attributes it to lack of expertise on the part of officials, failure of the press to perform its watchdog function, and antipathy to the cities and their poor. "Aid for the States: Is Revenue Sharing the Answer?" *Review of Politics*, 3: 43–50.

29. See Advisory Commission on Intergovernmental Relations (ACIR), *Urban America and the Federal System*, and The Ford Foundation, *The Near Side of Federalism: Improving State and Local Governments* (New York: The Ford Foundation, Jan. 1972), pp. 31–41.

30. Statement to the President of the United States by the Congressional Black Caucus, Mar. 25, 1971. Excerpt quoted from the *Review of Black Political Economy*, 1 (Winter/ Spring 1971): 106.

31. For an analysis of "the perverse ways in which we determine the priorities of American politics," see Duane Lockard, *The Perverted Priorities of American Politics* (New York: Macmillan Co., 1971).

32. Leonard Opperman, "Aid for the States," p. 49.

33. The National Black Political Convention in March 1972 called for this kind of structure. For an analysis of the convention and its recommendations as contained in the *Black Political Agenda;* See "It's Nation Time," in Special Issue, National Conference of Black Political Scientists *Newsletter* on the Black Political Convention, ed. by Marguerite Ross Barnett, May 1972.

Savings, Voluntary Taxes, and the National Fund

Richard F. America

In the late 1960s and early 1970s there were many indications of growing interest in and need for organized capital accumulation in Afro-America. Many groups have held conferences at which plans and programs were discussed but could not be implemented for lack of massive funding. Groups interested in the arts, in political action, health, education, criminal justice, commercial development, and so on, generate a constant stream of proposals, many of which are worthwhile and almost all of which call for heavy, ongoing financial support.

All of these activities underscore the need for dramatically increased savings in many forms and for organized fund raising and capital accumulation in a few well-planned, well-managed institutions.

The development and security of Afro-America over the next thirty years will require the harnessing of its financial resources. Such saving and investment will occur in many forms—commercial and noncommercial. Savings account deposits in black financial institutions as well as the retained earnings of black-controlled corporations will contribute to savings. Indeed, increased savings in mattresses, socks, cookie jars, and piggy banks are also desirable if these ultimately find their way into black institutions for investment and do not simply become deferred consumption. But our interest here is in the potential of savings in the form of internal charity of what might be thought of as voluntary taxation. Such savings will probably be an important component of any successful comprehensive development effort.

Events in the past decade have brought many people to the realization that if they are serious about accelerating the development of their communities and institutions they will, of necessity, have to develop various forms of central treasuries. These will first have to be successfully demonstrated in a few localities before consolidated national fund raising can be undertaken.

We are all aware of several sophisticated and apparently effective national fund raising efforts on behalf of Meharry Medical School, the

United Negro College Fund (UNCF), the Voter Education Project, the NAACP Special Contributions Fund, and the NAACP Legal Defense and Education Fund among others. And from time to time there are one-shot appeals in legal emergencies or in support of the victims of natural disasters. But a requirement for an annual national program that successfully reaches and effectively appeals to all 7 to 8 million households and all the businesses in Afro-America still remains. A basic principle is clear; Afro-America cannot permit itself to remain so financially dependent on government and established foundations and contributors for support of its ongoing or experimental programs.

One example of financial vulnerability can be found in the experience of many of the community action efforts of the Great Society program. In many places a kind of grass-roots community organization was undertaken to develop general cohesion and some broader democratic participation. Much of the early energy was generated through rallies against traditional downtown political figures and institutions. Movement to oppose City Hall was often generated over specific educational, service, or developmental issues. Some distortions, and even some demagogery crept into these processes.

But City Hall perceived the threat, which, ironically was funded by government. At the urging of many mayors, Congress then withdrew much of the necessary financial support from community organizing activities.

That was predictable. It is now widely understood to be unrealistic to expect white or general institutions to underwrite consistently the activities of black parties to the conflict, to the extent that the interests of Afro-America are in conflict with those of the general community. If political organization is considered to have some ongoing value, then funds for it will have to be found internally.

Tithing requirements, such as are frequently mentioned in connection with the Nation of Islam, have been the subject of some comment.[1] Also efforts like the "10–36" program of the large Zion Baptist Church and the Reverend Leon Sullivan in Philadelphia have attracted attention.[2] Historically, religious sanctions or charismatic leadership have succeeded in inducing heavy savings increases by groups of people who, because of relatively low incomes and other socioeconomic characteristics, would have been expected to consume virtually all income. Lower-income black people, like lower-income people in general, theoretically have high marginal propensities to consume. But an effective appeal apparently can alter those patterns. The same may be true for middle-income households, which, because of relentless advertising and other stimuli, also tend to have trouble saving consistently from year to year.

The national savings rate appears to be in the range of 7 to 10 percent annually. The black rate appears to be lower than that in most years, although this is a complex subject. Some insight may be gained from the statistics set forth in Table 1. Notice that the comparison is between average family incomes. Since the upper range, the top 20 percent of the income distribution, is disproportionately white, the white average saving rate is pulled up.

TABLE 1
Comparative Savings in the United States, 1960–61

	Negro	White
Average income after taxes	$3840	$6169
Current consumption	3707	5609
Savings	133	560
Savings as percentage of income	3.5	9.1

Source: Gardner Ackley, *Macroeconomic Theory* (New York City: Macmillan Co.), 1961, p. 247.

According to Marcus Alexis, the highly regarded Northwestern economist, direct comparisons of savings by income categories suggest "evidence of higher savings (or lower dissavings) by blacks than by comparable income white families."[3] And "statistical data show regional differences in savings. Northern blacks save a larger proportion of their incomes than Northern whites with the same incomes."[4]

Alexis discusses at some length several hypotheses that attempt to explain this greater savings by blacks. For our purposes, however, despite possibly greater household savings by blacks over whites of comparable incomes, the overall black savings rate will have to increase as a proportion of total income if satisfactory development is to occur. The rate of 3 to 5 percent is probably too low for successful development. Of course the problem is compounded in that much of Afro-America's saving does not occur in its financial institutions and is diverted away from its investments into investments in the general economy. Little of the reverse flow has occurred, although it may be possible to stimulate white savings in black banks as they gain in strength and numbers.

But our particular focus here is on a specific type of saving that occurs in the form of charitable donations. Some interracial flows do occur here and presumably will continue. Blacks give to white-controlled efforts such as the United Fund and Red Cross, and whites give to the UNCF and the NAACP. There has been some controversy over allocation decisions in United Fund budgets in several cities, and some reforms have been made. But even if the United Funds did everything that could reasonably be asked, there would still be a need for a similar autonomous organization managing a reservoir of Afro-American funds for Afro-American programs—the National Fund.

(Officials of United Way of America have not been enthusiastic at the prospect of the National Fund. Their cooperation could be helpful, and certainly communication during start-up will be desirable to avoid any undue abrasion.)

There are issues on which it may be possible and desirable to develop something like Afro-American policy. If so, such issues deserve serious research in independent centers or elsewhere, and that is costly. Similarly, specific problems in education, housing, health, employment, transportation, law enforcement, public safety, and economic development could be more adequately addressed if major institutions like Howard, Atlanta, and Fisk Universities, for examples, could undertake more extensive serious research. Additional financial support to them, not just from alumni but from the broader community, perhaps through a National Fund, could help make that possible.

For these reasons and many others, Afro-America must increasingly fund its own development. Problems come quickly to mind concerning intragroup politics, personalities, collection, administration, disbursal, and safeguarding of large funds. There are difficulties to anticipate which are real enough. But the basic problems are subject to demonstrative and evaluative research.

The National Fund would contain a number of familiar elements similar to those of other national charitable organizations. The key problems will be recognized as marketing problems, which may be summarized as asking how to find a set of secular and technically effective substitutes for traditional charitable and religious commitment:

Endorsement: Who must vouch for the concept as well as for the organization, national and local, that collects and distributes? How shall the endorsement and even the visible participation be obtained from the major established senior leaders who may, for practical reasons, feel initial uncertainty about an association with the National Fund?[5]

Advertising: In collaboration with the best professional fund raisers and advertising consultants, which media, what mix?

Direct mail: How intensive the solicitation?

Broad base: How extensive? How many households—2, 4, 6, 8 million? How best to organize local campaigns and coordinate nationally? How best to reach the business community? And how best to use the payroll checkoff through major employers?

Appeal: What will produce the response? A request to give, or to save, or in some sense both? Or perhaps it can be presented as an opportunity to invest in progress and development. Or is it, after all, a matter of encouraging people to voluntarily tax themselves? Or would it be preferable to present it as an offer to consume, to purchase an intangible product—freedom, progress, security, development, and the like?

Obviously there is considerable professional market research needed to develop a sustained massive National Fund.

Many leaders have expressed the desire over the years to see community-wide support for annual fund-raising drives having the purpose of "raising money from the community for the Community."

There is no obvious reason why this cannot be accomplished in this decade, although there are sources of opposition, apparently including some major foundations[6] and executives of the major national multipurpose funds. Their opposition is significant, because they are in a position to make the launching of the National Fund either more or less difficult. The major foundations are especially important, because operating budgets in the Fund's early phases will require significant grant subsidies.

Looking ahead, what might be the magnitude of the financial potential of the National Fund? It is difficult to judge, but we can look at a variety of combinations of assumptions as to level of response and level of contribution. With conservative assumptions estimates can be derived in the $10 to 15 million range; with moderate assumptions, in the $20 to 30 million range; and, with optimistic ones, even higher, as can be seen in Table 2. Roughly, if we reckon total income in Afro-America at over $50 billion, one tenth of 1 percent of that is $50 million, and, given the savings rate, this might not be an unreasonable expectation after the Fund has achieved some operating history and wide respect as a sensible apparatus for internal philanthropic purposes.

TABLE 2
Estimates of Total Potential of Coordinated Local Efforts
in the National Fund

Number of Households in Millions	Percentage of Response	Total Contribution in Millions Estimated on the Basis of Average Contribution				
		$5	$10	$20	$30	$50
	10	$1	2	4	6	10
2	25	2.5	5	10	15	25
	50	5	10	20	30	50
	10	2	4	8	12	20
4	25	5	10	20	30	50
	50	10	20	40	60	100
	10	3	6	12	18	30
6	25	7.5	15	30	45	75
	50	15	30	60	90	150
	10	4	8	16	24	40
8	25	10	20	40	60	100
	50	20	40	80	120	200

A number of organizations have considered such a program. Indeed, there is in existence an effort known as the National Black United Fund which has sought to create a program together with several local funds now affiliated through it. This might evolve into the vehicle for the National Fund.

In any event, the problems of coordination and cooperation in the National Fund may strike some as staggering. It is no secret that there have been, historically, problems of mutual trust. We can reasonably assume for now that they are manageable, if not solvable.

The lesson is clear: It takes money to raise money. The catalytic agent to raise seed money to establish the structure and launch the Fund perhaps should be a business-oriented group, a group of civil rights and legal leaders, perhaps a group of athletes and entertainers[7] (frequently mentioned as people looking for ways to make worthwhile contributions to social reform and development), or a body of religious leaders. Such a group may already exist, but more likely it will have to be created.

A major benefit of the undertaking will be the pressure it exerts toward program developments throughout Afro-America. The Fund presumably will screen applications for financial assistance according to seriously applied standards of feasibility and soundness.

One reason that radicals and conservatives have adopted those postures is that they have tended to lack funds. For radicals, rhetoric often has been a substitute for constructive action. Conservative elements have tended to be preoccupied with pageantry, frivolity, and trivia—in part because meaningful activity is difficult without organized, reliable financial resources. The National Fund should, hopefully, lead to greater emphasis on careful program development by groups all along the ideological spectrum.

The success of a National Fund could have a dramatic impact on planning and growth throughout Afro-America.

NOTES

1. It has been reported that the expected level of support from adult members of the Nation of Islam is 10 percent of income.

2. Zion Baptist Church has organized a shopping center, various other commercial ventures, and some training programs using outside grants and leveraged equity capital raised largely from the 4,000-member member congregation.

3. Marcus Alexis, "Patterns of Black Consumption," *Journal of Black Studies,* Sept. 1970, pp. 59–63. See also Marcus Alexis, *Wealth Accumulation of Black and White Families: The Empirical Evidence: Comment.* Paper presented at a joint session of the American Economic Association and the American Finance Association, 1970.

4. There are several major organizations whose budgets come from membership dues, general and corporate contributions, United Fund support, and government and foundation grants. The NAACP and NUL are two of the strongest. These two might be reluctant to take any short-run risks by associating with a fledgling National Fund. Some of their long-standing sources of budget support, such as the United Fund, might for varying reasons express displeasure at the emergence of the NF, viewing it as in some way competitive. So there will be serious diplomatic problems in bringing the established senior leadership on board. But their participation can be of great significance at the onset, so every effort to gain it will be justified.

5. A program officer at a very large foundation mentioned in private conversation that he had discussed the concept of providing a grant to subsidize the early operations of such a Fund. He reported that a senior executive of the foundation had reservations appa-

rently based in part on his view that other groups had established fund-raising programs without foundation support. Aside from questions of fact, the underlying attitude suggested here is important and will have to be successfully met.

6. Many show business and sports figures have become associated with images of extravagant living and conspicuous consumption. This is unfortunate in celebrities of a community that probably needs a decade or so of voluntary semiausterity if it is to develop rapidly.

Several noted high-income athletes and entertainers have made a public point of their intention to initiate or carry out personal charitable programs. Muhammad Ali, Arthur Ashe, Kareem Abdul Jabbar, James Brown, Bill Cosby, Melvin Van Peebles, and Jim Brown are some of those who come to mind.

Fifty such persons at $20,000 each could be an effective foundation group for a National Fund. A carefully planned, one-shot contribution of $1 million from them could be matched by grants from foundations and others and could provide an effective initial operating capitalization for the Fund.

This group could thereby make possible the mechanism through which the 25 million people in Afro-America can thereafter systematically look after more of their own community needs.

A Proposal for Political Marketing

Charles Hampden-Turner

Political marketing offers a new way of assisting the economic development of poor communities and of creating opportunities for integrating political values with daily activities. Central to the concept of political marketing is the belief that the considerable purchasing power and growing political consciousness of liberals and radicals in America can be harnessed to assist in the generation of economic well-being for the poor.

Community development corporations represent an attempt to create independent institutions—owned and operated by residents of urban and rural poor communities—for stimulating the economic and social development of the poor. The strategy of political marketing is to urge liberal and radical consumers to provide a guaranteed market for the products and services of community development corporations. Consumer marketing organizations (CMOs) formed by the consumers would serve as vehicles for consumer expression and thus as a source of guidance to the community development corporations (CDCs) about their primary market. Through the CMOs and acts of "political" consumption, the consumers would be provided with new avenues for political expression and for making political values more relevant to their lives.

Political Marketing and Community Development Corporations

There are presently about fifty community development corporations in operation across the nation. Their efforts, however, face staggering obstacles. CDCs must attempt to survive in an economy in which 80 percent of small businesses fail within three years. Private sources of capital are virtually nonexistent, not only because of tight money but also because of the risks and uncertainties of new black enterprises, ingrained patterns of discrimination against minority borrowers, and an unwillingness to become involved in novel and experimental ventures. Equally serious are the lack of skills in poor communities—aggravated by the shortage of funds for worker training—and the dearth of managerial talent. (In a survey of Harvard Business School students, I discovered that black MBAs, although well-informed about CDCs, were lured away by salary offers from large corporations ranging from $13,000–25,000).

Even with sufficient capital and talent, community development corporations could not afford to rely on the limited purchasing power of inner-city consumers. CDCs must therefore compete in a larger market, into which entry has become increasingly difficult—particularly for enterprises which are not well-financed, well-connected, or experienced. In the few instances where CDCs have found capital and an assured market, they have generally been forced to rely on the patronage of large corporations or public-spirited banks. In these situations commercial viability may have been achieved but only at the price of political impotence and increased dependence upon local elites.

It seems clear that community development corporations have little chance of competing with corporate leaders who have resources a thousand times greater and who shape the rules of the game which they dominate. The only hope may be to create a different game.

Political marketing is an attempt to frame the rules for a new game. It assumes that the very factors which impede economic development in poor communities can become the basis of a competitive advantage. In essence, it assumes that concern for the plight of the poor is marketable.

A common function of advertising is artificial differentiation, and the amount spent on advertising a product is often inversely proportional to any real difference between the product and its competition. Reaching a market is largely a matter of creating an image. Experienced advertising executives know that "you don't sell the sausage; you sell the sizzle." Unlike such advertising, which is largely an attempt to appeal to the self-centered values of conspicuous consumption and gratification, political marketing would focus on the people behind the product, their oppression, their cooperative effort, and their hopes for freedom. The sizable minority of Americans— mostly young, affluent, middle-class—who are already commited to supporting the poor in their struggle for a decent life thus represent an enormous potential market.

Political marketing would offer the consumer an opportunity to use his purchasing power to serve the needs of others as well as his own. In contrast to the trivial materialism of traditional advertising, it would offer nothing less than an invitation to help people get out of poverty. We have seen nearly half a million people travel to Washington, D.C., to march for peace, and increasing numbers are protesting racism and pollution. Thus, it is not inconceivable that several million people might go a few blocks out of their way, or pay a little more, in response to an appeal based upon their political and social ideals.

The possibility of having an assured consumer market and of eliciting new brand loyalties suggests that the logical enterprise for the community development corporations would be wholesaling. While the profit margins in traditional wholesaling are often small, especially when the wholesaler provides only storage and distribution services, the potential for profit in "brand management" is considerable. The CDCs could market the goods of several manufacturers under their own brand name—"Liberation," for example—and could establish a national coordinating organization—Liberation, Incorporated—to handle negotiations with manufacturers and large retail chains and to direct national brand advertising campaigns.

Wholesaling could assist in overcoming a number of the economic obstacles facing a new CDC. Wholesaling requires relatively little capital, and the necessary skills can be taught in a short time. Unlike retailing, it is not restricted to a neighborhood market, and it can be performed by persons with little access to land or raw materials. In terms of performing the distributive function, the inner-city is well located geographically. Economies of scale can generally be achieved at a smaller size of operation in wholesaling than in manufacturing. Wholesaling goods manufactured by others would enable community development corporations to respond to a rapidly expanding demand in the event that Liberation brand marketing was successful; if CDCs were initially engaged in manufacturing, on the other hand, their greatly limited ability to produce might result in the loss of important opportunities to capture a larger segment of the market.

Most important, wholesaling offers the prospect of vertical integration into the manufacturing process once the pattern of demand has stabilized. With an assured market and a full order book, CDCs would have less difficulty raising large sums of capital. With access to capital, gradual vertical expansion would be possible. For example, a community development corporation might be engaged in distributing laundry soap, already boxed. If successful, it could then manufacture its own boxes, filling them with the same product. Later, it could begin to manufacture the product itself. With numerous lines of merchandise to expand into, the CDC could concentrate on those with the best markets, the simplest manufacturing process, etc. It could use the prices at which goods are being supplied by big manufacturers as a benchmark against which to measure its own ability to produce the goods efficiently. Such opportunities for expansion and for retention of increasingly large shares of the profit margin would provide a continual incentive for economic growth and development.

Would large corporations contract to supply CDC wholesalers? Corporations are already under some pressure to assist black economic development. Businessmen are increasingly anxious to demonstrate that "the system works," and, at first glance, a contract with a community corporation promises a conventional solution. Even President Nixon has spoken approvingly of CDCs as examples of "community capitalism." Indeed, a number of manufacturers already work with CDCs in "turn-key" operations, in which subsidiaries are established in the inner-city and then turned over to the community.

But we need not only rely on the altruism of the corporations. When a wholesaler places an order, the supplier will generally fill it. Manufacturers do not generally avoid an opportunity for profit, particularly one that has added public relations value. And there would always be the prospect of competitors reaping the benefits if they refused. Even if no more than 1 percent of the nation's manufacturers cooperated, it would be sufficient to establish a network of CDC wholesalers.

Finally, wholesaling occupies a strategic position in the economy. If political marketing succeeded in winning the brand loyalty of politically conscious, organized consumers, Liberation, Incorporated, would have a strong bargaining position vis-à-vis manufacturers. And once the brand name was welded into the distribution pipeline, any attempt to dislodge it could cause an uproar.

Consumer Marketing Organizations

An important ally of community development corporations in their attempt to capture a portion of the market would be the consumer marketing organizations and, on a national level, their coordinating organization. Local CMO members could put pressure on retailers to stock all Liberation brand products and insure that such products were prominently displayed. At the request of a CDC, they would provide a "commando" sales force for soliciting institutional orders, pledges to buy, free publicity, and local support. In particular, CMO members from university communities could demand that their schools purchase from CDCs. The poor could thus end up the beneficiaries of much of the rapidly growing education industry, which, if Ivan Illich is right, presently represents a grossly regressive allocation of resources.

Through the CMOs, consumers would express their preferences for products and, in effect, would provide market research for the CDCs. At both the national and local levels, the CMOs could assist in the development and implementation of advertising, marketing and political strategies.

The successful marketing of the Liberation brand name will very likely depend upon the consumers' confidence that Liberation Products meet their political criteria. Thus, the national CMO coordinating body would have to be given the right to accept or reject products before they could carry the Liberation trademark. All new products would have to be agreed upon by the national CMO and Liberation, Incorporated. Moreover, the national CMO could require that a description of the particular CDC marketing a product be carried on the label or in accompanying literature, or otherwise made available. While the CMO would not be in the position of judging the internal conduct of the CDCs, it would insure that the relevant information was available to consumers concerned about those matters.

The relationship between the CMOs and the development corporations would represent an "arm's-length" alliance between the poor and largely white, middle-class consumers, each organizing their own constituency to give maximum aid and trade to the other. That relationship would give effect to one of the vital lessons of the sixties: poor people desire and need to organize and guide themselves; and though alliances between the poor and the concerned middle class may be necessary, the latter must not be allowed to dominate them. Political marketing, then, would be founded on an equitable relationship—of mutual strengths, needs, and interests—in which initiative would not be wrenched from the poor and development of an independent political and economic base would not be frustrated.

One underlying source of strength and tension in the CDC–CMO relationship would be the reciprocal influence of two types of radicalism. Social research seems to indicate that middle-class radicals are strongly oriented toward abstract ideals and moral principles, while the radicalism of the poor is more concerned with material wants and concrete gains. Whereas the former group is prone to losing touch with reality, poor people are faced with the temptation to compromise principle for the sake of short-run expediency. Hopefully, the interdependence of the two sides will keep these tendencies in check and motivate them to cooperate. Mutuality is essential.

Competitive Prospects

Competing against bigger, richer, and more powerful corporations will require overcoming established brand loyalties. Brand loyalty, that subtle province of motivational research and subliminal persuasion, relies heavily on the fact that the thousands of trivial acts in our lives are based upon subconscious habit rather than conscious choice. The sheer idiocy of advertising is often quite deliberate, based on the theory that habits are formed when people quickly dismiss appeals from conscious reflection.

If people can be induced to make conscious choices, their brand loyalties can be undermined. By making brand selection into a sociopolitical issue, the move from subconscious to conscious choice might be effected. So as to distract the consumer from these issues as little as possible, the products marketed in the early stages should be intrinsically dull. They should also be quick-turnover items. The more frequent the acts of purchasing, the greater the consumer's feeling of participation and the more readily new brand loyalty could be established.

An enormous amount of money, energy, and mendacity goes into establishing the myth that branded products are worth four or five times the price of unbranded equivalents. Liberation, Incorporated, would compete not only through political marketing, emphasizing the people behind the products, but also by challenging the blatant abuses of hard sell advertising. It could then charge prices equivalent to those of branded products, asking the consumer to give consciously to the poor what he earlier relinquished unknowingly to large corporations.

Moreover, the very size and power of competing corporations could be turned against them. There would be no way for a corporation which values and radiates size, wealth, glamour, and power to satisfy people who do not share such values—once the issues were drawn and alternatives made available. For consumers who are predisposed to respond to the underdog appeal from the organized poor, the competitors' advertisements would only serve to advertise their unfair advantage. A comparable occurrence was General Motors' attempt to smear Ralph Nader, which only enhanced his image and dramatized his criticisms.

A significant competitive advantage for Liberation products would be the efficiency of its advertising expenditures. Advertising is most effective when there is a congruence between content and advertising matter, and so left-of-center publications would be natural advertising vehicles for Liberation products. Whereas a firm advertising a wart-removing substance in *TV Guide* is faced with the fact that fewer than 3 percent of the readers will be wart-conscious when they flip the page, close to 75 percent of the readers of *The New Republic* might respond to political marketing—particularly if they received editorial comment.

As mentioned above, the CMOs could provide the additional competitive advantage of a free, highly motivated selling force. Moreover, once the CDCs begin to integrate vertically, the nation's university communities, which are likely to be the locations of the initial and strongest consumer organizations, could provide a very valuable resource—intellectual labor. Millions of dollars worth of patents, techniques, and discoveries pour out of American universities every year, and they need not enrich giant corporations alone. I believe that many scientists and engineers could be convinced to steer an increasing volume of their technological innovations toward counter-institutions. The inventors might not become as rich, but they would gain stature among their peers and students. The climate of opinion among the younger staff in universities would seem ripe for this development.

The Needs of Political Consumers

Political marketing is as much a proposal to satisfy the needs of political consumers as it is a plan for assisting the cause of minority economic development. In my recently published book, *Radical Man*, I considered the motivating forces of the new middle-class radicalism in America, and, with the help of research findings from the social sciences, I tried to identify personal fulfillment needs which seemed to be frustrated. Among them were: 1) the need for political and cultural self-expression, and 2) the desire to reconcile contradictions. Political marketing is designed to help satisfy these frustrated needs.

Through the consumer marketing organizations, consumers would be able to translate their political concerns into product standards, ideas for new products, and ideas for marketing appeals. Through political marketing, moral principles and ideas could be "acted out," and social conscience could be translated into action. The grape boycott, despite the negative nature of refusing to buy as opposed to buying, was a positive and successful effort of this kind.

For some, political marketing offers an extra, alternative avenue of political and cultural self-expression. And for others who, like the young, are disenfranchised—in terms of both voting rights in the political arena and influence on the decision-making processes of the institutions they inhabit—it offers the only means of self-expression. At least in part, political marketing is intended to give young people a meaningful lever of choice that could be exercised from their early teens onward.

Political marketing could be integrated with the political life of the left by making support of the Liberation counter-institutions a part of every major rally or campaign. Demonstrations could conclude with groups of people going down shopping streets buying Liberation products as they went, pointedly passing by retailers who did not stock them. Every major act of Nixonian politics could be used to boost the support of the CDCs and lessen the patronage of those companies which, at best, conduct business-as-usual as the problems of our society worsen. Public outcries such as those that followed events like Jackson State and Kent State, the murder of Fred Hampton, the delivery of arms to the current regime in Greece, and the invasion of Cambodia, could include information about, and appeals to buy, Liberation products.

Within the context of political marketing, the possibilities for reconciling contradictions are very great. For example, we have already seen how political marketing could be traditional enough to work within the mainstream of the American economy yet radical enough to contribute to a real breakthrough in the economic development of poor communities.

Political marketing would make possible the reconciliation of materialism and humanitarianism. Instead of glorifying consumption and making it the symbol of achievement, status, and well-being, political marketing would extol the contribution the acts of consumption could make toward the solution of social problems. The products themselves, and the purely consumptive dimension, would be de-emphasized in comparison to the human beings who would be supplying them and who would be sustained by their consumption.

Political marketing would also create the opportunity for fusing social purpose and commercial jobs. For example, most advertising copywriters, commercial artists, and directors of television commercials are hopelessly compromised and trivialized as people. "Serious" writers, artists, composers and film-makers usually ostracize their commercial counterparts, yet, in an important sense, they also are compromised in our society. They are tolerated but are carefully isolated from commerce and politics. Thus, creative persons today have a choice: they can bend their talents to the greater glory of the "Breakfast with the Built-in Bounce" and have some impact on the economy and the lives of common men, or they can exist in a gilded ghetto of literary salons and talk shows, offering witty and irreverent comments which the wider culture will applaud and then ignore for as many years as it wishes.

The choice between impact without personal integrity and some measure of integrity with extremely limited impact is an unenviable choice and, I think, an unnecessary one. The choice reflects the existing dichotomy between the humanistic concerns of literary and artistic talents and the essentially exploitative nature of commercial advertising. In the context of political marketing, however, advertising would have political and social impact and would be an integral part of the efforts of the poor to make economic progress.

Political marketing would end the contradiction between voluntary, spare-time "do-goodism" and self-interested business-as-usual. We would no longer need to think of idealism and cooperatism as somehow impractical. Similarly, the dichotomy between private and public life would also be transcended as politics and life style are united. In the end, the reconciliation of dichotomies like these would develop in individuals the inner unity and integrity which they increasingly desire.

Radical Social Change through the Transformation of Commercial Relationships

A radical proposal is one that goes to the root of a situation. One of the roots of our culture and society is the commerical relationship. Alter its context and its meaning for people, and the complexion of society might be fundamentally altered.

For Marx, the "relations of production"—primarily between the industrial proletariat and the owners of capital—comprised the most influential and formative aspect of economic life. But today, the number of people involved in industrial production has decreased markedly, and the economies of mass production are no longer the chief cutting edge of capitalist competition. Most people are involved in supplying goods and services, and businesses compete for and retain the allegiance of their employees and consumers by massive campaigns to project an image. (Except for marginal differences between products or companies, such images and messages celebrate the same values.) This new focus on the consumer aspect has had several profound effects on economic life, which is ripe for change through political marketing.

First, the commercial relationship has tended to become inauthentic. Manufacturers hire advertising agencies to discover what images and symbols will lead people to buy their products. In addition to their instrumental and manipulative qualities, commerical appeals are designed to disguise a product's shortcomings or limitations—products that cause lung tumors are often advertised in the context of spring days and mountain streams, and those with a reputation for shoddiness are frequently presented in luxury surroundings.

Second, commercial relationships are less a form of cooperation than of mutual egotism. The seller gets the money; the buyer gets the product. What the purchase means to the other is usually a matter of complete indifference to either. There has simply been a coincidence of self-interest. "Customer relations" are usually confined to ensuring the prospect of repeat sales, and where repeat sales are unlikely—as in the door-to-door selling of encyclopedias—the sales techniques are generally ruthless. In tightly organized small communities, commercial relationships are usually controlled by the network of social relationships; but in the anonymity of urban mass culture, the true viciousness of the purely commercial relationship comes into its own.

Third, the commercial relationship is often an exceedingly unequal one. When organized business deals with unorganized consumers, there is no dialogue. Business firms define the range of choice and styles of products; the consumer says "yes" or "no" totally within the context decreed by business. The power to formulate alternatives is not shared at all. Not surprisingly, therefore, the consumer suffers from a trivialization of choice. And the thousands of commercial messages to which he is exposed all stimulate and reinforce the same narrow vein of acquisitiveness.

How would political marketing transform the moral imbecility of existing commercial relationships? Authenticity would be increased because of the integrity of the Liberation brand name and the worth of the goals it would stand for. Mutual egotism and the mere coincidence of self-interest would give way to genuine cooperation because consumer support of Liberation products would have a beneficial effect on the lives of the poor. And if Liberation, Incorporated, proved successful enough to go into production, the commercial relationship would become more equal. Through local CMOs, consumers, for the first time, would be able to help create and choose the kinds of products supplied to them.

Once they had tasted freedom and personal creativity, consumers would no longer tolerate the paternalism and instrumentalism of traditional marketing. Those who can choose between levels of moral existence, who by the selective support of certain organizations can help nudge the course of social history, will not lightly regress to suckling on the latest taste-sensation. The success of the CMOs could represent the beginning of the end of corporate-dominated consumption.

The Effect on Communications Media

In the long run, political marketing could transform television commercials and newspaper advertising from trivial and distracting invitations to narcissism to continued reminders of our obligation to other men and of the real pleasure of successfully helping them.

Many liberals and radicals are hostile to television and other advertising *per se*, ignoring how incredibly influential it could be if the content of the messages ever rose above the level of the spurious. The morality currently being inculcated through television advertising holds that self-gratification is deservedly achieved by those who most nearly correspond to conventional role models and images. The conservative, racist, and sexist ramifications of this conditioning are obvious. Nostalgic affection is inspired for those stereotypical images idealized by the Silent Majority, while increasing degrees of disgust are evoked for those who deviate. Thus, the cruelty of advertisements falls upon all those who cannot or will not conform to the role models—blacks, people with unconventional features, people unfulfilled by the roles of consumer and housewife, and people too poor to consume on the idealized scale. The morality of the person who shouts "Get a haircut" to young peace marchers is taught to him and reinforced by his television set.

The content of the actual programs corresponds to these values, except that what is stressed is the maintenance of harmony among a number of conventional roles. In program after program, conventional virtue is threatened by dark-complexioned or hirsute characters who are foiled in the nick of time by Muscular Armericanism—in the shape of sheriffs, policemen, secret agents, and various embodiments of authoritative violence. Such endings pave the way for the conventional role models in the commercials which follow.

The advertising that would promote the political marketing concept, however, would have a different thrust and might have an effect on the medium itself. While traditional advertising needs programs with happy endings in order to set the consumer up for thoughtless consumption, advertising for political marketing would require programs and stories with unresolved crises, manifest contradictions, and real-life dilemmas which would invite the active participation and intervention of the political consumer. Television stories depicting the true agonies of poverty and racism would be followed by commercials for politically motivated buying that would contribute to the solution of social problems.

Not the least of the impacts of political marketing would be its effect upon the economics of publishing and broadcasting. The necessity of pleasing advertisers has almost certainly pulled the media to the right and dampened the fires of controversy. Former Senator Joseph Clark, for example, was unable to get any mass-circulation magazines to publish his views on truth-in-advertising, nor could Dr. Benjamin Spock find a large magazine to print his articles on peace until he was indicted. Because the advertising for political marketing would *need* controversy, non-sugar-coated treatments of unsolved problems and radical proposals in order to galvanize the consuming public, it would be a countervailing force to most advertisers.

The effect that political marketing could have on journals like *The New Republic* and *The Nation*, which are nearly bereft of advertising support, would be even more substantial. It is conceivable that these left-wing periodicals, recognizing a good thing, would carry free advertising supplements for Liberation products in the launch stage, later charging a fee that would lower their own prices, raise their circulations, and bring political marketing to more people.

A Contribution to the Democratic Process

In many ways, political marketing can be seen as an opportunity to add new dimensions to the meaning of democracy in America. It would create a mode of decentralized decision-making, an alternative forum for political activity to the over-centralized Washington arena. It would enable consumers to give selective support to different groups in the society, not only through the Liberation brand name in general but also within the family of Liberation products.

Political marketing is actually more democratic than electoral politics, for democracy ultimately depends upon the concern, support and respect that citizens show for one another. If one man is ten times more concerned than another, democratic society cannot afford to restrict that concern to the yanking of a lever on a voting machine. A just, cooperative society must allow the fullest expression to those who have the greatest cooperative impulses. Political marketing enables every consumer to take effective political action every day by purposefully utilizing the time and money which he presently spends on self-centered consumption. He would ''vote'' as often as he shopped, and he would shop as selectively as he cared.

As a system of redistributing income, political marketing is more democratic than taxation. Taxpayers feel that a large portion of what they earn and therefore ''deserve'' is taken away and given as hand-outs to ''people who won't work as hard as they do.'' In a sense, the complainers are right: there is no joy in giving to others through the taxation system. Money is demanded peremptorily, and one has little effective control over its use. And the taxes fall hardest on those people barely above the poverty line. Political marketing, in effect, asks those who are the most willing to shoulder the financial burden of helping the disadvantaged. Since liberals and radicals in this country are preponderantly upper-middle-class, such a system would represent a fairer distribution of the burden. It would be fairer, too, because it would be voluntary.

Conclusion

Political marketing specifies no ultimate political state. Rather, it suggests ways in which commerical relationships can be more equal, more authentic, more cooperative, and more capable of incorporating nonmaterialistic values. What people would do with those improved relationships is not for us to decide. Through applied psychology, we may be able to create conditions which will enable more people to choose more freely, but we cannot know or predict what use they will make of their choices. My own hope is that we would learn how to live coopera-tively. But this proposal is not a magic formula that will make man cooperative. It is only a system that would make possible experimenta-tion in the construction and development of cooperative counter-institutions.

I suggest that one prototype consumer-marketing organization be established. Others will learn from its successes and mistakes. When additional CMOs arise—supporting, perhaps, new towns, communes, rehabilitation communities similar to Synanon or Daytop, and even con-ventional businesses converting from defense work, as well as CDCs—we may be able to build a nationwide organization within which we can find abundant opportunity to be free men making free decisions.

A Planning Model for Black Community Development

June G. Hopps

When urban unrest and violence was at a high peak during the late sixties, public concern and debate began to focus on conditions of life in black communities. The impact of the rapid population growth of blacks in central cities, the blocked opportunity structure they must confront, the racist practices of societal institutions, and a plethora of other causes, theories and rationales, have been put forth as explanations of the "state" of the black community. This paper asserts that despite the volume of dialogue and massive program interventions such as Model Cities, Economic Opportunity programs, and Black Capitalism Programs, the basic conditions of economic life have not materially changed for the majority of the black population. A basic assumption of this paper is that there is need for blacks to devise more strategies for black community development which can form the basis of serious debate among those concerned with the future of the black community. It is suggested that the black community must provide for its own salvation if it is to avoid the debilitating consequences of shifts in national political priorities and the whimsical nature of white public consciousness.

As a contribution to the stock of strategies for black economic development, we put forth in this paper a planning model which we call Linked Cluster Economic Development (LCED). It acknowledges kinship with a long tradition of activist scholarship, exemplified in the early efforts of Booker T. Washington and W. E. B. DuBois, the later activities of the Black Muslims under the leadership of Elijah Muhammed, and the more recent contribution of Professor Frank Davis of Howard University, Washington, D.C.

Problem Areas in Black Community Economic Development Efforts

Social planners in urban economic development face many problems that are unique to the black community. The black community has shown phenomenal resistance to structural change. Programs such as public housing, urban renewal, neighborhood development model cities, and corporate expansion in black areas—once the reformer's panacea—have not had positive impact. As black economic development continues to be viewed as a workable interventive strategy some problem areas that planners must confront tend to surface. These include issues of sovereignty; ghetto markets; human capital limitations; social capital limitations; horizontal structures and social capital; and the black-white trade imbalance. Though none of these issues is new, it will be worthwhile to review them very briefly, for one of the key features of the LCED is that it tries to deal simultaneously with all of these problems.

Sovereignty

It is an undisputable fact that successful economic development occurs in sovereign nations. We hypothesize that while sovereignty is not a sufficient condition for economic development, nonetheless, it may very well be a necessary condition for economic progress to take place on a broad front. The black community is not sovereign. It is a colony, with the special feature that it is geographically and institutionally imbedded in the metropolitan country. Strategies for gaining self-determination have not been clearly elucidated or generally embraced by blacks. There are varying thrusts toward self-determination arising out of such different orientations as nationalism, integration, or separation. The forceful movement of blacks for political power in both central cities and rural southern communities represents a major step toward self-determination.[1] The thrust for community control of schools, municipal services and recreation is another example of the urgency with which blacks view self-determination. Likewise, the recent expansion in economic development as symbolized by community development corporations reflects a similar theme.

The ghetto market

The size or volume of exchange engaged in by the black community is equal to 6.7 percent of the aggregate personal income of the nation, spent by approximately 11 percent of the nation's population. Black businesses, however, do not fully exploit the market but have traditionally operated primarily in personal services and marginal retail enterprises. Most of these businesses operate below the minimum size at which technology becomes effective. As a result, they resort to the use of the cheapest labor and inferior raw materials. But even these devices fail to generate sufficient profits for capital accumulation and business expansion.

Human capital

Human capital refers to the investment in individuals that influences their future monetary and psychic income.[2] An individual's stock of human capital is an investment in the same sense that physical capital is an investment. Some crucial human capital items include schooling, on the job training, and medical care.

Investment in human capital has not been as adequate for blacks as it has been for whites. For example, a recent U.S. Department of Labor report stated that 30 percent of the black male civilian labor force has only an elementary education as compared with less than 20 percent for whites; less than 50 percent of the nonwhites have graduated from high school as opposed to almost 70 percent for whites.[3] In 1968, the average earnings of white high-school dropouts was still higher than the average earnings of a nonwhite high school graduate.[4]

Social capital

The low investment in human capital for blacks is compounded by lack of access to social capital. Social capital is defined as the aggregate savings of society.[5] It is available to citizens through schools and universities, recreational facilities, hospitals and clinics. Much of a society's social capital is transmitted through informal social and political systems—the family, neighborhood, union hall, and the company executive board room. Discrimination and patterns of racism in education, housing, and employment have denied blacks equal access to social capital.

The lack of access to the social capital accumulated by society also has a direct effect on doing business in the black community. The black entrepreneur is confronted with higher fixed operating costs than his counterpart in the white community. This higher operating cost is a result of inferior and often nonexistent police protection, inferior municipal services, and higher insurance premiums. Additionally, land and rental costs are high because of the ghetto's high population density, further magnifying the burden to be borne by the black entrepreneur.

Horizontal-vertical structures and social capital

One way of altering the social capital dilemma is for blacks to move aggressively toward forming both horizontal and vertical organizational structures. The general purpose of these structures would be to exert collective action on communal needs. A specific agenda would include:

1. Defining general economic goals and developing strategies to achieve them.
2. Defining financial needs and developing strategies for tapping contracts, sheltered markets, low-interest capital, grants-in-aid, etc., and for demanding greater commitment to redevelopment of the ghetto.
3. Eliminating some of the fierce competition for funds and property.

4. Developing schemes for pooling resources in order to develop, train, and share skilled manpower resources.
5. Developing appropriate communication links with political leaders so that they can receive information on legislation that deals with economic development.
6. Developing strategies for attacking the crime problem and enlisting support of local citizens, police, etc., in an effort to eliminate, or at least reduce, a situation that has extracted large amounts of resources from the new ghetto economic development efforts.

The black-white trade balance

Trade relations between the black and white sectors are characterized by (a) export of low-wage labor by blacks to the white economy, (b) practically zero imports of commodities by the white economy from blacks, and (c) imports of almost 100 percent of black commodity requirements from the white economy.

Trade balance would dictate that, as a minimum, black labor exports pay for black commodity imports. But all profits derived from the employment of black labor belong to the white community. When one adds the interest payments by blacks on white-owned investments (housing, business establishments, business loans, consumer loans, professional equipment, etc.) in the black community, the direction of flow of the balance of payments is obviously against the black sector.

All of the limitations discussed above have serious effects on the black economy. One would be hard-pressed indeed to provide a consensus priority ranking of these issues. Thus, it would seem that a full-scale assault should be made on all of these problems simultaneously. This is precisely the framework within which the LCED plan has been devised and hence the framework within which its objectives and methods can be understood.

Linked Cluster Economic Development

"Linked clusters" is proposed as a new economic development approach for the black community.[6] In the present context a cluster defines a group of "dynamically interacting" and "economically stabilized" business enterprises. Each business enterprise will be referred to as an element of the cluster. The cluster thus consists of a group of firms, judiciously pre-selected, whose inputs and outputs are interconnected in such a fashion as to optimize the economic performance of the group as a whole, rather than to maximize profits of a single member of the group.

Figure 1 illustrates a simplified diagram of the sales/procurement interactions of a three-element cluster. We see from the figure that a portion of the sales and procurement by each element of the cluster occurs within the cluster. We may now show explicitly that this interaction is favorable to the cluster.

First, we define an approximate profit relation for a given element of the cluster, say element #1. We define it for purposes of the present illustration as: Net of #1 *equals* total sales of #1 *minus* total procurements of #1 *minus* operational costs of #1. The sales and procurements of element #1 may be separated into external and internal components, so that we may alternatively express Net of #1

$$N_1 = S_{12} + S_{13} - P_{12} - P_{13} + S_1 - P_1 - O_1$$
$$= (\Sigma S_{1k} - (\Sigma P_{1k}) + S_1 - P_1 - O_1$$
$$\quad k \neq 1 \quad\quad k \neq 1$$

What we emphasize in this equation is that the procurements within the cluster by element #1 enter negatively in the equation and act to reduce the net or profit of element #1. If, however, we consider the net with respect to the complete clusters, i.e., N1+N2+N3=N, we find that

$$N = S_{12} + S_{13} + S_{21} + S_{23} + S_{31} + S_{32}$$
$$- P_{12} - P_{13} - P_{21} - P_{23} - P_{31} - P_{32}$$
$$+ S_1 + S_2 + S_3 - P_1 - P_2 - P_3 - O_1 - O_2 - O_3.$$

As indicated in the figure, however, $P_{12} = -S_{21}$, etc. That is, all procurements within the cluster are reflected as sales with respect to the overall cluster. Thus,

$$N = \Sigma (S_n - P_n - O_n) + \Sigma \Sigma (S_{nk}),$$
$$\quad n \quad\quad\quad\quad\quad\quad n \neq k$$
$$\text{where } n, k, = 1,2,3.$$

To extend the above analysis to a more general cluster configuration we simply let n and k run through all the positive integers up to some arbitrary number.

The meaning of the above analysis is clear: of the nine procurement entries for our three-element cluster, each of which acts to reduce the profit of the cluster elements when considered individually, six of these take on the character of sales or profit-increasing entries when the cluster itself is considered. This conversion of a loss, with respect to an element, to a gain, with respect to the cluster, lies at the heart of our linked cluster approach.

The concept of linking becomes clear on the basis of foregoing discussion. If a portion of the external procurements made by a specific cluster is from one or more different clusters, then we obtain an effective gain

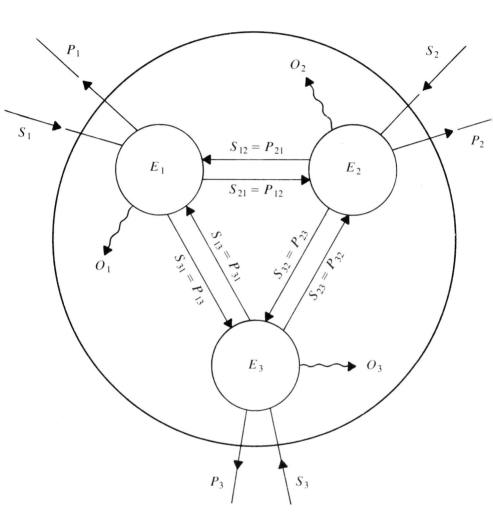

Definitions of symbols:
E_1, E_2, E_3 = elements of the cluster.
S_1, S_2, S_3 = sales "external" to the cluster by elements 1, 2 and 3 respectively.
P_1, P_2, P_3 = procurements "external" to the cluster by elements 1, 2 and 3 respectively.
O_1, O_2, O_3 = operational costs (labor, loss, etc.) for elements 1, 2 and 3 respectively.
S_{nk} = sales by n^{th} element of the cluster *to* the kth element of that cluster.
P_{nk} = procurements by n^{th} element of the cluster *from* the kth element of that cluster.

Fig. 1. Sales-procurement interaction for three-element cluster.

with respect to the system of clusters. This process of connection we call linking and our additional economic gain is in respect to the system of linked clusters.

The optimizing process will be affected by the initial choices of cluster elements, the intrinsic parasitic effect of certain interactions between the cluster elements, and other constraints imposed upon the optimization itself. As a result, it would be virtually impossible to give an a priori optimization rule for a cluster of arbitrary size. Rather, this paper takes a planning stance, and in the next section we develop a generalized organizational framework or plan within which these initial choices may be made, the constrained optimization performed, and the general LCED approach effected.

Before developing the plan, it is perhaps useful to give some qualitative consideration on some of the problems connected with the optimization idea. One such problem is the initial choice of cluster elements. This choice must be largely dictated by the potential for coupling of the elements themselves. Yet, this choice must be constrained by the level of technical expertise that may presently be found in the black community. Certainly General Motors and U.S. Steel would make ideal coupled elements, but such a pair is not presently in the domain of possible choices available to the black community.

In terms of the optimization over the cluster, we may make some general statements based upon the general formula given for the cluster as a whole. We would like to maximize sales, minimize procurements, and minimize operational cost. Although we emphasize the cluster, we nev-

Fig. 2. Hypothetical cluster based on dry cleaning.

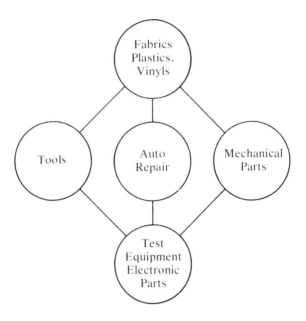

Fig. 3. Hypothetical cluster based on auto repair.

ertheless are constrained by the desirability of having each element profitable, although not necessarily maximally so.

Figures 2 and 3 depict hypothetical but realistic clusters based upon the typical ghetto businesses of dry cleaning and auto repair. Though we do not suggest that these examples are optimum, they should nonetheless provide the reader with a practical frame of reference within which many of the ensuing ideas may be viewed.

The administrative plan for LCED together with the optimized cluster concept represents the two main thrusts of this paper.

Administrative Framework for LCED

The plan presented in this section illustrates how the Linked Cluster Economic Development concept should be put into operation. The economic aspects of the plan are not totally unique, but the overall plan does represent a departure from previous proposals. The plan deals specifically with the difficult reality that the economic problems of blacks have critical political and social dimensions. Even more crucially, the plan comes to grips with another impending reality; namely, that the economic salvation of blacks is a cross to be borne solely by the black community itself. In contrast, consider the analysis of Davis, which calls for an approximately $40 billion initial input from the federal government.[7] We take the position in this paper that the time is at hand for planning based on a pragmatic premise.

The overall structure of the LCED plan is depicted schematically in Figure 4. It identifies basic organizational units and their relationships. The detailed description of the organizational units—their make-up, functions, etc.—is presented in the following discussion.

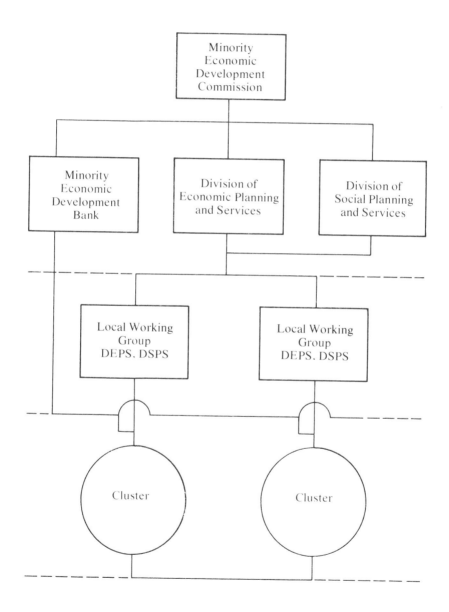

Fig. 4. General structure of LCED plan.

Minority Economic Development Commission (MEDC)

The Minority Economic Development Commission (MEDC) should be the unit designated as the executive and policy-making body responsible for the overall development and administration of the plan. Members of the board should be clear that their purpose is to represent the interest of the black community. Since their function will be to oversee the planning and delivery of economic development programs for the black community, the members must be subject to some form of recall. Officials should come from each state; the mechanism for election or appointment could be worked out locally. Also there should be a fixed number of appointments from the Black Political Caucus.

The second administrative level is composed of three subexecutive level agencies, each responsible for a critical phase of the overall plan. The Minority Economic Development Bank (MEDB) is to be established for the dual purposes of raising funds for a national black economic development effort and making available loans to new and existing black enterprises. The MEDB will differ in several respects from conventional banks. It will solicit direct financial contributions from individuals and organizations to be used for the funding of black enterprises. It will promote receiving fixed and regular percentages of the dividends on individual savings accounts held in local banks throughout the country through formal agreement of the individual and the local bank. This amounts to a "savings dividend deduction plan." It will promote direct handling of savings accounts which, in order to minimize manpower requirements, should be in excess of certain specified minimum amounts.

In all cases, emphasis should be placed upon soliciting funds from black individuals and organizations. Funds from foundations, church-related groups, the government, and other white institutions should be accepted only if they forfeit any role in policy decision making. Otherwise, they will dominate the organization by virtue of their wealth and technology. Above all, their presence will cause blacks to minimize the need for control of their institutions.

It is possible that one of the existing black banks could assume the financial management responsibility initially. It is conceivable, and possibly desirable, that the MEDB be established around an already existing black bank. In such a case, the chosen bank would be compensated by the MEDB for supplemental staff to handle its specific account, with actual fund raising and disbursment decisions being strictly the responsibility of the Minority Economic Development Commission.

Decisions on the nature, amount, and recipients of the fund made available to the MEDC will be based upon the recommendations of the Division of Economic Planning and Services (DEPS). This group forms the backbone of the LCED plan. The departmental functions can, for the purpose of descriptive clarity, be divided into two primary categories, each of which has several sublevels. They are the (1) cluster function, including design, locations, monitoring, and dynamic stabilization; and (2) linkage function, including design, monitoring, and dynamic stabilization.

This department must be staffed by the best talent (preferably black) available. Its staff will be composed of experts in the field of social planning, economics, and business services (e.g., corporate finance, marketing and marketing research, production and operations management, corporate law, and industrial relations). In addition, the staff should consist of expert programmers and data analysts.

The cluster group, whose work dominates the initial phases of the LCED plan, will be responsible for the design of cluster systems which are optimum with respect to business potential and economic interaction. On the basis of analysis of market potentials, available technical skills, etc., one or more business clusters will be given priority designations for selected cluster location target areas. The match-ups having been determined, their realization is secured in two ways. First, by recommendations to the MEDB these priorities also become the bank's funding priorities for the designated target areas. Secondly, blacks in the designated target areas will be recruited by the department's contingent of the Local/Regional Working Group. Recruited blacks will be recommended to the MEDB for loans. The funding priorities should provide the leverage necessary to polarize the business interests of a sufficient number of blacks so that the optimized cluster schemes may be implemented in the designated areas. It is here that LCED makes contact with the concept of sovereignty. As regards the ultimate objective of black economic development the net effects of the funding provide leverage in substantially the same manner as that of sovereignty. This leverage therefore provides what may be termed an economically induced pseudo-sovereignty.

Once the clusters are operational the department's local team members become monitors. Specified sets of data are collected on each element of the cluster, the data being communicated by local team members to central department headquarters for analysis. Desirable adjustments, as determined by the central group, are re-recommended to local team members for implementation. In this way, the clusters may be dynamically stabilized and the chances for success of each element optimized. Local team members will help coordinate mutual endeavors, e.g., combined procurements, shipping, etc., which results in cost and other benefits to each of the cluster elements.

It should be pointed out that there is some evidence, on a much smaller scale of course, that the availability of technical assistance greatly increases the success factor for a wide variety of black businesses.[8]

The linkage group performs functions which are to a large extent exactly analogous to those of the cluster group. Their primary task, however, is of delocalization, linking not only cluster elements, but sometimes complete sets of clusters which are located in different regions. This function is of course not operative during the initial stages of LCED.

The function also would include designing feasible "linkage enterprises," such as crate and container manufacturing and transportation. As with the MEDB, this department could benefit from establishment around existing structures. For example, the department could be established so that it is closely associated in function and location with the school of business of a black university. This would mean additional resources for the DEPS, (e.g., of graduate student manpower). On the other hand, DEPS would be a valuable training ground where black business students in black business schools could learn black business.

The Division of Social Planning Services (DSPS) functions primarily as lobbyist at the national, state, and local levels for black business interests. It will work to secure many of the social and human capital components that are lacking in the black community. One major task area will be securing the passage and just implementation of legislation, at all levels, that is favorable to black business. In this regard, the National Black Political Caucus could serve as a valuable ally, since its primary goal is to see that legislation favorable to the black community is enacted. An area where blacks have not benefited like other interest groups in the American political scene is in the dissemination of information on legislative proposals. Close affiliation with the Caucus would help alleviate this situation. There would also be a relationship with state legislators.

Though there are many established organizations working to secure for the black community various components of social capital (e.g., medical, educational, and recreational facilities) there are many other areas that more directly relate to the operational costs of businesses that will receive the main attention of DSPS. Examples are excessive insurance costs, or the complete lack of insurance, in inner city areas; high and unjust real estate purchase and rental costs; unfair central-city tax burdens; inadequate transportation, police, and fire protection; etc. Again, there are existing groups (e.g., NAACP, Urban League, and CORE) to which this function may be appended.

The local working team also contains DSPS staff who maintain direct communications with the central body. DSPS's contingent of the local team will be involved in initial phases in some aspects of the establishment of clusters, e.g., site plans, insurance, or negotiations.

Conclusions

Economic advancement through planned efforts is viewed as the basis for initiating and sustaining structural change in the black community. The LCED plan suggests that integration does not hold the immediate key to black community ills. The ghetto continues to exist despite the trickle of blacks who move beyond it yearly. The majority of inner-city blacks cannot escape it. As has been shown in many studies, intervention efforts by the federal government have been a dismal failure. In fact, many of those efforts, such as the Nixon Black Capitalism doctrine, must be classified as a cruel hoax.

The present plan asserts that the impetus, financial aid, leadership, and technical expertise must come from the black community if the economic development of the black community is to proceed with dispatch and avoid the pitfalls of neo-colonialism. Leadership must come from talented black men and women. Expertise and dedication must replace rhetoric. This top black talent must be recruited and rewarded in much the same sense as the civil rights warriors of the early 1960s were rewarded. The LCED plan is comprehensive and provides an efficient framework for the utilization of available black expertise, the rapid extension of black entrepreneurial skills, the accelerated accumulation of human and social capital, and the generation of funds for black economic development within the black community.

A striking feature of the LCED plan is that it is optimistic in regard to the ability of blacks to take charge of their economic destiny in this country. It views even the short-term future, of black economic development as potentially quite positive. Though oriented towards the future, it is to some extent a reflection of some past efforts at black economic development made, not by government, white businesses and foundations, but most importantly by blacks themselves. Many of the basic issues that this plan addresses, and that any other such plan must, are the same as those that confronted such outstanding black scholars as Booker T. Washington and W. E. B. DuBois. There is much to be learned from their attempts, though not totally successful, to deal with these problems.

Finally, what organization could possibly take on such an awesome task as implied by LCED? Political considerations notwithstanding, an immediate recommendation would be that existing national black organizations with the technical, fund-raising and organizational skills they have amassed over the decades be utilized to as great an extent as possible. Such groups to be utilized would include the NAACP, Urban League, CORE, and PUSH. Black traditional business institutions such as banks and insurance companies should be incorporated into the fund-raising network. Black educational institutions offering graduate training in economics and the business sciences could be incorporated, with mutual benefit, into the scheme for delivering expert technical services to the cluster elements proposed in the plan. The scheme for the delivery of social and political planning services may be aided in an analogous manner. The necessary coalition is therefore definable; the remaining question then is who can effect it?

Of existing black groups, it appears that the Black Congressional Caucus would most likely have the required scope of influence necessary to effect such a coalition. The Caucus also would apparently have a motivation to do so, since black economic development is an issue with which it has recently been particularly concerned.

We should not be naïve about the difficulty of overcoming political and ideological conflicts and rivalries between existing black organizations which would be required in such a coalition. We must bear in mind, however, that economic forces have proven themselves time and time again, even in a conflict as intense as the Cold War, to be effective in negating or moderating political and ideological differences.

NOTES

1. The number of elected black officials has shown a steady increase. In 1968 there were 29 black mayors, in 1971 there were 81; in 1962 there were 52 blacks in state legislatures, in 1971 there were 198. Source: U.S., Department of Labor, Bureau of Labor Statistics, *The Social and Economic Status of Negroes in the United States,* Report 394 (Washington, D.C.: By the Bureau, 1970), p. 142.

2. Gary Becker, *Human Capital,* National Bureau of Economic Research (New York: Columbia University Press, 1964), pp. 1–3.

3. U.S., Bureau of the Census, *The Social and Economic Status of Negroes in the U.S., 1970* (Washington, D.C.: U.S. Government Printing Office, 1970).

4. *Economic Report of the President, 1969* (Washington, D.C.: U.S. Government Printing Office, 1969), p. 167.

5. Courtney Blackman, "An Eclectic Approach to the Problem of Black Economic Development," *Review of Black Political Economy,* 2, no. 1 (1971): 20–21.

6. Examples of existing black firms which may form clusters are discussed in June G. Hopps, "A Study of Ghetto Economic Corporations," Ph.D. dissertation (Waltham, Mass.: Brandeis University) pp. 140–46, and Roland Warren, *Community in America* (Chicago, Ill.: Rand McNally, 1963). See chapters 8 and 9 for discussion of Horizontal and Vertical Structures.

7. Frank G. Davis, *The Economics of Black Community Development* (Chicago, Ill.: Markham Publishing Co., 1972).

8. CREED (Community Resources for the Encouragement of Economic Development), a Columbus, Ohio, organization, has been effective in helping black businesses become viable through the provision of technical assistance.

Topics for Discussion

1. The implementation of many proposals for black economic development, whether individual or community oriented, is hampered by the lack of funds or by the restrictions placed on the use of available funds. Discuss how the financial problems of black economics can be solved in view of the following obstacles:
   A. The low savings rates generally associated with low incomes.
   B. Materialism and other highly consumption-oriented stimuli (especially those aimed at middle-income blacks, who often possess fewer assets than whites with comparable incomes).
   C. The preponderance of black savings being held in white-controlled institutions which support investments often totally unrelated to black economic development and, in some cases, contrary to black economic development.

   Design a proposal for overcoming the obstacles above, for increasing the black savings rate, and for using black savings for investment and research projects that would be subject to black surveillance and control.

2. The problems of black economic development include not only the number of black businesses but also the types of businesses. How can the structure and infrastructure of black businesses be improved for the advantages of diversification and synergism? To what extent can existing black businesses and organizations be incorporated towards such an improvement?

3. How can proponents of black economic development more effectively utilize various routine government activities (such as procurement, research and development support, information-gathering systems, etc.)?

4. How can environmental (demographic, economic, technological, etc.) changes be monitored to help identify and exploit potential opportunities (or risks) for black people?

Suggested Readings

Daniels, B. "A Conceptual Framework for Analyzing the Feasibility of a Development Banking System to Support Community Economic Development." Cambridge, Mass.: Center for Community Economic Development, 1973.

Davis, Frank G. *The Economics of Black Community Development: An Analysis and Program for Autonomous Growth and Development.* Chicago, Ill.: Markham Publishing Company, 1972.

"How AMA Might Help Develop Minority Business." Paper presented to American Marketing Association Educator's Conference, 1969.

McLaurin, D. *The Ghediplan.* New York: Human Resources Administration, City of New York, 1968.

Niedercorn, John. H. "A Neo-Mercantilist Model for Maximizing Ghetto Income." *The Review of Black Political Economy,* 1, no. 3 (Winter/Spring 1971).

Venable, A.S. *Building Black Business: An Analysis and a Plan.* New York: Earl G. Graves Publishing Co., Inc., 1972, distributed by Thomas Y. Crowell Co., New York.